Systems Benchmarking

Samuel Kounev • Klaus-Dieter Lange
Jóakim von Kistowski

Systems Benchmarking

For Scientists and Engineers

 Springer

Samuel Kounev
University of Würzburg
Würzburg, Germany

Jóakim von Kistowski
DATEV eG
Nürnberg, Germany

Klaus-Dieter Lange
Hewlett Packard Enterprise
Houston, TX, USA

ISBN 978-3-030-41707-9   ISBN 978-3-030-41705-5   (eBook)
https://doi.org/10.1007/978-3-030-41705-5

This Springer imprint is published by the registered company Springer Nature Switzerland AG
The registered company address is: Gewerbestrasse 11, 6330 Cham, Switzerland

Foreword by David Patterson

In January of 2010, I met Sam and Klaus at the inaugural International Conference on Performance Engineering (ICPE), in San Jose, USA. I gave the keynote address "Software Knows Best: Portable Parallelism Requires Standardized Measurements of Transparent Hardware" to an audience where half was from the industry and half from academia. That was by design, since in their roles as co-founders and steering committee members of ICPE, they drove to establish this forum for sharing ideas and experiences between industry and academia. Thus, I was not surprised to see that their book "Systems Benchmarking—For Scientists and Engineers" has the same underlying tone: to foster the integration of theory and practice in the field of systems benchmarking.

Their work is twofold: Part I can be used as a textbook for graduate students as it introduces the foundations of benchmarking. It covers:

- the fundamentals of benchmarking,
- a refresher of probability and statistics,
- benchmark metrics,
- statistical measurements,
- experimental design,
- measurement techniques,
- operational analysis and basic queueing models,
- workloads, and
- benchmark standardization.

Part II features a number of concrete applications and case studies based on input from leading benchmark developers from consortia such as the Standard Performance Evaluation Corporation (SPEC) or the Transaction Processing Performance Council (TPC). It describes a broad range of state-of-the-art benchmarks, their development, and their effective use in engineering and research. In addition to covering classical performance benchmarks—including CPU, energy efficiency, virtualization, and storage benchmarks—the book looks at benchmarks and measurement methodologies for evaluating elasticity, performance isolation, and security aspects.

Moreover, some further topics related to benchmarking are covered in detail, such as resource demand estimation.

The authors also ventured to share some insightful retrospectives in regard to benchmark development in industry-standard bodies, as they have been active in SPEC for many years. The information about the formation and growth of SPEC and TPC over the last 30 years is valuable when starting new leading initiatives like Embench or MLPerf.

One of my observations is that benchmarks shape a field, for better or for worse. Good benchmarks are in alignment with real applications, but bad benchmarks are not, forcing engineers to choose between making changes that help end users or making changes that only help with marketing.

This book should be required reading for anyone interested in making good benchmarks.

Berkeley, CA, USA   *David Patterson*
January 2020   2017 ACM A.M. Turing Award Laureate

Foreword by John R. Mashey

I am delighted to write a foreword for this thorough, comprehensive book on theory and practice of benchmarking. I will keep it short, so people can quickly start on the substantial text itself.

Creating good benchmarks is harder than most imagine. Many have been found to have subtle flaws or have become obsolete. In addition, benchmark audiences differ in their goals and needs. Computer system designers use benchmarks to compare potential design choices, so they need benchmarks small enough to simulate before creating hardware. Software engineers need larger examples to help design software and tune its performance. Vendors want realistic benchmarks that deter gimmicks by competitors. They dislike wasting time on those they know to be unrepresentative. Buyers might like to run their own complete workloads, but that is often impractical. They certainly want widely reported, realistic benchmarks they trust that correlate with their own workloads. Researchers like good, relevant examples they can analyze and use in textbooks.

In the 1980s, benchmarks were still often confusing and chaotic, driven by poor examples and much hype. Vendors boasted of poorly defined MIPS, MFLOPS, or transactions, and universities often studied tiny benchmarks. Luckily, the last few decades have seen huge progress, some contributed by the authors themselves. From personal experience, the close interaction of academia and industry has long been very fruitful. The three authors have extensive experience combining academic research, industrial practice, and the nontrivial methods to create good industry-standard benchmarks on which competitors can agree.

I am especially impressed by the pervasive balance of treatments in this book. It aims to serve as both a handbook for practitioners and a textbook for students. It certainly is the former and if I were still teaching college, I would use it as a text.

It starts with the basics of benchmarks and their taxonomies, then covers the theoretical foundations of benchmarking: statistics, measurements, experimental design, and queueing theory. That is very important, from experience giving guest lectures, where I have often found that many computer science students had not studied the relevant statistical methods, even at very good schools. The theory is properly complemented with numerous case studies.

The book explores the current state of the art in benchmark developments, but as important, provides crucial context by examining decades of benchmark evolution, failures and successes. It recounts histories of changes from scattered benchmarks to the more disciplined efforts of industry–academic consortia, such as the Transaction Processing Performance Council (TPC) and especially the Standard Performance Evaluation Corporation (SPEC), both started in late 1988. Much was learned not just about benchmarking technology and good reporting, but in effective ways to organize such groups. Both organizations are still quite active, three decades later, an eternity in computing. Chapter 10's history of the SPEC CPU benchmarks' evolution is especially instructive.

From history and long-established benchmarks, the book then moves to modern topics—energy efficiency, virtualization, storage, web, cloud elasticity, performance isolation in complex data centers, resource demand estimation, and research in software and system security. Some of these topics were barely imaginable for benchmarking when we started SPEC in 1988 just to create reasonable CPU benchmarks!

This is a fine book by experts. It offers many good lessons and is well worth the time to study.

Portola Valley, CA, USA   *John R. Mashey*
January 2020   SPEC Co-Founder and
                                      Former Silicon Graphics VP/Chief Scientist

Preface

> "To measure is to know... If you cannot measure it, you cannot improve it."
> —*William Thomson—Lord Kelvin (1824–1907),*
> *Scottish engineer, mathematician, and physicist*

> "You can't control what you can't measure."
> —*Tom DeMarco, American software engineer, author,*
> *and consultant on software engineering topics*

Theme

A benchmark is a tool coupled with a methodology for evaluating and comparing systems, or components thereof, with respect to specific characteristics, such as performance, energy efficiency, reliability, or security. Modern benchmarks are increasingly complex applications, sometimes composed of hundreds of thousands of lines of code, combined with detailed specifications describing the benchmarking process and evaluation methodology.

Traditional benchmarks have been focused on evaluating performance, typically understood as the amount of useful work accomplished by a system (or component) compared to the time and resources used. Ranging from simple benchmarks, targeting specific hardware or software components, to large and complex benchmarks focusing on entire systems (e.g., information systems, storage systems, cloud platforms), performance benchmarks have contributed significantly to improve successive generations of systems. Beyond traditional performance benchmarking, research on dependability benchmarking has increased in the past two decades. Dependability captures "the trustworthiness of a system that allows reliance to be justifiably placed on the service it delivers."[1] Due to the increasing relevance of security issues, secu-

---

[1] International Federation for Information Processing (IFIP) Working Group 10.4

rity benchmarking has also become an important research field. Finally, resilience benchmarking faces challenges related to the integration of performance, dependability, and security benchmarking as well as to the adaptive characteristics of the systems under consideration. Resilience encompasses all attributes of the quality of "working well in a changing world that includes faults, failures, errors, and attacks."[2]

Compared to traditional software, benchmark development has different goals and challenges. While in the past two decades numerous benchmarks have been developed, very few contributions focusing on the underlying concepts and foundations of benchmarking have been published.[3]

The best-known publication on benchmarking is Gray's *The Benchmark Handbook*.[4] The book presents a detailed description of several benchmarks and discusses the need for domain-specific benchmarks defining four specific criteria they must fulfill:

1. **Relevance:** A benchmark should measure the performance of the typical operation within the problem domain.
2. **Portability:** A benchmark should be easy to implement on many different systems and architectures.
3. **Scalability:** A benchmark should be scalable to cover small and large systems.
4. **Simplicity:** A benchmark should be understandable to avoid lack of credibility.

The criteria benchmarks should fulfill are further discussed by Huppler.[5] The questions, what a "good" benchmark should look like and which aspects should be kept in mind from the beginning of the development process, are discussed in detail and five key criteria are presented:

1. **Relevance:** A benchmark has to reflect something important.
2. **Repeatable:** It should be possible to reproduce the results by running the benchmark under similar conditions.
3. **Fair and Portable:** It should be possible for all systems compared to participate equally.
4. **Verifiable:** There should be confidence that the documented results are real. This can, for example, be assured by reviewing results by external auditors.
5. **Economical:** The cost of running the benchmark should be affordable.

The increasing size and complexity of modern systems make the engineering of benchmarks that fulfill the above criteria a challenging task. This book covers the theoretical and abstract foundations necessary for gaining a deep understanding

---

[2] Bondavalli, A. et al. (2009). Research Roadmap—Deliverable D3.2, AMBER—Assessing, Measuring and Benchmarking Resilience. EU FP7 ICT-216295 Coordination and Support Action (CSA).

[3] Vieira, M. et al. (2012). "Resilience Benchmarking". In: Resilience Assessment and Evaluation of Computing Systems. Springer-Verlag: Berlin, Heidelberg, pp. 283–301.

[4] Gray, J., ed. (1993). The Benchmark Handbook: For Database and Transaction Systems. 2nd Edition. Morgan Kaufmann.

[5] Huppler, K. (2009). "The Art of Building a Good Benchmark". In: Performance Evaluation and Benchmarking. Vol. 5895. Lecture Notes in Computer Science. Springer-Verlag: Berlin, Heidelberg, pp. 18–30.

of benchmarking and the benchmark engineering process. It also provides a high number of practical applications and concrete examples of modern benchmarks and their development processes.

Goals, Prerequisites, and Target Audience

The aim of the book is to serve both as a handbook and as a textbook on benchmarking of systems and components used as building blocks of modern Information and Communication Technologies (ICT) applications. Benchmarks enable educated purchasing decisions and play an important role as evaluation tools during system design, development, and maintenance. In research, benchmarks play an integral part in the evaluation and validation of new approaches and methodologies.

Benchmarking evolved from the need to be able to compare different systems fairly in order to make an informed purchasing decision. Without fair and representative benchmarks, such decisions are often made based on performance indicators provided by manufacturers; however, such proprietary performance indicators are often unreliable, as they may be specifically tailored to showcase the strengths of a given product or to even exploit weaknesses of competing products. Driven by the need for tools enabling fair and reliable comparisons of systems, a number of benchmarks, benchmarking methodologies, and benchmark standardization bodies have emerged. Since then, benchmarks have found broad acceptance in industry and academia. They now are employed in many fields of testing, some of which go beyond the original purpose of competitive system comparisons. These fields include regulatory programs, research evaluation, and testing during system design and development.

With benchmarking becoming an ever more pervasive topic extending far beyond the core audience of people with a computer science background, we identify the need for a book that both explains the fundamentals of benchmarking and provides detailed examples of modern benchmarks and their methodologies. The conception, design, and development of benchmarks require a thorough understanding of benchmarking fundamentals beyond the understanding of the System Under Test (SUT), including statistics, measurement techniques, metrics, and relevant workload characteristics. This book fills the identified gap covering the aforementioned areas in depth. It describes how to determine relevant system characteristics to measure, how to measure these characteristics, and how to aggregate the measurement results into a metric. Further, the aggregation of metrics into scoring systems is an additional challenging topic that is discussed and explained in detail. Finally, the book covers the topic of workload characterization and modeling.

The book is intended to serve as a reference that provides practical and theoretical foundations as well as an in-depth look at modern benchmarks and benchmark development. It is intended to serve two audiences. First, it can be used as a *handbook* for professionals and researchers who work in areas related to benchmarking. It provides an up-to-date point of reference for existing work as well as the latest results, research challenges, and future research directions. Second, it can be used as a *textbook* for lecturers and students of graduate and postgraduate courses on any of the many subjects that relate to benchmarking. While the reader is assumed to be generally acquainted with the principles and practices of computer science, as well as software and systems engineering, no specific expertise in any subfield of these disciplines is required.

The book is based on experiences that have been gained over the past 14 years in teaching a regular graduate course on performance engineering and benchmarking. The course, developed by Prof. Samuel Kounev, has been held at four different European universities since 2006, including University of Cambridge, Polytechnic University of Catalonia, Karlsruhe Institute of Technology (KIT), and University of Würzburg. The book is based on the broad range of materials that have been collected in this time frame and the extensive experience gained from teaching this course over the years. In addition, the book reflects much of the authors' experiences gained from benchmark development in industry and academia over the past 20 years.

Book Organization and Outline

The book is structured into two parts: foundations and applications. The first part introduces the foundations of benchmarking as a discipline, covering the three fundamental elements of each benchmarking approach: metrics, workloads, and measurement methodology. The second part of the book focuses on different application areas, presenting contributions in specific fields of benchmark development. These contributions address the unique challenges that arise in the conception and development of benchmarks for specific systems or subsystems. They also demonstrate how the foundations and concepts of the first part of the book are being used in existing benchmarks. A number of concrete applications and case studies are presented, based on input from leading benchmark developers from consortia such as the Standard Performance Evaluation Corporation (SPEC) and the Transaction Processing Performance Council (TPC).

Chapter 1 starts by providing a definition of the term "benchmark" followed by definitions of the major system quality attributes that are typically subject of benchmarking. After that, a classification of the different types of benchmarks is provided, followed by an overview of strategies for performance benchmarking. Finally, the quality criteria for good benchmarks are discussed in detail, and the chapter is wrapped up with a discussion of application scenarios for benchmarks.

Chapter 2 briefly reviews the basics of probability and statistics while establishing the statistical notation needed for understanding some of the chapters in the book. The chapter is not intended as an introduction to probability and statistics but rather as a quick refresher, assuming that the reader is already familiar with the basic concepts. While basic probability and statistics is essential for understanding Chapters 4, 5, 7, and 17, we note that it is not a prerequisite for understanding the other chapters in the book.

Chapter 3, devoted to benchmark metrics, starts by defining the basic concepts: metric, measure, and measurement. It then introduces the different measurement scales, which allow one to classify the types of values assigned by measures. Next, definitions of the most common performance metrics are presented. The chapter continues with a detailed discussion of the quality attributes of good metrics. Finally, the different types of averages are introduced while showing how they can be used to define composite metrics and aggregate results from multiple benchmarks.

Chapter 4 is dedicated to experimental measurements, introducing statistical approaches to quantify the variability and precision of measurements. The chapter starts by introducing the most common indices of dispersion for quantifying the variability, followed by defining basic concepts such as accuracy, precision, and resolution of measurements. A model of random errors is introduced and used to derive confidence intervals for estimating the mean of a measured quantity of interest based on a sample of measurements. Finally, statistical tests for comparing alternatives based on measurements are introduced.

Chapter 5 covers the topic of experimental design, that is, the process of planning a set of experiments coupled with a statistical analysis procedure in order to understand and explain the variation of information under some specified conditions (factors). Starting with the case of one factor, the analysis of variance (ANOVA) technique from statistics is introduced; it is then generalized to multiple factors that can be varied independently. Following this, the Plackett–Burman design is introduced and compared with the ANOVA technique. Finally, a case study showing how experimental design can be applied in practice is presented.

Chapter 6 looks at the different measurement techniques that can be used in practice to derive the values of common metrics. While most presented techniques are useful for performance metrics, some of them can also be applied for other types of metrics. The chapter starts with a brief introduction to the basic measurement strategies. It then looks at interval timers and performance profiling, which provides means to measure how much time a system spends in different states. Following this, call path tracing is introduced—a technique for extracting a control flow graph of an application. Finally, the chapter is wrapped up with an overview of commercial and open-source monitoring tools for performance profiling and call path tracing.

Chapter 7 starts by introducing operational analysis, an approach to evaluate a system's performance based on measured or known data by applying a set of basic quantitative relationships known as operational laws. Operational analysis can be seen as being part of queueing theory, which provides general methods to analyze the queueing behavior of one or more service stations. The chapter provides a brief introduction to the basic notation and principles of queueing theory. While queueing theory is used in many different domains, from manufacturing to logistics, in this chapter, the focus is on performance evaluation of computer systems. Nevertheless, the introduced concepts and mathematical models are relevant for any processing system where some generic assumptions hold.

Chapter 8 is devoted to benchmark workloads considering their properties and characteristics in the context of workload generation. The chapter starts with a classification of the different workload facets and artifacts. The distinction between executable and non-executable parts of a workload is introduced as well as the distinction between natural and artificial workloads. The rest of the chapter introduces the different types of workload descriptions that can be used for batch workloads and transactional workloads as well as for open and closed workloads. The challenges of generating steady-state workloads and workloads with varying arrival rates are discussed. Finally, the chapter concludes with a brief introduction of system-metric-based workload descriptions.

Chapter 9 concludes Part I with an overview of benchmark standardization efforts in the area of computer systems and information technology (IT). In an effort to provide and maintain fair industry standards for measuring system-level and component-level performance of computer systems, industry-standard consortia such as the Standard Performance Evaluation Corporation (SPEC) and the Transaction Processing Performance Council (TPC) were established in 1988. In 1998, the Storage Performance Council (SPC) was founded with a focus on storage benchmarks. The chapter provides an overview of benchmark standardization efforts within SPEC and TPC; a brief overview of SPC can be found in Chapter 13.

Chapter 10, the first chapter in Part II, presents an overview and retrospective on the development and evolution of one of the industry's most popular standard benchmarks for computing systems—the SPEC CPU benchmark suite—designed to stress a system's processor, memory subsystem, and compiler. The original version of this benchmark was released in 1989, and since then, five new generations have been released. The chapter describes these benchmarks and shows how they have influenced the computer industry over the years, helping to boost computing performance by several orders of magnitude. For the latest benchmark, SPEC CPU2017, details on the benchmark architecture, workloads, metrics, and full disclosure report are provided.

The measurement and benchmarking of server energy efficiency has become an ever more important issue over the last decades. To this end, Chapter 11 describes a rating methodology developed by SPEC for evaluating the energy efficiency of servers. The methodology was first implemented in the SPECpower_ssj2008 benchmark and later extended with more workloads, metrics, and other application areas for the SPEC Server Efficiency Rating Tool (SERT). The SERT suite was developed to fill the need for a rating tool that can be utilized by government agencies in their regulatory programs, for example, the U.S. Environmental Protection Agency (EPA) for the use in the Energy Star program for servers. The chapter provides an overview of both SPECpower_ssj2008 and SERT.

Chapter 12 provides an overview of established benchmarks for evaluating the performance of virtualization platforms, which are widely used in modern data centers. The chapter focuses on the SPEC VIRT series of industry-standard benchmarks while also considering the VMmark benchmark by VMware. The discussed benchmarks provide users with the capability of measuring different virtualization solutions on either single-host or multi-host platforms, using workloads and methodologies that are designed for fair comparisons. They have been used by hardware and software vendors to showcase, analyze, and design the latest generations of virtualization products.

Next, Chapter 13 looks at benchmarks specifically designed to evaluate the performance of storage systems and storage components. The chapter presents a brief history of the SPEC System File Server (SFS) benchmarks and takes a closer look at SPEC SFS 2014. It then introduces the benchmarks from the Storage Performance Council (SPC) and the IOzone file system benchmark. Finally, the Flexible I/O Tester (fio) is presented, showing some examples of how it can be used to measure I/O performance.

Chapter 14 switches the context to research benchmarks. The chapter introduces TeaStore, a test and reference application intended to serve as a benchmarking framework for researchers evaluating their work. Specifically, TeaStore is designed to be used in one of the three target domains: evaluation of software performance modeling approaches; evaluation of run-time performance management techniques, such as autoscalers; and evaluation of server energy efficiency, power models, and optimization techniques. TeaStore is designed as a distributed microservice-based application. Its use is demonstrated by a case study, analyzing the energy efficiency of different deployments and showing the nontrivial power and performance effects placement decisions can have.

Chapter 15 is dedicated to the evaluation of the elasticity of cloud platforms. The chapter starts by presenting a set of intuitively understandable metrics that support evaluating both the accuracy and the timing aspects of elastic behavior. The focus is on Infrastructure-as-a-Service (IaaS) clouds; however, the presented approach can also be applied in the context of other types of cloud platforms. The chapter outlines an elasticity benchmarking approach—called Bungee—that explicitly takes into account the performance of the underlying hardware infrastructure and its influence on the elastic behavior. In combination with the proposed metrics, this enables an independent quantitative evaluation of the actual achieved system elasticity.

Cloud computing enables resource sharing at different levels of a data center infrastructure, based on server virtualization, application containerization, or multi-tenant software architectures. However, due to the sharing of resources, if a customer generates increasing load on the system beyond the expected level, this may impact the performance observed by other customers. To this end, Chapter 16 presents metrics to quantify the degree of performance isolation a system provides. It also presents a case study showing how the metrics can be used in real life. The metrics presented in this chapter and in the previous chapter, as well as the thought process to create them, serve as practical examples illustrating the metric attributes and principles introduced in Chapter 3.

Chapter 17 builds on the foundations introduced in Chapters 6 and 7; it presents a survey, systematization, and evaluation of different approaches to the statistical estimation of resource demands, which play a key role in operational analysis and queueing theory. While the direct measurement of resource demands is feasible in some systems, it requires an extensive instrumentation of the application. The chapter presents generic methods to approximate resource demands without relying on dedicated instrumentation of the application. These methods are an example of using an indirect measurement strategy as discussed in Chapter 6. Resource demands

are considered in the context of computing systems; however, the presented methods
are also applicable to other types of systems.

Finally, the last chapter of Part II, Chapter 18, is dedicated to benchmarking of
computer security mechanisms, which are crucial for enforcing the properties of
confidentiality, integrity, and availability of system data and services. To minimize
the risk of security breaches, methods for evaluating security mechanisms in a
realistic and reliable manner are needed. The chapter surveys and systematizes the
existing knowledge and current practices in the area. The discussions in this chapter
are relevant for the evaluation of a wide spectrum of security mechanisms, such as
intrusion detection systems, firewalls, and access control systems.

Book's Website

A website will be maintained at http://www.benchmarking-book.com to keep readers
informed about new developments and supplementary materials related to this book.

Acknowledgements

Many people have contributed to the preparation and writing of this book.

First of all, we would like to thank our coauthors of chapters in Part II:
Jeremy A. Arnold, André Bauer, John Beckett, James Bucek, Ken Cantrell,
Don Capps, Alexander Carlton, Simon Eismann, Sorin Faibish, Johannes Grohmann,
Nikolas Roman Herbst, Rouven Krebs, Mary Marquez, Aleksandar Milenkoski,
David Morse, Nick Principe, David Schmidt, Norbert Schmitt, Simon Spinner, and
Sitsofe Wheeler.

Thanks also to Karl Huppler and Meikel Poess who contributed to Section 9.3
of Chapter 9, providing an overview of benchmarking efforts by the Transaction
Processing Performance Council (TPC).

We are especially thankful to David Lilja from the University of Minnesota for
providing us with many practical examples that were used in Chapters 3–6; we also
greatly appreciate his support by sharing materials from his course on computer
systems performance measurement, which served as a basis and inspiration for the
work on these chapters. We are grateful to Lizy Kurian John from the University
of Texas at Austin for providing illustrative examples on the aggregation of results
from multiple benchmarks, which were included in Chapter 3 (Section 3.5.3.1). We
are further grateful to Daniel Menascé from George Mason University whose books
on performance modeling and evaluation inspired the work in Chapter 7.

Fabian Brosig provided support in writing the initial version of some parts of
Section 7.2 in Chapter 7. Johannes Grohmann and André Bauer contributed a case
study on experimental design, which was included in Section 5.6 of Chapter 5.
Johannes Grohmann also contributed to Chapter 6 (Section 6.4 on event tracing),

while Simon Eismann helped with the illustrative examples on operational analysis in Chapter 7 (Section 7.1).

We are also indebted to many of our friends, colleagues, and students who carefully read individual chapter drafts and suggested changes that improved the readability and accuracy of the text.

The following colleagues from industry provided feedback on chapters in the second part of the book: Walter Bays, Hansfried Block, Karla Orozco Bucek, John Henning, Scott Hinchley, Supriya Kamthania, Mukund Kumar, Kris Langenfeld, Pranay Mahendra, John R. Mashey, Luis Mendoza, Sriranga Nadiger, Daniel Pol, Jesse Rangel, Nishant Rawtani, Jeff Reilly, David Reiner, Sanjay Sharma, and Rajesh Tadakamadla. Further, the following members of the Chair of Software Engineering at the University of Würzburg provided feedback on individual chapters of the book: André Bauer, Lukas Beierlieb, Simon Eismann, Johannes Grohmann, Stefan Herrnleben, Lukas Iffländer, Christian Krupitzer, Veronika Lesch, Thomas Prantl, Norbert Schmitt, and Marwin Züfle.

Samuel Kounev would like to thank the many students of his graduate course on performance engineering and benchmarking over the past 13 years who contributed through their thought-provoking questions and remarks on many of the topics presented in the book. He also appreciates the help of his teaching assistants for this course Nikolas R. Herbst and Marwin Züfle who contributed by developing many exercises and examples, some of which are used in the book.

Special thanks go to Lorrie Crow Kimble for copy editing the manuscript and helping us to ensure consistent writing style. Thanks also to Tobias Loos who helped in the typesetting process very early in the project.

We would also like to thank our editor, Ralf Gerstner from Springer, for his patience and support throughout this project over the past few years. Further, the anonymous reviewers selected by Springer provided very helpful and in-depth feedback on the initial version of our manuscript, which helped us to greatly improve both the content and the presentation. The help by the staff at Springer in preparation of the book is also appreciated.

Finally, we thank David Patterson and John R. Mashey for reviewing our manuscript and writing a foreword for the book.

Würzburg, Germany   *Samuel Kounev*
Houston, TX, USA   *Klaus-Dieter Lange*
Nürnberg, Germany   *Jóakim von Kistowski*

July 2020

Contents

About the Authors

Samuel Kounev is a Professor of Computer Science and Chair of Software Engineering at the University of Würzburg (Germany). He has been actively involved in the Standard Performance Evaluation Corporation (SPEC), the largest standardization consortium in the area of computer systems benchmarking, since 2002. He serves as the elected chair of the SPEC Research Group (https://research.spec.org), which he initiated in 2010 with the goal of providing a platform for collaborative research efforts between academia and industry in the area of quantitative system evaluation. Samuel is also Co-founder and Steering Committee Co-chair of several conferences in the field, including the ACM/SPEC International Conference on Performance Engineering (ICPE) and the IEEE International Conference on Autonomic Computing and Self-Organizing Systems (ACSOS). He has published extensively in the area of systems benchmarking, modeling, and evaluation of performance, energy efficiency, reliability, and security.

Klaus-Dieter Lange is a Distinguished Technologist at Hewlett Packard Enterprise (HPE), where he started his professional career in 1998, with a focus on performance and workload optimization, industry-standard benchmark development, server efficiency, and the design of secure enterprise solutions. He has been active in several of the SPEC Steering and Sub-committees since 2005; he serves on the SPEC Board of Directors and has been on the ICPE Steering Committee since its inception. Klaus is the founding chair of the SPECpower Committee, which under his technical leadership developed and maintains among others the SPECpower_ssj2008 benchmark, the SPEC PTDaemon, and the Server Efficiency Rating Tool (SERT) suite.

Jóakim von Kistowski is a software architect at DATEV eG, where he focuses on software performance and load testing, driving benchmarking method adoption, software architecture, software testing and evaluation. Jóakim has a strong SPEC background, actively contributing to the SPECpower Committee and serving as elected chair of the SPEC RG Power Working Group.

Part I
Foundations

Chapter 1
Benchmarking Basics

"One accurate measurement is worth a thousand expert opinions."
—*Grace Hopper (1906–1992), US Navy Rear Admiral*

"From a user's perspective, the best benchmark is the user's own application program."
—*Kaivalya M. Dixit (1942–2004), Former SPEC President*

This chapter provides a definition of the term "benchmark" followed by definitions of the major system quality attributes that are typically subject of benchmarking. After that, a classification of the different types of benchmarks is provided, followed by an overview of strategies for performance benchmarking. Finally, the quality criteria for good benchmarks are discussed in detail, and the chapter is wrapped up by a discussion of application scenarios for benchmarks.

1.1 Definition of Benchmark

The term benchmark was originally used to refer to "a mark on a workbench used to compare the lengths of pieces so as to determine whether one was longer or shorter than desired."[1] In computer science, a benchmark refers to "a test, or set of tests, designed to compare the performance of one computer system against the performance of others."[1] Performance, in this context, is typically understood as the amount of useful work accomplished by a system compared to the time and resources used. Better performance means more work accomplished in shorter time and/or using less resources. Depending on the context, high performance may involve one or more of the following: high responsiveness when using the system, high processing rate, low amount of resources used, or high availability of the system's

---

[1] SPEC Glossary: https://www.spec.org/spec/glossary

© Springer Nature Switzerland AG 2020
S. Kounev et al., *Systems Benchmarking*, https://doi.org/10.1007/978-3-030-41705-5_1

services. While systems benchmarking has traditionally been focused on evaluating performance in this classical sense (amount of work done vs. time and resources spent), in recent years, the scope of benchmarking has been extended to cover other properties beyond classical performance aspects (see Section 1.2). Examples of such properties include system reliability, security, or energy efficiency. Modern benchmarks can thus be seen as evaluating performance in a broader sense, that is, "the manner in which or the efficiency with which something reacts or fulfills its intended purpose."[2]

In line with this development, we use the following definition of the term benchmark in this book:

Definition 1.1 (Benchmark) A benchmark is a tool coupled with a methodology for the evaluation and comparison of systems or components with respect to specific characteristics, such as performance, reliability, or security.

We refer to the entity (i.e., system or component) that is subject of evaluation as *System Under Test (SUT)*. This definition is a variation of the definition provided by Vieira et al. (2012). A more narrow interpretation of this definition was formulated by Kistowski et al. (2015), where the competitive aspects of benchmarks are stressed (i.e., "a standard tool for the competitive evaluation and comparison of competing systems"), reflecting the fact that competitive system evaluation is the primary purpose of standardized benchmarks as developed by the Standard Performance Evaluation Corporation (SPEC) and the Transaction Processing Performance Council (TPC). To distinguish from tools for non-competitive system evaluation and comparison, such tools are often referred to as *rating tools* or *research benchmarks*. Rating tools are primarily intended as a common method of evaluation for research purposes, regulatory programs, or as part of a system improvement and development approach. Rating tools can also be standardized and should generally follow the same design and quality criteria as standard benchmarks. SPEC's Server Efficiency Rating Tool (SERT), for example, has been designed and developed using a similar process as the SPECpower_ssj2008 benchmark. The term *research benchmark* is used mostly by SPEC's Research Group[3] to refer to standard scenarios and workloads that can be used for in-depth quantitative analysis and evaluation of existing products as well as early prototypes and research results.

Each benchmark is characterized by three key aspects: *metrics*, *workloads*, and *measurement methodology*. The metrics determine what values should be derived based on measurements to produce the benchmark results. The workloads determine under which usage scenarios and conditions (e.g., executed programs, induced system load, injected failures / security attacks) measurements should be performed to derive the metrics. Finally, the measurement methodology defines the end-to-end process to execute the benchmark, collect measurements, and produce the benchmark results.

---

[2] Random House Webster's Unabridged Dictionary

[3] SPEC Research Group: https://research.spec.org

1.2 System Quality Attributes

As discussed above, systems benchmarking has evolved to cover properties beyond classical performance aspects, such as system reliability, security, or energy
efficiency. According to the ISO/IEC 25010:2011 standard, *system quality* can be
described in terms of the attributes shown in Figure 1.1. We distinguish between external and internal quality attributes. *External quality* attributes describe the view of
the system users, for example, performance, reliability, and usability. *Internal quality* attributes describe the view of the system developers, typically reflected in the
attribute *maintainability*, which captures the degree of effectiveness and efficiency
with which the system can be modified.

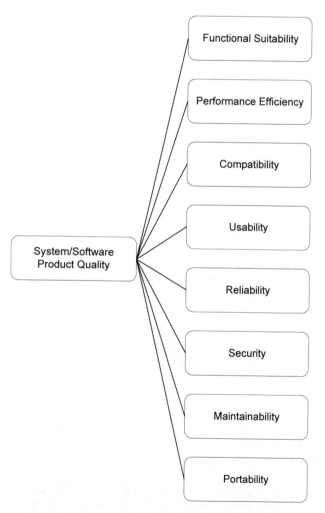

Fig. 1.1: System quality attributes according to ISO/IEC 25010:2011

In the following, we provide a brief overview of the major quality attributes targeted for evaluation by modern benchmarks.

Performance As discussed in Section 1.1, performance in its classical sense captures the amount of useful work accomplished by a system compared to the time and resources used. Typical performance metrics, which will be introduced more formally and discussed in detail in Chapter 3, include response time, throughput, and utilization. Very briefly, *response time* is the time it takes a system to react to a request providing a respective response; *throughput* captures the rate at which requests are processed by a system measured in number of completed requests (operations) per unit of time; and *utilization* is the fraction of time in which a resource (e.g., processor, network link, storage device) is used (i.e., is busy processing requests).[4]

Scalability Scalability is the ability to continue to meet performance requirements as the demand for services increases and resources are added (Smith and Williams, 2001).

Elasticity Elasticity is the degree to which a system is able to adapt to workload changes by provisioning and deprovisioning resources in an autonomic manner, such that at each point in time, the available resources match the current demand as closely as possible (Herbst et al., 2013).

Energy Efficiency Energy efficiency is the ratio of performance over power consumption. Alternatively, energy efficiency can be defined as a ratio of work performed and energy expended for this work.

Availability Availability is the readiness for correct service (Avizienis et al., 2004). In practice, the availability of a system is characterized by the fraction of time that the system is up and available to its users (Menascé et al., 2004), that is, the probability that the system is up at a randomly chosen point in time. The two main reasons for unavailability are system failures and overload conditions.

Reliability Reliability is the continuity of correct service (Avizienis et al., 2004). In practice, the reliability of a system is characterized by the probability that the system functions properly over a specified period of time (Trivedi, 2016).

Security Security is a composite of the attributes of *confidentiality*, *integrity*, and *availability* (Avizienis et al., 2004). Confidentiality is the protection of data against its release to unauthorized parties. Integrity is the protection of data or services against modifications by unauthorized parties. Finally, availability, in the context of security, is the protection of services such that they are ready to be used when needed. Enforcing security typically requires encrypting data, which in many cases may have a significant performance overhead.

Dependability The notion of dependability and its terminology have been established by the International Federation for Information Processing (IFIP) Working Group 10.4, which defines dependability as "the trustworthiness of a computing system that allows reliance to be justifiably placed on the service it delivers." Dependability is an integrative concept that includes the following attributes (Laprie, 1995):

---

[4] We use the term *request* in a general sense meaning any unit of work executed by a system that has a distinct start and end time, for example, a request sent through a browser to open a web page, a database transaction, a network operation like transferring a data packet, or a batch job executed by a mainframe system.

availability (readiness for correct service), *reliability* (continuity of correct service), *safety* (absence of catastrophic consequences on the users and the environment), *confidentiality* (absence of unauthorized disclosure of information), *integrity* (absence of improper system alterations), and *maintainability* (ability to undergo modifications and repairs).

Resilience Resilience encompasses all attributes of the quality of "working well in a changing world that includes faults, failures, errors, and attacks" (Vieira et al., 2012). Resilience benchmarking merges concepts from performance, dependability, and security benchmarking. In practice, resilience benchmarking faces challenges related to the integration of these three concepts and to the adaptive characteristics of the system under test.

1.3 Types of Benchmarks

Computer benchmarks typically fall into three general categories: *specification-based*, *kit-based*, and *hybrid*. Furthermore, benchmarks can be classified into *synthetic benchmarks*, *microbenchmarks*, *kernel benchmarks*, and *application benchmarks*.

Specification-based benchmarks describe functions that must be realized, required input parameters, and expected outcomes. The implementation to achieve the specification is left to the individual running the benchmark. Kit-based benchmarks provide the implementation as a required part of official benchmark execution. Any functional differences between products that are allowed to be used for implementing the benchmark must be resolved ahead of time. The individual running the benchmark is typically not allowed to alter the execution path of the benchmark.

Specification-based benchmarks begin with a definition of a business problem and a set of specific requirements to be addressed by the benchmark. The key criteria for this definition are the relevance topics discussed in Section 1.5 and novelty. Such benchmarks have the advantage of allowing innovative software to address the business problem of the benchmark by proving that the specified requirements are satisfied by the new implementation (Huppler and Johnson, 2014). On the other hand, they require substantial development prior to running the benchmark and may have challenges proving that all requirements of the benchmark are met.

Kit-based benchmarks may appear to restrict some innovative approaches to a business problem, but have the advantage of providing near "load and go" implementations that greatly reduce the cost and time required to run the benchmark. For kit-based benchmarks, the "specification" is used as a design guide for the creation of the kit. For specification-based benchmarks, the "specification" is presented as a set of rules to be followed by a third party who will implement and run the benchmark. This allows for substantial flexibility in how the benchmark's business problem will be resolved—a principal advantage of specification-based benchmarks.

A hybrid of the specification-based and kit-based approaches may be necessary if the majority of the benchmark can be provided in a kit, but there is a desire to allow some functions to be implemented at the discretion of the individual running the benchmark. While both specification-based and kit-based approaches have been successful in the past, current trends favor kit-based development.

The differences between synthetic benchmarks, microbenchmarks, kernel benchmarks, and application benchmarks are discussed next based on the classification by Lilja (2000). To evaluate the performance of a system with respect to a given characteristic, the system must execute some sort of program, as defined by the benchmark *workload*. Since the user is ultimately interested in how the system will perform when executing *his* application, the best program to run is obviously the user's application itself. Unfortunately, in practice this is usually infeasible, as a significant amount of time and effort may be required to port the application to the SUT. Also, one may be interested in comparing different systems to determine which one is most suitable for developing a new application. Since, in such a case, the application will not exist yet, it cannot be used as a workload for benchmarking. Given these observations, one is often forced to rely on making measurements while executing a different program than the user's application. Depending on the type of benchmark program used, benchmarks can be classified into synthetic benchmarks, microbenchmarks, kernel benchmarks, or application benchmarks.

Synthetic benchmarks are artificial programs that are constructed to try to mimic the characteristics of a given class of applications. They normally do this by executing mixes of operations carefully chosen to elicit certain system behavior and/or to match the relative mix of operations observed in the considered class of applications. The hope is that if the induced system behavior and/or the executed operation mixes are similar, the performance observed when running the benchmark would be similar to the performance obtained when executing an actual application from the respective class. The major issue with synthetic benchmarks is that they do not capture the impact of interactions between operations caused by specific execution orderings. Furthermore, such benchmarks often fail to capture the memory-referencing patterns of real applications. Thus, in many cases, synthetic benchmarks fail to provide representative workloads exhibiting similar performance to real applications from the respective domain. However, given their flexibility, synthetic benchmarks are useful for tailored system analysis allowing one to measure the limits of a system under different conditions.

Microbenchmarks are small programs used to test some specific part of a system (e.g., a small piece of code, a system operation, or a component) independent of the rest of the system. For example, a microbenchmark may be used to evaluate the performance of the floating-point execution unit of a processor, the memory management unit, or the I/O subsystem. Microbenchmarks are often used to determine the maximum performance that would be possible if the overall system performance were limited by the performance of the respective part of the system under evaluation.

Kernel benchmarks (also called program kernels) are small programs that capture the central or essential portion of a specific type of application. A kernel benchmark typically executes the portion of program code that consumes a large fraction of the total execution time of the considered application. The hope is that since this code is executed frequently, it captures the most important operations performed by the actual application. Given their compact size, kernel benchmarks have the advantage that they are normally easy to port to different systems. On the downside, they may fail to capture important influencing factors since they may ignore important system components (e.g., operating system or middleware) and may not stress the memory hierarchy in a realistic manner.

Application benchmarks are complete real application programs designed to be representative of a particular class of applications. In contrast to kernel or synthetic benchmarks, such benchmarks do real work (i.e., they execute real, meaningful tasks) and can thus more accurately characterize how real applications are likely to behave. However, application benchmarks often use artificially small input datasets in order to reduce the time and effort required to run the benchmarks. In many cases, this limits their ability to capture the memory and I/O requirements of real applications. Nonetheless, despite this limitation, application benchmarks are usually the most effective benchmarks in capturing the behavior of real applications.

1.4 Performance Benchmarking Strategies

As discussed in the beginning of this chapter, in classical performance benchmarking, a benchmark is defined as a test, or set of tests, designed to compare the performance of one system against the performance of others. The term *performance* in this context is understood as the amount of useful work accomplished by a system compared to the time and resources used. Better performance means more work accomplished in shorter time and/or using less resources.

In classical performance benchmarking, three different benchmarking strategies can be distinguished (Lilja, 2000): (1) *fixed-work benchmarks*, which measure the time required to perform a fixed amount of work; (2) *fixed-time benchmarks*, which measure the amount of work performed in a fixed period of time; and (3) *variable-work and variable-time benchmarks*, which vary both the amount of work and the execution time.

1.4.1 Fixed-Work Benchmarks

Let W_i be the "amount of work" done by System i in a measurement interval T_i. The amount of work done can be seen as an event count, where each event represents a completion of a unit of work.

The *system speed* (execution rate) is defined as $R_i = W_i/T_i$. Assuming that we run a fixed-work benchmark on two systems, that is, $W_1 = W_2 = W$, it follows that the speedup of the second system relative to the first is given by[5]

---

[5] We formally introduce and discuss the metric *speedup* in more detail in Chapter 3 (Section 3.3).

$$S = \frac{R_2}{R_1} = \frac{\frac{W}{T_2}}{\frac{W}{T_1}} = \frac{T_1}{T_2}. \tag{1.1}$$

Thus, the time T_i a system needs to execute W units of work can be used to compare the performance of systems. The performance of a system typically depends on the performance of multiple system components (e.g., CPU, main memory, I/O subsystem) that are used during operation. The main issue with fixed-work benchmarks is that they introduce an intrinsic performance bottleneck limiting how much the performance can be improved by improving only a single component of the system.

To illustrate this, assume that a system is optimized by improving the performance of its most important performance-influencing component (e.g., its CPU). The system's execution time can be broken down into two parts: time spent processing at the component under optimization and time spent processing at other components unaffected by the optimization. Assume that the performance of the optimized component is boosted by a factor of q. Let T be the time the system needs to execute W units of work before the optimization is applied, and let T' be the time it needs to execute the same workload after the optimization is applied. Let α be the fraction of time in which the optimized component is executing. $(1 - \alpha)$ will then correspond to the fraction of time spent on components and activities unaffected by the optimization. Figure 1.2 illustrates the impact of the optimization on the overall benchmark execution time (Lilja, 2000).

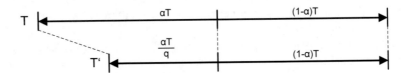

Fig. 1.2: Impact of optimizing a single system component

We observe that the overall system speedup that can be achieved through the described kind of optimization is limited:

$$S = \frac{T}{T'} = \frac{T}{\frac{\alpha T}{q} + (1 - \alpha)T} = \frac{1}{1 - \alpha\left(1 - \frac{1}{q}\right)}, \tag{1.2}$$

$$\lim_{q \to \infty} S = \lim_{q \to \infty} \frac{1}{1 - \alpha\left(1 - \frac{1}{q}\right)} = \frac{1}{1 - \alpha}. \tag{1.3}$$

Equation (1.3) is known as *Amdahl's law*. It introduces an upper bound on the overall performance improvement that can be achieved by improving the performance of a single component of a system. Given this upper bound, fixed-work benchmarks are not very popular in the industry since they have an intrinsic performance bottleneck limiting how much performance improvement can be achieved by optimizing a given system component.

1.4.2 Fixed-Time Benchmarks

To address the described issue, fixed-time benchmarks do not fix the amount of work W_i and instead measure the amount of work that can be processed in a fixed period of time. The amount of work that a system manages to process in the available time is used to compare the performance of systems.

This idea was first implemented in the SLALOM benchmark (Gustafson, Rover, et al., 1991), which runs an algorithm for calculating radiosity.[6] The performance metric is the accuracy of the answer that can be computed in 1 min. The faster a system executes, the more accurate the result obtained in 1 min would be. The advantage of this approach is that the problem being solved is automatically scaled to the capabilities of the system under test.

Fixed-time benchmarks address the described scalability issue of fixed-work benchmarks. Whatever part of the execution is optimized, it would lead to saving some time, which can then be used for processing further units of work improving the benchmark result.

To show this, we consider the same scenario as above but with a fixed execution time. Let T_f be the fixed time period for which the benchmark is executed. Given that the optimized part of the execution is running q times faster, if we imagine running the same amount of work without the optimization, the respective execution time would be q times longer. This is illustrated in Figure 1.3, sometimes referred to as the scaled version of Amdahl's law (Lilja, 2000). The benchmark execution time is compared against a hypothetical scenario (T_h) where the same amount of work is processed without the optimization.

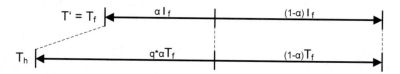

Fig. 1.3: Scaled version of Amdahl's law

We observe that unlike the case for fixed-work benchmarks, this time there is no upper bound on the speedup that can be achieved:

$$S = \frac{T_h}{T_f} = \frac{\alpha q T_f + (1 - \alpha)T_f}{T_f} = \alpha q + (1 - \alpha), \tag{1.4}$$

$$\lim_{q \to \infty} S = \lim_{q \to \infty} [\alpha q + (1 - \alpha)] = \infty. \tag{1.5}$$

---

[6] Radiosity is a global illumination algorithm used in 3D computer graphics rendering.

1.4.3 Variable-Work and Variable-Time Benchmarks

Fixed-work benchmarks are most intuitive in terms of our expectation of how improvements in system performance should impact the execution time of an application. Fixed-time benchmarks, on the other hand, have the advantage that the problem solved is automatically scaled to reflect the capabilities of the system under test. Finally, there are also variable-work and variable-time benchmarks, which fix neither the available time T nor the amount of work W (Lilja, 2000). The metric is defined as a function of T and W.

An example of a benchmark that follows this strategy is the HINT benchmark (Gustafson and Snell, 1995). It defines a mathematical problem to be solved and uses the quality of the provided solution as a basis for evaluation. The assumption is that the solution quality can be improved continually if additional time for computations is available. The ratio of the provided solution quality to the time used to achieve this quality is used as a performance metric.

The specific problem considered in the HINT benchmark is to find rational upper and lower bounds for the integral

$$\int_0^1 \frac{1-x}{1+x}dx. \tag{1.6}$$

The classical interval subdivision technique is used to find the two bounds by dividing the interval $[0, 1]$ into subintervals and counting the number of squares in the area completely below the curve and those in the area including the curve. The solution quality is then defined as $1/(u-l)$, where u and l are the computed upper and lower bounds, respectively. The metric quality improvements per second (QUIPS) is then computed by dividing the quality of the solution by the execution time in seconds. By fixing neither the execution time nor the amount of work to be processed, maximum flexibility is provided to evaluate the performance of systems with different behavior and performance bottlenecks.

1.5 Benchmark Quality Criteria

Benchmark designers must balance several, often conflicting, criteria in order to be successful. Several factors must be taken into consideration, and trade-offs between various design choices will influence the strengths and weaknesses of a benchmark. Since no single benchmark can be strong in all areas, there will always be a need for multiple workloads and benchmarks (Skadron et al., 2003).

It is important to understand the characteristics of a benchmark and determine whether or not it is applicable for a particular situation. When developing a new benchmark, the goals should be defined so that choices between competing design criteria can be made in accordance with those goals to achieve the desired balance.

Several researchers and industry participants have listed various desirable charac-teristics of benchmarks (Gustafson and Snell, 1995; Henning, 2000; Huppler, 2009; Kistowski et al., 2015; Sim et al., 2003; Skadron et al., 2003). The contents of the lists vary based on the perspective of the authors and their choice of terminol-ogy and grouping of characteristics, but most of the concepts are similar. The key characteristics can be organized in the following five groups:

1. **Relevance:** how closely the benchmark behavior correlates to behaviors that are of interest to users,
2. **Reproducibility:** producing consistent results when the benchmark is run with the same test configuration,
3. **Fairness:** allowing different test configurations to compete on their merits without artificial limitations,
4. **Verifiability:** providing confidence that a benchmark result is accurate, and
5. **Usability:** avoiding roadblocks for users to run the benchmark in their test envi-ronments.

All benchmarks are subject to these same criteria, but each category includes additional issues that are specific to the individual benchmark, depending on the benchmark's goals. In the following, the individual criteria are discussed in more detail based on Kistowski et al. (2015).

1.5.1 Relevance

"Relevance" is perhaps the most important characteristic of a benchmark. Even if the workload was perfect in every other regard, it will be of minimal use if it does not provide relevant information to its consumers. Yet relevance is also a characteristic of how the benchmark results are applied; benchmarks may be highly relevant for some scenarios and of minimal relevance for others. For the consumer of benchmark results, an assessment of a benchmark's relevance must be made in the context of the planned use of the benchmark results. For the benchmark designer, relevance means determining the intended usage scenarios of the benchmark and then designing the benchmark to be relevant for those usage scenarios (SPECpower Committee, 2014).

A general assessment of the relevance of a benchmark or workload involves two dimensions: (1) the breadth of its applicability and (2) the degree to which the workload is relevant in a given area. For example, an XML parsing benchmark may be highly relevant as a measure of XML parsing performance, somewhat relevant as a measure of enterprise server application performance, and not at all relevant for graphics performance of 3D games. Conversely, a suite of CPU benchmarks such as SPEC CPU2017 may be moderately relevant for a wide range of comput-ing environments. Benchmarks that are designed to be highly relevant in a specific area tend to have narrow applicability, while benchmarks that attempt to be appli-cable to a broader spectrum of uses tend to be less meaningful for any particular scenario (Huppler, 2009).

Scalability is an important aspect of relevance, particularly for server benchmarks. Most relevant benchmarks are multiprocess and/or multithreaded in order to be able to take advantage of the full resources of the server (Skadron et al., 2003). Achieving scalability in any application is difficult; for a benchmark, the challenges are often even greater because the benchmark is expected to run on a wide variety of systems with significant differences in available resources. Benchmark designers must also strike a careful balance between avoiding artificial limits to scaling and behaving like real applications, which often have scalability issues of their own.

1.5.2 Reproducibility

Reproducibility is the capability of the benchmark to produce the same results consistently for a particular test environment. It includes both run-to-run consistency and the ability for another tester to independently reproduce the results in another but identical environment.

Ideally, a benchmark result should be a function of the hardware and software configuration, so that the benchmark is a measure of the performance of that environment; if this were the case, the benchmark would have perfect consistency. In reality, the complexity inherent in a modern computer system introduces significant variability in the performance of an application. This variability is introduced by several factors, including things such as the timing of thread scheduling, dynamic compilation, physical disk layout, network contention, and user interaction with the system during the run (Huppler, 2009). Energy-efficiency benchmarks often have additional sources of variability due to power management technologies dynamically making changes to system performance and temperature changes affecting power consumption.

Benchmarks can address this run-to-run variability by running workloads for long enough periods of time (or executing them multiple times successively) in order to include representative samples of these variable behaviors. Some benchmarks require submission of several runs with scores that are near each other as evidence of consistency. Benchmarks also tend to run in steady state[7], unlike more typical applications, which have variations in load due to factors such as the usage patterns of users.

The ability to reproduce results in another test environment is largely tied to the ability to build an identical environment. Industry-standard benchmarks require results submissions to include a description of the test environment, typically including both hardware and software components as well as configuration options. Similarly, published research that includes benchmark results generally adds a description of the test environment that produced those results. However, in both of these cases,

---

[7] Generally, a system or a process is considered to be in a steady state if the variables that define its behavior are unchanging in time (Gagniuc, 2017). In the context of benchmarking, typically, the variables that define the workload executed on the system under test are considered.

the description may not provide enough detail for an independent tester to be able to assemble an identical environment.

Hardware must be described in sufficient detail for another person to obtain identical hardware. Software versions must be stated so that it is possible to use the same versions when reproducing the result. Tuning and configuration options must be documented for firmware, operating system, and application software so that the same options can be used when rerunning the test. Unfortunately, much of this information cannot be automatically obtained in a reliable way, so it is largely up to the tester to provide complete and accurate details.

TPC benchmarks require a certified auditor to audit results and ensure compliance with reporting requirements. SPEC uses a combination of automatic validation and committee reviews to establish compliance.

1.5.3 Fairness

Fairness ensures that systems can compete on their merits without artificial constraints. Because benchmarks always have some degree of artificiality, it is often necessary to place some constraints on test environments in order to avoid unrealistic configurations that take advantage of the simplistic nature of the benchmark.

Benchmark development requires compromises among multiple design goals; a benchmark developed by a consensus of experts is generally perceived as being more fair than a benchmark designed by a single company. While "design by committee" may not be the most efficient way to develop a benchmark, it does require that compromises are made in such a way that multiple interested parties are able to agree that the final benchmark is fair. As a result, benchmarks produced by organizations such as SPEC and TPC (both of which comprise members from industry as well as academic institutions and other interested parties) are generally regarded as fair measures of performance.

Benchmarks require a variety of hardware and software components to provide an environment suitable for running them. It is often necessary to place restrictions on what components may be used. Careful attention must be placed on these restrictions to ensure that the benchmark remains fair. Some restrictions must be made for technical reasons. For example, a benchmark implemented in Java requires a Java Virtual Machine (JVM) and an operating system and hardware that supports it. A benchmark that performs heavy disk I/O may effectively require a certain number of disks to achieve acceptable I/O rates, which would therefore limit the benchmark to hardware capable of supporting that number of disks.

Benchmark *run rules*, which specify the requirements that have to be fulfilled in order to produce a compliant benchmark result, often require the used hardware and software to meet some level of support or availability. While this restricts what components may be used, it is actually intended to promote fairness. Because benchmarks are by nature simplified applications, it is often possible to use simplified software to run them; this software may be quite fast because it lacks features that may be required by real applications. For example, enterprise servers typically require certain security features in their software which may not be directly exercised by benchmark applications; software that omits these features may run faster than software that includes them, but this simplified software may not be usable for the customer base to which the benchmark is targeted. Rules regarding software support can be a particular challenge when using open source software, which is often supported primarily by the developer community rather than commercial support mechanisms.

Both of these situations require a careful balance. Placing too many or inappropriate limits on the configuration may disallow results that are relevant to some legitimate situations. Placing too few restrictions can pollute the pool of published results and, in some cases, reduce the number of relevant results because vendors cannot compete with the "inappropriate" submissions.

Portability is an important aspect of fairness. Some benchmarks, such as TPC-C, provide only a specification and not an implementation of the benchmark, allowing vendors to implement the specification using whatever technologies are appropriate for their environment (as long as the implementation is compliant with the specification and other run rules). Other benchmarks, such as those from SPEC, provide an implementation that must be used. Achieving portability with benchmarks written in Java is relatively simple; for C and C++, it can be more difficult (Henning, 2000).

If the benchmark allows code to be recompiled, rules must be defined to state what compilation flags are allowed. SPEC CPU2017 defines *base results* (with minimal allowed compilation flags) and *peak results* (allowing the tester to use whatever compilation flags they would like). Similarly, Java benchmarks may put limits on what JVM command line options may be used.

In some cases, multiple implementations may be required to support different technologies. In this case, it may be necessary (as with SPECweb2009) for results with different implementations to be assigned to different categories so they cannot be compared with each other.

Benchmark run rules often include stipulations on how results may be used. These requirements are intended to promote fairness when results are published and compared, and they often include provisions that require certain basic information to be included any time that results are given. For example, SPECpower_ssj2008 requires that if a comparison is made for the power consumption of two systems at the 50% target load level, the performance of each system at the 50% load level as well as the overall `ssj_ops/watt` value must also be stated.

SPEC has perhaps the most comprehensive fair use policy, which further illustrates the types of fair use issues that benchmarks should consider when creating their run rules.[8]

---

[8] SPEC fair use rules: https://www.spec.org/fairuse.html

1.5.4 Verifiability

Within the industry, benchmarks are typically run by vendors who have a vested interest in the results. In academia, results are subjected to peer review and interesting results will be repeated and built upon by other researchers. In both cases, it is important that benchmark results are verifiable so that the results can be deemed trustworthy.

Good benchmarks perform some amount of self-validation to ensure that the workload is running as expected and that run rules are being followed. While a workload might include configuration options intended to allow researchers to change the behavior of the workload, standard benchmarks typically limit these options to some set of compliant values, which can be verified at run time. Benchmarks may also perform some functional verification that the output of the test is correct; these tests could detect some cases where optimizations (e.g., experimental compiler options) are producing incorrect results.

Verifiability is simplified when configuration options are controlled by the benchmark or when these details can be read by the benchmark. In this case, the benchmark can include the details with the results. Configuration details that must be documented by the user are less trustworthy since they could have been entered incorrectly.

One way to improve verifiability is to include more details in the results than are strictly necessary to produce the benchmark's metrics. Inconsistencies in this data could raise questions about the validity of the data. For example, a benchmark with a throughput metric might include response time information in addition to the transaction counts and elapsed time.

1.5.5 Usability

Most users of benchmarks are technically sophisticated, making ease of use less of a concern than it is for more consumer-focused applications; however, there are several reasons why ease of use is important. One of the most important ease of use features for a benchmark is self-validation. This was already discussed in terms of making the benchmark verifiable. Self-validating workloads give the tester confidence that the workload is running properly.

Another aspect of ease of use is being able to build practical configurations for running the benchmark. For example, one of the top TPC-C results has a system under test with over 100 distinct servers, over 700 disk drives, 11,000 SSD modules (with a total capacity of 1.76 petabytes), and a system cost of over $30 million. Of the 18 non-historical accepted TPC-C results published between January 1, 2010 and August 24, 2013, the median total system cost was $776.627. Such configurations are not economical for most potential users (Huppler, 2009).

Accurate descriptions of the system hardware and software configuration are critical for reproducibility but can be a challenge due to the complexity of these descriptions. Benchmarks can improve ease of use by providing tools to automatically extract the relevant information required for generating the descriptions.

1.6 Application Scenarios for Benchmarks

While benchmarking has traditionally been focused on competitive system evaluation and comparison, over the past couple of decades the scope of benchmarking has evolved to cover many other application scenarios. In the following, a brief overview of the main application scenarios for modern benchmarks is given. Benchmarks are considered in a broad sense including tools for non-competitive system evaluation (i.e., rating tools or research benchmarks).

As discussed in Section 1.1, systems benchmarking has traditionally been focused on evaluating performance in a classical sense (amount of work done vs. time and resources spent); however, in recent years, the scope of systems benchmarking has been extended to cover other properties beyond classical performance aspects, such as system reliability, security, or energy efficiency.

Generally, benchmarks are used to evaluate systems with respect to certain quality attributes of interest. In Section 1.2, we provided an overview of the major system quality attributes that may be subject of evaluation using benchmarks.

We refer to the entity (e.g., end user or vendor) that employs a benchmark to evaluate a system under test (SUT) as *benchmarker*. The SUT could be a hardware or software product (or service), or it could be an end-to-end application comprising multiple hardware and software components. Figure 1.4 shows the different scenarios of what the benchmarker could be with respect to his goals and intentions.

In the first scenario, the benchmarker is a customer interested to buy the SUT who uses the benchmark to compare and rank competing products offered by different vendors or to determine the size and capacity of a specific system to be purchased.

In the second scenario, the benchmarker is a vendor who sells the SUT to customers and is using the benchmark to showcase its quality for marketing purposes. Industry-standard benchmarks and standardization bodies provide means to evaluate and showcase a product's quality on a level playing field. The benchmarker might also be interested to receive an official certificate issued by a certification agency, attesting a given quality level (e.g., energy-efficiency standard).

In the next scenario, the benchmarker is in the process of developing, deploying, or operating the SUT. In this scenario, one might be using the benchmark for stress or regression testing, for system optimization or performance tuning, for system sizing and capacity planning, or for validating a given hardware and software configuration. In this scenario, the benchmark may also be used as a blueprint demonstrating programming best practices and design patterns as a guidance for the development of a new system architecture.

Finally, the benchmarker may be a researcher using the benchmark as a representative application to evaluate novel system architectures or approaches to system development and operation.

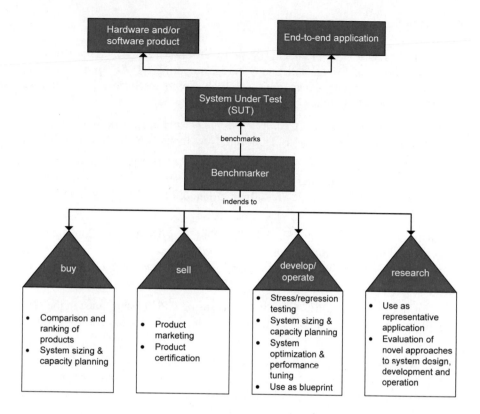

Fig. 1.4: Application scenarios for benchmarks

1.7 Concluding Remarks

In this chapter, we introduced the fundamental concepts and terminology used in systems benchmarking. We provided a definition of the term "benchmark" followed by definitions of the major system quality attributes that are typically subject of benchmarking. We distinguished between external and internal system quality attributes. After that, we presented a classification of the different types of benchmarks, followed by an overview of strategies for performance benchmarking. Finally, the quality criteria for good benchmarks, such as relevance, reproducibility, fairness, verifiability, and usability, were discussed in detail. While benchmarking has traditionally been focused on competitive system evaluation and comparison, over the past couple of decades, the scope of benchmarking has evolved to cover many other application scenarios. In the final section of this chapter, we provided an overview of the application scenarios for benchmarks discussing both their use in industry and their use in the research and academic community.

References

Avizienis, A., Laprie, J.-C., Randell, B., and Landwehr, C. (2004). "Basic Concepts and Taxonomy of Dependable and Secure Computing". *IEEE Transactions on Dependable and Secure Computing*, 1(1). IEEE Computer Society: Los Alamitos, CA, USA, pp. 11–33 (cited on p. 6).

Gagniuc, P. A. (2017). *Markov Chains: From Theory to Implementation and Experimentation*. John Wiley & Sons: Hoboken, New Jersey, USA (cited on p. 14).

Gustafson, J., Rover, D., Elbert, S., and Carter, M. (1991). "The Design of a Scalable, Fixed-Time Computer Benchmark". *Journal of Parallel and Distributed Computing*, 12(4). Academic Press, Inc.: Orlando, FL, USA, pp. 388–401 (cited on p. 11).

Gustafson, J. and Snell, Q. (1995). "HINT: A New Way To Measure Computer Performance". In: *Proceedings of the 28th Annual Hawaii International Conference on System Sciences*. (Wailea, Hawaii, USA). Vol. 2. IEEE, pp. 392–401 (cited on pp. 12, 13).

Henning, J. L. (2000). "SPEC CPU2000: Measuring CPU Performance in the New Millennium". *Computer*, 33(7). IEEE: New Jersey, USA, pp. 28–35 (cited on pp. 13, 16).

Herbst, N. R., Kounev, S., and Reussner, R. (2013). "Elasticity in Cloud Computing: What it is, and What it is Not". In: *Proceedings of the 10th International Conference on Autonomic Computing (ICAC 2013)*. (San Jose, CA, USA). USENIX, pp. 23–27 (cited on p. 6).

Huppler, K. (2009). "The Art of Building a Good Benchmark". In: *Performance Evaluation and Benchmarking—First TPC Technology Conference (TPCTC 2009), Revised Selected Papers*. Ed. by R. O. Nambiar and M. Poess. Vol. 5895. Lecture Notes in Computer Science. Springer-Verlag: Berlin, Heidelberg, pp. 18–30 (cited on pp. 13, 14, 17).

Huppler, K. and Johnson, D. (2014). "TPC Express - A New Path for TPC Benchmarks". In: *Performance Characterization and Benchmarking—5th TPC Technology Conference (TPCTC 2013), Revised Selected Papers*. Ed. by R. O. Nambiar and M. Poess. Vol. 8391. Lecture Notes in Computer Science. Springer-Verlag: Berlin, Heidelberg, pp. 48–60 (cited on p. 7).

Kistowski, J. von, Arnold, J. A., Huppler, K., Lange, K.-D., Henning, J. L., and Cao, P. (2015). "How to Build a Benchmark". In: *Proceedings of the 6th ACM/SPEC International Conference on Performance Engineering (ICPE 2015)*. (Austin, TX, USA). ACM: New York, NY, USA, pp. 333–336 (cited on pp. 4, 13).

Laprie, J.-C. (1995). "Dependable Computing: Concepts, Limits, Challenges". In: *Proceedings of the 25th International Symposium on Fault-Tolerant Computing (FTCS 1995)*. (Pasadena, CA, USA). IEEE Computer Society: Washington, DC, USA, pp. 42–54 (cited on p. 6).

Lilja, D. J. (2000). *Measuring Computer Performance: A Practitioner's Guide.* Cambridge University Press: Cambridge, UK (cited on pp. 8–12).

Menascé, D. A., Almeida, V. A., and Dowdy, L. W. (2004). *Performance by Design: Computer Capacity Planning By Example.* Prentice Hall: Upper Saddle River, NJ, USA (cited on p. 6).

Sim, S. E., Easterbrook, S., and Holt, R. C. (2003). "Using Benchmarking to Advance Research: A Challenge to Software Engineering". In: *Proceedings of the 25th International Conference on Software Engineering (ICSE 2003).* (Portland, Oregon). IEEE Computer Society: Washington, DC, USA, pp. 74–83 (cited on p. 13).

Skadron, K., Martonosi, M., August, D. I., Hill, M. D., Lilja, D. J., and Pai, V. S. (2003). "Challenges in Computer Architecture Evaluation". *Computer,* 36(8). IEEE Computer Society: Los Alamitos, CA, USA, pp. 30–36 (cited on pp. 12–14).

Smith, C. U. and Williams, L. G. (2001). *Performance Solutions: A Practical Guide to Creating Responsive, Scalable Software.* Addison-Wesley Professional Computing Series. Addison-Wesley: Boston, USA (cited on p. 6).

SPECpower Committee (2014). *Power and Performance Benchmark Methodology V2.2.* Gainesville, VA, USA: Standard Performance Evaluation Corporation (SPEC) (cited on p. 13).

Trivedi, K. S. (2016). *Probability and Statistics with Reliability, Queuing and Computer Science Applications.* Second Edition. John Wiley and Sons Ltd.: Hoboken, New Jersey (cited on p. 6).

Vieira, M., Madeira, H., Sachs, K., and Kounev, S. (2012). "Resilience Benchmarking". In: *Resilience Assessment and Evaluation of Computing Systems.* Ed. by K. Wolter, A. Avritzer, M. Vieira, and A. van Moorsel. Springer-Verlag: Berlin, Heidelberg, pp. 283–301 (cited on pp. 4, 7).

Chapter 2
Review of Basic Probability and Statistics

"Statistics are like alienists—they will testify for either side."
—*Fiorello La Guardia (1882-1947), 99th Mayor of NYC*

"It is easy to lie with statistics. It is hard to tell the truth without statistics."
—*Andrejs Dunkels (1939-1998), Swedish mathematics teacher, mathematician, and writer*

In this chapter, we briefly review the basics of probability and statistics while establishing the statistical notation needed for understanding some of the chapters in the book. The chapter is not intended as an introduction to probability and statistics but rather as a quick refresher assuming that the reader is already familiar with the basic concepts. While basic probability and statistics is essential for understanding Chapters 4, 5, 7, and 17, we note that it is not a prerequisite for understanding the other chapters in the book.

Much of the world around us is not *deterministic*, but it is rather governed by random processes of which the behavior is hard to predict. Consider an online banking application hosted on a server inside a data center. The application processes requests sent from users over the Internet. Although the set of possible requests that may arrive is finite and known, we cannot know *for certain* how many requests of each type will arrive at a given point in time. Moreover, since the server resources (e.g., processors) are shared, it is hard to predict the processing time of a request given that it depends on how many other requests are processed concurrently. This makes it impossible to tell for certain what will happen next. A process like the one described is referred to as *stochastic*. There is a vast theory to predict the behavior of stochastic processes. In the following, we review the basics of probability and statistics, including random variables and distribution functions, which form the basis for stochastic models. For a detailed introduction to probability and statistics, we refer the reader to Walpole et al. (2016). An in-depth treatment of the mathematical foundations of probability and measure theory can be found in Billingsley (2012).

© Springer Nature Switzerland AG 2020
S. Kounev et al., *Systems Benchmarking*, https://doi.org/10.1007/978-3-030-41705-5_2

2.1 Basic Concepts

We start by introducing some basic concepts and respective notation from probability and statistics.

> **Definition 2.1 (Experiment, Sample Space, Sample Point)** An *experiment* (or *random experiment*) is a process of which the outcome is uncertain. The set of possible outcomes of an experiment is called the *sample space* and is usually denoted by S. The individual outcomes themselves are called *sample points* in the sample space.

Example 2.1 Consider the experiment of tossing a die one time. The sample space is $S = \{1, 2, 3, 4, 5, 6\}$.

Example 2.2 Consider the experiment of measuring the processing time of a database transaction. In theory, the sample space S is the set of positive real numbers; that is, $S = \mathbb{R}^+$.

> **Definition 2.2 (Event, Probability)** Any subset A of the sample space S, that is, $A \subset S$, or equivalently any statement of conditions that defines a collection of certain sample points, is referred to as *event*. The *probability function* $P(\cdot)$ assigns to each event a real number between 0 and 1 (referred to as its *probability*) while satisfying the following three Kolmogorov axioms: (i) For any event A, $P(A) \geq 0$; (ii) $P(S) = 1$; and (iii) if $A_1, A_2, A_3, \ldots$ is a countable sequence[a] of *mutually exclusive* events[b] (i.e., $A_j \cap A_k = \emptyset$ whenever $j \neq k$), it follows that $P(A_1 \cup A_2 \cup A_3 \cup \ldots) = P(A_1) + P(A_2) + P(A_3) + \ldots$.
>
> ---
>
> [a] *Countable* means that the number of elements is either finite or countably infinite, where the latter means that the elements can be put in a one-to-one correspondence with the natural numbers.
>
> [b] Two or more events are *mutually exclusive* if it is impossible for two or more such events to occur at the same time; that is, the occurrence of any one of them implies that the others will not occur.

> **Definition 2.3 (Random Variable)** A *random variable* is a function that assigns a real number to each point in the sample space S. It is common to denote random variables by capital letters (e.g., X or Y) and the concrete values that they take on in a particular experiment by lowercase letters (e.g., x or y).

Example 2.3 Consider the experiment of tossing a pair of dice. The sample space S is the set $\{(1, 1), (1, 2), \ldots, (6, 6)\}$, where (i, j) corresponds to getting i on the first die and j on the second die. We define X as the random variable equal to the product of the two dice so that X assigns the value $x \times y$ to the outcome (x, y). For example, X will be equal to 12 if the outcome is $(3, 4)$.

A random variable X is said to be *discrete* if the number of possible values of X is countable (i.e., either finite or countably infinite).

Definition 2.4 (Probability Mass Function—PMF) The *probability mass function (PMF)* $p(x)$ of a discrete random variable X is defined as

$$p(x) = p_x \stackrel{\text{def}}{=} P(X = x). \tag{2.1}$$

It follows that

$$\sum_x p_x = 1. \tag{2.2}$$

An example of a probability mass function for a discrete random variable is shown in Figure 2.1.

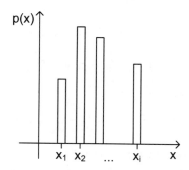

Fig. 2.1: Example of a PMF for a discrete random variable

Next, we consider random variables that can take on an uncountably infinite number of different values (e.g., all real numbers in a given interval). Such random variables are called *continuous* random variables.

Definition 2.5 (Probability Density Function—PDF) For a continuous random variable X, it is assumed that there exists a nonnegative function $f(x)$ called *probability density function (PDF)* (or simply density function) such that for any interval $[a, b]$

$$P(X \in [a, b]) = \int_a^b f(x)dx \quad \text{and} \quad \int_{-\infty}^{+\infty} f(x)dx = 1. \tag{2.3}$$

An example of a probability density function for a continuous random variable is shown in Figure 2.2.

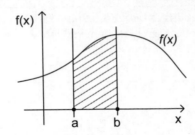

Fig. 2.2: Example of a PDF for a continuous random variable

2.2 Distributions of Random Variables

For a given value of x, the probability mass function $p(x)$ of a discrete random variable X gives us the probability of the random variable taking on the value of x. For a continuous random variable, the probability of the random variable taking on a given value x is

$$P(X = x) = P(X \in [x, x]) = \int_x^x f(y)dy = 0. \tag{2.4}$$

Thus, the value of the probability density function $f(x)$ does not directly correspond to the probability of the random variable taking on the value of x. However, the value of $f(x)$ still provides an indication of the likelihood of the random variable taking on a value close to x. Indeed, if $\Delta x > 0$, then

$$P(X \in [x, x + \Delta x]) = \int_x^{x+\Delta x} f(y)dy, \tag{2.5}$$

which is the area under $f(x)$ between x and $x + \Delta x$. Consequently, the value of a continuous random variable X is more likely to fall in an interval above which $f(x)$ is high than in an interval of the same width above which $f(x)$ is low.

Definition 2.6 (Cumulative Distribution Function—CDF) The *cumulative distribution function (CDF)* or simply distribution function $F(x)$ of the random variable X is defined such that

$$F(y) \overset{\text{def}}{=} P(X \le y) = \begin{cases} \sum\limits_{x \le y} p_x & \text{for } X \text{ discrete,} \\[2em] \int\limits_{-\infty}^{y} f(x)dx & \text{for } X \text{ continuous.} \end{cases} \tag{2.6}$$

A distribution function $F(x)$ has the following properties:

$0 \leq F(x) \leq 1$ for all x,

$F(x)$ is nondecreasing, that is, if $x_1 \leq x_2$ then $F(x_1) \leq F(x_2)$, $\qquad$ (2.7)

$\lim_{x \to \infty} F(x) = 1$ and $\lim_{x \to -\infty} F(x) = 0$ (since X takes on only finite values).

From the definition of the distribution function $F(x)$, it can be shown that under some mild technical assumptions $f(x) = F'(x)$. For an interval $[a, b]$, it then follows that

$$P(X \in [a, b]) = \int_a^b f(x)dx = F(b) - F(a). \qquad (2.8)$$

Definition 2.7 (Mean) The *mean* μ (also referred to as *expected value*) of a random variable X is defined as

$$\mu = E[X] \stackrel{\text{def}}{=} \begin{cases} \sum_x x p_x & \text{for } X \text{ discrete,} \\ \int_{-\infty}^{+\infty} x f(x)dx & \text{for } X \text{ continuous.} \end{cases} \qquad (2.9)$$

The mean is one *measure of central tendency* of the distribution of a random variable. An alternative measure of central tendency is the *median* $x_{0.5}$ defined as the smallest value of x such that $F_X(x) \geq 0.5$, where $F_X(x)$ is the distribution function of X. For a continuous random variable X, $F_X(x_{0.5}) = 0.5$. In cases where a random variable X may take on very large or very small values with low probability, the median is generally considered to be a better measure of central tendency than the mean, since extreme values (despite being unlikely to occur) may greatly affect the mean, whereas they do not affect the median in a similar way.

Definition 2.8 (Variance) The *variance* σ_X^2 of a random variable X is defined as

$$\sigma_X^2 = \text{Var}(X) = \sigma^2[X] \stackrel{\text{def}}{=} \begin{cases} \sum_x (x - \mu)^2 p_x & \text{for } X \text{ discrete,} \\ \int_{-\infty}^{+\infty} (x - \mu)^2 f(x)dx & \text{for } X \text{ continuous.} \end{cases} \qquad (2.10)$$

The variance is a *measure of dispersion* of the random variable about its mean, so that the larger the variance, the more likely the random variable will take on values far from its mean.

It is easy to show that the following relation holds:

$$\text{Var}(X) = E[(X - \mu)^2] = E[X^2] - E[X]^2. \qquad (2.11)$$

> **Definition 2.9 (Standard Deviation)** The *standard deviation* σ_X of a random variable X is defined as
>
> $$\sigma_X = \sigma[X] \stackrel{\text{def}}{=} \sqrt{\text{Var}(X)}. \tag{2.12}$$

Looking at the definition of variance, given that it is defined based on the *squared* deviation of the values of the random variable from its mean, it is expressed in square units. In contrast, the standard deviation, as the square root of the variance, is a measure of dispersion expressed in the same units as the random variable, which makes it easier to work with and interpret.

2.3 Independent and Dependent Random Variables

So far, we considered only one random variable at a time; however, in practice one often must deal with n random variables $\{X_1, X_2, ..., X_n\}$ at the same time.

If $\{X_1, X_2, ..., X_n\}$ are discrete random variables, the function

$$p(x_1, x_2, ..., x_n) = P(X_1 = x_1, X_2 = x_2, ..., X_n = x_n) \tag{2.13}$$

is called *joint probability mass function* of $\{X_1, X_2, ..., X_n\}$.

> **Definition 2.10 (Independent Random Variables—Discrete Case)** The discrete random variables $\{X_1, X_2, ..., X_n\}$ are *independent* if
>
> $$p(x_1, x_2, ..., x_n) = p_{X_1}(x_1)p_{X_2}(x_2)...p_{X_n}(x_n), \tag{2.14}$$
>
> where $p_{X_i}(x_i)$ is the probability mass function of the random variable X_i.

If $\{X_1, X_2, ..., X_n\}$ are continuous random variables, they are referred to as *jointly continuous* if there exists a nonnegative function $f(x_1, x_2, ..., x_n)$, called *joint probability density function* of $\{X_1, X_2, ..., X_n\}$, such that for all sets of real numbers $A_1, A_2, ..., A_n$,

$$P(X_1 \in A_1, X_2 \in A_2, ..., X_n \in A_n) = \int_{A_1} \int_{A_2} ... \int_{A_n} f(x_1, x_2, ..., x_n)dx_1 dx_2...dx_n.$$
$$\tag{2.15}$$

> **Definition 2.11 (Independent Random Variables—Continuous Case)** The continuous random variables $\{X_1, X_2, ..., X_n\}$ are *independent* if they have a joint probability density function computed as
>
> $$f(x_1, x_2, ..., x_n) = f_{X_1}(x_1)f_{X_2}(x_2)...f_{X_n}(x_n), \tag{2.16}$$
>
> where $f_{X_i}(x_i)$ is the probability density function of the random variable X_i.

Intuitively, the random variables $\{X_1, X_2, ..., X_n\}$ are independent if knowing the values of a subset of them reveals nothing about the distribution of the remaining random variables. If $\{X_1, X_2, ..., X_n\}$ are not independent, we say that they are *dependent*.

It can be easily shown that the mean of a linear combination of the random variables $\{X_1, X_2, ..., X_n\}$ is equal to the same linear combination of the means of the random variables; that is,

$$E\left[\sum_{i=1}^{n} a_i X_i\right] = \sum_{i=1}^{n} a_i E[X_i].$$ (2.17)

The above equation does not require that the random variables $\{X_1, X_2, ..., X_n\}$ be independent. However, if they are independent, it can also be shown that the variance of a linear combination of the random variables is equal to the respective linear combination of the variances of the random variables with squared coefficients; that is,

$$\mathsf{Var}\left(\sum_{i=1}^{n} a_i X_i\right) = \sum_{i=1}^{n} a_i^2 \mathsf{Var}(X_i).$$ (2.18)

We now consider measures that characterize the dependence between two random variables X and Y.

Definition 2.12 (Covariance) The *covariance* between the random variables X and Y is a measure of their (linear) dependence and is defined as follows:

$$\mathsf{Cov}(X, Y) = C_{XY} \stackrel{\text{def}}{=} E\left[(X - \mu_X)(Y - \mu_Y)\right] = E[XY] - \mu_X \mu_Y,$$ (2.19)

where μ_X and μ_Y are the mean values of the random variables X and Y, respectively.

From the definition of covariance, it is obvious that $\mathsf{Cov}(X, Y) = \mathsf{Cov}(Y, X)$ and $\mathsf{Cov}(X, X) = \mathsf{Var}(X)$.

If $\mathsf{Cov}(X, Y) = 0$, we say that the random variables X and Y are *uncorrelated*. It can be easily shown that if X and Y are independent, then it follows that they are also uncorrelated; that is, $\mathsf{Cov}(X, Y) = 0$. Two uncorrelated variables, however, must not necessarily be independent.

If $\mathsf{Cov}(X, Y) > 0$, we say that X and Y are *positively correlated*, which implies that the events $\{X > \mu_X\}$ and $\{Y > \mu_Y\}$ tend to occur together, and also the events $\{X < \mu_X\}$ and $\{Y < \mu_Y\}$ tend to occur together.

If $\mathsf{Cov}(X, Y) < 0$, we say that X and Y are *negatively correlated*, which implies that the events $\{X > \mu_X\}$ and $\{Y < \mu_Y\}$ tend to occur together, and also the events $\{X < \mu_X\}$ and $\{Y > \mu_Y\}$ tend to occur together.

In the case of positively correlated random variables, if one variable has a large value, the other is likely to have a large value as well. For negatively correlated random variables, if one variable has a large value, the other is likely to have a small value instead.

Definition 2.13 (Correlation) Given that the covariance is not a dimensionless quantity, its interpretation as a measure of dependence between two random variables X and Y poses difficulties. Therefore, often the *correlation* is used instead, which is defined as follows:

$$\text{Cor}(X, Y) = \rho_{XY} \overset{\text{def}}{=} \frac{\text{Cov}(X, Y)}{\sigma_X \sigma_Y}, \tag{2.20}$$

where σ_X and σ_Y are the values of the standard deviation for the random variables X and Y, respectively.

It can be easily shown that $-1 \leq \text{Cor}(X, Y) \leq 1$. If $\text{Cor}(X, Y)$ is close to 1, then the random variables X and Y are highly positively correlated, whereas if $\text{Cor}(X, Y)$ is close to -1, they are highly negatively correlated.

2.4 Random Samples and Some Important Statistics

The totality of the observations with which we are concerned in an experiment is commonly referred to as *population*. Each observation in a population is a value of a random variable X with some probability distribution $f(x)$. The field of *statistical inference* is concerned with drawing conclusions about a population when it is impractical to observe the entire population. In such cases, a subset of the population, referred to as a *sample*, is observed and used to estimate relevant characteristics of the population. If our inferences from the sample to the population are to be valid, the sample must be chosen such that it is *representative* of the population. A sampling procedure that consistently overestimates or underestimates a characteristic of the population is said to be *biased*. To avoid bias in the sampling procedure, observations in a sample should be made independently and at random, resulting in a *random sample*. More formally, the concept of random sample is captured in the following definition:

Definition 2.14 (Random Sample) A set of independent and identically distributed random variables $\{X_1, X_2, ..., X_n\}$ with a common distribution function $F(x)$ is said to constitute a *random sample* of size n from a population with distribution function $F(x)$, or equivalently, from any random variable X with distribution function $F(x)$. A set of specific observed values $\{x_1, x_2, ..., x_n\}$ of the random variables $\{X_1, X_2, ..., X_n\}$ can be considered to be n independent measurements of some quantity distributed according to their common distribution. In this context, the term random sample is also used to refer to any such set of n observed values $\{x_1, x_2, ..., x_n\}$ from the respective distribution.

Definition 2.15 (Statistic) A *statistic* is any function of the random variables that make up a random sample.

When considering a random sample from a given random variable with an unknown underlying distribution, some of the most common statistics used in practice are the sample mean, sample variance, and sample standard deviation.

Definition 2.16 (Sample Mean) The *sample mean* $\bar{X}$ of a random sample $\{X_1, X_2, ..., X_n\}$ is defined as

$$\bar{X} \stackrel{\text{def}}{=} \frac{\sum_{i=1}^{n} X_i}{n}. \tag{2.21}$$

The statistic $\bar{X}$ assumes the value $\bar{x} = \sum_{i=1}^{n} x_i/n$ when X_1 takes on the value x_1, X_2 takes on the value x_2, and so on. It is a common practice that the value of a statistic in a given instance of an experiment is given the same name as the statistic. As an example, the term sample mean is used to refer to both the statistic $\bar{X}$ and its computed value $\bar{x}$.

Definition 2.17 (Sample Variance) The *sample variance* S^2 of a random sample $\{X_1, X_2, ..., X_n\}$ is defined as

$$S^2 \stackrel{\text{def}}{=} \frac{\sum_{i=1}^{n} (X_i - \bar{X})^2}{n - 1}. \tag{2.22}$$

Definition 2.18 (Sample Standard Deviation) The *sample standard deviation* S of a random sample $\{X_1, X_2, ..., X_n\}$ is defined as the square root of the sample variance S^2.

As usual, the computed values of S^2 and S for a given sample are denoted using lower case characters s^2 and s, respectively.

Definition 2.19 (Estimator, Point Estimate) An *estimator* is a statistic $\hat{\Theta}$ that provides an approximation of a given parameter θ of a population (e.g., mean or standard deviation). A *point estimate* of the respective parameter θ is a single value $\hat{\theta}$ of the respective statistic $\hat{\Theta}$.

The sample mean $\bar{x}$ is a point estimate of the mean μ of the respective distribution, whereas the sample variance s^2 and sample standard deviation s are point estimates of the variance σ^2 and standard deviation σ, respectively. As a general rule of thumb in statistics, if a sample has at least 30 elements, then the sample variance can be considered a good estimate of the population variance (Walpole et al., 2016).[1]

Definition 2.20 (Unbiased Estimator) The estimator $\hat{\Theta}$ of the parameter θ of a population is said to be an *unbiased estimator* of θ if $E[\hat{\Theta}] = \theta$.

---

[1] Although this rule is typically assumed to apply, the reader is warned to use it with some caution since it is easy to show examples of distributions where it does not apply.

It is often preferable to come up with an interval within which we would expect the value of the unknown population parameter to lie. Such an interval is called *interval estimate* of the population parameter.

> **Definition 2.21 (Interval Estimate)** An *interval estimate* of a given parameter θ of a population is an interval of the form $\hat{\theta}_L < \theta < \hat{\theta}_U$, where $\hat{\theta}_L$ and $\hat{\theta}_U$ depend on the value of the statistic $\hat{\Theta}$ for a particular sample as well as on the distribution of $\hat{\Theta}$.

2.5 Important Continuous Distributions and Central Limit Theorem

One of the most common continuous probability distributions in statistics is the *Normal distribution* (also called Gaussian, Gauss, or Laplace–Gauss distribution).

> **Definition 2.22 (Normal distribution)** The probability density function of the *Normal distribution* with parameters μ and σ^2 is defined as
>
> $$f(x) = \frac{1}{\sqrt{2\pi\sigma^2}} e^{-\frac{(x-\mu)^2}{2\sigma^2}}, \qquad (2.23)$$
>
> where μ is the mean and σ^2 is the variance of the distribution. When a random variable is normally distributed with mean μ and variance σ^2, we will use the following notation:
>
> $$X \sim N(\mu, \sigma^2). \qquad (2.24)$$

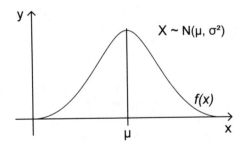

Fig. 2.3: Example of a Normal distribution

A random variable with a Normal distribution is said to be *normally distributed* and is referred to as *normal deviate*. Figure 2.3 shows an example density function of a normally distributed random variable. The Normal distribution is sometimes informally called the *bell curve*. However, we note that many other distributions are also bell-shaped (e.g., the Cauchy distribution or the Student *t*-distribution).

If the random variables $\{X_1, X_2, ..., X_n\}$ are independent and normally distributed $X_i \sim N\left(\mu_i, \sigma_i^2\right) \mid i \in \{1, \ldots, n\}$, it can be easily shown that any linear combination of the random variables is also normally distributed. From Equations (2.17) and (2.18), it then follows that

$$Y = \sum_{i=1}^{n} a_i X_i \sim N\left(\sum_{i=1}^{n} a_i \mu_i, \sum_{i=1}^{n} a_i^2 \sigma_i^2\right). \qquad (2.25)$$

Similarly, based on Equation (2.25), it can be shown that if $X \sim N\left(\mu_i, \sigma_i^2\right)$, then

$$Z = \left(\frac{X - \mu}{\sigma}\right) \sim N(0, 1). \qquad (2.26)$$

The random variable Z has a Normal distribution with mean 0 and variance 1. This distribution is referred to as *standard Normal distribution*.

In statistics (e.g., in the context of hypothesis testing), it is often required to find a symmetrical interval around the mean of the standard Normal distribution, such that the respective area under the density function is equal to a specified target value. To facilitate this, in most statistics textbooks, statistical tables are provided that list so-called *critical values* of the standard Normal distribution. The critical value z_α is typically defined as a value such that the area under the standard Normal density function to the right of that value is equal to α (see Figure 2.4). The respective area is called *right tail* of the distribution. For symmetry reasons, the area to the left of the value $-z_\alpha$, referred to as *left tail* of the distribution, is also equal to α. It follows that the central area under the curve between $-z_\alpha$ and z_α is equal to $1 - 2\alpha$. In other words, the probability of a random variable with standard Normal distribution taking on a value in the interval $[-z_\alpha, z_\alpha]$ is given by $1 - 2\alpha$. The values $-z_\alpha$ and z_α are often referred to as *lower critical value* and *upper critical value* of the standard Normal distribution, respectively.

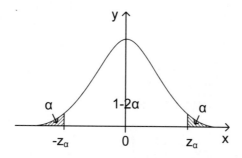

Fig. 2.4: Critical values of the standard Normal distribution

The Normal distribution is often used in practice because of the *Central Limit Theorem (CLT)*, which is generally considered to be the most important result in probability theory. In its classical form, the theorem states, in effect, that a sum of a "large number" of values from any distribution with a finite positive variance will be approximately normally distributed. What is meant by a large number is not explicitly defined; however, 30 or higher is typically considered large enough (Lilja, 2000; Walpole et al., 2016). If the distribution is not too different from a Normal distribution, a number higher than six or seven is often considered sufficient to apply the CLT.[2] Below, we present the classical CLT more formally.

Theorem 2.1 (Central Limit Theorem) *Let $\{X_1, X_2, ..., X_n\}$ be a set of independent and identically distributed random variables with finite mean μ and finite positive variance $\sigma^2 > 0$. If $\bar{X}$ and Z_n are defined as*

$$\bar{X} = \frac{\sum_{i=1}^{n} X_i}{n} \qquad Z_n = \frac{\bar{X} - \mu}{\sqrt{\sigma^2/n}} \qquad (2.27)$$

then as n tends to infinity, the distribution function $F_n(z) = P(Z_n \leq z)$ of the random variable Z_n converges to the standard Normal distribution $N(0, 1)$. In other words, if n is large enough, the random variable Z_n will be approximately normally distributed with mean 0 and variance 1, regardless of the underlying distribution of the X_i's. Equivalently, for large n, the sample mean $\bar{X}$ will be approximately normally distributed with mean μ and variance σ^2/n.

A random variable whose logarithm is normally distributed is said to have a *Log-normal distribution*. Such a variable is generated by collections of small multiplicative effects, rather than the additive effects that generate Normal distributions. The mathematics of the Log-normal distribution are relevant to the widespread use of the geometric mean for aggregating speedup ratios in modern benchmarks, a procedure discussed in detail in Chapter 3, Section 3.5.3.2.

Another important distribution that we will use in this book is the *t-distribution*, also called *Student t-distribution*.

Definition 2.23 (t-distribution) The probability density function of the *t-distribution* with parameter $n > 0$, referred to as *degrees of freedom*, is given by

$$f_n(x) = \frac{\Gamma\left(\frac{n+1}{2}\right)}{\sqrt{n\pi}\,\Gamma\left(\frac{n}{2}\right)} \left(1 + \frac{x^2}{n}\right)^{-\frac{n+1}{2}}, \qquad (2.28)$$

where $\Gamma(x)$ is the gamma function

$$\Gamma(x) = \int_0^{+\infty} t^{x-1} e^{-t}\, dt. \qquad (2.29)$$

---

[2] Similarly to the rule about the use of the sample variance as an estimate of the population variance, the reader is warned to use these rules with caution since it is easy to show examples of distributions where they do not apply.

The t-distribution was introduced in 1908 by W. S. Gosset. At that time, Gosset was working in an Irish brewery that did not allow its staff members to publish research results. To circumvent this, Gosset published his work under the name "Student." As a result, the distribution is commonly referred to as Student t-distribution or simply t-distribution.

The t-distribution is similar to the standard Normal distribution. While they are both bell-shaped and symmetric about a mean of zero, the t-distribution has a higher variance, which depends on the degrees of freedom n and is always greater than 1. As the sample size $n \to \infty$, the t-distribution converges to the standard Normal distribution.

The t-distribution is often used in the context of the following theorem:

Theorem 2.2 *Let $\{X_1, X_2, ..., X_n\}$ be a set of independent and normally distributed random variables with mean μ and variance σ^2; that is, $X_i \sim N(\mu, \sigma^2) \mid i \in \{1, \dots, n\}$. If $\bar{X}$ and S^2 are defined as*

$$\bar{X} = \frac{\sum_{i=1}^{n} X_i}{n} \qquad S^2 = \frac{\sum_{i=1}^{n} (X_i - \bar{X})^2}{n - 1} \qquad (2.30)$$

then the random variable

$$T = \frac{\bar{X} - \mu}{S/\sqrt{n}} \qquad (2.31)$$

has a t-distribution with $(n - 1)$ degrees of freedom.

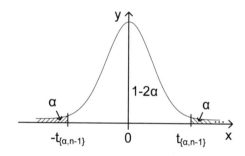

Fig. 2.5: Critical values of the t-distribution

Similarly to the standard Normal distribution, statistical tables listing *critical values* for the t-distribution can be found in most statistics textbooks. Critical values help to easily find a symmetrical interval around the mean of the t-distribution, such that the respective area under the density function is equal to a specified target value. The critical value $t_{\{\alpha, n-1\}}$ for a t-distribution with $(n - 1)$ degrees of freedom is a value such that the area under the respective density function to the right of that value is equal to α (see Figure 2.5). This area is referred to as *right tail* of the distribution, whereas the symmetrical area to the left of the value $-t_{\{\alpha, n-1\}}$ is referred to as *left tail* of the distribution. It follows that the central area under the curve between $-t_{\{\alpha,n-1\}}$ and $t_{\{\alpha,n-1\}}$ is equal to $1 - 2\alpha$. In other words, the probability of a random variable with t-distribution taking on a value in the interval $[-t_{\{\alpha,n-1\}}, t_{\{\alpha,n-1\}}]$ is given by $1 - 2\alpha$. The values $-t_{\{\alpha,n-1\}}$ and $t_{\{\alpha,n-1\}}$ are referred to as *lower critical value* and *upper critical value* of the t-distribution, respectively.

Finally, another distribution used later in this book is the F-distribution.

Definition 2.24 (F-distribution) The probability density function of the F-*distribution* with parameters d_1 and d_2 is given by

$$f(x; d_1, d_2) = \frac{\sqrt{\frac{(d_1 x)^{d_1} d_2^{d_2}}{(d_1 x + d_2)^{d_1 + d_2}}}}{x \, \mathrm{B}\left(\frac{d_1}{2}, \frac{d_2}{2}\right)}, \tag{2.32}$$

where $\mathrm{B}(a, b)$ is the beta function

$$\mathrm{B}(a, b) = \int_0^1 t^{a-1}(1-t)^{b-1} dt \tag{2.33}$$

for $a > 0$ and $b > 0$.

The F-distribution is often used in the context of the following theorem:

Theorem 2.3 *Let X_1 and X_2 be two independent and normally distributed random variables with variances σ_1^2 and σ_2^2, respectively. If S_1^2 and S_2^2 are the sample variances of two random samples of size n_1 and n_2 taken from X_1 and X_2, respectively, then the random variable*

$$F = \frac{S_1^2/\sigma_1^2}{S_2^2/\sigma_2^2} = \frac{\sigma_2^2 S_1^2}{\sigma_1^2 S_2^2} \tag{2.34}$$

has an F-distribution with $(n_1 - 1)$ and $(n_2 - 1)$ degrees of freedom.

The F-distribution is typically used to draw inferences about the population variances of two random variables.

2.6 The Bernoulli and Binomial Distributions

Consider an experiment consisting of n trials, called *Bernoulli trials*, each of which can result in two possible outcomes, a success or a failure. We define the random variable X_j for $j = 1, 2, ..., n$ to be equal to 1 if the jth trial resulted in a success, and equal to 0 if the jth trial resulted in a failure. The n Bernoulli trials constitute a *Bernoulli process* if they are independent and the probability of a trial resulting in success remains constant from trial to trial; that is, $P(X_j = 1) = p$ for $j = 1, 2, ..., n$. From the independence assumption, it follows that the joint probability mass function of the n trials $\{X_1, X_2, ..., X_n\}$ is given by

$$p(x_1, x_2, ..., x_n) = p_1(x_1)p_2(x_2)...p_n(x_n) \tag{2.35}$$

where

$$p_j(x_j) = p(x_j) = \begin{cases} p & \text{if } x_j = 1, \\ 1 - p & \text{if } x_j = 0, \\ 0 & \text{otherwise,} \end{cases} \tag{2.36}$$

for $j = 1, 2, ..., n$. For one trial, the distribution in Equation (2.36) is called the *Bernoulli distribution* with parameter p. The mean and variance of X_j are given by

$$E[X_j] = 0 \cdot (1 - p) + 1 \cdot p = p,$$
$$\text{Var}\left(X_j\right) = \left[0^2 \cdot (1 - p) + 1^2 \cdot p\right] - p^2 = p(1 - p). \tag{2.37}$$

Let X be the number of successes in n Bernoulli trials. The distribution of the random variable X is called the *Binomial distribution* and it has a probability mass function given by

$$p(x) = \begin{cases} \binom{n}{x}p^x(1 - p)^{n-x} & \text{for } x = 0, 1, ..., n \\ 0 & \text{otherwise.} \end{cases} \tag{2.38}$$

To understand the above formula, we represent the outcome of the n Bernoulli trials as an n-tuple of zeros and ones, where 0 stands for failure of the respective trial and 1 stands for success. Consider the n-tuple $t_1 = (0, 1, 1, 0, ..., 1)$ with k ones and $(n - k)$ zeros. The probability of the respective outcome is given by

$$P(t_1) = p^k(1 - p)^{n-k} \tag{2.39}$$

since we have n independent events, k of them occurring with probability p and the rest with probability $(1 - p)$. There are

$$\binom{n}{k} = \frac{n!}{k!(n - k)!} \tag{2.40}$$

possible n-tuples with k ones and $(n - k)$ zeros, each of them representing a possible outcome with probability given by Equation (2.39). Since these are exclusive events, the probability that one of them occurs, which corresponds to the probability of the random variable X taking on the value of k, is given by

$$P(X = k) = \binom{n}{k}p^k(1 - p)^{n-k}. \tag{2.41}$$

We will use the notation $X \sim B(p, n)$ to indicate that X has a Binomial distribution with parameters p and n.

It can be easily shown that

$$E[X] = pn, \qquad \text{Var}(X) = p(1-p)n. \tag{2.42}$$

The random variable $\hat{P} = X/n$ is an estimator of p. Indeed,

$$E[\hat{P}] = E[X/n] = E[X]/n = (pn)/n = p. \tag{2.43}$$

Thus, if n is large, we can estimate p using the sample proportion $\hat{p} = x/n$.

Theorem 2.4 (Normal Approximation to the Binomial Distribution)
If $X \sim B(p, n)$, then the limiting form of the distribution of

$$Z = \frac{X - np}{\sqrt{p(1-p)n}} \tag{2.44}$$

as $n \to \infty$ is the standard Normal distribution N(0,1).

The Normal distribution provides a very accurate approximation to the Binomial distribution when n is large and p is not very close to 0 or 1. It also provides a reasonably accurate approximation when n is small and p is close to 0.5.

One possible rule of thumb for determining when the approximation is good is: if $[pn \geq 5 \wedge (1-p)n \geq 5]$, then the Normal distribution provides a good approximation to the Binomial distribution.

2.7 Statistical Techniques for Parameter Estimation

In this section, we give an overview of statistical techniques that can be used to estimate parameters characterizing properties of a system or its workload from empirical observations (e.g., transaction resource demands as considered in Chapter 7).

2.7.1 Regression Analysis

Given a set of independent variables $\{X_1, X_2, ..., X_k\}$ and a dependent variable Y, linear regression aims to capture the relationship between the dependent variable and the independent variables with the linear model

$$Y = \beta_0 + \beta_1 X_1 + \beta_2 X_2 + \ldots + \beta_k X_k + \epsilon. \tag{2.45}$$

In regression analysis, Y is known as *response variable* and X_j for $1 \leq j \leq k$ as *control variables*. The goal is to determine the parameters β_j for $0 \leq j \leq k$ in such a way that the residuals ϵ are minimized with respect to a specific measure. Examples for such measures are the sum of squared residuals, used in *least squares (LSQ) regression*, or the sum of absolute differences, used in *least absolute deviation (LAD) regression*. To be able to determine a unique solution for the parameters β_j, at least n sets of known values $\{y, x_1, \ldots, x_k\}$ are required, where $n > k$. The above linear model can be formulated in matrix notation as (Chatterjee and Price, 1995)

$$\mathbf{Y} = \mathbf{X}\beta + \epsilon \tag{2.46}$$

where

$$\mathbf{X} = \begin{pmatrix} 1 & x_{1,1} & x_{1,2} & \cdots & x_{1,k} \\ 1 & x_{2,1} & x_{2,2} & \cdots & x_{2,k} \\ \vdots & \vdots & \vdots & & \vdots \\ 1 & x_{n,1} & x_{n,2} & \cdots & x_{n,k} \end{pmatrix}, \mathbf{Y} = \begin{pmatrix} y_1 \\ y_2 \\ \vdots \\ y_n \end{pmatrix}, \epsilon = \begin{pmatrix} \epsilon_1 \\ \epsilon_2 \\ \vdots \\ \epsilon_n \end{pmatrix} \text{ and } \beta = \begin{pmatrix} \beta_0 \\ \beta_1 \\ \vdots \\ \beta_k \end{pmatrix}.$$

$\mathbf{X}$ is called *control matrix* and $\mathbf{Y}$ is the *response vector*. We assume that the vector of error residuals ϵ is independent and identically distributed with mean $E[\epsilon] = 0$ and a constant variance. Then, we can conclude that $E[\mathbf{Y}] = \mathbf{X}\beta$. The parameter vector β needs to be estimated.

LSQ regression estimates the vector β by minimizing the sum of squared residuals. Hence, the following expression needs to be minimized:

$$\epsilon^T \epsilon = (\mathbf{Y} - \mathbf{X}\beta)^T (\mathbf{Y} - \mathbf{X}\beta). \tag{2.47}$$

The vector $\hat{\beta}$ that minimizes the previous expression can be calculated as follows (Chatterjee and Price, 1995):

$$\hat{\beta} = (\mathbf{X}^T \mathbf{X})^{-1} \mathbf{X}^T \mathbf{Y}. \tag{2.48}$$

2.7.2 Kalman Filter

Statistical filtering deals with the estimation of hidden states of a dynamic system from known system inputs and incomplete and noisy measurements (Kumar et al., 2009). In this context, the term *state* is defined as follows:

> The states of a system are those variables that provide a complete representation of the internal condition or status at a given instant of time. (Simon, 2006)

The term *dynamic system* implies that the state of the system changes over time. Different statistical filtering methods have been proposed. We describe the Kalman filter here in more detail because it is often used to estimate transaction resource demands.

Generally speaking, we can distinguish between discrete-time and continuous-time systems. Subsequently, we will focus on *discrete-time Kalman filters*. The notation we use is based on the one used by Kumar et al. (2009) and Simon (2006).

The system state $\mathbf{x}$ is a vector containing the variables that describe the internal state of a system. These variables cannot be directly observed. The Kalman filter estimates the vector $\mathbf{x}$ from a series of measurements $\mathbf{z}$. The system is described by two equations. The first equation describes how the system state evolves over time (Simon, 2006):

$$\mathbf{x}_k = \mathbf{F}_{k-1}\mathbf{x}_{k-1} + \mathbf{G}_{k-1}\mathbf{u}_{k-1} + \mathbf{w}_{k-1}. \tag{2.49}$$

The time advances in discrete steps. $\mathbf{x}_k$ is the system state at time step k, which is calculated from the previous system state $\mathbf{x}_{k-1}$ and the control vector $\mathbf{u}_{k-1}$ containing the inputs of the system. The matrices $\mathbf{F}$ and $\mathbf{G}$ are called *state transition model* and *control-input model*, respectively. The process noise $\mathbf{w}_{k-1}$ is assumed to be normally distributed with zero mean and covariance $\mathbf{Q}_k$.

The second equation describes the relationship between the system state $\mathbf{x}_k$ and the measurements $\mathbf{z}_k$ at time step k

$$\mathbf{z}_k = \mathbf{H}_k\mathbf{x}_k + \mathbf{v}_k. \tag{2.50}$$

The matrix $\mathbf{H}_k$ is the observation model, which maps the state space to the observation space. $\mathbf{v}_k$ is the observation noise, which is assumed to be Gaussian white noise with zero mean and covariance $\mathbf{R}_k$.

If the relation $\mathbf{z} = h(\mathbf{x})$ between system state and measurements is non-linear, *extended Kalman filter (EKF)* can be used. EKF approximates a linear model with the following output sensitivity matrix:

$$\mathbf{H}_k = \left[\frac{\partial h}{\partial x}\right]_{\hat{x}_{k|k-1}}. \tag{2.51}$$

The output sensitivity matrix is set to the Jacobian matrix of $h(\mathbf{x})$. The partial derivatives are evaluated with the current estimates of the system state. The vector $\hat{\mathbf{x}}_{n|m}$ represents the estimated system state $\hat{\mathbf{x}}$ at time step n given measurements $\{\mathbf{z}_1, \ldots, \mathbf{z}_m\}$.

The Kalman filter is a recursive estimator. It starts with an initial state and continuously updates its estimate as new measurements are obtained. At each time step k, the calculations depend only on the previous estimate $\hat{\mathbf{x}}_{k-1|k-1}$ and the current measurements vector $\mathbf{z}_k$ (Kumar et al., 2009). The internal state of the filter is represented by two variables, the state estimate $\hat{\mathbf{x}}_{k|k}$ and the error covariance matrix $\mathbf{P}_{k|k}$.

The error covariance matrix is a measure for the estimated accuracy of the state estimates (Kumar et al., 2009). At the beginning, the filter is initialized with given values for $\hat{\mathbf{x}}_{0|0}$ and $\mathbf{P}_{0|0}$.

The algorithm that calculates new state estimates consists of two phases: *predict* and *update* (Kumar et al., 2009). In the predict phase, a new state estimate $\hat{\mathbf{x}}_{k|k-1}$ is calculated with Equation (2.49). In the update phase, the prediction error of $\hat{\mathbf{x}}_{k|k-1}$ is determined according to the current measurements $\mathbf{z}_k$. Then, a corrected estimate $\hat{\mathbf{x}}_{k|k}$ is calculated. These two steps are carried out each time a new measurement sample vector becomes available.

Assuming a linear relationship between the measurements and the system state, and uncorrelated and normally distributed noise with zero mean, the Kalman filter is an optimal estimator. Since most systems are inherently nonlinear, EKF provides a linear approximation for cases with slightly nonlinear characteristics.

2.7.3 Maximum Likelihood Estimation

Consider a collection of independent and identically distributed random variables $\{Y_1, Y_2, ..., Y_n\}$, where θ are the parameters of their probability distribution, and a corresponding set of observed values $\{y_1, y_2, ..., y_n\}$ of the random variables. Then, the joint distribution is represented by the probability density function $f(y_1, y_2, ..., y_n|\theta)$. This function is also known as the *likelihood* $\mathbb{L}(\theta)$ stating the probability of observing the values $\{y_1, y_2, ..., y_n\}$ for a given θ. The joint distribution can be replaced by the product of the conditional probability of the individual observed values:

$$\mathbb{L}(\theta) = \prod_{i=1}^{n} f(y_i|\theta). \tag{2.52}$$

An equivalent representation that is often easier to solve is obtained by taking the logarithm of the likelihood function resulting in a sum of logarithms. This is known as the *log-likelihood function*.

The maximum likelihood estimate $\hat{\theta}$ is then defined as

$$\hat{\theta} = \max_{\theta} \mathbb{L}(\theta). \tag{2.53}$$

In case of complex likelihood functions, optimization algorithms (see Chapter 2, Section 2.7.5) are typically used to determine the maximum likelihood estimate.

2.7.4 Bayesian Inference

In the previous section, we described the maximum likelihood estimation method based on the frequentist interpretation of probability. In contrast, Bayesian inference introduces the concept of a prior distribution capturing assumptions and knowledge available before making observations. Suppose a vector of parameters θ and a vector $\mathbf{y}$ with observations, the *posterior distribution* $f(\theta|\mathbf{y})$ is given by

$$f(\theta|\mathbf{y}) = \frac{f(\mathbf{y}|\theta)f(\theta)}{f(\mathbf{y})}. \tag{2.54}$$

$f(\mathbf{y}|\theta)$ denotes the likelihood of observing $\mathbf{y}$ for a given θ. $f(\theta)$ is the prior distribution, and $f(\mathbf{y})$ is the marginal likelihood of the observations. Assuming fixed values for the observations $\mathbf{y}$, $f(\mathbf{y})$ can be seen as a normalization constant. The constant can be calculated using the following indefinite integral:

$$f(\mathbf{y}) = \int f(\mathbf{y}|\theta)f(\theta)d\theta. \tag{2.55}$$

However, the exact calculation of this integral, which requires to determine the joint posterior distribution, is intractable for most practical problems, especially in case of multi-variate posterior distributions. The Metropolis–Hastings algorithm (Hastings, 1970), a Markov Chain Monte Carlo (MCMC) algorithm for random sampling, allows us to approximate the posterior distribution without calculating the normalization constant. The algorithm only requires the availability of a function g that is proportional to a desired probability distribution. In case of Bayesian inference, the function g is the numerator in Equation (2.54).

The general idea of MCMC algorithms is to construct a Markov chain with an equilibrium distribution resembling the desired posterior distribution. Samples are generated by a random walk on this Markov chain. A sample is then the state of the Markov chain after a certain number of steps. Gibbs sampling (S. Geman and D. Geman, 1984) is a special case of the Metropolis–Hastings algorithm for highly multi-variate distributions. Suppose we want to obtain a sample $X = \{x_1, x_2, ..., x_n\}$ from the posterior distribution. Then, Gibbs sampling requires the availability of all conditional distributions $f(x_i|x_1, ..., x_{i-1}, x_{i+1}, ..., x_n)$. The conditional distributions may be calculated either exactly, or we rely on other random sampling algorithms for single-dimensional distributions, such as adaptive rejection sampling. In order to determine the sample in step t, a Gibbs sampler iterates over each component of vector $X^{(t)}$ and determines its value by sampling from $f(x_i^{(t)}|x_1^{(t)}, ..., x_{i-1}^{(t)}, x_{i+1}^{(t-1)}, ..., x_n^{(t-1)})$. Given a large set of samples resulting from the Gibbs sampler, we can approximate the expected value of the posterior distribution by averaging over all samples. It should be noted that consecutive samples from a Gibbs sampler are typically auto-correlated. Therefore, only every n-th sample should be included. Furthermore, samples at the beginning should be discarded as long as the underlying Markov chain is not in its equilibrium state.

2.7.5 Mathematical Optimization

Mathematical optimization techniques do not belong to the class of statistical estimation techniques; however, we consider them here since they are used often in the context of parameter estimation in combination with other techniques.

Generally speaking, an optimization problem is described by a *cost (objective) function* f with a domain $D \subseteq \mathbb{R}^n$ and a *constraint set* $\Omega \subseteq D$ (Dostál, 2009). The goal is either to minimize or to maximize the objective function. In the following, we assume that it should be minimized. Then, the optimization problem is also called *minimization problem* and can be solved by finding a value $\bar{x} \in \Omega$ such that

$$f(\bar{x}) \leq f(x), \; x \in \Omega. \tag{2.56}$$

Solutions of a minimization problem are called *(global) minimizers* (Dostál, 2009). In contrast to global minimizers, there are also *local minimizers*. A local minimizer $\bar{x}$ satisfies the condition

$$f(\bar{x}) \leq f(x), \; x \in \Omega, \; \|x - \bar{x}\| \leq \delta \tag{2.57}$$

for $\delta > 0$ (Dostál, 2009).

Optimization problems can be classified into different categories. There are *constrained* and *unconstrained* optimization problems. In the case of unconstrained optimization problems, there are no additional constraints in the constraint set; that is, $\Omega = D$. If additional equality and inequality constraints are given, we speak of constrained optimization. Depending on the degree of the objective function and the constraints, the following types of optimization problems exist:

- *linear programming* problems have a linear objective function and a set of linear equality and inequality constraints,
- *quadratic programming* problems have a quadratic objective function and a set of linear equality and inequality constraints, and
- *non-linear programming* problems can have any kind of non-linear objective function and/or non-linear constraints.

Different solution algorithms exist for the different types of optimization problems. Descriptions of possible solution algorithms can be found in Dostál (2009) and Nemhauser et al. (1989).

2.8 Concluding Remarks

In this chapter, we reviewed the basics of probability and statistics while establishing the statistical notation needed for understanding some of the chapters in the book. This chapter is not intended as an introduction to probability and statistics but rather as a quick refresher assuming that the reader is already familiar with the basic concepts. For a detailed introduction to probability and statistics, we refer the reader to Walpole et al. (2016). An in-depth treatment of the mathematical foundations of probability and measure theory can be found in Billingsley (2012).

References

Billingsley, P. (2012). *Probability and Measure*. Anniversary Edition. Wiley Series in Probability and Statistics. John Wiley & Sons, Inc.: Hoboken, New Jersey, USA (cited on pp. 23, 43).

Chatterjee, S. and Price, B. (1995). *Praxis der Regressionsanalyse*. Second Edition. Oldenbourg Wissenschaftsverlag: Munich, Germany (cited on p. 39).

Dostál, Z. (2009). *Optimal Quadratic Programming Algorithms: With Applications to Variational Inequalities*. Vol. 23. Springer Optimization and Its Applications. Springer US: New York City, USA (cited on pp. 42, 43).

Geman, S. and Geman, D. (1984). "Stochastic Relaxation, Gibbs Distributions, and the Bayesian Restoration of Images". *IEEE Transactions on Pattern Analysis and Machine Intelligence*, PAMI-6(6). IEEE: Piscataway, New Jersey, USA, pp. 721–741 (cited on p. 42).

Hastings, W. K. (1970). "Monte Carlo Sampling Methods Using Markov Chains and Their Applications". *Biometrika*, 57(1). Oxford University Press on behalf of Biometrika Trust: Oxford, UK, pp. 97–109 (cited on p. 42).

Kumar, D., Tantawi, A. N., and Zhang, L. (2009). "Real-Time Performance Modeling for Adaptive Software Systems with Multi-Class Workload". In: *Proceedings of the 17th Annual Meeting of the IEEE/ACM International Symposium on Modelling, Analysis and Simulation of Computer and Telecommunication Systems (MASCOTS 2009)*. (London, UK). IEEE Computer Society: Washington, DC, USA, pp. 1–4 (cited on pp. 39, 40).

Lilja, D. J. (2000). *Measuring Computer Performance: A Practitioner's Guide*. Cambridge University Press: Cambridge, UK (cited on p. 34).

Nemhauser, G. L., Kan, A. R., and Todd, M., eds. (1989). *Optimization*. Vol. 1. Handbooks in Operations Research and Management Science. Elsevier Science: Amsterdam, The Netherlands (cited on p. 43).

Simon, D. (2006). *Optimal State Estimation: Kalman, H Infinity, and Nonlinear Approaches*. John Wiley & Sons: Hoboken, New Jersey, USA (cited on pp. 39, 40).

Walpole, R. E., Myers, R. H., Myers, S. L., and Ye, K. E. (2016). *Probability & Statistics for Engineers & Scientists*. Ninth Edition. Pearson Education: London, UK (cited on pp. 23, 31, 34, 43).

Chapter 3
Metrics

"Measurements are not to provide numbers but insight."
—*Ingrid Bucher*

"It is much easier to make measurements than to know exactly what you are measuring."
—*J. W. N. Sullivan (1886-1937), English journalist and science writer*

This chapter starts by defining the basic concepts: metric, measure, and measurement. It then introduces the different scales of measurement, allowing one to classify the types of values assigned by measures. Next, definitions of the most common performance metrics are presented. The chapter continues with a detailed discussion of the quality attributes of good metrics. Finally, the different types of averages are introduced while showing how they can be used to define composite metrics and aggregate results from multiple benchmarks.

3.1 Definition of Metric

According to the Merriam-Webster dictionary, "a *metric* is a standard of measurement." The term *measurement* is defined as the assignment of values to objects or events according to some rules (Stevens, 1946, 1951). This definition originates from Stevens who claimed that any consistent and non-random assignment counts as measurement in the broad sense. A set of rules (i.e., a concrete process) for assigning values to the individual objects or events is referred to as a *measure*. Mathematically speaking, a measure is a function (a mapping) that maps the considered set of objects or events to a set of values. From a statistical point of view, a measure can be seen as a *variable* capturing the outcome of an experiment, that is, an observation of a property or characteristic of some event or object in the real world. In statistics, such variables are often referred to as *dependent variables* to distinguish them from

© Springer Nature Switzerland AG 2020
S. Kounev et al., *Systems Benchmarking*, https://doi.org/10.1007/978-3-030-41705-5_3

independent variables, which can be manipulated by the experimenter. While in mathematics, the term metric is explicitly distinguished from the term measure (the former referring to a *distance function*), in computer science and engineering, the terms metric and measure overlap in meaning and are often used interchangeably. One way to distinguish between them is looking at metrics as values that can be derived from some fundamental measurements comprising one or more measures.

Summarizing, we introduce the following definitions that will be used throughout the book:

Definition 3.1 (Measurement) A *measurement* is the assignment of values to objects or events by applying a given set of rules or a procedure referred to as a measurement process.

Definition 3.2 (Measure) A *measure* is a function (mapping) that maps a considered set of objects or events to a set of values. Each measure can also be seen as a *random variable* capturing the outcome of an experiment such as an observation of a property or characteristic of some event or object in the real world.

Definition 3.3 (Metric) A *metric* is a value derived from some fundamental measurements comprising one or more measures. In the context of benchmarking, metrics are used to characterize different properties of the system under test (SUT), such as performance, reliability, or security.

Definition 3.4 (Composite Metric) A *composite metric* is a metric whose value is derived by combining other metrics (elementary or previously defined composite metrics). The combined metrics may characterize different system properties, or they may capture measurements of the same property but under different conditions.

3.2 Scales of Measurement

Stevens (1946) defines four scales of measurement—nominal, ordinal, interval, and ratio—which can be used to classify the types of values assigned by different measures.

A measure with a *nominal scale*, also called qualitative scale, assigns values that are simple categories or names (rather than numerical quantities), which can be used to partition a set of objects into groups or subsets. Measurements made on nominal scales are often called categorical data or qualitative data. For example, processors can be divided into groups based on their manufacturer (Intel, AMD, IBM, etc.). Numbers may be used as identifiers of the different processor manufacturers; however, such numbers are simple labels and they do not have numerical value or meaning. Consequently, no mathematical computations (addition, subtraction, etc.) may be performed on nominal measures.

A measure with an *ordinal scale* assigns values that have an inherent ordering, which can be used to sort the set of objects in a given order. For example, a set of

Intel Core i series processors can be sorted into first, second, and third generation. Note that such ordering can be seen as a ranking; however, it does not allow for characterizing the relative degree of difference between the individual objects. The difference between the first and second place does not necessarily have the same meaning as the difference between the second and third place. We know that third generation is faster than second, and second faster than first; however, we do not know how much faster they are.

A measure with an *interval scale* assigns values that have an inherent ordering where the distances, or intervals, between the values are meaningful. With an ordinal scale, one value can only be greater than, less than, or equal to another, whereas with an interval scale, the difference between values is quantified in scale points that have a consistent meaning across the scale. An example of a measure with an interval scale is processor temperature measured in degrees centigrade. This scale has meaningful intervals. A given increase in heat produces the same increase in degrees no matter where we are on the scale; however, a zero on the centigrade scale does not indicate an absence of the quantity we are measuring (temperature). This distinguishes interval scales from ratio scales.

A *ratio scale* is an interval scale with a meaningful (unique and non-arbitrary) zero point corresponding to a point at which the quantity measured is absent. For a ratio scale, the same ratio at two places on the scale carries the same meaning, allowing one to compare values by considering the ratio between them. As an example, a duration of 1 h is equivalent to 3/4 h + 1/4 h. Coming back to the example of processor temperature expressed in a centigrade scale, the latter is not a ratio scale since it has an arbitrary zero point. However, if we express temperature in the Kelvin scale, it will then have an absolute zero point. Also, if a temperature measured on the Kelvin scale is twice as high as another, then the former would have twice the kinetic energy of the latter. This makes the Kelvin scale a ratio scale. Measurements in the physical sciences and engineering are typically done on ratio scales, for example, mass, length, volume, time duration, or power consumption. Informally, many ratio scales can be seen as specifying a count of something ("how many") or an amount/magnitude ("how much") of something.

The above classification of scales into four categories (i.e., nominal, ordinal, interval, and ratio) can be further refined, introducing a distinction between linear and logarithmic interval scales and between ratio scales with and without a natural unit (Stevens, 1959). A ratio scale with a natural unit is often referred to as *absolute scale*. Examples of natural units are those used for counting discrete objects and for representing probabilities.

The considered measurement scales are increasingly informative. Each scale adds a given aspect not considered in the previous scales. At the lowest level, the nominal scale simply names or categorizes objects (responses). The ordinal scale adds an ordering. The interval scale adds meaning to differences between values (intervals) across the scale; that is, the same difference at two places on the scale has the same meaning. The ratio scale adds a meaningful absolute zero point, introducing a meaning to the ratios of values across the scale; that is, the same ratio at two places on the scale also carries the same meaning. Finally, the absolute scale adds a natural unit.

The measurement scales can also be differentiated with respect to the families of transformations that measures of the respective types can be subjected to without loss of empirical information. For example, empirical relations represented on ratio scales are invariant under multiplication by a positive number (e.g., multiplication by 1,000 converts from seconds to milliseconds). Linear interval scales are invariant under both multiplication by a positive number and a constant shift; for example, the formula $T_C \frac{9}{5} + 32 = T_F$ can be used to convert temperature from Celsius to Fahrenheit. Ordinal scales are invariant under any transformation function that is monotonic and increasing, and nominal scales are invariant under any one-to-one substitution. Finally, absolute scales allow no transformation other than identity.

Table 3.1: Hierarchy of measurement scales

Scale	Mapping	Transformations	Operations	Statistics	Example
Nominal	Unordered 1:1	Any 1:1 substitution	$=,\neq$	Mode, frequencies	Processor type: $0 = Intel$, $1 = AMD$, $2 = Other$
Ordinal	+ ordering	Monotonic and increasing	$\ldots, <,>$	Median, percentiles	Complexity: $0 = low$, $1 = medium$, $2 = high$
Interval	+ distance function	$M' = aM + b$ $(a > 0)$	$\ldots, +,-$	Mean, standard deviation	Temperature in Celsius or Fahrenheit: $T_F = T_C \frac{9}{5} + 32$
Ratio	+ unit and zero point	$M' = aM$ $(a > 0)$	$\ldots, *, /$	Geometric mean, coeff. of variation	Temperature in Kelvin scale, time to execute an instruction
Absolute	+ natural unit	Only identity $M' = M$			Num. of transistors in a processor, probability of a cache miss

Table 3.1 summarizes the most important characteristics of the different measurement scales. It shows the type of mapping used in each scale, the possible transformations without loss of information, the mathematical operations that can be performed on measurements, some possible statistics that can be applied to analyze measurements, and some concrete examples of measures with different scales. The different statistics are introduced and discussed in detail in Section 3.5.1 and in Chapter 4 (Section 4.1). Next, we introduce the most common metrics used to characterize the performance behavior of a system.

3.3 Performance Metrics

As discussed in Chapter 1, performance in its classical sense is understood as the amount of useful work accomplished by a system compared to the time and resources used. Better performance means more work accomplished in shorter time and/or using less resources. Depending on the context, high performance may involve one or more of the following: high responsiveness when using the system, high processing rate, low amount of resources used, or high availability of the system's services. To characterize the performance behavior of a system, performance metrics are used.

Definition 3.5 (Performance Metric) A value derived from some fundamental measurements that characterizes a given performance-related property of a system.

The fundamental measurements from which performance metrics are typically derived can be classified into three groups (Lilja, 2000):

- Count of how often a certain event occurs
- Duration of a time interval
- Size of some parameter

For example, in the context of a database system, one may be interested in the number of database transactions executed in a given observation interval (count), how much time a transaction needs to complete (duration), and the amount of data it writes to the database (size). From such measurements, one can derive different performance metrics. If the measured count, time, or size value itself is of interest, it can be used directly as a performance metric. Often, however, basic measurements are not used directly, but combined using a formula to calculate a given quantity of interest. For example, event counts are typically normalized to a common time basis by dividing the number of observed events in a given time interval by the length of the interval. The result is a *rate metric*, which allows comparing measurements made over different time intervals.

3.3.1 Speedup and Relative Change

The term *speed* is used to refer to any kind of rate metric. Let W_i be the "amount of work" done by a System i in a measurement interval T_i assuming that the system is processing during the whole interval. The amount of work done W_i can be seen as an event count, where each event represents a completion of a unit of work. We use the term *request* to refer to any unit of work with a distinct start and end time (e.g., a system operation or service offered to clients as part of a given use case, a request sent through a browser to open a web page, a database transaction, a network operation like transferring a data packet, or a batch job executed by a mainframe system).

The *system speed* as a rate metric R_i is defined as

$$R_i = \frac{W_i}{T_i}. \tag{3.1}$$

Assuming sequential processing where the units of work do not overlap, the time M_i for processing a unit of work is given by

$$M_i = \frac{T_i}{W_i}. \tag{3.2}$$

Considering two different systems observed in the measurement interval T_i, we define the terms *speedup* and *relative change* as follows (Lilja, 2000):

Definition 3.6 (Speedup) The speedup $S_{2,1}$ of System 2 with respect to System 1 is defined as

$$S_{2,1} = \frac{R_2}{R_1} = \frac{M_1}{M_2}. \tag{3.3}$$

Definition 3.7 (Relative Change) The relative change $\Delta_{2,1}$ of System 2 with respect to System 1 is defined as

$$\Delta_{2,1} = \frac{R_2 - R_1}{R_1}. \tag{3.4}$$

If $\Delta_{2,1} > 0$, System 2 is faster than System 1. If $\Delta_{2,1} < 0$, System 2 is slower than System 1.

3.3.2 Basic Performance Metrics

The most common basic performance metrics used in practice are: response time, throughput, and utilization.

Definition 3.8 (Response Time) Response time is the time R, usually measured in seconds, it takes a system to react to a request providing a respective response. The response time includes the time spent waiting to use various resources (e.g., processors, storage devices, networks), often referred to as *congestion time*.

Definition 3.9 (Throughput) Throughput is the rate X at which requests are processed by a system, measured in the number of completed requests (operations) per unit of time. The throughput is a function of the load placed on the system (i.e., number of incoming requests per second) and of the maximum system capacity.

Definition 3.10 (Utilization) Utilization is the fraction of time U in which a resource (e.g., processor, network link, storage device) is used (i.e., it is busy processing requests).

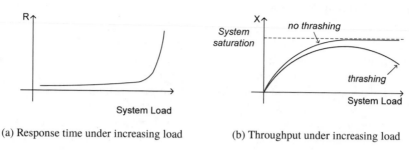

(a) Response time under increasing load   (b) Throughput under increasing load

Fig. 3.1: Response time and throughput under increasing load

Figure 3.1 illustrates the behavior of the metrics response time and throughput as the load placed on the system increases. We assume a static system configuration; that is, no resources are being added using techniques such as elastic autoscaling discussed in Chapter 15. Response time rises steadily up to a given point and then increases rapidly after that. Throughput increases up to a given maximum and then either stabilizes after that or may start to slightly drop. The point at which the system throughput reaches its maximum is referred to as *system saturation*. Ideally, if the load increases beyond the saturation point, the system throughput should remain stable. However, in many systems, the throughput may start to drop—an effect referred to as *thrashing*. Thrashing is normally caused by increasing system overhead due to activities such as memory paging or contention for software resources (e.g., database locks, operating system threads, network connections).

Response time, throughput, and utilization are generic performance metrics that can be applied to any system that processes some units of work. However, system performance is inherently a multi-dimensional property, as most systems comprise different types of resources and offer multiple services, which may exhibit different performance. Therefore, in performance benchmarking, typically composite metrics are used to summarize the overall system performance with a single number. They are derived from elementary metrics like response time, throughput, and utilization. For a metric to be fair and reliable, it has to possess several fundamental properties. In the next section, we look at the attributes that make it possible to distinguish good metrics from bad metrics.

3.4 Quality Attributes of Good Metrics

Different metrics can be used to quantify a given system property under evaluation. Not all such metrics are good in the sense of providing insight into the system behavior and helping to make informed decisions. In this section, we describe six fundamental attributes that characterize the quality of a benchmark metric. We start with a motivating example.

3.4.1 Motivating Example

Consider the following hypothetical scenario: A service provider has to select a server platform for a new application that is planned to be launched. The provider is considering three different servers as possible candidates. A benchmark is used to evaluate their performance in order to select the best server for the target application. The benchmark executes two different programs that represent the two main types of workload that will be executed on the server. For each program, the execution time is measured on each server. The two programs used as benchmark workloads are assumed to be equally important; it is assumed that, in real life, each of them is expected to run 50% of the time while consuming half of the server's processing resources. One way to define the benchmark metric is to use the average of the execution times of the two programs. Table 3.2 shows some example results of running the benchmark. The execution times of the two programs on the three servers are shown.

Table 3.2: Example benchmark results using average of execution times as a metric

	Server 1	Server 2	Server 3
Program A	10 s	10 s	5 s
Program B	1,000 s	500 s	1,000 s
Average	505 s	255 s	502.5 s

The benchmark results make the impression that Server 2 is the fastest, followed by Server 3 and Server 1. However, if we look more closely, we see that this impression is misleading. Let us use Server 1 as a baseline and compare the performance of Server 2 and Server 3 against it. Compared to Server 1, Server 2 exhibits the same execution time for Program A and half the execution time for Program B. When it comes to Server 3, it is the other way around; it exhibits the same execution time for Program B and half the execution time for Program A. Server 2 is twice as fast for Program B, whereas Server 3 is twice as fast for Program A. However, under the assumption that each program is executed 50% of the time, it should not make a difference whether the performance of Program A or Program B is boosted by a factor of two. This is illustrated in Figure 3.2.[1]

As we can see from the figure, Server 2 and Server 3 save the same amount of time compared to Server 1. Thus, their performance can be considered to be equivalent for the target application and the decision of which one to select can be made based on the price.

---

[1] Note that, in real life, multiple executions of Program A and Program B can occur in an arbitrary order; for simplicity of the illustration, in Figure 3.2, we have assumed that the repeated execution of Program A is completed first before execution of Program B starts.

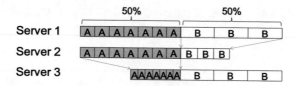

Fig. 3.2: Behavior of Server 2 and Server 3 compared to Server 1 used as a baseline

The example shows that the selection of the average program execution time as a benchmark metric leads to misleading results. One way to address this issue is to use a different metric based on speedup. The advantage of using speedup is that the actual absolute values of the execution items are irrelevant and only the relative differences play a role. Thus, speeding up one of the programs by a factor of two will have the same effect on the overall application performance, no matter which of the two programs is optimized. Instead of using the execution time as a basis for our metric, we use the speedup comparing to Server 1 as a reference. Table 3.3 shows the results if we use the average speedup as a benchmark metric.

Table 3.3: Behavior of Server 2 and Server 3 compared to Server 1
using speedup instead of execution time

	Server 1	Server 2	Server 3
Program A	1	1	2
Program B	1	2	1
Average	1	1.5	1.5

As we can see, using speedup as a basis for our metric, we now obtain results that show the same performance for Server 2 and Server 3. However, there is a subtle issue here that has to be addressed. We selected Server 1 as a reference server providing a baseline against which we compared the other servers. The question arises whether we would have obtained the same results if we had selected one of the other two servers to use as a reference. Table 3.4 shows the resulting performance rankings when using Server 2 and Server 3 as reference servers, respectively.

As we can see, the rankings are not consistent, implying that the metric *average speedup* may be easily manipulated by selecting a different server to use as a baseline for computing the relative speedups. The solution to this issue is to use the geometric mean as the average value instead of the arithmetic mean, which is normally used by default. The geometric mean has the property of ensuring consistent rankings when averaging normalized data such as speedups. As shown in Table 3.5, the results are consistent, independently of which server is chosen as a reference. We will formally introduce the different averages (i.e., means) and discuss their differences in Section 3.5. The takeaway point from the above example is that the selection of

Table 3.4: Ranking of the three servers based on the average
speedup with different reference systems

(a) Speedup relative to Server 1

	Server 1	Server 2	Server 3
Average	1	1.5	1.5
Rank	2	1	1

(b) Speedup relative to Server 3

	Server 1	Server 2	Server 3
Average	0.75	1.25	1
Rank	3	1	2

(c) Speedup relative to Server 2

	Server 1	Server 2	Server 3
Average	0.75	1	1.25
Rank	3	2	1

Table 3.5: Ranking of the three servers based on the
geometric mean of speedups

(a) Speedup relative to Server 1

	Server 1	Server 2	Server 3
Geometric mean	$\sqrt{1}$	$\sqrt{2}$	$\sqrt{2}$
Rank	2	1	1

(b) Speedup relative to Server 3

	Server 1	Server 2	Server 3
Geometric mean	$\sqrt{0.5}$	$\sqrt{1}$	$\sqrt{1}$
Rank	2	1	1

(c) Speedup relative to Server 2

	Server 1	Server 2	Server 3
Geometric mean	$\sqrt{0.5}$	$\sqrt{1}$	$\sqrt{1}$
Rank	2	1	1

benchmark metrics is critically important to ensure valid comparisons and fairness. Improper metric selection may lead to misleading results and respective purchasing decisions. This begs the question of what constitutes a good benchmark metric.

3.4.2 Quality Attributes

We now will describe six fundamental attributes that characterize the quality of a benchmark metric (Lilja, 2000). These attributes have been specifically discussed in the context of performance metrics; however, they can also be applied generally to any benchmark metric.

Easy to measure The easier a metric is to measure, the more likely it is that it will be used in practice and that its value will be correctly determined.

Repeatable Repeatability implies that if the metric is measured multiple times using the same procedure, the same value is measured. In practice, small differences are usually acceptable; however, ideally, a metric should be deterministic when measured multiple times.

Reliable A metric is considered reliable if it ranks systems consistently with respect to the property that is subject to evaluation. In other words, if System A performs better than System B with respect to the property under evaluation, then the values of the metric for the two systems should consistently indicate this (e.g., higher value meaning better score).

Linear A metric is linear if its value is linearly proportional to the degree to which the system under test exhibits the property under evaluation. For example, if a performance metric is linear, then a twice as high value of the metric should indicate twice as good performance. Linear metrics are intuitively appealing since humans typically tend to think in linear terms.

Consistent A metric is consistent if it has the same units and the same precise definition across different systems or configurations of the same system.

Independent A metric is independent if its definition and behavior are not subject to influence by proprietary interests of different vendors or manufacturers aiming to gain competitive advantage by defining the metric in a way that favors their products or services.

To illustrate the described attributes, we consider three classical metrics for characterizing processor performance: clock rate, MIPS, and MFLOPS.

The *clock rate* refers to the frequency at which a processor's central clock is running and is often used as an indicator of a processor's speed. It is normally measured in clock cycles per second or its equivalent, the unit hertz (Hz). The speed of modern CPUs is typically advertised in gigahertz (GHz), where 1 GHz is equal to 10^9 Hz. With respect to the described six quality attributes of good performance metrics, we can say that clock rate is repeatable (it is constant for a given processor[2]),

---

[2] Note that modern processors support dynamic frequency scaling where the clock rate may vary depending on the workload. Repeatability here refers to the fact that the clock rate behaves consistently under a given workload and configuration.

easy to measure (it is included in the processor's technical specification), consistent (its value is precisely defined across systems), and independent (its definition cannot be influenced by manufacturers). However, given its limited scope, clock rate is both non-linear and unreliable as a performance metric. Indeed, a processor with a faster clock rate does not necessarily imply better overall performance given that the clock rate ignores many important performance-relevant aspects, such as how much computation is actually performed in each clock cycle as well as the interaction of the processor with the memory and I/O subsystems.

MIPS is a rate metric for processor performance capturing the *millions of instructions executed per second*. It is intended to allow direct comparison of the processor speed by considering the execution of an instruction as a measure of useful work done. The MIPS metric is easy to measure, repeatable, and independent. However, it is not linear, since twice as high a MIPS rate does not necessarily result in boosting performance by a factor of two. Moreover, MIPS is neither reliable nor consistent. The root of the problem with MIPS is that the amount of computation (useful work) executed with a single instruction varies significantly for different instruction set architectures (ISA). For example, a reduced instruction set computer (RISC) architecture has a small set of simple and general instructions, whereas a complex instruction set computer (CISC) architecture typically has a large set of complex and specialized instructions. With CISC, a single instruction can execute several low-level operations (e.g., read data from main memory into a processor register, perform an arithmetic operation, and store the result of the operation into main memory). The fact that instructions are not defined consistently across different processor architectures renders the MIPS metric both inconsistent and unreliable as an indicator of processor performance.

MFLOPS is another rate metric for processor performance, which captures the *millions of floating-point operations executed per second*. MFLOPS is an attempt to address the drawbacks of MIPS by using floating-point operations as a measure of useful work done. A floating-point operation is an arithmetic operation on two floating-point numbers. The results of such operations are clearly more comparable across different processor architectures than the results of individual instructions. On the other hand, other operations like those operating on integer values are just as important for the overall processor performance. In real-life applications, floating-point operations represent only part of the executed programs. The MFLOPS metric ignores other types of operations, which makes it biased by capturing only one aspect of processor performance. The MFLOPS metric is easy to measure and repeatable; however, it does not possess the other four attributes of good metrics. This is because it is not completely clear how floating-point operations should be counted. Different processor architectures execute floating-point operations differently and sometimes such operations are executed as part of the execution of other operations. Processor manufacturers may use different rules for what is counted as floating-point operation, which makes the metric fail to meet the criteria for consistency and independence. For reasons similar to the other two considered metrics, MFLOPS is also neither a linear nor reliable performance metric.

Table 3.6: Quality attributes of clock rate, MIPS, and MFLOPS

	Easy to measure	Repeatable	Reliable	Linear	Consistent	Independent
Clock rate	✓	✓	✗	✗	✓	✓
MIPS	✓	✓	✗	✗	✗	✓
MFLOPS	✓	✓	✗	✗	✗	✗

Table 3.6 summarizes the evaluation of the metrics clock rate, MIPS, and MFLOPS with respect to the described quality attributes (Lilja, 2000).

3.5 From Measurements to Metrics

In Section 3.1, we defined *metric* as a value that can be derived from some fundamental measurements comprising one or more measures. Each measure can be seen as a *random variable* capturing the outcome of an experiment such as an observation (measurement) of a property or characteristic of some event or object in the real world.

Typically, measurements vary when repeated multiple times. Thus, a set of measured values $\{x_1, x_2, ..., x_n\}$ is considered a sample from a random variable X with an unknown distribution. Metrics are often computed from the sample using statistics that allow one to summarize the measurements and/or characterize a property of the underlying population (i.e., the probability distribution of the random variable X).

Consider the response time of a request to a web server. Sending n requests to the web server and measuring their response times result in a set of n measurements $\{x_1, x_2, ..., x_n\}$ forming a sample from the response time distribution. Computing the average $\overline{x} = \frac{1}{n} \sum_{i=1}^{n} x_i$ of the n measurements allows summarizing the measurements with a single value that can then be used as a performance metric.

3.5.1 Types of Averages

The most common way to summarize a sample of measurements is to compute an average value and use it as a metric characterizing the measured property or characteristic. Informally, an average is a middle or typical value that lies in the center of the interval where most measurements are distributed. In statistics, different types of averages are used, typically referred to as *indices of central tendency*. The most common types of averages are the sample *mean*, *median*, and *mode*. The mean normally refers to the *arithmetic mean*; however, there are also other types of means such as the *harmonic mean* and the *geometric mean*.

For a sample of measurements $\{x_1, x_2, ..., x_n\}$, Table 3.7 shows the different types of average values and how they are defined.

Table 3.7: Most common types of averages (indices of central tendency)

Average value	Definition
Arithmetic mean	$\bar{x} = \frac{1}{n} \sum_{i=1}^{n} x_i$
Harmonic mean	$\overline{x_H} = \frac{n}{\sum_{i=1}^{n} \frac{1}{x_i}}$
Geometric mean	$\overline{x_G} = \sqrt[n]{x_1 x_2 \cdots x_n} = \left(\prod_{i=1}^{n} x_i\right)^{\frac{1}{n}}$
Median	The value that lies in the middle when the measurements are in sorted order (if there are an even number of values, the arithmetic mean of the two values in the middle is taken)
Mode	The value that occurs most often

The geometric mean can also be expressed as the exponential of the arithmetic mean of logarithms as follows:

$$\overline{x_G} = \left(\prod_{i=1}^{n} x_i\right)^{\frac{1}{n}} = \exp\left[\frac{1}{n} \sum_{i=1}^{n} \ln(x_i)\right] \tag{3.5}$$

assuming that $x_1, x_2, ..., x_n > 0$. More generally,

$$\overline{x_G} = \left(\prod_{i=1}^{n} x_i\right)^{\frac{1}{n}} = (-1)^m \exp\left[\frac{1}{n} \sum_{i=1}^{n} \ln|x_i|\right], \tag{3.6}$$

where m is the number of negative numbers.

The arithmetic mean is the most common average used to summarize a sample of measurements. As an index of central tendency, it normally lies in the center of the interval where most measurements are distributed; however, one drawback of the arithmetic mean is that it is quite sensitive to outliers in the measurements. Outliers may introduce a bias that distorts the intuition of central tendency. Consider the example given in Figure 3.3. First, a sample of measurements without outliers is shown; then, the same sample with one added outlier is shown. As we can see, the outlier has significant impact on the arithmetic mean, which in this case does not serve as a good index of central tendency. The median, however, is much less influenced by the presence of outliers as shown in the figure. The differences between the arithmetic mean, harmonic mean, and geometric mean are discussed in detail in Section 3.5.2.

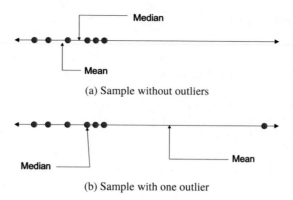

(a) Sample without outliers

(b) Sample with one outlier

Fig. 3.3: Impact of outliers on the arithmetic mean

The *median* is the "middle" value defined as a value such that half of the values are above and half are below that value. The median can be determined by sorting the values and taking the value that lies in the middle of the sorted set. If the number of measurements n is odd, the middle value can be uniquely determined. If n is even, the median is computed as the arithmetic mean of the two values that lie in the middle of the sorted set.

Finally, the *mode* is the value that occurs most often. The mode may not be unique if multiple values happen to occur with the same frequency. The mode is typically used when the measured values represent distinct types/categories (i.e., for categorical data in nominal scale as introduced in Section 3.2).

The standard definitions of means assume that all measurements are equally important. If that is not the case, one can use weights to represent the relative importance of measurements. Each measured value x_i is assigned a weight $w_i \in (0, 1)$. The weights are assumed to add up to one; that is, $\sum_{i=1}^{n} w_i = 1$.

Table 3.8 shows the weighted versions of the mean values (arithmetic, harmonic, and geometric).

Table 3.8: Weighted means

Average value	Definition
Weighted arithmetic mean	$\overline{x_{A,w}} = \sum_{i=1}^{n} w_i x_i$
Weighted harmonic mean	$\overline{x_{H,w}} = \dfrac{1}{\sum_{i=1}^{n} \frac{w_i}{x_i}}$
Weighted geometric mean	$\overline{x_{G,w}} = \prod_{i=1}^{n} x_i^{w_i}$

3.5.2 Composite Metrics

So far, we used statistics to summarize a sample of measurements corresponding to the same underlying measured system property. In other words, we considered repeated measurements of the same underlying measure, that is, a sample from a random variable characterizing a given system property.

Another common scenario in benchmarking is when multiple different metrics need to be aggregated into a single value in order to summarize the results. Such a metric is called a *composite metric* (see Section 3.1) since its values are derived by combining other metrics (elementary metrics or previously defined composite metrics). The combined metrics may characterize different system properties, or they may capture measurements of the same property but under different conditions (e.g., measurement of response time under different workloads).

A composite metric is typically defined as a mean value (arithmetic, harmonic, or geometric) of a set of elementary metrics. The arithmetic mean is commonly used when the sum of raw values has a physical meaning, for example, when the aggregated metrics represent measured times (durations). Similarly, the harmonic mean is also used when the sum of raw values has a physical meaning; however, it is typically used to summarize metrics that represent measured rates. Finally, the geometric mean is commonly used when the product of raw values has a physical meaning, such as in the case of averaging speedups.

Similar to our motivating example in Section 3.4.1, consider two programs A and B executed on two different computers X and Y. Assume that program A runs twice as fast on computer Y compared to X, whereas program B runs at half the speed compared to X, so that the speedup of A is 2 and the speedup of B is 0.5. Calculating the arithmetic mean of the two speedups results in $(2 + 0.5)/2 = 1.25$, whereas the geometric mean is $\sqrt{2 \times 0.5} = 1$. Assuming that the two programs are executed for the same amount of time, the geometric mean provides an average speedup value that has a physical meaning. Speeding up half of the execution by a factor of two, while at the same time slowing down the other half by the same factor, results in an overall speedup of 1 (no change). As we saw in Section 3.4.1, the geometric mean can be used to compute a mean value of a set of speedup ratios that is consistent regardless of the choice of reference (i.e., the denominator in the ratios). It is a shortcut for using the logarithms of the ratios, computing their arithmetic mean, and then applying the exponential function to return to the linear scale, while hoping that the logarithms are symmetrically (or even better, normally) distributed (Mashey, 2004). In Section 3.5.3.2, we discuss the properties of the geometric mean in more detail.

The design of good composite metrics, providing a level playing field for comparing systems, is challenging. The main challenge stems from the fact that when multiple metrics are combined into a single value, normally information is lost. For example, as discussed in Section 3.3, in performance benchmarking, different types of metrics are used, such as response time, throughput, and resource utilization, each characterizing a different aspect of the system performance. Given that performance is inherently multi-dimensional, it is often not straightforward how to weight the individual performance metrics when combining them into a single composite metric.

Also, systems are often specialized for running specific types of workloads. Thus, a system may perform great for one type of workload and bad for others. Combining performance metrics for different types of workloads into a single composite metric leads to losing such information.

Consider the example in Table 3.9. The execution times of five programs on three different servers are shown. The last row shows the arithmetic mean of the measured execution times on each server. Although the systems exhibit significant performance differences when running the different programs, the arithmetic mean of the execution times is constant. Thus, when using the arithmetic mean as a composite performance metric, the three servers are indistinguishable.

Table 3.9: Execution times of five programs on three different servers

Program	Server 1	Server 2	Server 3
1	50 s	100 s	500 s
2	200 s	400 s	600 s
3	250 s	500 s	500 s
4	400 s	800 s	800 s
5	5,000 s	4,100 s	3,500 s
Arithmetic mean	1,180 s	1,180 s	1,180 s

One way to better reflect the different performance of the three servers is to consider the frequency with which the different programs are expected to be executed in practice. If information on the execution frequency of the respective workloads is available, this information can be used to assign different weights to the execution times for each program and thus come up with a more representative composite metric. Table 3.10 shows the weighted arithmetic means of the execution times of the five programs on the different servers. As we can see, Server 1 performs best, followed by Server 2 and Server 3. Thus, by using the weighted arithmetic mean to take into account the execution frequencies of the different workloads, we obtain a composite metric that better captures the differences between the three systems.

We note that weighted means are normally quite sensitive to the choice of weights. Table 3.11 shows the performance of Server 1 for two different execution frequencies. As we can see, the server exhibits very different performance behavior when the execution frequencies change.

Table 3.10: Weighted means of the execution times of the five programs

Program	Execution frequency	Server 1	Server 2	Server 3
1	50%	50 s	100 s	500 s
2	30%	200 s	400 s	600 s
3	10%	250 s	500 s	500 s
4	5%	400 s	800 s	800 s
5	5%	5,000 s	4,100 s	3,500 s
Weighted arithmetic mean		380 s	465 s	695 s

Table 3.11: Performance of Server 1 under varying execution frequencies

Program	Execution time	Execution frequency 1	Execution frequency 2
1	50 s	50%	25%
2	200 s	30%	5%
3	250 s	10%	10%
4	400 s	5%	5%
5	5,000 s	5%	55%
Weighted arithmetic mean		380 s	2,817.5 s

3.5.3 Aggregating Results from Multiple Benchmarks

In the previous section, we briefly explained how composite metrics can be used to summarize results from multiple different measurement experiments testing the system behavior under different conditions (e.g., when running different types of workloads). This is common in benchmarking since modern benchmark suites are often composed of multiple benchmarks that exercise different aspects of the system. Each benchmark has its own metric or a set of metrics. The results from the individual benchmarks are normally aggregated into one or more high-level composite metrics.

Ideally, when aggregating metrics from multiple benchmarks, each benchmark metric should be weighted according to the fraction of time in which the workload emulated by the respective benchmark is expected to run in the user's target application scenario. For example, consider a benchmark suite composed of three benchmarks: image processing, encryption, and compression. Each of the three benchmarks measures and reports its own MIPS metric. For a user whose actual workload is expected to be encryption for 90% of the time, image processing for 5%, and compression for 5%, the weighted arithmetic mean with weights 0.9, 0.05, and 0.05 can be used to aggregate the MIPS metrics measured for the three workloads into a single overall MIPS metric. If each benchmark is expected to run for an equal period of time, one can use a simple (unweighted) arithmetic mean of the MIPS. While this works in the case of MIPS, as we show in the following, using the arithmetic mean to aggregate metrics from multiple benchmarks does not always produce a reliable metric.

3.5.3.1 Aggregating Ratio Metrics

Many performance metrics are defined as ratio A/B of two measured quantities A and B, for example, the metrics MIPS and MFLOPS we discussed in Section 3.4.2 as well as all speedup metrics (Section 3.3). Some further examples of ratio metrics include cycles per instruction (CPI), instructions per cycle (IPC), cache miss rates, cache hit rates, and branch miss-prediction rates. Based on the examples provided in John (2004) and John (2006), in this section, we show how ratio metrics corresponding to multiple benchmarks from a benchmark suite can be aggregated to summarize the system performance with a single number.

Consider a benchmark suite composed of n benchmarks. Assume that a ratio metric A/B is measured for each of the benchmarks in the suite. In this section, we show how the metrics can be aggregated to present a summary of the performance over the entire suite. While we focus on performance metrics, the principles we present can also be generalized to other metrics that are defined as ratios. We start with MIPS as an example. Assume that each of the benchmarks in the benchmark suite reports its individual result $MIPS_i = c_i/t_i$ for $i = 1, 2, ..., n$, where c_i is the instruction count of the ith benchmark (in millions) and t_i is the execution time of the ith benchmark.

The overall MIPS metric of the benchmark suite is the MIPS metric when the n benchmarks are considered as part of a single application:

$$Overall\ MIPS = \frac{\sum_{i=1}^{n} c_i}{\sum_{i=1}^{n} t_i}. \tag{3.7}$$

We now show that the overall MIPS of the benchmark suite can be obtained by:

- a weighted harmonic mean (WHM) of the MIPS of the individual benchmarks weighted according to the instruction counts or
- a weighted arithmetic mean (WAM) of the MIPS of the individual benchmarks weighted according to the execution times.

Indeed, if the weight of the ith benchmark according to instruction count is denoted as $w_i^c = \frac{c_i}{\sum_{k=1}^{n} c_k}$, then the WHM with weights corresponding to instruction counts is given by

$$\frac{1}{\sum_{i=1}^{n} \frac{w_i^c}{MIPS_i}} = \frac{1}{\frac{1}{\sum_{k=1}^{n} c_k} \sum_{i=1}^{n} \frac{c_i}{MIPS_i}} = \frac{\sum_{k=1}^{n} c_k}{\sum_{i=1}^{n} \frac{c_i}{MIPS_i}} =$$

$$= \frac{\sum_{k=1}^{n} c_k}{\sum_{i=1}^{n} \frac{c_i t_i}{c_i}} = \frac{\sum_{k=1}^{n} c_k}{\sum_{i=1}^{n} t_i} = Overall \ MIPS. \tag{3.8}$$

Similarly, if the weight of the ith benchmark according to execution time is denoted as $w_i^t = \frac{t_i}{\sum_{k=1}^{n} t_k}$, then the WAM with weights corresponding to execution times is given by

$$\sum_{i=1}^{n} \left(w_i^t MIPS_i \right) = \frac{1}{\sum_{k=1}^{n} t_k} \sum_{i=1}^{n} (t_i MIPS_i) =$$

$$= \frac{1}{\sum_{k=1}^{n} t_k} \sum_{i=1}^{n} \left(t_i \frac{c_i}{t_i} \right) = \frac{\sum_{i=1}^{n} c_i}{\sum_{k=1}^{n} t_k} = Overall \ MIPS. \tag{3.9}$$

Table 3.12: Example benchmark suite with five benchmarks (John, 2004)

Benchmark	Instruction count (in millions)	Execution time (s)	Individual MIPS
1	500	2	250
2	50	1	50
3	200	1	200
4	1,000	5	200
5	250	1	250

Consider the example in Table 3.12. The results of running a benchmark suite comprising five benchmarks are shown. For each benchmark, the instruction count, the execution time, and the individual MIPS rating are shown.

The weights of the benchmarks with respect to instruction counts are

$$\left(\frac{500}{2000}, \frac{50}{2000}, \frac{200}{2000}, \frac{1000}{2000}, \frac{250}{2000} \right) = (0.25, 0.025, 0.1, 0.5, 0.125). \tag{3.10}$$

The weights of the benchmarks with respect to execution times are

$$\left(\frac{2}{10}, \frac{1}{10}, \frac{1}{10}, \frac{5}{10}, \frac{1}{10} \right) = (0.2, 0.1, 0.1, 0.5, 0.1). \tag{3.11}$$

WHM of individual MIPS (weighted with instruction counts):

$$\frac{1}{\frac{0.25}{250} + \frac{0.025}{50} + \frac{0.1}{200} + \frac{0.5}{200} + \frac{0.125}{250}} = 200. \tag{3.12}$$

WAM of individual MIPS (weighted with execution times):

$$(250 \times 0.2) + (50 \times 0.1) + (200 \times 0.1) + (200 \times 0.5) + (250 \times 0.1) = 200. \tag{3.13}$$

$$Overall \; MIPS = \frac{\sum_{i=1}^{n} c_i}{\sum_{i=1}^{n} t_i} = \frac{2000}{10} = 200. \tag{3.14}$$

Generalizing the presented example, we can formulate the following theorem:

Theorem 3.1 *Given a benchmark suite made of n benchmarks that use a ratio metric defined as A/B, where A and B are two measures, the values of the metric for the individual benchmarks can be aggregated into a single overall metric by using either: (1) the harmonic mean with weights corresponding to the measure in the numerator or (2) the arithmetic mean with weights corresponding to the measure in the denominator.*

Corollary 3.1 *If A is weighted equally among the benchmarks, the simple (unweighted) harmonic mean can be used. If B is weighted equally among the benchmarks, the simple (unweighted) arithmetic mean can be used.*

Tables 3.13 and 3.14 show some examples of how the above theorem and corollary can be applied to some common metrics used in the computer architecture domain.

Table 3.13: Examples of aggregating ratio metrics (John, 2004)

Metric	Appropriate mean value to aggregate metrics over a benchmark suite	
A/B	WAM weighted with Bs	WHM weighted with As
IPC	WAM weighted with cycles	WHM weighted with inst. count
CPI	WAM weighted with inst. count	WHM weighted with cycles
MIPS	WAM weighted with time	WHM weighted with inst. count
MFLOPS	WAM weighted with time	WHM weighted with FLOP count
Cache hit rate	WAM weighted with the number of references to cache	WHM weighted with number of cache hits
Transactions per minute	WAM weighted with execution times	WHM weighted with proportion of transactions for each benchmark
Speedup	WAM weighted with execution times of each benchmark in the enhanced system	WHM weighted with execution times of each benchmark in the baseline system

Table 3.14: Use of simple (unweighted) means (John, 2004)

Metric	To aggregate metrics over a benchmark suite:	
	Simple arithmetic mean valid?	Simple harmonic mean valid?
A/B	If Bs are equal	If As are equal
IPC	If equal cycles in each benchmark	If equal inst. count in each benchmark
CPI	If equal inst. count in each benchmark	If equal cycles in each benchmark
MIPS	If equal times in each benchmark	If equal inst. count in each benchmark
MFLOPS	If equal times in each benchmark	If equal FLOPS in each benchmark
Cache hit rate	If equal number of references to cache for each benchmark	If equal number of cache hits in each benchmark
Transactions per minute	If equal times in each benchmark	If equal number of transactions in each benchmark
Speedup	If equal execution times in each benchmark in the enhanced system	If equal execution times in each benchmark in the baseline system

3.5.3.2 Aggregating Normalized Values

Consider the motivating example we presented in Section 3.4.1. A benchmark suite composed of two programs, which we can consider as separate benchmarks, was run on three different servers. The execution times of the two benchmarks were measured on each server and used to compute a composite metric summarizing the server performance. We assumed that no information is available about the fraction of time in which the two workloads emulated by the benchmarks are expected to run in the user's application scenario. The two workloads were therefore treated as equally important assuming that they will be executed for the same fraction of time. In other words, it was assumed that at a randomly chosen point of time, the probability that the first workload is running is equal to the probability that the second workload is running. We showed that using the arithmetic mean to aggregate the execution times of the two benchmarks leads to a composite metric that does not reflect the actual server performance and is therefore unreliable.

When using the arithmetic mean of execution times, large absolute values have a higher influence on the overall result. To address this problem, we computed the speedup of the different servers with respect to a selected reference server and used the speedup as a basis for our metric instead of the execution time. The advantage of using speedup is that the actual absolute values of the execution times are irrelevant and only the relative differences play a role. Thus, speeding up one of the two benchmarks by a given factor would have the same effect on the overall performance, no matter which benchmark is selected. Furthermore, when comparing speedups, the choice of a reference server does not influence the results; that is, the ratio of two speedups is independent of the server chosen as a reference (Lilja, 2000). This is shown in Equation (3.15), where $ExecTime_A$ and $ExecTime_B$ denote the execution times on two arbitrary servers and $ExecTime_{ref}$ denotes the respective execution time on the server used as a baseline.

$$\frac{Speedup_A}{Speedup_B} = \frac{\frac{ExecTime_{ref}}{ExecTime_A}}{\frac{ExecTime_{ref}}{ExecTime_B}} = \frac{ExecTime_B}{ExecTime_A}. \tag{3.15}$$

While the use of speedup resolved part of the issue, we showed in Section 3.4.1 that if the arithmetic mean is used to compute the average speedup for the two benchmarks, the resulting rankings of the three servers depend on the choice of the reference system. Thus, a composite metric based on the arithmetic mean of speedups may be easily manipulated by selecting a different server as a baseline. The solution was to use the geometric mean to compute the mean speedup. The geometric mean has the property that it ensures consistent rankings when averaging normalized data, such as speedups. In the following, we elaborate a bit more on this property.

Consider the example in Table 3.15 where the execution times of five benchmarks executed on three different servers are shown. The table shows the raw execution times as measured when running the benchmarks as well as the execution times normalized to Server 1 and Server 2, respectively. The geometric mean is used as a composite metric summarizing the results for each server. As we can see, in all three cases the geometric mean provides consistent rankings of the three servers, independent of the server chosen as a baseline for the normalization.

It can be easily shown that not only are the rankings consistent, but also the ratios of geometric means corresponding to different servers are independent of the baseline used for normalization. We denote with x_i and y_i the results of the i-th benchmark (in our case, measured execution times) for two selected servers x and y. We denote with r_i the respective benchmark results for a reference server used as a baseline for normalization. Equation (3.16) shows the ratio of the geometric means $\overline{x_G}$ and $\overline{y_G}$ of the benchmark results for the two servers. As we can see, the ratio of the geometric means is independent of the server used for normalization.

$$\frac{\overline{x_G}}{\overline{y_G}} = \frac{\left(\prod_{i=1}^{n} \frac{x_i}{r_i}\right)^{\frac{1}{n}}}{\left(\prod_{i=1}^{n} \frac{y_i}{r_i}\right)^{\frac{1}{n}}} = \frac{\left(\prod_{i=1}^{n} \frac{1}{r_i}\right)^{\frac{1}{n}} \left(\prod_{i=1}^{n} x_i\right)^{\frac{1}{n}}}{\left(\prod_{i=1}^{n} \frac{1}{r_i}\right)^{\frac{1}{n}} \left(\prod_{i=1}^{n} y_i\right)^{\frac{1}{n}}} = \frac{\left(\prod_{i=1}^{n} x_i\right)^{\frac{1}{n}}}{\left(\prod_{i=1}^{n} y_i\right)^{\frac{1}{n}}}. \tag{3.16}$$

The most prominent example of a benchmark suite that uses the geometric mean to aggregate metrics from multiple benchmarks is SPEC CPU, which is introduced in detail in Chapter 10. Since its first version (SPEC CPU89), this benchmark has followed the same approach to derive composite metrics summarizing the performance of a CPU under test. SPEC CPU includes a number of different benchmarks, each running a different type of workload (e.g., GNU C compiler, video compression, ray tracing). The benchmarks are executed on the CPU under test. The results are then normalized by computing the speedup with respect to a standardized reference machine, the results of which are provided by SPEC. In SPEC's terminology, the

Table 3.15: Ranking of three servers based on the geometric mean with different
reference systems

(a) Execution times of five benchmarks executed on three different servers

Benchmark	Server 1	Server 2	Server 3
1	417	244	134
2	83	70	70
3	66	153	135
4	39,449	33,527	66,000
5	772	368	369
Geometric mean	586	503	499
Rank	3	2	1

(b) Execution times normalized to Server 1

Benchmark	Server 1	Server 2	Server 3
1	1.0	0.59	0.32
2	1.0	0.84	0.85
3	1.0	2.32	2.05
4	1.0	0.85	1.67
5	1.0	0.48	0.48
Geometric mean	1.0	0.86	0.85
Rank	3	2	1

(c) Execution times normalized to Server 2

Benchmark	Server 1	Server 2	Server 3
1	1.71	1.0	0.55
2	1.19	1.0	1.0
3	0.43	1.0	0.88
4	1.18	1.0	1.97
5	2.10	1.0	1.0
Geometric mean	1.17	1.0	0.99
Rank	3	2	1

speedup when applied to the execution time is referred to as *SPECratio*. The normalized results (SPECratios) for the different benchmarks are aggregated by computing their geometric mean, which is reported as an overall metric.

The same approach is followed in all SPEC CPU benchmark suites including the latest, SPEC CPU 2017. The latter offers 43 benchmarks, organized into four suites (SPECspeed 2017 Integer, SPECspeed 2017 Floating Point, SPECrate 2017 Integer, SPECrate 2017 Floating Point) that focus on different types of compute intensive workloads. Each suite is a set of benchmarks that is run as a group to produce one of the overall metrics. SPEC CPU 2017 uses both execution time (SPECspeed) and throughput (SPECrate) metrics that are measured and normalized to a reference machine. The respective ratios for the benchmarks in each of the four suites are then averaged using the geometric mean, which is reported as the overall metric for the respective suite.

The motivation to use normalized metrics combined with geometric mean is that each of the benchmarks should be treated as equally important; that is, the workloads modeled by the different benchmarks are assumed to be equally represented in customer applications. The geometric mean is used to compute the overall metric, so that the results are independent of the reference machine used by SPEC. The intent is that improvements in each benchmark are encouraged and rewarded equally. In other words, a 20% improvement in one benchmark should have the same effect on the overall mean as a 20% improvement on any of the other benchmarks, and another 20% improvement on that benchmark should have the same effect as the last 20% improvement. This ensures that no one benchmark in the suite becomes more important than any of the others in the suite.

3.6 Concluding Remarks

This chapter started by defining the basic concepts: metric, measure, and measurement. While in mathematics, the term metric is explicitly distinguished from the term measure, in computer science and engineering, the terms metric and measure overlap in meaning and are often used interchangeably. One way to distinguish between them is looking at metrics as values that can be derived from some fundamental measurements comprising one or more measures. We introduced four scales of measurement—nominal, ordinal, interval, and ratio—which can be used to classify the types of values assigned by different measures. After that, we defined the most common performance metrics—response time, throughput, and utilization—while also introducing the terms speedup and relative change.

We showed that not all metrics that can be used to quantify a given system property under evaluation are good in the sense of providing insight into the system behavior and helping to make informed decisions. To distinguish good metrics from bad, we described six fundamental attributes that characterize the quality of a benchmark metric: easy to measure, repeatable, reliable, linear, consistent, and independent. Following this, we introduced the different types of averages (i.e., indices of central tendency): arithmetic mean, harmonic mean, geometric mean, median, and mode. We showed how average values can be used to define composite metrics that summarize results from multiple different measurement experiments testing the system behavior under different conditions. This is common in benchmarking since modern benchmark suites are often composed of multiple benchmarks that exercise different aspects of the system. Each benchmark has its own metric or a set of metrics. The results from the individual benchmarks are normally aggregated into one or more high-level composite metrics. The chapter concluded by discussing approaches to aggregate results from multiple benchmarks.

References

John, L. K. (2004). "More on Finding a Single Number to Indicate Overall Performance of a Benchmark Suite". *ACM SIGARCH Computer Architecture News*, 32(1). ACM: New York City, NY, USA, pp. 3–8 (cited on pp. 63–66).

– (2006). "Aggregating Performance Metrics Over a Benchmark Suite". In: *Performance Evaluation and Benchmarking*. Ed. by L. K. John and L. Eeckhout. CRC Press, Taylor & Francis Group, LLC, pp. 47–58 (cited on p. 63).

Lilja, D. J. (2000). *Measuring Computer Performance: A Practitioner's Guide*. Cambridge University Press: Cambridge, UK (cited on pp. 49, 50, 55, 57, 66).

Mashey, J. R. (2004). "War of the Benchmark Means: Time for a Truce". *ACM SIGARCH Computer Architecture News*, 32(4). ACM: New York, NY, USA (cited on p. 60).

Stevens, S. S. (1946). "On the Theory of Scales of Measurement". *Science*, 103(2684), pp. 677–680 (cited on pp. 45, 46).

– (1951). "Mathematics, Measurement, and Psychophysics". In: *Handbook of Experimental Psychology*. Ed. by S. S. Stevens. John Wiley & Sons: Hoboken, New Jersey, USA, pp. 1–49 (cited on p. 45).

– (1959). "Measurement, psychophysics, and utility". In: *Measurement: Definitions and Theories*. Ed. by C. Churchman and P. Ratoosh. John Wiley & Sons: Hoboken, New Jersey, USA, pp. 18–63 (cited on p. 47).

Chapter 4
Statistical Measurements

> "A man with one watch knows what time it is; a man with two watches is never quite sure."
>
> —*Lee Segall*

In the previous chapter, we saw that the design of good benchmark metrics that possess the quality attributes presented in Chapter 3 (Section 3.4.2) is challenging. So far, we focused on ensuring that metrics are reliable and independent from influences of vendors. In this chapter, we focus on the quality attributes *easy to measure* and *repeatable*.

In Chapter 3 (Section 3.1), we defined *metric* as a value that can be derived from measurements of one or more measures that evaluate some properties or characteristics of events or objects in the real world. Typically, the properties or characteristics of interest cannot be measured directly and can only be estimated statistically. Each measure can therefore be seen as a *random variable* capturing the outcome of an experiment, that is, an observation (measurement) of a given property or characteristic of an event or object.

This chapter introduces statistical approaches for quantifying the variability and precision of measurements. The chapter starts by introducing the most common indices of dispersion for quantifying the variability, followed by defining basic concepts such as accuracy, precision, and resolution of measurements as well as the distinction between systematic and random measurement errors. A model of random errors is introduced and used to derive confidence intervals for estimating the mean of a measured quantity of interest based on a sample of measurements. After that, the special case where the quantity of interest is defined as a proportion is considered. Finally, statistical tests for comparing alternatives based on measurements are introduced. The cases of paired and unpaired observations are covered separately.

© Springer Nature Switzerland AG 2020
S. Kounev et al., *Systems Benchmarking*, https://doi.org/10.1007/978-3-030-41705-5_4

4.1 Measurement as a Random Experiment

The process of measurement can be seen as a random experiment in which the values of the respective measures of interest are observed. Typically, measurements vary when repeated multiple times. Thus, a set of measured values $\{x_1, x_2, ..., x_n\}$ is considered a sample from a random variable X with an unknown distribution. Metrics are often computed from the sample using statistics that allow one to summarize the measurements while at the same time characterizing properties of the underlying population (i.e., the distribution of the random variable X).

Indices of central tendency A sample of measurements is normally summarized by computing an average value, also referred to as *index of central tendency*, and using it as a metric characterizing the measured property or characteristic of interest. As introduced in Chapter 3 (Section 3.5), the most common indices of central tendency are the sample *mean*, *median*, and *mode*. When speaking of the sample mean, the *arithmetic mean* is assumed. Further indices of central tendency include the *harmonic mean* and the *geometric mean*. In this chapter, we focus on the sample mean, since it is the standard index of central tendency used in statistics when considering a sample $\{x_1, x_2, ..., x_n\}$ from a random variable X. The sample mean is defined as

$$\bar{x} = \frac{1}{n} \sum_{i=1}^{n} x_i. \tag{4.1}$$

The sample mean is an estimate of the mean $\mu = E[X]$ of the random variable X, also called *expected value* of X.

Indices of dispersion While the indices of central tendency aim to provide a middle or typical value that lies in the center of the interval where most measurements are distributed, they do not provide information about the variability of the measurements. Figure 4.1 shows two histograms corresponding to samples from two different random variables. While the respective distributions have the same sample mean, they obviously have different shape, the second one exhibiting much higher variability. The sample mean does not provide any information on how "spread out" the measurements are. To quantify the variability of measurements, different statistics are used, referred to as *indices of dispersion*. Table 4.1 shows the most common indices of dispersion for a sample of measurements $\{x_1, x_2, ..., x_n\}$ with their definitions.

The most common indices of dispersion are the sample *variance*, *standard deviation*, and *coefficient of variation (COV)*. The sample variance s^2 for a sample of size n has $(n - 1)$ degrees of freedom. As mentioned in Chapter 2 (Section 2.4), the sample variance is an estimate of the variance σ^2 of the random variable X, also denoted as $\text{Var}(X)$ or σ_X^2. In general, the *degrees of freedom* of an estimate of a statistical parameter are equal to the number of independent pieces of information used as input in the estimation minus the number of parameters used as intermediate steps. The sample variance for a sample of size n has $(n - 1)$ degrees of freedom, because it is computed from n random values minus one parameter estimated as intermediate step (i.e., the sample mean).

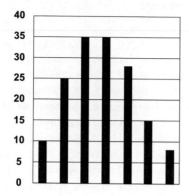 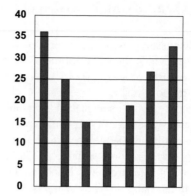

Fig. 4.1: Example of distributions with different variability

Table 4.1: Most common indices of dispersion for a sample of measurements

Index of dispersion	Definition
Range	$\max\limits_{1 \leq i \leq n}(x_i) - \min\limits_{1 \leq i \leq n}(x_i)$
Maximum distance from the mean	$\max\limits_{1 \leq i \leq n}(\lvert x_i - \bar{x}\rvert)$
Sample variance s^2	$s^2 = \frac{\sum_{i=1}^{n}(x_i - \bar{x})^2}{n-1}$
Sample standard deviation s	$s = \sqrt{s^2}$
Coefficient of variation (COV)	$\mathrm{COV} = s/\bar{x}$

It can be shown that the following equation holds:

$$s^2 = \frac{\sum_{i=1}^{n}(x_i - \bar{x})^2}{n-1} = \frac{n\sum_{i=1}^{n}x_i^2 - (\sum_{i=1}^{n}x_i)^2}{n(n-1)}. \tag{4.2}$$

The second formula allows us to compute the variance using one pass through the data, which is normally more convenient to implement.

The sample variance is derived based on the squared distance of the observed values x_i from the sample mean. Given that the square of the distance is taken, the resulting quantity is in "units-squared" compared to the mean. This makes it hard to compare the variance to the mean. The sample standard deviation is computed as the square root of the variance and thus has the same units as the mean. This allows setting the standard deviation in relation to the mean. Finally, the coefficient of variation (COV) compares the relative size of the standard deviation to the mean value and is thus a dimensionless quantity.

4.2 Quantifying Precision of Measurements

As discussed previously, the process of measurement can then be seen as an experiment in which the values of the respective measures of interest are observed. A set of measured values $\{x_1, x_2, ..., x_n\}$ is considered a sample from a population, that is, a random variable X with an unknown distribution. Metrics are often computed from the sample using statistics that allow summarizing the measurements while at the same time quantifying certain properties of the underlying population.

In reality, the actual measured quantity is characterized by the probability distribution of the random variable X. The sample mean $\bar{x}$, typically used to summarize a sample of measurements, is interpreted as an estimate of the mean $\mu = E[X]$ of the random variable X. The mean μ is the main index of central tendency characterizing the distribution of the measurements. Since the distribution is unknown, μ is also unknown and it can be only approximated using the sample mean $\bar{x}$. However, since measurements vary when repeated multiple times, the computed sample mean also varies. This introduces *uncertainty* into our measurements raising the question of how good the sample mean $\bar{x}$ serves as approximation of the population mean μ? Answering this question is the topic of the rest of this section.

4.2.1 Experimental Errors

The variability in experimental measurements, which introduces uncertainty, is referred to as *noise*. The noise is caused by different sources of variability, referred to as *errors*. We distinguish between systematic errors and random errors (Lilja, 2000).

Systematic errors are the result of some oversight or mistake in the measurement process introducing some bias into the measurements. For example, a change in the temperature may cause a clock period to drift, affecting time measurements. Similarly, if the experimenter fails to ensure an identical system state in the beginning of each experiment (e.g., by forgetting to clear the cache or to reload the database), this may introduce bias into the measurements. Systematic errors typically produce a constant or a slowly varying bias.

Random errors, on the other hand, result from limitations in the measurement tools and random processes within the system. They are unpredictable, non-deterministic, and unbiased, in the sense that they may equally likely cause higher or lower values to be measured. While systematic errors depend on the skills of the experimenter and can be controlled, random errors typically can be neither controlled nor completely eliminated. A number of random processes in modern computer systems may affect measurements such as CPU caching, process scheduling and synchronization, data contention, virtual memory paging, virtual machine scheduling, and network packet collisions. While random errors normally cannot be completely eliminated, their influence can be analyzed and quantified using statistical methods, as we show in the rest of this chapter.

To give an example of a random error, we consider an interval timer. Most interval timers are implemented using a counter variable incremented on each tick of a system clock. Figure 4.2 shows an example of an interval timer reporting a different duration of the same event, depending on the exact starting point of the measurement. Repeated measurements of the same event duration will lead to values $X \pm \Delta$. This effect is referred to as *quantization effect*.

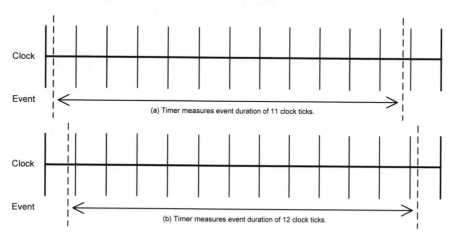

Fig. 4.2: Example of random errors caused by quantization effect in interval timers

The measurement process itself, including the employed measurement tools, can be characterized by three properties that influence the quality of the measurements: accuracy, precision, and resolution (Lilja, 2000).

The *accuracy* is the absolute difference between the true value of interest and the mean of the actual value being measured. In other words, the accuracy is an indicator of how close the mean μ of the distribution of measurements is to the true value we are trying to measure. Ideally, there will be no difference between the two; however, due to systematic errors in the measurement process, often the two values are not identical. For example, in the case of a timer, the accuracy determines how close the timer's measurements match the standard measurement of time based on agreed-upon standards and reference clocks.

The *precision* characterizes the repeatability of measurements obtained through the respective measurement approach. Higher variability leads to more scatter in the measurements. The high variability translates into higher variance σ^2 of the random variable X, resulting in lower precision of the measurement process. The precision depends on the amount of random errors in the measurements. The more sources of random errors, the lower the precision of measurements. Unlike accuracy, which is up to the skills of the experimenter, the precision of measurements can be quantified using statistical methods, as will be shown later in this chapter.

Finally, the *resolution* is the smallest difference between two possible measured values, that is, the smallest change in the measured quantity that can be detected

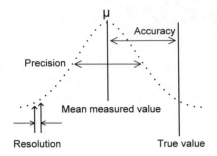

Fig. 4.3: Distribution of measurements—accuracy, precision, and resolution

by the measurement process. For example, for interval timers, the resolution is the period of time between two clock ticks, which determines the minimum amount of time that can be measured. As discussed above, the quantization effect is caused by the limited resolution of interval timers. Figure 4.3 illustrates the concepts of accuracy, precision, and resolution.

4.2.2 A Model of Random Errors

Consider a measurement experiment resulting in obtaining the sample $\{x_1, x_2, ..., x_n\}$ from the random variable X, representing the measured quantity of interest. The measurements are influenced by a number of error sources causing noise in the measurements. As a simplification, let us first assume one source of error (e.g., quantization effect) that leads to shifting the measured value by e units to the left or to the right with equal probability. This is shown in Table 4.2a. Now consider two or three independent sources of errors, each of them behaving in the same way. The possible measured values and their probabilities are shown in Tables 4.2b and 4.2c, respectively. Figure 4.4 shows the distribution of measurements.

The effect of multiple error sources on the measurements can be generalized for n independent error sources as shown in Figure 4.5 (Lilja, 2000). Starting with a value x, each error source shifts the value either to the left or to the right with an equal probability. The $n + 1$ possible resulting values $r_k = x - (n - 2k)e$ for $k = 0, 1, ..., n$ that can be measured are shown at the bottom. For each of the possible values, the probability of the measurement experiment resulting in the respective value is proportional to the number of paths from the initial value x to the respective value at the bottom of the diagram. Each path can be seen as a sequence of "going left" $(-e)$ vs. "going right" $(+e)$ decisions (n Bernoulli trials with probability 0.5) for n independent error sources, that is, a Bernoulli process. We denote with $p = 0.5$ the probability of "going right." The final measured value r_k depends on the number of "going right" decisions k in the sequence (ranging from 0 to n). For each possible number of decisions to go right ($k = 0, 1, ..., n$), $\binom{n}{k}$ possible orderings exist

Table 4.2: Effects of multiple error sources

(a) Effect of one error source

Error	Measured value	Probability
-e	x-e	$\frac{1}{2}$
+e	x+e	$\frac{1}{2}$

(b) Effect of two error sources

Error 1	Error 2	Measured value	Probability
-e	-e	x-2e	$\frac{1}{4}$
-e	+e	x	$\frac{1}{4}$
+e	-e	x	$\frac{1}{4}$
+e	+e	x+2e	$\frac{1}{4}$

(c) Effect of three error sources

Error 1	Error 2	Error 3	Measured value	Probability
-e	-e	-e	x-3e	$\frac{1}{8}$
+e	-e	-e	x-1e	$\frac{1}{8}$
-e	+e	-e	x-1e	$\frac{1}{8}$
-e	-e	+e	x-1e	$\frac{1}{8}$
+e	+e	-e	x+1e	$\frac{1}{8}$
+e	-e	+e	x+1e	$\frac{1}{8}$
-e	+e	+e	x+1e	$\frac{1}{8}$
+e	+e	+e	x+3e	$\frac{1}{8}$

corresponding to different paths, all leading to the same final point in the diagram (measured value). Each of these paths occurs with probability $p^k(1-p)^{(n-k)}$. Thus, the probability of measuring the value $r_k = x - (n - 2k)e = x + ke - (n - k)e$, corresponding to k decisions to go right, is given by

$$P(X = r_k) = \binom{n}{k} p^k (1 - p)^{(n-k)} \tag{4.3}$$

for $k = 0, 1, ..., n$ and $p = 0.5$, assuming equal probability of going left or right. The above probabilities correspond to the Binomial distribution with parameters p and n. The introduced model is very simple given the simplifying assumption of error sources being independent and each error source having similar behavior.

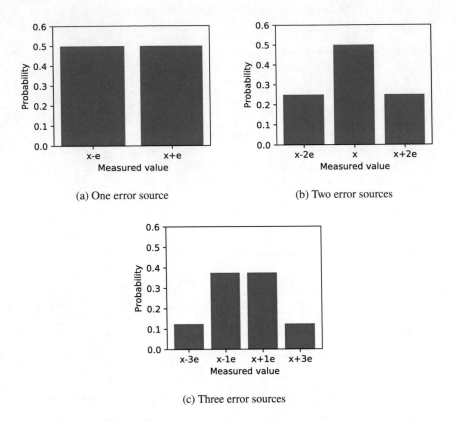

(a) One error source   (b) Two error sources

(c) Three error sources

Fig. 4.4: Distribution of measurements for one to three error sources

Nonetheless, we can conclude that for n error sources, the measurements would follow an approximate Binomial distribution.

Now let us assume that the number of error sources becomes large (i.e., $n \to \infty$). From statistics, we know that the Binomial distribution converges towards Normal distribution when the number of trials n tends towards infinity (see Chapter 2, Section 2.6). Since in practice the number of error sources is large, measurements are commonly assumed to follow a Normal distribution (Lilja, 2000). In other words, a measurement experiment can be seen as a random experiment in which a sample $\{x_1, x_2, ..., x_n\}$ from a normally distributed random variable X with parameters μ and σ^2 is obtained. By the definition of a sample, the individual measurements can be seen as independent and identically distributed (IID) Normal random variables $\{X_1, X_2, ..., X_n\}$ with parameters μ and σ^2. The Normal distribution, plotted in Figure 4.6, is one of the most common distributions used in statistics (see Chapter 2, Section 2.5).

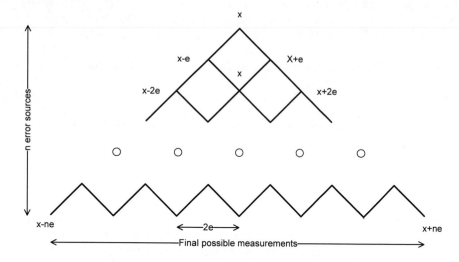

Fig. 4.5: Simple model of *n* error sources and their effect on the
measurements (Lilja, 2000)

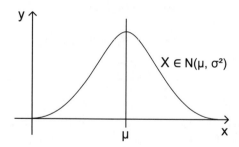

Fig. 4.6: Modeling measurements with the Normal distribution

4.2.3 Estimating Means

Consider a measurement experiment modeled as a sample $\{X_1, X_2, ..., X_n\}$ from
a normally distributed random variable X with parameters μ and σ^2; that is,
$X \sim N(\mu, \sigma^2)$. As discussed in the previous sections, the individual measurements
can be seen as independent and identically distributed (IID) Normal random variables
$\{X_1, X_2, ..., X_n\}$ with parameters μ and σ^2.

The actual measured quantity is characterized by the probability distribution
of the random variable X. While we assume that X is normally distributed, its
parameters μ and σ^2 are unknown. The sample mean $\overline{x}$ provides a *point estimate*
of the mean $\mu = E[X]$. However, since measurements vary when repeated multiple
times, the computed sample mean also varies. This raises the question of how good

the sample mean $\bar{x}$ serves as an approximation of the population mean μ? The answer to this question depends on the precision of the measurements. In the rest of this section, we show how the precision can be quantified by deriving an *interval estimate* for μ.

An interval estimate for μ is defined as an interval $[c_1, c_2]$ such that

$$P(c_1 \leq \mu \leq c_2) = 1 - \alpha, \tag{4.4}$$

where $\alpha \in (0, 1)$ is a parameter referred to as *significance level*. Usually, a symmetric interval is used so that

$$P(\mu < c_1) = P(\mu > c_2) = \frac{\alpha}{2}. \tag{4.5}$$

Such an interval $[c_1, c_2]$ is called *confidence interval (CI)* for the mean μ with *confidence level* $(1 - \alpha) \times 100\%$. Typical values used for α are 0.1 or 0.05 corresponding to confidence levels of 90% and 95%, respectively. We will now show how an interval $[c_1, c_2]$ that satisfies Equation (4.5) can be derived from the sample of measurements.

4.2.3.1 CI Based on the Normal Distribution

Let us first assume that we have at least 30 measurements (i.e., $n \geq 30$). The sample mean

$$\overline{X} = \frac{\sum_{i=1}^n X_i}{n} \tag{4.6}$$

can be seen as a random variable defined as a linear combination of the random variables $\{X_1, ..., X_n\}$, which are assumed to be normally distributed with parameters μ and σ^2. It follows (see Chapter 2, Section 2.5) that the sample mean is also normally distributed with parameters μ and σ^2/n, that is,

$$X_i \sim N(\mu, \sigma^2) \Rightarrow \overline{X} \sim N(\mu, \sigma^2/n). \tag{4.7}$$

The random variable

$$Z = \frac{\overline{X} - \mu}{\sqrt{\frac{\sigma^2}{n}}} \tag{4.8}$$

will then have a standard Normal distribution, that is, $Z \sim N(0, 1)$ (see Chapter 2, Section 2.5), from which it follows that

$$P\left(-z_{\alpha/2} \leq Z \leq z_{\alpha/2}\right) = 1 - \alpha, \tag{4.9}$$

where $z_{\alpha/2}$ is the upper $\alpha/2$ critical value of the standard Normal distribution (as illustrated in Figure 4.7).

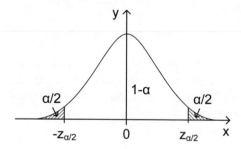

Fig. 4.7: Standard Normal distribution

Interpreting Equation (4.9), after some rearrangements, we obtain

$$P\left(-z_{\alpha/2} \leq \frac{\overline{X} - \mu}{\sqrt{\frac{\sigma^2}{n}}} \leq z_{\alpha/2}\right) = 1 - \alpha$$

$$P\left(\overline{X} - z_{\alpha/2}\sqrt{\frac{\sigma^2}{n}} \leq \mu \leq \overline{X} + z_{\alpha/2}\sqrt{\frac{\sigma^2}{n}}\right) = 1 - \alpha. \qquad (4.10)$$

As a general rule of thumb in statistics, if a sample from a random variable X has at least 30 elements, then the sample variance

$$S^2 = \frac{\sum_{i=1}^{n}(X_i - \overline{X})^2}{n - 1} \qquad (4.11)$$

can be considered to be a good estimate of the variance σ^2 of X (see Section 2.4 in Chapter 2).

Given that we assumed a sample size of $n \geq 30$, we can thus replace σ^2 with S^2 in Equation (4.10) obtaining

$$P\left(\overline{X} - z_{\alpha/2}\sqrt{\frac{S^2}{n}} \leq \mu \leq \overline{X} + z_{\alpha/2}\sqrt{\frac{S^2}{n}}\right) = 1 - \alpha. \qquad (4.12)$$

Equation (4.12) provides a confidence interval $[c_1, c_2]$ as per Equation (4.4), such that $P(c_1 \leq \mu \leq c_2) = 1 - \alpha$, where

$$c_1 = \overline{x} - z_{\alpha/2}\sqrt{\frac{s^2}{n}} \quad \text{and} \quad c_2 = \overline{x} + z_{\alpha/2}\sqrt{\frac{s^2}{n}}. \qquad (4.13)$$

The quantity $\sqrt{s^2/n}$ is an estimate of the standard deviation of the sample mean $\sigma_{\overline{X}} = \sqrt{\sigma^2/n}$, which is commonly referred to as *standard error* of the mean. Denoting the estimate of the standard error as $SE_{\overline{X}} = \sqrt{s^2/n}$, the confidence interval can also be expressed as

$$c_1 = \overline{x} - z_{\alpha/2}SE_{\overline{X}} \quad \text{and} \quad c_2 = \overline{x} + z_{\alpha/2}SE_{\overline{X}}. \tag{4.14}$$

The interval $[c_1, c_2]$ is an *approximate* $100(1 - \alpha)\%$ confidence interval (CI) for the mean μ. It is approximate because we made some simplifications above, such as estimating σ^2 with S^2. The larger the number of measurements n, the more accurate the resulting confidence interval would be.

4.2.3.2 CI Based on the *t*-distribution

So far, we assumed a sample size of at least 30 measurements. We now relax this assumption and consider the case when $n < 30$. In that case, we generally cannot assume that the sample variance S^2 provides a good estimate of the population variance σ^2. Thus, we cannot use the confidence interval in Equation (4.12). However, a similar confidence interval based on the *t*-distribution can be derived.

Since $X_i \sim N(\mu, \sigma^2)$, it follows that

$$T = \frac{\overline{X} - \mu}{\sqrt{\frac{S^2}{n}}} \tag{4.15}$$

has a *t*-distribution with $(n - 1)$ degrees of freedom (see Chapter 2, Section 2.5, Theorem 2.2). From this, it follows that

$$P\left(-t_{\{\alpha/2,n-1\}} \leq T \leq t_{\{\alpha/2,n-1\}}\right) = 1 - \alpha, \tag{4.16}$$

where $t_{\{\alpha/2,n-1\}}$ is the upper $\alpha/2$ critical value of the *t*-distribution with $(n - 1)$ degrees of freedom. Interpreting Equation (4.16), after some rearrangements, we obtain

$$P\left(-t_{\{\alpha/2,n-1\}} \leq \frac{\overline{X} - \mu}{\sqrt{\frac{S^2}{n}}} \leq t_{\{\alpha/2,n-1\}}\right) = 1 - \alpha$$

$$P\left(\overline{X} - t_{\{\alpha/2,n-1\}}\sqrt{\frac{S^2}{n}} \leq \mu \leq \overline{X} + t_{\{\alpha/2,n-1\}}\sqrt{\frac{S^2}{n}}\right) = 1 - \alpha. \tag{4.17}$$

Equation (4.17) provides a confidence interval $[c_1, c_2]$ as per Equation (4.4), such that $P(c_1 \leq \mu \leq c_2) = 1 - \alpha$, where

$$c_1 = \overline{x} - t_{\{\alpha/2,n-1\}}\sqrt{\frac{s^2}{n}} \quad \text{and} \quad c_2 = \overline{x} + t_{\{\alpha/2,n-1\}}\sqrt{\frac{s^2}{n}}. \tag{4.18}$$

As discussed in Chapter 2, Section 2.5, the *t*-distribution is similar to the standard Normal distribution (see Figure 4.8); they are both bell-shaped and symmetric about a mean of zero. The t-distribution is generally more "spread out" (i.e., it has greater variance); however, it converges to the standard Normal distribution when n tends to infinity.

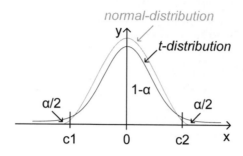

Fig. 4.8: t-distribution

The confidence interval quantifies the precision of the measurements. The wider the interval, the less repeatable the measurements are expected to be and the more uncertainty there will be in the accuracy of the sample mean as an estimate of the mean of the underlying population.

In the derivation of the two confidence intervals, based on the Normal distribution and on the t-distribution, respectively, we assumed that measurements are normally distributed random variables. Even though, as argued in Section 4.2.2, this assumption is reasonable and it is typically made for measurement experiments, the derivation of the two confidence intervals is not dependent on this assumption. This can be shown by applying the Central Limit Theorem (CLT). As introduced in Chapter 2, Section 2.5, the latter states that a sum of a "large number" of values from any distribution with a finite positive variance will be approximately normally distributed. What is meant by a large number is not explicitly defined; however, 30 or higher is typically considered large enough (Lilja, 2000; Walpole et al., 2016). If the distribution is not too different from a Normal distribution, a number higher than six or seven is often considered sufficient to apply the CLT.[1]

In the case of $n \geq 30$, the assumption of normally distributed measurements $\{X_1, ..., X_n\}$ was used in Equation (4.7) in order to claim that the sample mean is normally distributed. However, based on the CLT, the sample mean, given that it is computed as a sum of values, can be assumed to be normally distributed without requiring that the individual measurements $\{X_1, ..., X_n\}$ are themselves normally distributed. Equation (4.7) would thus still hold, and the approximate confidence interval based on the Normal distribution remains valid and can be used.

In the case of $n < 30$, we could possibly try to normalize the measurements by grouping them into groups of six or more and using the sample mean of each group

---

[1] The reader is warned to use these rules with caution since it is easy to show examples of distributions where they do not apply.

as input measurement. By the CLT, the sample means are going to be approximately normally distributed, which allows us to apply Equation (4.16) and complete the derivation of the confidence interval based on the t-distribution as was shown above. We emphasize that this is only an approximation and the quality of the approach becomes better as the sample size grows.

Table 4.3 shows the formulas for the two confidence intervals we derived based on the Normal distribution and the t-distribution.

Table 4.3: Confidence intervals for the mean μ based on the
Normal distribution and t-distribution

Number of measurements	Confidence interval $[c_1, c_2]$
$n \geq 30$	$c_1 = \overline{x} - z_{\alpha/2}\sqrt{\frac{s^2}{n}} \qquad c_2 = \overline{x} + z_{\alpha/2}\sqrt{\frac{s^2}{n}}$
$n < 30$	$c_1 = \overline{x} - t_{\{\alpha/2,n-1\}}\sqrt{\frac{s^2}{n}} \quad c_2 = \overline{x} + t_{\{\alpha/2,n-1\}}\sqrt{\frac{s^2}{n}}$

Example Consider an experiment in which the response time of a web service is measured. A sample of eight measurements shown in Table 4.4 is obtained.

Table 4.4: A sample of eight response time measurements

Measurement	Measured value (s)
1	8.0
2	7.0
3	5.0
4	9.0
5	9.5
6	11.3
7	5.2
8	8.5

The sample mean is computed as

$$\overline{x} = \frac{\sum_{i=1}^{n} x_i}{n} = 7.94 \tag{4.19}$$

and the sample standard deviation as

$$s = \sqrt{\frac{\sum_{i=1}^{n}(x_i - \bar{x})^2}{n-1}} = 2.14. \qquad (4.20)$$

We consider two cases $\alpha = 0.1$ and $\alpha = 0.05$ corresponding to confidence levels of 90% and 95%, respectively. Applying the formulas presented above for $\alpha = 0.1$:

$$\alpha = 0.1 \Rightarrow p = \alpha/2 = 0.1/2 = 0.05 \qquad\qquad df = (n-1) = 7$$

$$t_{\{p,df\}} = t_{\{0.05,7\}} = 1.895 \qquad\qquad\qquad\qquad\qquad\qquad (4.21)$$

$$c_1 = 7.94 - \frac{1.895(2.14)}{\sqrt{8}} = 6.5 \qquad c_2 = 7.94 + \frac{1.895(2.14)}{\sqrt{8}} = 9.4$$

we obtain a 90% confidence interval $[6.5, 9.4]$ for the mean μ.

Similarly, applying the formulas for $\alpha = 0.05$:

$$\alpha = 0.05 \Rightarrow p = \alpha/2 = 0.05/2 = 0.025 \qquad\qquad df = (n-1) = 7$$

$$t_{\{p,df\}} = t_{\{0.025,7\}} = 2.365 \qquad\qquad\qquad\qquad\qquad\qquad (4.22)$$

$$c_1 = 7.94 - \frac{2.365(2.14)}{\sqrt{8}} = 6.1 \qquad c_2 = 7.94 + \frac{2.365(2.14)}{\sqrt{8}} = 9.7$$

we obtain a 95% confidence interval $[6.1, 9.7]$ for the mean μ.

Table 4.5 shows the tabulated data for the critical values of the t-distribution used in the above computations.

Table 4.5: Critical values of t-distribution with df degrees of freedom

(a) $\alpha = 0.1, p = 0.05, df = 7$

df	p 0.10	0.05	0.025
...	...	...	...
5	1.476	2.015	2.517
6	1.440	1.943	2.447
7	1.415	1.895	2.365
...	...	...	...
∞	1.282	1.645	1.960

(b) $\alpha = 0.05, p = 0.025, df = 7$

df	p 0.10	0.05	0.025
...	...	...	...
5	1.476	2.015	2.517
6	1.440	1.943	2.447
7	1.415	1.895	2.365
...	...	...	...
∞	1.282	1.645	1.960

The two confidence intervals are shown in Figure 4.9 together with the respective density function of the t-distribution. The semantic of the 90% confidence interval is that there is 90% chance that the population mean lies in the interval $[6.5, 9.4]$.

Similarly, there is 95% chance that the population mean lies in the interval [6.1, 9.7]. As we can see, the second interval is wider. This makes sense intuitively. Given that both intervals are derived from the same underlying measurements with no additional data available, a higher confidence level would naturally result into a wider interval.

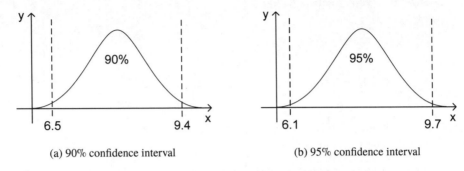

(a) 90% confidence interval   (b) 95% confidence interval

Fig. 4.9: Semantics of the two confidence intervals

4.2.3.3 Indirect Measurement

Sometimes the quantity of interest cannot be measured directly, for example, due to limited resolution of the measurement tool. As introduced in Section 4.2.1, the resolution is the smallest change in the measured quantity that can be detected by the measurement process. For example, if the execution time of an operation is shorter than the period of time between two clock ticks, an interval timer will not be able to measure the operation execution time. In such a case, an *indirect measurement* approach can be applied (Lilja, 2000).

   To illustrate this, we stick to the example with measuring the execution time of a very short operation. In this case, one can measure the total time for several consecutive repetitions of the operation and divide this time by the number of repetitions to calculate the mean time for one execution. Denote with T_j the total time for k_j consecutive executions of the operation. The mean time for one execution is then given by

$$\overline{x}_j = \frac{T_j}{k_j}. \tag{4.23}$$

   By repeating the above procedure n times, we obtain a sample $\{\overline{x}_1, \overline{x}_2, \ldots, \overline{x}_n\}$ of estimated times for one execution of the operation. We assume that the number of executions k_j for $j = 1, \ldots, n$ are chosen high enough, such that the resolution of the used interval timer can measure the cumulative times T_j.

   We can now use the formulas for deriving a confidence interval, Equations (4.13) and (4.18), by applying them to the sample of n mean values $\{\overline{x}_1, \overline{x}_2, \ldots, \overline{x}_n\}$. While this approach provides a workaround for the issue, the normalization has a penalty. On the one hand, the sample size is reduced leading to loss of information. On the other hand, we obtain a confidence interval for the mean value of the aggregated operations, as opposed to the individual operations themselves. This leads to reducing the variation and thus the resulting confidence interval might be more narrow than it would have been if applied to the measured runtimes of single executions.

4.2.3.4 Determining the Number of Measurements Needed

The confidence intervals we derived (summarized in Table 4.3) were computed for a given sample of n measurements. From the formulas, we see that the width of the confidence intervals is inversely proportional to $\sqrt{n}$. The higher the number of measurements, the smaller the resulting confidence intervals. In practice, an experimenter will be interested to know how many measurements one needs to conduct in order to obtain a confidence interval with a given target maximum width. We now show how the experimenter can determine how many measurements are needed to obtain the desired confidence interval.

Let us assume that the experimenter needs a confidence interval $[c_1, c_2]$ of length $2e\overline{x}$ expressed relative to the center of the interval $\overline{x}$, where e is a parameter specifying the targeted maximum half-width. For simplicity, we assume that at least 30 measurements will be obtained and the confidence interval based on the Normal distribution will be used. Given that confidence intervals are symmetric around the mean, we can write down the following equation that must be satisfied:

$$(c_1, c_2) = ((1 - e)\overline{x}, (1 + e)\overline{x}) = \left(\overline{x} - z_{\alpha/2}\frac{s}{\sqrt{n}}, \ \overline{x} + z_{\alpha/2}\frac{s}{\sqrt{n}}\right). \tag{4.24}$$

Solving this equation for n, we obtain

$$z_{\alpha/2}\frac{s}{\sqrt{n}} = \overline{x}e \Rightarrow n = \left(\frac{s \cdot z_{\alpha/2}}{\overline{x}e}\right)^2. \tag{4.25}$$

We now have an estimate of the required number of measurements; however, to apply the formula in Equation (4.25), we need the sample mean $\overline{x}$ and the standard deviation s. To solve this, one should proceed as follows: First an experiment with a small number of measurements (at least 30) is conducted to obtain an estimate for $\overline{x}$ and s. The estimates are then inserted into Equation (4.25) to determine how many measurements in total are needed to obtain the desired confidence interval width. Then the experiment is continued until the target number of measurements is reached. The final sample of measurements is then used to derive the confidence interval.

Example Assume that, based on 30 measurements, we found: $\overline{x} = 7.94$ s and $s = 2.14$ s. To obtain a 90% confidence interval that the true mean is within 3.5% of the sample mean (i.e., $e = 0.035$), we apply the formula in Equation (4.25):

$$n = \left(\frac{z_{\alpha/2}s}{\overline{x}e}\right)^2 = \left(\frac{1.6449(2.14)}{7.94(0.035)}\right)^2 = 160.44. \tag{4.26}$$

We conclude that we need 161 measurements to obtain a confidence interval with the desired target width.

4.2.4 Estimating Proportions

In the previous section, we considered a general measurement experiment modeled as a sample $\{X_1, X_2, ..., X_n\}$ from a random variable X. The actual measured quantity is characterized by the probability distribution of the random variable X. The two most important parameters of the distribution are the mean μ and the standard deviation σ. We showed how to derive point estimates for μ and σ as well as interval estimates (i.e., confidence intervals) for μ.

We now look at a more specific type of measurement experiment in which the quantity of interest to be measured is defined as a *proportion*. Assume we have a large collection of objects and we would like to estimate the proportion of objects that satisfy a given property by examining a random sample from the collection. A similar scenario arises when the frequency with which a specific event occurs (out of a given set of possible events) should be estimated by counting the number of times the respective event occurs. For example, one may be interested in measuring the fraction of time in which a system is in a given state (e.g., operating system running in kernel mode) by examining the system state at a set of randomly selected points in time. Each observation of the system state can then be seen as an event of a given type (e.g., kernel mode vs. user mode) and the goal is to estimate the proportion of events of the respective type of interest.

We model the above experiment as a sequence of n Bernoulli trials (Lilja, 2000). We examine a sample of n objects/events from the set of all possible objects/events. Each time we examine an object, we have a Bernoulli experiment with two possible outcomes: the object/event satisfies the respective property of interest (success) or the object/event does not satisfy it (failure). Let p be the probability of success. We assume that the successive Bernoulli trials are independent. Consider the random variable X defined as the number of successes in the n trials, that is, the number of objects/events from the sample that satisfy the property of interest. We know that X will have a Binomial distribution $B(p, n)$ with parameters p and n (see Chapter 2, Section 2.6). The actual quantity of interest that we would like to estimate is the parameter p of the Binomial distribution, which corresponds to the proportion of objects/events that satisfy the respective property. In the following, we will show how to derive a confidence interval for p.

Given that X has a Binomial distribution with parameters p and n, we know that

$$E[X] = pn \qquad \sigma^2[X] = p(1 - p)n. \tag{4.27}$$

The random variable $\hat{P} = X/n$ is an estimator of p. Indeed, $E[\hat{P}] = E[X/n] = E[X]/n = (pn)/n = p$. Thus, if n is large, we can estimate p using the sample proportion $\hat{p} = x/n$. Assuming in addition that $[\hat{p}n \geq 5 \wedge (1 - \hat{p})n \geq 5]$, we can approximate the Binomial distribution with a Normal distribution (see Chapter 2, Section 2.6):

$$X \sim B(p, n) \Rightarrow X \approx N(pn, p(1 - p)n). \tag{4.28}$$

Since we can estimate p with $\hat{p}$, we can approximate the variance $\sigma^2[X] = p(1 - p)n$ with $\hat{p}(1 - \hat{p})n$ such that

$$X \approx N(pn, \hat{p}(1 - \hat{p})n). \tag{4.29}$$

From the above equation, it follows that $Z = (X - E[X])/\sigma[X] \sim N(0, 1)$ (see Chapter 2, Section 2.5). Interpreting this, we obtain

$$P\left(-z_{\alpha/2} \leq Z \leq z_{\alpha/2}\right) \approx 1 - \alpha$$

$$P\left(-z_{\alpha/2} \leq \frac{X - pn}{\sqrt{\hat{p}(1 - \hat{p})n}} \leq z_{\alpha/2}\right) \approx 1 - \alpha$$

$$P\left(X - z_{\alpha/2}\sqrt{\hat{p}(1 - \hat{p})n} \leq pn \leq X + z_{\alpha/2}\sqrt{\hat{p}(1 - \hat{p})n}\right) \approx 1 - \alpha \tag{4.30}$$

$$P\left(\hat{p} - z_{\alpha/2}\sqrt{\frac{\hat{p}(1 - \hat{p})}{n}} \leq p \leq \hat{p} + z_{\alpha/2}\sqrt{\frac{\hat{p}(1 - \hat{p})}{n}}\right) \approx 1 - \alpha.$$

We found an interval $[c_1, c_2]$ such that $P(c_1 \leq p \leq c_2) = 1 - \alpha$, where

$$c_1 = \hat{p} - z_{\alpha/2}\sqrt{\frac{\hat{p}(1 - \hat{p})}{n}} \quad \text{and} \quad c_2 = \hat{p} + z_{\alpha/2}\sqrt{\frac{\hat{p}(1 - \hat{p})}{n}}. \tag{4.31}$$

The interval $[c_1, c_2]$ is an *approximate* $100(1 - \alpha)\%$ confidence interval for the probability p, which represents the proportion we wanted to estimate. It is approximate because we made some simplifications above, such as approximating the Binomial distribution with a Normal distribution. The larger the number of measurements n, the more accurate the resulting confidence interval would be.

4.2.4.1 Determining the Number of Measurements Needed

The confidence interval we derived—Equation (4.31)—was computed for a given sample of n measurements. We now show how the experimenter can determine how many measurements one needs to conduct in order to obtain a confidence interval with a given target maximum width. Let us assume that the experimenter needs a confidence interval $[c_1, c_2]$ of length $2e\hat{p}$ expressed relative to the center of the interval $\hat{p}$, where e is a parameter specifying the targeted maximum half-width. Given that confidence intervals are symmetric around the mean, we can write down the following equation that must be satisfied:

$$(1 - e)\hat{p} = \hat{p} - z_{\alpha/2}\sqrt{\frac{\hat{p}(1 - \hat{p})}{n}} \Rightarrow e\hat{p} = z_{\alpha/2}\sqrt{\frac{\hat{p}(1 - \hat{p})}{n}}. \tag{4.32}$$

Solving this equation for n, we obtain

$$n = \frac{z_{\alpha/2}^2 \hat{p}(1 - \hat{p})}{(e\hat{p})^2}. \tag{4.33}$$

We now have an estimate of the required number of measurements; however, to apply the formula in Equation (4.33), we need the sample proportion $\hat{p} = x/n$. To solve this, first an experiment with a small number of measurements (at least 30) is conducted to obtain an initial estimate $\hat{p}$. The estimate is then inserted into Equation (4.33) to determine how many measurements in total are needed to obtain the desired confidence interval width. Then the experiment is continued until the target number of measurements is reached. The final sample of measurements is then used to derive the confidence interval.

Alternatively, an upper bound for n based on the *absolute error* $(e\hat{p})$ can be obtained as follows:

$$\hat{p}(1 - \hat{p}) = -(\hat{p}^2 - \hat{p}) = \frac{1}{4} - \left(\hat{p}^2 - \hat{p} + \frac{1}{4}\right) = \frac{1}{4} - \left(\hat{p} - \frac{1}{2}\right)^2 \leq \frac{1}{4} \tag{4.34}$$

$$n = \frac{z_{\alpha/2}^2 \hat{p}(1 - \hat{p})}{(e\hat{p})^2} \leq \frac{z_{\alpha/2}^2}{4(e\hat{p})^2}.$$

Example Consider an experiment aiming to estimate how much time a processor (CPU) spends executing operating system (OS) code. The execution is interrupted every 10 ms updating two counters: (1) the number of times x, the processor's program counter (PC) register is observed to point to an instruction within OS code and (2) the total number of interrupts n. After running the experiment for 1 min, the values of the two counters are as follows: $n = 6000$, $x = 658$. Using the formulas in Equation (4.31), we obtain the following 95% confidence interval for the probability p of executing OS code:

$$(c_1, c_2) = \hat{p} \mp z_{\alpha/2}\sqrt{\frac{\hat{p}(1 - \hat{p})}{n}} =$$

$$= 0.1097 \mp 1.96\sqrt{\frac{0.1097(1 - 0.1097)}{6000}} = (0.1018, 0.1176). \tag{4.35}$$

Based on these results, we can claim with 95% confidence that the processor spends between 10.2% and 11.8% of its time executing OS code. Now, assume that we would like to have a confidence interval of half-length $\hat{p}0.5\%$, that is, $e = 0.005$. We use Equation (4.33) to determine how long the experiment must be run to collect enough measurements:

$$\hat{p} = \frac{x}{n} = \frac{658}{6000} = 0.1097$$

$$n = \frac{z_{\alpha/2}^2 \hat{p}(1 - \hat{p})}{(e\hat{p})^2} = \frac{(1.960)^2(0.1097)(1 - 0.1097)}{[0.005(0.1097)]^2} = 1{,}247{,}102. \tag{4.36}$$

Under the assumption that the execution is interrupted every 10 ms, we will need to run the experiment for 3.46 h to collect enough measurements.

4.3 Comparing Alternatives

So far, we considered a measurement experiment modeled as a sample $\{x_1, x_2, ..., x_n\}$ from a random variable X representing the measured quantity of interest. We showed that measurements are typically influenced by errors causing noise, and we introduced confidence intervals, which help to quantify the precision of measurements. The precision indicates how good the sample mean $\bar{x}$ serves as approximation of the true mean of the underlying population μ. The wider the confidence interval, the less repeatable the measurements are expected to be, and the more uncertainty there will be when the sample mean is used as an estimate of the measured quantity of interest.

Now consider a scenario where two systems need to be compared with respect to a given property that can be measured experimentally (Lilja, 2000). Two separate measurement experiments are conducted resulting in two sets of measurements, one for each of the two systems under study. This scenario occurs in practice when, for example, two different systems are compared to determine which one is better with respect to a considered property of interest. Another example is when a change is made to a system and the new system is compared with the original one to determine the impact of the change. Given the presence of random errors and the uncertainty they introduce in experimental measurements, the goal is to determine whether differences observed in the measurements are statistically significant or if they are simply due to random noise. Note that *statistical significance* should not be confused with actual importance. Scientists have argued that in many cases this may lead to overhyped claims or overlooked effects. For further discussion of this issue, we refer the reader to Amrhein et al. (2019).

In the rest of this section, we will assume that two sets of measurements are collected corresponding to the two *alternatives* that need to be compared. We denote the individual measurements as random variables $\{X_{1,1}, ..., X_{1,n_1}\}$ for the first alternative and $\{X_{2,1}, ..., X_{2,n_2}\}$ for the second alternative.

We will distinguish between two cases:

- *non-corresponding measurements* (also referred to as *unpaired observations*), when the two sets of measurements are independent and
- *before-and-after comparisons* (also referred to as *paired observations*), when the two sets of measurements are not independent.

4.3.1 Non-corresponding Measurements

In the case of non-corresponding measurements, we consider the measurements within each set as independent and identically distributed (IID) random variables with variances σ_1^2 and σ_2^2, respectively. In other words, each set of measurements is modeled as a sample from an unknown distribution and the two samples are assumed to be independent. By the Central Limit Theorem (CLT), the sample means of the two sets of measurements

$$\overline{X}_i = \frac{1}{n_i} \sum_{j=1}^{n_i} X_{i,j} \quad \text{for } i \in \{1, 2\} \tag{4.37}$$

are approximately normally distributed. Therefore, the difference of the two means $\overline{X} = \overline{X}_1 - \overline{X}_2$ is also approximately normally distributed being a linear combination of normally distributed random variables:

$$\overline{X} \sim N(\mu, \sigma_{\overline{X}}^2) \Rightarrow Z = \frac{\overline{X} - \mu}{\sigma_{\overline{X}}} \sim N(0, 1). \tag{4.38}$$

Interpreting Equation (4.38), we apply the same approach as in Section 4.2.3.1; see Equation (4.9) and the following derivations. If $n_1 \geq 30$ and $n_2 \geq 30$, after applying the approach from Section 4.2.3.1, we arrive at the following confidence interval $[c_1, c_2]$ for the *difference of means* $\overline{X}$:

$$c_1 = \overline{x} - z_{\alpha/2} s_{\overline{X}} \quad \text{and} \quad c_2 = \overline{x} + z_{\alpha/2} s_{\overline{X}}, \quad \text{where } s_{\overline{X}} = \sqrt{\frac{s_1^2}{n_1} + \frac{s_2^2}{n_2}}, \tag{4.39}$$

where s_1^2 and s_2^2 are the sample variances of the two sets of measurements and the quantity $s_{\overline{X}}$ is an estimate of the standard deviation $\sigma_{\overline{X}}$ of the random variable $\overline{X}$. To show this, we recall that the variance σ^2 of a linear combination of independent random variables is equal to the same linear combination of the variances of the individual random variables with squared coefficients; see Equation (2.18) in Chapter 2, Section 2.3. Applying this rule, we observe that

$$\sigma_{\overline{X}}^2 = \text{Var}\left(\overline{X}_1 - \overline{X}_2\right) = 1^2 \text{Var}\left(\frac{\sum_{j=1}^{n_1} X_{1,j}}{n_1}\right) + (-1)^2 \text{Var}\left(\frac{\sum_{j=1}^{n_2} X_{2,j}}{n_2}\right) =$$

$$= \frac{1}{n_1^2}\sum_{j=1}^{n_1}\text{Var}\left(X_{1,j}\right) + \frac{1}{n_2^2}\sum_{j=1}^{n_2}\text{Var}\left(X_{2,j}\right) = \frac{n_1\sigma_1^2}{n_1^2} + \frac{n_2\sigma_2^2}{n_2^2} = \frac{\sigma_1^2}{n_1} + \frac{\sigma_2^2}{n_2}. \tag{4.40}$$

Assuming that $n_1 \geq 30$ and $n_2 \geq 30$, we can approximate the variances σ_1^2 and σ_2^2 with the sample variances s_1^2 and s_1^2 of the two sets of measurements. Thus, from Equation (4.40), it follows that the quantity

$$s_{\overline{X}}^2 = \frac{s_1^2}{n_1} + \frac{s_2^2}{n_2} \tag{4.41}$$

is an estimate of the variance $\sigma_{\overline{X}}^2$ from which it follows that the quantity $s_{\overline{X}}$ is an estimate of the standard deviation $\sigma_{\overline{X}}$ of $\overline{X}$.

If $n_1 < 30$ and $n_2 < 30$, we can follow a similar approach as in Section 4.2.3.2 assuming that the measurements $X_{i,j}$ are approximately normally distributed and using the t-distribution. Under this assumption, it can be shown that the following confidence interval $[c_1, c_2]$ for the difference of means $\overline{X}$ is valid (Walpole et al., 2016):

$$c_1 = \overline{x} - t_{\{\alpha/2, n_{df}\}}s_{\overline{X}} \quad \text{and} \quad c_2 = \overline{x} + t_{\{\alpha/2, n_{df}\}}s_{\overline{X}},$$

$$\text{where } n_{df} \approx \frac{\left(\frac{s_1^2}{n_1} + \frac{s_2^2}{n_2}\right)^2}{\frac{\left(s_1^2/n_1\right)^2}{n_1-1} + \frac{\left(s_2^2/n_2\right)^2}{n_2-1}}. \tag{4.42}$$

Based on the above derivations, we can follow the following procedure to determine if there is a statistically significant difference between the two sets of measurements and the respective alternatives they represent:

1. Compute the means of the two sets of measurements $\overline{X}_1$ and $\overline{X}_2$ using Equation (4.37).

2. Compute the difference of means $\overline{X} = \overline{X}_1 - \overline{X}_2$.

3. Compute an estimate of the standard deviation $s_{\overline{X}}$ of the difference of means $\overline{X}$ using Equation (4.41).

4. Compute confidence interval $[c_1, c_2]$ for this difference using Equation (4.39) if $n_1 \geq 30, n_2 \geq 30$ and Equation (4.42), otherwise.

5. If $0 \notin [c_1, c_2]$, it can be concluded that there is a statistically significant difference between the two alternatives.

The two confidence intervals we derived for the difference of means $\overline{X}$ are shown in Table 4.6.

Table 4.6: Confidence intervals for the difference of means $\overline{X}$

Number of measurements	Confidence interval $[c_1, c_2]$
$n_1 \geq 30$ and $n_2 \geq 30$	$(c_1, c_2) = \overline{x} \mp z_{\alpha/2} s_{\overline{X}}$, where $s_{\overline{X}} = \sqrt{\dfrac{s_1^2}{n_1} + \dfrac{s_2^2}{n_2}}$
$n_1 < 30$ and $n_2 < 30$	$(c_1, c_2) = \overline{x} \mp t_{\{\alpha/2, n_{df}\}} s_{\overline{X}}$, where $n_{df} \approx \dfrac{\left(\frac{s_1^2}{n_1} + \frac{s_2^2}{n_2}\right)^2}{\frac{\left(s_1^2/n_1\right)^2}{n_1-1} + \frac{\left(s_2^2/n_2\right)^2}{n_2-1}}$

The described procedure is known as *(unpaired) t-test*. Note that in case the zero point lies inside the derived confidence interval, that is, $0 \in [c_1, c_2]$, no conclusion can be drawn from the test. In other words, one cannot interpret the result of the test as evidence that there is no statistically significant difference between the two alternatives.

Example Consider an experiment in which the processing time of a job is measured when executed on two different servers. A sample of measurements is collected for each server. We assume that the measurements are approximately normally distributed. The first sample has 12 measurements with mean $\overline{x}_1 = 1243$ s and standard deviation $s_1 = 38.5$; the second sample has 7 measurements with mean $\overline{x}_2 = 1085$ s and standard deviation $s_2 = 54.0$. To determine if there is a statistically significant difference between the measurements on the two servers, in the following, we apply the above described *t-test* to derive a 90% confidence interval for the difference of means based on Equation (4.42):

$$\overline{x} = \overline{x}_1 - \overline{x}_2 = 1243 - 1085 = 158$$

$$s_{\overline{X}} = \sqrt{\frac{38.5^2}{12} + \frac{54^2}{7}} = 23.24$$

$$n_{df} = \frac{\left(\frac{38.5^2}{12} + \frac{54^2}{7}\right)^2}{\frac{\left(\frac{38.5^2}{12}\right)^2}{12-1} + \frac{\left(\frac{54^2}{7}\right)^2}{7-1}} = 9.62 \Rightarrow 10 \tag{4.43}$$

$$[c_1, c_2] = \overline{x} \mp t_{\{\alpha/2, n_{df}\}} s_{\overline{X}}$$

$$t_{\{\alpha/2, n_{df}\}} = t_{\{0.05, 10\}} = 1.813$$

$$[c_1, c_2] = 158 \mp 1.813(23.24) = [116, 200].$$

Given that $0 \notin [116, 200]$, we conclude that there is a statistically significant difference between the two sets of measurements.

Special Case A special case applies when only a few measurements are available (i.e., $n_1 < 30$ or $n_2 < 30$) but the measurements are approximately normally distributed *and* either $\sigma_1 = \sigma_2$ or $n_1 = n_2$. It can be shown that the following confidence interval $[c_1, c_2]$ for the difference of means $\overline{X}$ is then valid (Walpole et al., 2016):

$$[c_1, c_2] = \overline{x} \mp t_{\{\alpha/2, n_{df}\}} s_p \sqrt{\frac{1}{n_1} + \frac{1}{n_2}}$$

$$n_{df} = n_1 + n_2 - 2 \qquad s_p = \sqrt{\frac{s_1^2(n_1 - 1) + s_2^2(n_2 - 1)}{n_1 + n_2 - 2}}. \tag{4.44}$$

This confidence interval is typically tighter than the general one obtained through the standard *t-test* we described above.

4.3.2 Before-and-After Comparisons

In the case of before-and-after comparisons (also referred to as paired observations), the measurements within each set are not independent. This scenario occurs, for example, when the effect of an optimization is evaluated by measuring its impact on a given system metric when applied to a set of systems. Two corresponding measurements of the respective metric are collected for each system: one without the optimization and one with the optimization. Another example is when a set of benchmarks are run on two systems and two corresponding measurements of a given metric of interest are collected for each benchmark.

We assume that the measurements can be grouped into corresponding pairs (b_i, a_i) for $i = 1, 2, ..., n$, where b_i is referred to as *before* measurement and a_i as *after* measurement. We consider the set of differences $d_i = b_i - a_i$ for $i = 1, 2, ..., n$ as a random sample from a population of differences that we shall assume to be approximately normally distributed with mean $\mu_D = \mu_1 - \mu_2$ and standard deviation σ_D. We denote with $\overline{d}$ the sample mean of the differences $d_i = b_i - a_i$ and with s_d the sample standard deviation. Applying the formulas from Section 4.2.3 (Table 4.3) to the sample of measurements d_i for $i = 1, 2, ..., n$, we obtain the confidence intervals for the *mean of differences* $\overline{d}$ shown in Table 4.7.

Table 4.7: Confidence intervals for the mean of differences $\overline{d}$

Number of measurements	Confidence interval $[c_1, c_2]$
$n \geq 30$	$(c_1, c_2) = \overline{d} \mp z_{\alpha/2} \frac{s_d}{\sqrt{n}}$
$n < 30$	$(c_1, c_2) = \overline{d} \mp t_{\{\alpha/2, n-1\}} \frac{s_d}{\sqrt{n}}$

As previously, if $0 \notin [c_1, c_2]$, it can be concluded that there is a statistically significant difference between the two alternatives. In case $0 \in [c_1, c_2]$, no conclusion can be drawn from the test.

Example Consider an experiment aiming to evaluate the effect of implementing an operating system (OS) kernel optimization on the response time of a system call (in microseconds). The optimization is applied to six installations of the OS on identical hardware. Two measurements are collected for each of the six installations: one before applying the optimization and one after applying the optimization. The measurements are shown in Table 4.8.

The mean of differences is $\overline{d} = -1$; the standard deviation is $s_d = 4.15$. Given that the mean of differences is negative, it appears that the optimization resulted in slightly worse performance (i.e., higher response time). However, we notice that the standard deviation is large, which introduces uncertainty. To determine if there is a statistically significant difference between the measurements before and after the optimization, we calculate a 95% confidence interval for the mean of differences $\overline{d}$ based on the t-distribution:

$$t_{\{\alpha/2, n-1\}} = t_{\{0.025, 5\}} = 2.571$$

$$(c_1, c_2) = \overline{d} \mp t_{\{\alpha/2, n-1\}} \frac{s_d}{\sqrt{n}} = -1 \mp 2.571 \left(\frac{4.15}{\sqrt{6}} \right) = [-5.36, 3.36].$$

(4.45)

Given that $0 \in [c_1, c_2]$, we cannot claim with 95% confidence that the optimization introduces statistically significant performance improvement.

Table 4.8: Response time of a system call on six OS installations
before and after applying a kernel optimization

Measurement (i)	Before (b_i)	After (a_i)	Difference ($d_i = b_i - a_i$)
1	85	86	-1
2	83	88	-5
3	94	90	4
4	90	95	-5
5	88	91	-3
6	87	83	4

4.3.3 Comparing Proportions

We showed how confidence intervals can be used to determine if there is a statistically significant difference between the means of two sets of measurements, corresponding to two alternatives. We now look at the case where the quantity of interest that is subject to comparison is defined as a *proportion*. This scenario occurs, for example, when we consider two collections of objects and would like to compare the proportion of objects that satisfy a given property by examining a random sample from each collection. Similarly, one may be interested in comparing the fraction of time in which two systems are in a given state (e.g., operating system running in kernel mode) by examining the state of each system at a set of randomly selected points in time. Each observation of the system state can then be seen as an event of a given type (e.g., kernel mode vs. user mode) and the goal is to compare the proportion of events of the respective type of interest.

The above scenario can be mathematically modeled as two sequences of Bernoulli trials (Lilja, 2000). For each of the two alternatives, we examine a sample of n_i, $i = \{1, 2\}$ objects/events from the set of all possible objects/events. Each time we examine an object, we have a Bernoulli experiment with two possible outcomes: the object/event satisfies the respective property of interest (success) or the object/event does not satisfy it (failure). Let p_i be the probability of success. We assume that the successive Bernoulli trials are independent. Consider the random variables X_i for $i = \{1, 2\}$ defined as the number of successes in the n_i trials, that is, the number of objects/events from the sample that satisfy the property of interest. We know that X_i will have a Binomial distribution $B(p_i, n_i)$ with parameters p_i and n_i (see Chapter 2, Section 2.6). The actual quantity of interest that we would like to estimate is $p_1 - p_2$, that is, the difference between the two proportions under comparison. In the following, we will show how to derive a confidence interval for $p_1 - p_2$.

Given that X_i has a Binomial distribution with parameters p_i and n_i, we know that

$$E[X_i] = p_i n_i \qquad \text{Var}(X_i) = p_i(1 - p_i)n_i. \tag{4.46}$$

The random variable $\hat{P}_i = X_i/n_i$ is an estimator of p_i. Indeed, $E[\hat{P}_i] = E[X_i/n_i] = E[X_i]/n_i = (p_i n_i)/n_i = p_i$. If n_1 and n_2 are large, we can estimate p_i using the sample proportion $\hat{p}_i = x_i/n_i$. Assuming in addition that $[\hat{p}_i n_i \geq 5 \wedge (1 - \hat{p}_i)n_i \geq 5]$, we can approximate the Binomial distribution with Normal distribution (see Chapter 2, Section 2.6):

$$X_i \sim B(p_i, n_i) \Rightarrow X_i \approx N(p_i n_i, p_i(1 - p_i)n_i) \Rightarrow X_i \approx N(p_i n_i, \hat{p}_i(1 - \hat{p}_i)n_i). \tag{4.47}$$

Let $\hat{P} = \hat{P}_1 - \hat{P}_2 = (X_1/n_1) - (X_2/n_2)$. The mean of $\hat{P}$ is

$$E[\hat{P}] = E\left[\frac{X_1}{n_1} - \frac{X_2}{n_2}\right] = \frac{E[X_1]}{n_1} - \frac{E[X_2]}{n_2} = p_1 - p_2. \tag{4.48}$$

Interpreting Equation (4.47), after some rearrangements, we derive a confidence interval for the mean of $\hat{P}$ as follows:

$$X_i \approx N(p_i n_i, \hat{p}_i(1 - \hat{p}_i)n_i) \Rightarrow \frac{X_i}{n_i} \approx N\left(p_i, \frac{\hat{p}_i(1 - \hat{p}_i)}{n_i}\right)$$

$$\hat{P} = \frac{X_1}{n_1} - \frac{X_2}{n_2} \approx N\left(p_1 - p_2, \frac{\hat{p}_1(1 - \hat{p}_1)}{n_1} + \frac{\hat{p}_2(1 - \hat{p}_2)}{n_2}\right)$$

$$P\left(-z_{\alpha/2} \leq \frac{\hat{P} - (p_1 - p_2)}{\sqrt{\frac{\hat{p}_1(1-\hat{p}_1)}{n_1} + \frac{\hat{p}_2(1-\hat{p}_2)}{n_2}}} \leq z_{\alpha/2}\right) = 1 - \alpha$$

$$P\left(\hat{P} - z_{\alpha/2}\sqrt{\frac{\hat{p}_1(1 - \hat{p}_1)}{n_1} + \frac{\hat{p}_2(1 - \hat{p}_2)}{n_2}} \leq p_1 - p_2 \leq \hat{P} + z_{\alpha/2}\sqrt{\frac{\hat{p}_1(1 - \hat{p}_1)}{n_1} + \frac{\hat{p}_2(1 - \hat{p}_2)}{n_2}}\right) =$$

$$= 1 - \alpha.$$

$$\tag{4.49}$$

We found an interval $[c_1, c_2]$ such that $P(c_1 \leq p_1 - p_2 \leq c_2) = 1 - \alpha$, where

$$[c_1, c_2] = \hat{p} \mp z_{\alpha/2}s_p, \quad \text{where} \quad s_p = \sqrt{\frac{\hat{p}_1(1 - \hat{p}_1)}{n_1} + \frac{\hat{p}_2(1 - \hat{p}_2)}{n_2}}. \tag{4.50}$$

The interval $[c_1, c_2]$ is an *approximate* $100(1-\alpha)\%$ confidence interval for $p_1 - p_2$, that is, the difference between the two proportions under comparison. It is approximate because we made some simplifications above, such as approximating the Binomial distribution with a Normal distribution. As previously, if $0 \notin [c_1, c_2]$, it can be concluded that there is a statistically significant difference between the two alternatives. Otherwise, if $0 \in [c_1, c_2]$, no conclusion can be drawn from the test.

Example Consider a scenario where two versions of an operating system (OS) are compared with respect to the fraction of time the system is executing OS code. The first OS is run for 3.5 h during which it is interrupted 1,300,203 times and observed 142,892 times to execute OS code. Similarly, the second OS was interrupted 999,382 times and observed 84,876 times to execute OS code. Applying the formula from Equation (4.50), we obtain the following confidence interval for the difference between the fraction of time the system is executing OS code when running the two OS versions:

$$n_1 = 1,300,203 \qquad x_1 = 142,892 \qquad \hat{p}_1 = 0.1099$$

$$n_2 = 999,382 \qquad x_2 = 84,876 \qquad \hat{p}_2 = 0.0849$$

(4.51)

$$\hat{p}_1 - \hat{p}_2 = 0.0250 \qquad s_p = 0.0003911$$

$$[c_1, c_2] = [0.0242, 0.0257].$$

Given that the confidence interval does not include 0, we conclude that there is a statistically significant difference between the two OS versions.

4.4 Concluding Remarks

This chapter introduced statistical approaches for quantifying the variability and precision of measurements. We started by introducing the most common indices of dispersion for quantifying the variability (sample variance, standard deviation, and coefficient of variation), followed by defining basic concepts such as accuracy, precision, and resolution of measurements as well as the distinction between systematic and random measurement errors. A model of random errors was introduced and used to derive confidence intervals for estimating the mean of a measured quantity of interest based on a sample of measurements. We briefly discussed an indirect measurement approach for cases where the quantity of interest cannot be measured directly due to limited resolution of the measurement tool. After that, the special case where the quantity of interest is defined as a proportion was considered. Finally, statistical tests for comparing alternatives based on measurements were introduced. The cases of paired and unpaired observations were covered separately.

References

Amrhein, V., Greenland, S., and McShane, B. (2019). "Scientists Rise Up Against Statistical Significance". *Nature*, 567(7748). Springer Nature Limited, pp. 305–307 (cited on p. 91).

Lilja, D. J. (2000). *Measuring Computer Performance: A Practitioner's Guide*. Cambridge University Press: Cambridge, UK (cited on pp. 74–76, 78, 79, 83, 86, 88, 91, 97).

Walpole, R. E., Myers, R. H., Myers, S. L., and Ye, K. E. (2016). *Probability & Statistics for Engineers & Scientists*. Ninth Edition. Pearson Education: London, UK (cited on pp. 83, 93, 95).

Chapter 5
Experimental Design

> "No amount of experimentation can ever prove me right;
> a single experiment can prove me wrong."
> —*Albert Einstein (1879-1955)*

In Chapter 4, we showed how two systems can be compared with respect to a given measurable property by conducting a *t-test* to determine if there is a statistically significant difference between the systems. The procedure we introduced there falls under the broad topic of *experimental design*, also referred to as *design of experiments*. Experimental design is the process of planning a set of experiments, coupled with a statistical analysis procedure, in order to understand and explain the variation of information under some specified conditions hypothesized to have influence on the variation. During the experiments, typically one or more input variables (factors) are systematically changed to observe the impact they have on one or more response variables (metrics). Experimental design begins by setting concrete objectives for the experimental study and selecting the input variables for the study. A good experimental design aims to optimize the amount of "information" that can be obtained for a given amount of experimental effort. This involves planning experiments to ensure that the right type of data and a sufficient sample size are collected to answer the research questions of interest in an objective and efficient manner.

This chapter introduces the foundations of experimental design. Starting with the case of one factor, the analysis of variance technique from statistics is introduced, followed by the method of contrasts for comparing subsets of alternatives. The analysis of variance technique is then generalized to two factors that can be varied independently, and after that, it is generalized to *m* factors. Following this, the Plackett–Burman fractional factorial design is introduced and compared with the full-factorial analysis of variance technique. Finally, a case study showing how experimental design can be applied in practice is presented.

© Springer Nature Switzerland AG 2020
S. Kounev et al., *Systems Benchmarking*, https://doi.org/10.1007/978-3-030-41705-5_5

5.1 One-Factor Analysis of Variance

We start by generalizing the method we introduced in Chapter 4 (Section 4.3) for comparing two alternatives. Imagine there are more than two alternative systems that need to be compared with respect to a given measurable property of interest. The goal is to design a set of experiments and an analysis procedure to determine if there is a statistically significant difference between the systems.[1] A naive approach would be to compare the systems two-by-two by applying the method from Chapter 4. This has the disadvantage that, as the number of alternatives increases, the number of confidence intervals that need to be computed rapidly increases. A more robust approach is to use the general technique from statistics called *analysis of variance (ANOVA)*. In the specific scenario we are considering, where n alternative systems need to be compared, we speak of *one-factor* analysis of variance, which is sometimes also referred to as *one-factor experimental design* or *one-way classification*. The choice of system is considered to be an input variable, whereas the considered property of interest is the response variable under study. We speak of one factor since there is one input variable. We assume that for each alternative, a sample of measurements of the response variable is obtained. We further assume that the errors in the measurements for the different alternatives are independent and normally distributed with equal variance for all alternatives. We refer the reader to Walpole et al. (2016) for a discussion of the relevance and implications of these assumptions.

The ANOVA technique aims to separate the total variation observed in all of the measurements into two components (Lilja, 2000):

1. Variation *within* each alternative, assumed to be caused by random errors in the measurements and
2. Variation *between* the alternatives, assumed to be caused both by real differences between the alternatives and by random errors.

The aim of ANOVA is to determine if the magnitude of the second component of the observed variation is significantly larger in a statistical sense than the magnitude of the first component. In other words, ANOVA provides a statistical test to determine if the observed differences between the measured mean values for the alternatives are due to real differences between the alternatives, or they are simply due to measurement errors.

Assume that we have k alternatives and for each of them, n measurements are collected. We denote with y_{ij} the ith measurement for the jth alternative (see Table 5.1). As stated above, we assume that the measurement errors for the different alternatives are independent and normally distributed with equal variance for each of the alternatives.

---

[1] As mentioned in Chapter 4, Section 4.3, *statistical significance* should not be confused with actual importance, which as discussed in Amrhein et al. (2019) may lead to overhyped claims or overlooked effects.

Table 5.1: Measurements for all alternatives

Measure-ments	Alternatives					
	1	2	...	j	...	k
1	y_{11}	y_{12}	...	y_{1j}	...	y_{1k}
2	y_{21}	y_{22}	...	y_{2j}	...	y_{2k}
...	...	...	...	...	...	...
i	y_{i1}	y_{i2}	...	y_{ij}	...	y_{ik}
...	...	...	...	...	...	...
n	y_{n1}	y_{n2}	...	y_{nj}	...	y_{nk}

We denote with $\bar{y}_{.j}$ the mean of the measurements within the jth alternative (i.e., the mean of the measurements in the jth column of Table 5.2a) and with $\bar{y}_{..}$ the overall mean of the measurements for all alternatives (see Table 5.2b):

$$\bar{y}_{.j} = \frac{\sum_{i=1}^{n} y_{ij}}{n}, \tag{5.1}$$

$$\bar{y}_{..} = \frac{\sum_{j=1}^{k} \sum_{i=1}^{n} y_{ij}}{kn} = \frac{\sum_{j=1}^{k} \bar{y}_{.j}}{k}. \tag{5.2}$$

Each measurement y_{ij} can be represented as

$$y_{ij} = \bar{y}_{.j} + e_{ij} \tag{5.3}$$

where e_{ij} stands for *measurement error* and is defined as the deviation of the measured value from the mean of the measurements for the respective alternative (i.e., the column mean). Similarly, the column means can be represented as

$$\bar{y}_{.j} = \bar{y}_{..} + \alpha_j \tag{5.4}$$

where α_j is called *effect* of alternative j and is defined as the deviation of the column mean from the overall mean (see Table 5.2c). Each individual measurement can then be represented as the sum of the overall mean plus the effect of the respective alternative plus the measurement error:

$$y_{ij} = \bar{y}_{.j} + e_{ij} = \bar{y}_{..} + \alpha_j + e_{ij}. \tag{5.5}$$

From Equations (5.3)–(5.5), it follows that

$$\begin{aligned} e_{ij} &= y_{ij} - \bar{y}_{.j} \\ \alpha_j &= \bar{y}_{.j} - \bar{y}_{..} \\ t_{ij} &= \alpha_j + e_{ij} = y_{ij} - \bar{y}_{..} \end{aligned} \tag{5.6}$$

Table 5.2: Column means, overall mean, and effects

(a) Column means

Measure-ments	Alternatives					
	1	2	...	j	...	k
1	y_{11}	y_{12}	...	y_{1j}	...	y_{1k}
2	y_{21}	y_{22}	...	y_{2j}	...	y_{2k}
...	...	...	...	...	...	...
i	y_{i1}	y_{i2}	...	y_{ij}	...	y_{ik}
...	...	...	...	...	...	...
n	y_{n1}	y_{n2}	...	y_{nj}	...	y_{nk}
Col. mean	$y_{.1}$	$y_{.2}$	...	$y_{.j}$	...	$y_{.k}$

(b) Overall mean

Measure-ments	Alternatives					
	1	2	...	j	...	k
1	y_{11}	y_{12}	...	y_{1j}	...	y_{1k}
2	y_{21}	y_{22}	...	y_{2j}	...	y_{2k}
...	...	...	...	...	...	...
i	y_{i1}	y_{i2}	...	y_{ij}	...	y_{ik}
...	...	...	...	...	...	...
n	y_{n1}	y_{n2}	...	y_{nj}	...	y_{nk}
Col. mean	$y_{.1}$	$y_{.2}$	...	$y_{.j}$	...	$y_{.k}$

(c) Effects

Measure-ments	Alternatives					
	1	2	...	j	...	k
1	y_{11}	y_{12}	...	y_{1j}	...	y_{1k}
2	y_{21}	y_{22}	...	y_{2j}	...	y_{2k}
...	...	...	...	...	...	...
i	y_{i1}	y_{i2}	...	y_{ij}	...	y_{ik}
...	...	...	...	...	...	...
n	y_{n1}	y_{n2}	...	y_{nj}	...	y_{nk}
Col. mean	$y_{.1}$	$y_{.2}$	...	$y_{.j}$	...	$y_{.k}$
Effect	α_1	α_2	...	α_j	...	α_k

We define the following three sums SSE, SSA, and SST:

$$SSE = \sum_{j=1}^{k} \sum_{i=1}^{n} (e_{ij})^2 = \sum_{j=1}^{k} \sum_{i=1}^{n} (y_{ij} - \bar{y}_{.j})^2, \tag{5.7}$$

$$SSA = n \sum_{j=1}^{k} (\alpha_j)^2 = n \sum_{j=1}^{k} (\bar{y}_{.j} - \bar{y}_{..})^2, \tag{5.8}$$

$$SST = \sum_{j=1}^{k} \sum_{i=1}^{n} (t_{ij})^2 = \sum_{j=1}^{k} \sum_{i=1}^{n} (y_{ij} - \bar{y}_{..})^2. \tag{5.9}$$

The three sums (SSE, SSA, and SST) are called *sums of squares of differences*, and they each characterize some part of the variation observed in the measurements. SSE characterizes the variation due to measurement errors within the individual alternatives. SSA characterizes the variation due to the effects of the different alternatives plus measurement errors across alternatives. SST characterizes the total variation in all measurements.

By expanding SST and observing that $\sum_{j=1}^{k} \alpha_j = 0$, it can be easily shown that

$$SST = SSA + SSE. \tag{5.10}$$

The above equation separates the total variation observed in the measurements into two components: (1) variation due to the effects of alternatives plus measurement errors (SSA) and (2) variation due to measurement errors within alternatives (SSE). The next step is to determine if the magnitude of the first component (SSA) is larger in a statistical sense than the magnitude of the second component (SSE). If that is the case, we can conclude that the observed differences between the measurements for the different alternatives are due to real differences between the alternatives, as opposed to measurement errors. The question is how to compare the magnitude of SSA and SSE in a statistical sense. One simple approach would be to consider the two ratios:

1. SSA/SST: fraction of total variation explained by differences among the alternatives plus measurement errors,
2. SSE/SST: fraction of total variation due to measurement errors only.

While the two ratios provide some indication, some further analysis is needed to determine if the difference between SSA and SSE is statistically significant. We now show how this can be done using the F-test from statistics. The F-test provides a method to compare two sample variances in a statistical sense using the F-distribution. The F-test compares the ratio of two sample variances $F = s_1^2/s_2^2$ with the critical value $F_{[1-\alpha;df(num),df(denom)]}$ of the F-distribution, where α is the significance level, $df(num)$ is the degrees of freedom of the variance in the numerator of the ratio, and $df(denom)$ is the degrees of freedom of the variance in the denominator of the ratio. If the computed F-ratio is greater than the respective critical value, the conclusion is that it can be claimed with $(1-\alpha) \times 100\%$ confidence level that the difference between the two variances is statistically significant.

Coming back to the three sums of squares of differences SSE, SSA, and SST, looking at Equations (5.7)–(5.9), we notice that the way the sums are defined, they resemble the computation of sample variances (see Table 4.1 in Chapter 4) for one or more samples. Indeed, looking at SSE, we notice that the values whose squares are summed are differences between a sample of n measurements y_{ij} for $i = \{1, 2, ..., n\}$ and their mean value $\bar{y}_{.j}$. Dividing by the degrees of freedom $(n-1)$, we obtain the variance of the respective sample. k such variances are summed for $j = \{1, 2, ..., k\}$. Similarly, looking at SSA, we notice that the values whose squares are summed are differences between a sample of k measurements $\bar{y}_{.j}$ for $j = \{1, 2, ..., k\}$ and their mean value $\bar{y}_{..}$. Dividing by the degrees of freedom $(k-1)$, we obtain the variance of the respective sample. Finally, the values whose squares are summed in SST are differences between a sample of kn measurements y_{ij} for $i = \{1, 2, ..., n\}$, $j = \{1, 2, ..., k\}$ and their mean value $\bar{y}_{..}$. Dividing by the degrees of freedom $(kn-1)$, we obtain the variance of the respective sample.

Based on the above observations, we can convert the three sums, SSE, SSA, and SST, into sample variances by dividing them by the respective degrees of freedom. The resulting variances are called *mean square values* and are calculated as follows:

$$s_e^2 = \frac{SSE}{k(n-1)}, \qquad s_a^2 = \frac{SSA}{k-1}, \qquad s_t^2 = \frac{SST}{kn-1}. \tag{5.11}$$

We now apply the F-test to the ratio of variances $F = s_a^2/s_e^2$. If the computed F is greater than the critical value $F_{[1-\alpha;k-1,k(n-1)]}$ of the F-distribution, the conclusion is that it can be claimed with $(1-\alpha) \times 100\%$ confidence level that the variation due to actual differences in the alternatives plus measurement errors (SSA) is larger in a statistical sense than the variation due to measurement errors only (SSE). In other words, it can be claimed that the observed differences between the measurements for the different alternatives are due to real differences between the alternatives, as opposed to measurement errors. Table 5.3 summarizes the one-factor ANOVA.

Table 5.3: Summary of one-factor ANOVA

Variation	Alternatives	Error	Total
Sum of squares	SSA	SSE	SST
Degrees of freedom	$k-1$	$k(n-1)$	$kn-1$
Mean square value	$s_a^2 = \frac{SSA}{k-1}$	$s_e^2 = \frac{SSE}{k(n-1)}$	$s_t^2 = \frac{SST}{kn-1}$
Computed F	s_a^2/s_e^2		
Tabulated F	$F_{[1-\alpha;k-1,k(n-1)]}$		

Example Consider an experiment aiming to compare the execution time of three different alternative implementations of an algorithm. A sample of five measurements is collected for each alternative as shown in Table 5.4. The table shows the means of the three samples and the respective computed effects for each alternative.

Table 5.5 summarizes the results from applying the one-factor ANOVA technique. Given that the computed F statistic is greater than the tabulated F critical value, we conclude with 95% confidence that the observed differences among the three implementations of the algorithm are statistically significant.

The ratio $SSA/SST = 0.7585/0.8270 = 0.917$ indicates that 91.7% of the observed total variation in the measurements is due to differences among the three alternatives plus measurement errors. The ratio $SSE/SST = 0.0685/0.8270 = 0.083$ indicates that 8.3% of the total variation in the measurements is due to measurement errors (random noise).

Table 5.4: One-factor ANOVA example

Measure-ments	Alternatives			Overall mean
	1	2	3	
1	0.0972	0.1382	0.7966	
2	0.0971	0.1432	0.5300	
3	0.0969	0.1382	0.5152	
4	0.1954	0.1730	0.6675	
5	0.0974	0.1383	0.5298	
Col. mean	0.1168	0.1462	0.6078	0.2903
Effects	-0.1735	-0.1441	0.3175	

Table 5.5: Results of applying the one-factor ANOVA technique

Variation	Alternatives	Error	Total
Sum of squares	$SSA = 0.7585$	$SSE = 0.0685$	$SST = 0.8270$
Degrees of freedom	$k - 1 = 2$	$k(n - 1) = 12$	$kn - 1 = 14$
Mean square value	$s_a^2 = 0.3793$	$s_e^2 = 0.0057$	
Computed F	$0.3793/0.0057 = 66.4$		
Tabulated F	$F_{[0.95;2,12]} = 3.89$		

5.2 Method of Contrasts

While ANOVA provides a statistical test to determine if the observed differences between the considered alternatives are statistically significant, it does not provide any information on where exactly these differences are. For this purpose, a so-called *method of contrasts* can be used that allows us to compare subsets of alternatives, for example, {A} vs. {B} or {A, B} vs. {C}.

A *contrast* is defined as a linear combination of effects of alternatives:

$$c = \sum_{j=1}^{k} w_j \alpha_j, \quad \text{where} \quad \sum_{j=1}^{k} w_j = 0. \tag{5.12}$$

Contrasts are used to compare effects of a subset of the alternatives. For example, assuming that there are three alternatives and the first two of them should be compared, one can use the following contrast for this purpose:

$$c = (1)\alpha_1 + (-1)\alpha_2 + (0)\alpha_3 = \alpha_1 - \alpha_2$$
$$(w_1 = 1, \quad w_2 = -1, \quad w_3 = 0). \tag{5.13}$$

The contrast is defined such that for all alternatives that should be included in the comparison, a non-zero weight w_j is used. For the remaining, the weight is set to zero. Under the assumption that the variation due to errors is equally distributed among the kn total measurements, it can be shown that the following confidence interval for the contrast c is valid (Walpole et al., 2016):

$$(c_1, c_2) = c \mp t_{\{\alpha/2, k(n-1)\}} s_c, \tag{5.14}$$

where

$$s_c = \sqrt{\frac{\sum_{j=1}^{k} (w_j^2 s_e^2)}{kn}} \quad \text{and} \quad s_e^2 = \frac{SSE}{k(n-1)}. \tag{5.15}$$

As usual, if $0 \notin [c_1, c_2]$, it can be concluded that there is a statistically significant difference between the alternatives included in the contrast. Otherwise, if $0 \in [c_1, c_2]$, no conclusion can be drawn from the test.

5.3 Two-Factor Full Factorial Designs

We now generalize the ANOVA technique to two factors that can be varied at the same time. Consider the following example based on Lilja (2000): Table 5.6 shows the measured average transaction processing time for different levels of concurrency (Factor A) and varying amounts of main memory (Factor B) installed in a server running an online transaction processing (OLTP) system. The concurrency level specifies the average number of transactions processed concurrently at a point in time.

Table 5.6: Two-factor ANOVA example (Lilja, 2000)

	B (GB)		
A	32	64	128
1	0.25	0.21	0.15
2	0.52	0.45	0.36
3	0.81	0.66	0.50
4	1.50	1.45	0.70

The goal is to determine if the two considered factors (level of concurrency and amount of main memory) have a statistically significant impact on the transaction processing time. One possible approach would be to vary one factor at a time and apply the one-factor ANOVA technique from the previous section. We could, for example, fix Factor B to 64 GB and vary Factor A, and then fix Factor A to 3 and vary Factor B. This would reduce the number of configurations to be considered from 12 to 6. However, using this approach, we would not be able to determine if there is any interaction between the two factors; in other words, to determine if the selected combination of values of the two factors itself has an influence. Looking at the table, we see that for $A = 4$, the response time decreases non-linearly with B; however, when $A < 4$, the response time appears to be more directly correlated to B.

A more robust approach to the above described problem is to apply a generalized version of the one-factor ANOVA technique introduced in Section 5.1. In the following, we introduce a *two-factor* analysis of variance, also referred to as *two-factor experimental design* or *two-way classification*.

We assume that there are two *input variables (factors)* that are varied: Factor A and Factor B. The goal is to determine the effects of each input variable as well as the effect of the interaction between the two variables and the magnitude of the experimental error. As previously, the measured output value (i.e., the considered property of interest) is referred to as *response variable*. For each factor, the specific values of the respective input variable are referred to as *levels*, which can be either continuous (e.g., bytes) or discrete (e.g., type of system) values.

For every combination of input values of the factors, a sample of measurements of the response variable is obtained; that is, the experiment is repeated n times, where each repetition is referred to as *replication*. Multiple replications are needed in order to be able to determine the impact of the measurement errors. We assume that the errors in the measurements for the different combinations of levels for the factors are independent and normally distributed with equal variance for all combinations. Again, we refer the reader to Walpole et al. (2016) for a discussion of the relevance and implications of these assumptions. We will speak of *interactions* between factors when the effect of one factor depends on the level of another factor.

The two-factor ANOVA aims to separate the total variation observed in all of the measurements into the following components (Lilja, 2000):

1. Variation due to Factor A plus measurement errors,
2. Variation due to Factor B plus measurement errors,
3. Variation due to interaction of A and B (AB) plus measurement errors, and
4. Variation due to measurement errors only.

The aim of the two-factor ANOVA is to determine if the magnitude of the first three components of the observed variation is significantly larger in a statistical sense than the magnitude of the last component. In other words, ANOVA provides a statistical test to determine if the observed differences between the measured mean values for the different combinations of factor levels are due to real influences of the factors, or they are simply due to measurement errors.

Assume that there are a possible input levels for Factor A and b possible input levels for Factor B. For each combination of input levels, n measurements are collected resulting in $a \times b \times n$ total measurements. We denote with y_{ijk} the kth measurement for the combination of Factor A set to level i and Factor B set to level j (Table 5.7). As stated above, we assume that the measurement errors for the different experiments are independent and normally distributed with equal variance for each experiment.

Table 5.7: Measurements for all combinations of factor levels

It can be easily shown that each individual measurement can be broken down into the following components:

Mean of all measurements: $\bar{y}_{...} = \dfrac{\sum_{i=1}^{a} \sum_{j=1}^{b} \sum_{k=1}^{n} y_{ijk}}{abn}$,

Effect of Factor A: $\alpha_i = \bar{y}_{i..} - \bar{y}_{...}$

$$\text{where} \quad \sum_{i=1}^{a} \alpha_i = 0,$$

Effect of Factor B: $\beta_j = \bar{y}_{.j.} - \bar{y}_{...}$

$$\text{where} \quad \sum_{j=1}^{b} \beta_j = 0,$$

Effect of interaction btw. A and B: $\gamma_{ij} = \bar{y}_{ij.} - \bar{y}_{i..} - \bar{y}_{.j.} + \bar{y}_{...}$

$$\text{where} \quad \sum_{i=1}^{a} \gamma_{ij} = 0 \quad \sum_{j=1}^{b} \gamma_{ij} = 0,$$

Measurement error: e_{ijk}.

(5.16)

Each measurement can then be represented as the sum of the above components:

$$y_{ijk} = \bar{y}_{...} + \alpha_i + \beta_j + \gamma_{ij} + e_{ijk}. \tag{5.17}$$

Similarly to the one-factor ANOVA, we define the following *sums of squares of differences*, each characterizing some part of the variation observed in the measurements:

$$SSA = bn \sum_{i=1}^{a} (\bar{y}_{i..} - \bar{y}_{...})^2,$$

$$SSB = an \sum_{j=1}^{b} (\bar{y}_{.j.} - \bar{y}_{...})^2,$$

$$SSAB = n \sum_{i=1}^{a} \sum_{j=1}^{b} (\bar{y}_{ij.} - \bar{y}_{i..} - \bar{y}_{.j.} + \bar{y}_{...})^2, \qquad (5.18)$$

$$SSE = \sum_{i=1}^{a} \sum_{j=1}^{b} \sum_{k=1}^{n} (y_{ijk} - \bar{y}_{ij.})^2,$$

$$SST = \sum_{i=1}^{a} \sum_{j=1}^{b} \sum_{k=1}^{n} (y_{ijk} - \bar{y}_{...})^2.$$

SSA characterizes the variation due to Factor A plus measurement errors, SSB characterizes the variation due to Factor B plus measurement errors, and SSAB characterizes the variation due to the interaction of A and B plus measurement errors. SSE characterizes the variation due to measurement errors only, and finally, SST characterizes the total variation in all measurements. By expanding SST and noticing that all of the cross-product terms are zero, while also taking into account that effects add up to zero, it can be easily shown that the following equation, referred to as *sum-of-squares identity*, holds:

$$SST = SSA + SSB + SSAB + SSE. \qquad (5.19)$$

Each of the sums of squares of differences can be transformed into a set of sample variance computations (see Table 4.1 in Chapter 4) by dividing the respective sum by the degrees of freedom. To determine the degrees of freedom, we consider how many sample variances are computed in each sum of squares and how many values there are in each sample. This results in the following degrees of freedom (df) for each sum of squares:

$$\begin{aligned} df(SSA) &= a - 1, \\ df(SSB) &= b - 1, \\ df(SSAB) &= (a - 1)(b - 1), \\ df(SSE) &= ab(n - 1), \\ df(SST) &= abn - 1. \end{aligned} \qquad (5.20)$$

We notice that the sum-of-squares identity applies also when considering the respective degrees of freedom:

$$df(SST) = df(SSA) + df(SSB) + df(SSAB) + df(SSE). \qquad (5.21)$$

It can be shown that the sums of squares of differences can alternatively be computed using the following formulas:

$$SSA = \frac{\sum_{i=1}^{a} S_{i..}^2}{bn} - \frac{S_{...}^2}{abn}, \qquad SSB = \frac{\sum_{j=1}^{b} S_{.j.}^2}{an} - \frac{S_{...}^2}{abn},$$

$$SSAB = \frac{\sum_{i=1}^{a} \sum_{j=1}^{b} S_{ij.}^2}{n} - \frac{\sum_{i=1}^{a} S_{i..}^2}{bn} - \frac{\sum_{j=1}^{b} S_{.j.}^2}{an} + \frac{S_{...}^2}{abn},$$

$$SST = \sum_{i=1}^{a} \sum_{j=1}^{b} \sum_{k=1}^{n} y_{ijk}^2 - \frac{S_{...}^2}{abn},$$

$$SSE = SST - SSA - SSB - SSAB,$$

$$\text{where} \quad S_{...} = \sum_{i=1}^{a} \sum_{j=1}^{b} \sum_{k=1}^{n} y_{ijk}, \qquad S_{i..} = \sum_{j=1}^{b} \sum_{k=1}^{n} y_{ijk}, \qquad S_{.j.} = \sum_{i=1}^{a} \sum_{k=1}^{n} y_{ijk}.$$

$$(5.22)$$

Dividing the sums of squares of differences by the respective degrees of freedom, we obtain the *mean square values*. Similarly to the one-dimensional case, we now apply the F-test to the ratios of variances $F_a = s_a^2/s_e^2$, $F_b = s_b^2/s_e^2$, and $F_{ab} = s_{ab}^2/s_e^2$. If the computed F is greater than the respective critical value of the F-distribution, the conclusion is that it can be claimed with $(1 - \alpha) \times 100\%$ confidence level that the variation due to the effect of the respective factor (SSA, SSB) or interaction between factors (SSAB) plus measurement errors is larger in a statistical sense than the variation due to measurement errors only, SSE. In other words, it can be claimed that the observed differences between the measurements for the different combinations of factor levels are due to real differences, as opposed to measurement errors. Table 5.8 summarizes the two-factor ANOVA technique.

Table 5.8: Summary of two-factor ANOVA

Variation	A	B	AB	Error
Sum of squares	SSA	SSB	$SSAB$	SSE
Degrees of freedom	$a-1$	$b-1$	$(a-1)(b-1)$	$ab(n-1)$
Mean square value	$s_a^2 = \frac{SSA}{a-1}$	$s_b^2 = \frac{SSB}{b-1}$	$s_{ab}^2 = \frac{SSAB}{(a-1)(b-1)}$	$s_e^2 = \frac{SSE}{ab(n-1)}$
Computed F	$F_a = \frac{s_a^2}{s_e^2}$	$F_b = \frac{s_b^2}{s_e^2}$	$F_{ab} = \frac{s_{ab}^2}{s_e^2}$	
Tabulated F	$F_{[1-\alpha;(a-1);ab(n-1)]}$	$F_{[1-\alpha;(b-1);ab(n-1)]}$	$F_{[1-\alpha;(a-1)(b-1);ab(n-1)]}$	

Example Coming back to the motivating example in the beginning of this section, we now assume that for every combination of input values of the Factors A and B (level of concurrency and amount of main memory), a sample of two measurements of the transaction processing time (i.e., experiment replications) is collected. Table 5.9 shows the measurement results. For each combination of values for the Factors A and B, the respective two measurements of the transaction processing time are shown on two separate rows. Note that to be able to quantify the impact of the measurement errors, normally a bigger sample of measurements would be required; here, we show only two measurements for the sake of compactness. The goal was to determine if the two considered factors have a statistically significant impact on the transaction processing time. In addition to the two factors in isolation, we also consider the impact of the interaction between them.

Table 5.9: Two-factor ANOVA example

A	B (GB) 32	64	128
1	0.25	0.21	0.15
	0.28	0.19	0.11
2	0.52	0.45	0.36
	0.48	0.49	0.30
3	0.81	0.66	0.50
	0.76	0.59	0.61
4	1.50	1.45	0.70
	1.61	1.32	0.68

Table 5.10 summarizes the results from applying the two-factor ANOVA technique. Given that the computed F statistic is greater than the tabulated F critical value, we conclude with 95% confidence that the observed effects of the two factors, as well as the interaction between them, are statistically significant.

The ratios $SSA/SST = 77.6$ and $SSB/SST = 11.8$ indicate that 77.6% and 11.8% of the observed total variation in the measurements are due to the effects of Factor A (concurrency level) and Factor B (amount of main memory), respectively, plus measurement errors. The interaction between the two factors plus measurement errors is responsible for 9.9% ($SSAB/SST$) of the total variation. Finally, the ratio $SSE/SST = 0.7\%$ indicates that only 0.7% of the total variation in the measurements is due to measurement errors (random noise).

5.4 General m-Factor Full Factorial Designs

We now further generalize the ANOVA technique to m factors that can be varied at the same time (Lilja, 2000). We assume that there are m input variables (factors)

Table 5.10: Results of applying the two-factor ANOVA technique

Variation	A	B	AB	Error
Sum of squares	3.3714	0.5152	0.4317	0.0293
Degrees of freedom	3	2	6	12
Mean square value	1.1238	0.2576	0.0720	0.0024
Computed F	460.2	105.5	29.5	
Tabulated F	$F_{[0.95;3,12]} = 3.49$	$F_{[0.95;2,12]} = 3.89$	$F_{[0.95;6,12]} = 3.00$	

that are varied: A, B, C, and so on. The goal is to determine the effects of each input variable, the effect of the interaction between each combination of input variables, and the magnitude of the experimental error. As previously, the measured output value (i.e., the considered property of interest) is referred to as *response variable*, and for each factor, the specific values of the respective input variable are referred to as *levels*.

For every combination of input values of the factors, a sample of measurements of the response variable is obtained; that is, the experiment is repeated n times, where each repetition is referred to as *replication*. As previously, multiple replications are needed in order to be able to determine the impact of the measurement errors and we assume that the errors in the measurements for the different combinations of levels for the factors are independent and normally distributed with equal variance for all combinations. We will speak of *interactions* between factors when a given combination of factors, considered as a whole, has an impact on the measurement results.

Given that we have m factors, there are $2^m - 1$ possible combinations of factors whose effects can be considered:

$$m \text{ factors} \Rightarrow m \text{ main effects,}$$

$$\binom{m}{2} \text{ two-factor interactions,}$$

$$\binom{m}{3} \text{ three-factor interactions,} \qquad (5.23)$$

$$\cdots$$

$$\binom{m}{m} = 1 \ m\text{-factor interactions.}$$

As previously, for each combination of factors, we consider a respective *sum of squares of differences* that characterizes some part of the variation observed in the measurements: $SSA, SSB, SSC, ..., SSAB, SSAC, ...$ The degrees of freedom for a combination of factors is calculated by multiplying the degrees of freedom for the respective factors:

$$df(SSA) = (a-1),$$
$$df(SSB) = (b-1),$$
$$df(SSC) = (c-1),$$

$$\cdots$$

$$df(SSAB) = (a-1)(b-1), \qquad (5.24)$$
$$df(SSAC) = (a-1)(c-1),$$

$$\cdots$$

$$df(SSE) = abc(n-1),$$
$$df(SST) = abcn-1.$$

Dividing the sums of squares of differences by the respective degrees of freedom, we obtain the *mean square values* s_x^2. For a combination of factors x (a single factor or a set of factors), we can determine if its effect is statistically significant by applying the F-test to the ratios of mean square values $F_x = s_x^2/s_e^2$. If the computed F is greater than the respective critical value of the F-distribution, the conclusion is that it can be claimed with $(1-\alpha) \times 100\%$ confidence level that the variation due to the effect of the combination of factors x plus measurement errors is larger in a statistical sense than the variation due to measurement errors only, SSE. In other words, it can be claimed that the observed differences between the measurements for the different combinations of factor levels are due to real differences, as opposed to measurement errors.

In summary, the m-factor ANOVA technique proceeds as follows:

1. Calculate $(2^m - 1)$ sum of squares terms (SSx) and SSE,

2. Determine the degrees of freedom for each (SSx) and for SSE,

3. Calculate the mean square values s_x^2 and s_e^2,

4. Apply the F-test to the ratio $F_x = s_x^2/s_e^2$, and

5. If the computed F_x is greater than the critical value $F_{[1-\alpha;df(SSx),df(SSE)]}$, we conclude with $(1 - \alpha) \times 100\%$ confidence that the effect of the considered set of factors x is statistically significant.

The described m-factor full factorial design requires measuring the response variable for all possible combinations of values for the input variables (factors). In addition, each measurement is replicated n times to determine the effect of the measurement error. With m factors, v levels per factor, and n replications, we arrive at $v^m \times n$ measurement experiments that need to be conducted. As an example, for $m = 5$, $v = 4$, and $n = 3$, we arrive at $4^5 \times 3 = 3,072$ measurement experiments. Thus, the full factorial design requires a substantial amount of measurements even for a low number of factors. In many cases, it is not feasible to conduct measurements for all possible combinations of inputs. This limits the practical applicability of the full factorial m-factor ANOVA technique. In the rest of this chapter, we look at approaches to deal with this issue.

A straightforward approach to reduce the number of measurement experiments required by the full factorial m-factor ANOVA is to follow a two-step procedure as follows: In the first step, each factor is restricted to two possible levels (labeled *low* and *high*, respectively) and the normal ANOVA technique is applied to identify the factors with the highest impact. The two levels should ideally be chosen to cover the typical range of values of the respective factor. $n2^m$ measurement experiments are required and thus, this experiment design is often referred to as $n2^m$ *factorial design*. In the second step, the generalized full factorial design is applied to the identified factors with highest impact without restricting their levels in order to further investigate their influences. In many cases, however, this approach still incurs significant experimental effort. In the next section, we present a method for fractional factorial design that requires a significantly lower experimental effort. *Fractional factorial designs* are experimental designs that require only a carefully chosen subset (fraction) of the experiments of a full factorial design.

5.5 Fractional Factorial Designs: Plackett–Burman

Plackett–Burman (PB) designs were originally developed by Robin L. Plackett and J. P. Burman in 1946. They require $O(m)$ experiments for m factors instead of $O(v^m)$ as for full factorial designs. However, PB designs provide less detailed information than full factorial designs, as only the effects of the main factors are considered. An extension of the technique (PB designs with foldover) also covers two-factor interactions but no other arbitrary interactions. Figure 5.1 compares PB designs against the experimental designs discussed so far. The x-axis shows the cost in terms of number of required experiments; the y-axis shows the level of detail of the information provided by the respective design. *One-at-a-time* refers to the trivial approach of applying one-factor ANOVA while varying only one factor at a time. PB designs bridge the gap between low-cost/low-detail approaches, such as one-at-a-time, and high-cost/high-detail approaches, such as full factorial ANOVA designs. The advantage of PB designs is that they provide the most important information but at a very low cost comparable to the cost of the trivial one-at-a-time approach.

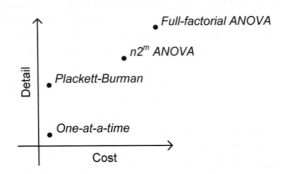

Fig. 5.1: Trade-off between cost and detail of experimental designs

We now introduce the PB design. Let X be the next multiple of four greater than the number of input variables m (factors). As an example, we assume that $X = 8$. For each input variable, two possible levels are considered (high and low) and carefully chosen to cover the typical range of values of the respective factor. Table 5.11 shows the *PB design matrix*, which has X rows and $(X - 1)$ columns. The columns correspond to the input variables. If $m < (X - 1)$, some dummy variables are used for the additional columns. Let us assume that $m = 7$. Each row represents a configuration of the input variables. For each input variable either -1 or $+1$ is indicated, corresponding to setting the respective factor to its low or high value, respectively. The first row is initialized with predefined values provided in Plackett and Burman (1946). Each subsequent row is initialized by a circular right shift of the preceding row. The last row is initialized with -1.

The choice of high and low values for each factor should be done carefully to avoid bias. For example, if the high and low values are selected to span a range of values that is too small, this may lead to underestimating the effect of the respective factor. Similarly, selecting a range that is too large may overestimate the effect. Ideally, the high and low values should represent the typical interval in which the values of the respective factor normally vary, excluding any outliers. For each row in the PB design matrix, the response variable is measured for the respective configuration of the input variables. The result is then entered into the last column of the matrix. Table 5.12 shows some example results.

Table 5.11: Example PB design matrix—initialization

Config	Factors							Response
	A	B	C	D	E	F	G	
1	+1	+1	+1	-1	+1	-1	-1	
2	-1	+1	+1	+1	-1	+1	-1	
3	-1	-1	+1	+1	+1	-1	+1	
4	+1	-1	-1	+1	+1	+1	-1	
5	-1	+1	-1	-1	+1	+1	+1	
6	+1	-1	+1	-1	-1	+1	+1	
7	+1	+1	-1	+1	-1	-1	+1	
8	-1	-1	-1	-1	-1	-1	-1	
Effect								

Table 5.12: Example PB design matrix—response variable

Config	Factors							Response
	A	B	C	D	E	F	G	
1	+1	+1	+1	-1	+1	-1	-1	9
2	-1	+1	+1	+1	-1	+1	-1	11
3	-1	-1	+1	+1	+1	-1	+1	2
4	+1	-1	-1	+1	+1	+1	-1	1
5	-1	+1	-1	-1	+1	+1	+1	9
6	+1	-1	+1	-1	-1	+1	+1	74
7	+1	+1	-1	+1	-1	-1	+1	7
8	-1	-1	-1	-1	-1	-1	-1	4
Effect								

The next step is to calculate the effects of each factor. This is done by multiplying the respective column in the matrix with the response column (vector multiplication). The result is entered in the last row as shown in Table 5.13.

$$\text{Effect}_A = (+1 \times 9) + (-1 \times 11) + (-1 \times 2) + \ldots + (-1 \times 4) = 65. \qquad (5.25)$$

The effects show the relative influence of the factors on the variation observed in the response variable. Note that only the magnitudes of the values are relevant; the signs are meaningless. Comparing the effects, the factors can be ranked from most important to least important. In our example, the following ranking is observed:

$$(C, D, E) \rightarrow F \rightarrow G \rightarrow A \rightarrow B. \qquad (5.26)$$

The presented base PB design does not provide any information about the impacts of interactions between factors. We now present an extended version of the PB design,

Table 5.13: Example PB design matrix—computing the effects

(a) Effect of Factor A

Config	Factors							Resp.
	A	B	C	D	E	F	G	
1	+1	+1	+1	-1	+1	-1	-1	9
2	-1	+1	+1	+1	-1	+1	-1	11
3	-1	-1	+1	+1	+1	-1	+1	2
4	+1	-1	-1	+1	+1	+1	-1	1
5	-1	+1	-1	-1	+1	+1	+1	9
6	+1	-1	+1	-1	-1	+1	+1	74
7	+1	+1	-1	+1	-1	-1	+1	7
8	-1	-1	-1	-1	-1	-1	-1	4
Effect	65							

(b) Effect of Factor B

Config	Factors							Resp.
	A	B	C	D	E	F	G	
1	+1	+1	+1	-1	+1	-1	-1	9
2	-1	+1	+1	+1	-1	+1	-1	11
3	-1	-1	+1	+1	+1	-1	+1	2
4	+1	-1	-1	+1	+1	+1	-1	1
5	-1	+1	-1	-1	+1	+1	+1	9
6	+1	-1	+1	-1	-1	+1	+1	74
7	+1	+1	-1	+1	-1	-1	+1	7
8	-1	-1	-1	-1	-1	-1	-1	4
Effect	65	-45						

(c) Effects of Factors C-G

Config	Factors							Resp.
	A	B	C	D	E	F	G	
1	+1	+1	+1	-1	+1	-1	-1	9
2	-1	+1	+1	+1	-1	+1	-1	11
3	-1	-1	+1	+1	+1	-1	+1	2
4	+1	-1	-1	+1	+1	+1	-1	1
5	-1	+1	-1	-1	+1	+1	+1	9
6	+1	-1	+1	-1	-1	+1	+1	74
7	+1	+1	-1	+1	-1	-1	+1	7
8	-1	-1	-1	-1	-1	-1	-1	4
Effect	65	-45	75	-75	-75	73	67	

referred to as *PB design with foldover*, which additionally quantifies the effects of two-factor interactions. The PB design matrix is expanded by adding X additional rows and initializing them with opposite signs to the ones in the original rows, as shown in Table 5.14. The response variable is measured for each of the new rows.

The effects are computed in the same way as previously but the additional X rows of the PB design matrix are also taken into account (the vectors whose product is taken are twice as long). The extended matrix now also allows computing the effects of two-factor interactions. For two arbitrary factors, the effect of the interaction between them is computed by first forming a vector of signs that are products of the respective signs for the two considered factors and then multiplying this vector with the *response* vector. For example, the effect of the interaction between Factors A and B is computed as follows:

$$\text{Effect}_{AB} = ((1 \times 1) \times 9) + ((-1 \times 1) \times 11) + ((-1 \times (-1)) \times 2) + \ldots + ((1 \times 1) \times 112) = -91. \tag{5.27}$$

The remaining effects of two-factor interactions can be computed in a similar way and can then be included in the ranking of the individual factors.

Table 5.14: Example PB design matrix with foldover

A	B	C	D	E	F	G	Resp.
+1	+1	+1	-1	+1	-1	-1	9
-1	+1	+1	+1	-1	+1	-1	11
-1	-1	+1	+1	+1	-1	+1	2
+1	-1	-1	+1	+1	+1	-1	1
-1	+1	-1	-1	+1	+1	+1	9
+1	-1	+1	-1	-1	+1	+1	74
+1	+1	-1	+1	-1	-1	+1	7
-1	-1	-1	-1	-1	-1	-1	4
-1	-1	-1	+1	-1	+1	+1	17
+1	-1	-1	-1	+1	-1	+1	76
+1	+1	-1	-1	-1	+1	-1	6
-1	+1	+1	-1	-1	-1	+1	31
+1	-1	+1	+1	-1	-1	-1	19
-1	+1	-1	+1	+1	-1	-1	33
-1	-1	+1	-1	+1	+1	-1	6
+1	+1	+1	+1	+1	+1	+1	112
191	19	111	-13	79	55	239	

The main advantage of the presented PB design is that it requires only $O(m)$ experiments for m factors. PB designs are often used to reduce the number of factors to the most significant ones. The full factorial ANOVA technique can then be applied to the reduced number of factors to explore their influences in more detail. Next, we present a case study illustrating this procedure.

5.6 Case Study

Having introduced several techniques for experimental design, in this section, we present a case study demonstrating how these techniques can be applied in practice. We look at the problem of tuning machine learning algorithms to optimize their performance. Machine learning algorithms typically offer a vast set of configuration parameters usually referred to as *hyperparameters*. Due to lack of expertise or lack of time, the average user does not configure these parameters and would usually leave them to their default values. However, tuning hyperparameters can massively influence the accuracy and performance of machine learning algorithms. Simply brute forcing all possible parameter combinations is impossible, or at least practically undesirable, due to the exponential explosion of parameter combinations to be searched. We therefore need to reduce the number of parameters to optimize. It is not trivial to determine which of the parameters have the most influence and how they interact with each other. This is therefore an excellent application scenario for experimental design.

In this example, we analyze one specific instance of a supervised machine learning algorithm. The task of supervised machine learning is usually described as follows (Russell and Norvig, 2009): A set of labeled training data T containing n training tuples $\{(y_1, x_1), \ldots, (y_n, x_n)\}$ is given. Each of these tuples (y_i, x_i) for $i \in 1, 2, \ldots, n$ labels a usually multi-dimensional feature vector x_i with a label y_i. The machine learning task that we focus on in this example is *classification*, which implies that there are l possible different classes for y_i. The task is to find a function $h : \mathbb{R}^k \mapsto \{1, 2, \ldots, x\}$, mapping from x_i to y_i. If h can be found, then h can be used to predict the label y_j for any new and unseen samples of x_j for $j > n$. Note that for simplicity, we assume all features to be from the domain of $\mathbb{R}$. The dimensionality of the input space k corresponds to the number of features.

One algorithm for solving such a machine learning task is the *random forest algorithm* (Breiman, 2001). The algorithm works by training a set of smaller *classifiers* (the so-called trees) with a subset of the training set and a randomized sub-feature-space. Each tree generates its own prediction, which is aggregated to the overall prediction of the whole forest. Like many other machine learning algorithms, random forest is highly configurable, allowing one to parameterize the number of underlying trees and how they are trained. The tree sub-classifiers have additional parameters that influence their training behavior. We use the implementation of Scikit learn (Pedregosa et al., 2011), which offers the list of tunable parameters shown in Table 5.15.

Table 5.15: List of relevant parameters available for optimization

Parameter	Datatype	Description
n_estimators	integer	The number of trees in the forest
criterion	enum	The function to measure the quality of a split
max_depth	integer	The maximum depth of the tree
min_samples_split	integer	The minimum number of samples required to split an internal node
min_samples_leaf	integer	The minimum number of samples required to be at a leaf node
min_weight_fraction_leaf	float	The minimum weighted fraction of the sum total of weights (of all input samples) required to be at a leaf node
max_features	enum	The number of features to consider when looking for the best split
max_leaf_nodes	integer	Grow trees with max_leaf_nodes in best-first fashion. Best nodes are defined in terms of relative reduction in impurity.
min_impurity_decrease	float	A node will be split if the split induces a decrease of the impurity greater than or equal to this value.
bootstrap	boolean	Whether bootstrap samples are used when building trees. If false, the whole dataset is used to build each tree.
class_weight	enum	Weights associated with classes

Understanding the exact meaning of these hyperparameters is not required for this example, as our goal here is to automatically identify the most important parameters by applying the statistical techniques introduced in this chapter. Table 5.16 defines a set of possible parameter settings that we use for our evaluation. These values are chosen based on experience and general rules of thumb.

Table 5.16: List of possible parameter values in our example

Parameter	Considered set of possible values
n_estimators	10, 25, 50, 100, 150
criterion	gini, entropy
max_depth	5, 10, 30, 10000
min_samples_split	2, 5, 10, 20, 30
min_samples_leaf	1, 5, 10, 20, 30
min_weight_fraction_leaf	0, 0.1, 0.2
max_features	sqrt, log2, none
max_leaf_nodes	5, 10, 10000
min_impurity_decrease	0, 0.1, 0.2, 0.3, 0.4
bootstrap	True, False
class_weight	balanced, balanced_subsample, none

5.6.1 Problem Statement

Let us now consider the following concrete example of a classification problem: A set of hard disk drives (HDDs) are installed as part of a storage system running in a data center. The goal is to predict whether an HDD is likely to fail within the next seven days. Being able to reliably predict such failures would enable us to proactively exchange faulty HDDs before any data gets corrupted.

We assume that monitoring data on the state of each HDD is collected at run time and fed into a machine learning algorithm in order to learn patterns in the data that indicate if a failure is likely to occur in the next 7 days. In this example, we have a classification problem with two classes (i.e., $l = 2$): (1) the HDD is "healthy" and (2) the HDD is likely to fail within the next 7 days. Assume that we have a training set T consisting of $n = 5,000$ training samples collected from historical data logs of HDD failures in the data center. Each sample contains a feature vector comprised of $k = 100$ values. These values are sensor metrics collected within an HDD that monitor the state of the drive; one example of such a dataset is the well-known S.M.A.R.T. monitoring system for HDDs.[2] Each of the training samples is assigned to one of the two classes, based on historical data revealing whether or not the respective HDD failed during the next 7 days.

---

[2] S.M.A.R.T. Monitoring Tools: https://sourceforge.net/projects/smartmontools

We can now use a random forest algorithm to learn the function h. However, the parameters in Table 5.15 heavily influence the performance of the random forest algorithm and are not trivial to configure.

We can evaluate the generated function h by splitting the given dataset of 5,000 samples into two sets: (1) a training set of 4,000 samples and (2) an evaluation set of 1,000 samples. By training our algorithm on the training set, we can evaluate how well h predicts the class of the remaining 1,000 samples. In our example, we use the F_1 score[3] of h on the 1,000 samples, a common practice in the area of machine learning. This process is called *cross validation* (Russell and Norvig, 2009) and can be used to obtain our response.

Now that we have a measure of how well h represents the data, we can simply try all parameter settings listed in Table 5.16 to find out which parameter values lead to the best results. However, as parameters may influence each other, we would need to test every combination of parameter settings. In our example, this would result in $5 \times 2 \times 4 \times 5 \times 5 \times 3 \times 3 \times 3 \times 5 \times 2 \times 3 = 810,000$ parameter combinations. Additionally, as the name *random* forest suggests, the training of the random forest is influenced by random factors. To cope with that, we need to repeat each experiment multiple times in order to ensure that random effects do not play a role. In our example, five repetitions provide sufficient confidence for the results. In total, we need to conduct $810,000 \times 5 = 4,050,000$ experiments if we want to do a full factorial design. Even if one experiment would take only one second to run, we still would need 1,125 h or over 46 days to evaluate all combinations of parameters. Note that the number of possible values dramatically impacts the number of combinations and the respective runtime of the algorithms. If we would add another parameter with four possible values, this would again quadruple the possible combinations. Therefore, this approach is often infeasible in practice.

Instead, we first apply the Plackett–Burman design in order to analyze the effects of the different parameters and reduce them to the most important ones, as shown in Figure 5.2. After that, we apply a full factorial ANOVA on the remaining parameters in order to analyze their impact in more detail. This allows us to filter more unimportant parameters and to cluster the remaining parameters into groups that influence each other and therefore need to be optimized together.

5.6.2 Plackett–Burman Design

We first apply a Plackett–Burman (PB) design. As described in Section 5.5, PB designs need significantly less experiments to analyze the impacts of different parameters. Hence, we apply a PB design to obtain a rough analysis of the parameters and to filter out the unimportant ones.

---

[3] The F_1 score is a standard measure used in machine learning to rate the classification performance of a learned function h by analyzing how many samples were correctly classified in relation to how many samples were wrongly classified (Russell and Norvig, 2009).

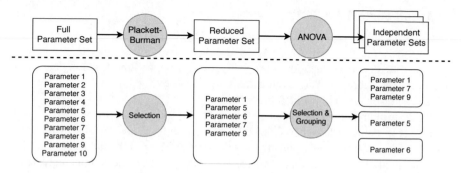

Fig. 5.2: Systematically reducing the set of hyperparameters using PB design
followed by ANOVA

In our case, we have 11 parameters available, which implies that our PB design consists of only 12 experiment runs. Recall that we always need a multiple of four. As minimum and maximum values of the parameters, we use the first and the last value in the value set provided in Table 5.16. After performing the experiments and adding all scores based on the respective response, we arrive at the ordering presented in Table 5.17.

Table 5.17: List of parameters sorted according to their corresponding
Plackett-Burman (PB) scores

Parameter	PB score
max_depth	0.011
bootstrap	0.031
criterion	0.049
min_samples_split	0.055
min_samples_leaf	0.087
class_weight	0.141
n_estimators	0.153
max_features	0.217
max_leaf_nodes	0.401
min_weight_fraction_leaf	0.407
min_impurity_decrease	1.901

Analyzing the results in Table 5.17, we conclude that the five most important parameters are n_estimators, max_features, max_leaf_nodes, min_weight_fraction_leaf, and min_impurity_decrease. Therefore, we continue with these parameters applying a full factorial ANOVA to further investigate their effects.

5.6.3 Full Factorial ANOVA

We apply a full factorial ANOVA on the identified most important parameters n_estimators, max_features, max_leaf_nodes, min_weight_fraction_leaf, and min_impurity_decrease. This requires us to evaluate $675 \times 5 = 3{,}375$ experiment series. The results are shown in Table 5.18.

First, it is interesting to note that all found significance values are actually highly significant (p-value of less than 0.001). Most other entities are very far away from any significance threshold (typically p-values of 0.01 or 0.05) and can thus be safely ignored. This means that the experiment results were quite conclusive and unambiguous for ANOVA.

From Table 5.18, we can furthermore draw the conclusion that the interaction between the three parameters min_weight_fraction_leaf, max_leaf_nodes, and min_impurity_decrease is important and should not be neglected. ANOVA shows that the response variable (the quality of our machine learning algorithm) highly depends on these parameters and their interactions with each other. This implies that it is not possible to optimize these influencing parameters independently of each other, which would save a lot of computation time. Instead, these three parameters must be optimized together given that the interactions between them are highly relevant.

Furthermore, ANOVA reveals that max_features actually does not have a statistically significant influence on the response variable or any statistically significant interaction with any of the other parameters. Hence, when optimizing the parameters, we can safely exclude the max_features parameter and thus save computation time. This is a bit surprising considering our previous result from the Plackett–Burman design, but it is probably due to random errors and influences.

Finally, the parameter n_estimators has a significant influence on the response. Unfortunately, the interaction between n_estimators and min_impurity_decrease is also significant. This is unfortunate, because it means that we need to account for interaction between the n_estimators parameter and the min_impurity_decrease parameter, which in turn interacts heavily with max_leaf_nodes and min_weight_fraction_leaf. Therefore, we have to consider all four parameters together when optimizing the performance of the machine learning algorithm. If n_estimators had no significant interactions with the other parameters, we could have optimized the two groups independently of each other. We could first optimize min_weight_fraction_leaf, max_leaf_nodes, and min_impurity_decrease in combination, and after optimizing them, we could start a separate optimization tuning the n_estimators parameter. Again, as we would not need to consider all combinations of these values, this would save a lot of computation time for the optimization.

5.6.4 Case Study Summary

We applied a Plackett–Burman design and a subsequent full factorial ANOVA to analyze the impact of hyperparameters on the performance of a selected machine

Table 5.18: Results of the ANOVA technique applied on the most important parameters; bold entries mark highly significant effects (*p*-value < 0.001); parameter interactions are denoted by the "&" sign

Parameter	*p*-value
n_estimators	**2.91e-14**
min_weight_fraction_leaf	**< 2e-16**
max_features	0.996354
max_leaf_nodes	**0.000219**
min_impurity_decrease	**< 2e-16**
n_estimators & min_weight_fraction_leaf	0.341666
n_estimators & max_features	0.995322
min_weight_fraction_leaf & max_features	0.958687
n_estimators & max_leaf_nodes	0.832510
min_weight_fraction_leaf & max_leaf_nodes	5.28e-05
max_features & max_leaf_nodes	0.996501
n_estimators & min_impurity_decrease	**< 2e-16**
min_weight_fraction_leaf & min_impurity_decrease	**< 2e-16**
max_features & min_impurity_decrease	0.990143
max_leaf_nodes & min_impurity_decrease	**3.91e-08**
n_estimators & min_weight_fraction_leaf & max_features	0.972791
n_estimators & min_weight_fraction_leaf & max_leaf_nodes	0.470147
n_estimators & max_features & max_leaf_nodes	0.999892
min_weight_fraction_leaf & max_features & max_leaf_nodes	0.990162
n_estimators & min_weight_fraction_leaf & min_impurity_decrease	0.182299
n_estimators & max_features & min_impurity_decrease	0.995795
min_weight_fraction_leaf & max_features & min_impurity_decrease	0.978592
n_estimators & max_leaf_nodes & min_impurity_decrease	0.518709
min_weight_fraction_leaf & max_leaf_nodes & min_impurity_decrease	**3.89e-09**
max_features & max_leaf_nodes & min_impurity_decrease	0.995688
n_estimators & min_weight_fraction_leaf & max_features & max_leaf_nodes	0.995791
n_estimators & min_weight_fraction_leaf & max_features & min_impurity_decrease	0.964687
n_estimators & min_weight_fraction_leaf & max_leaf_nodes & min_impurity_decrease	0.235314
n_estimators & max_features & max_leaf_nodes & min_impurity_decrease	0.999667
min_weight_fraction_leaf & max_features & max_leaf_nodes & min_impurity_decrease	0.998793
n_estimators & min_weight_fraction_leaf & max_features & max_leaf_nodes & min_impurity_decrease	0.997986

learning algorithm, namely random forest, on a given problem instance. Our analysis concludes that the four parameters min_weight_fraction_leaf, max_leaf_nodes, min_impurity_decrease, and n_estimators have influence on the response variable; that is, they have influence on the performance of the random forest algorithm for the given problem instance. Furthermore, they heavily interact with each other, which implies that they cannot be optimized in isolation and need to be optimized simultaneously. This required us to conduct 3,375 + 12 = 3,387 experiments, whereas evaluating all possible parameter combinations would have required 4,050,000 experiments. This is a relative saving of over 99.9%. The conclusion is that we should focus on optimizing these four parameters. The next step would then be to define an optimization problem using the four parameters and to then apply a search algorithm, for example, manual experimentation, brute forcing all combinations, or more sophisticated algorithms (Noorshams et al., 2013), in order to determine the best parameter combination.

5.7 Concluding Remarks

In this chapter, we introduced the foundations of experimental design. We focused on the analysis of variance (ANOVA) technique from statistics, starting with one-factor ANOVA and then generalizing to two factors and finally to m factors. The presented m-factor full factorial design requires conducting experiments for all possible combinations of values for the input variables (factors). In addition, each measurement must be replicated n times to determine the effect of the measurement error. Thus, the full factorial design requires substantial amount of measurements limiting its practical applicability.

We looked at approaches to deal with the above issue by using fractional factorial designs requiring only a fraction of the experiments of a full factorial design. After briefly describing $n2^m$ factorial designs, we focused on Plackett–Burman (PB) designs. The latter bridge the gap between low-cost/low-detail approaches, such as varying factors one-at-a-time, and high-cost/high-detail approaches, such as full factorial ANOVA designs. The advantage of PB designs is that they provide the most important information but at a very low cost similar to the cost of the trivial one-at-a-time approach.

Finally, having introduced several techniques for experimental design, we presented a case study demonstrating how these techniques can be applied in practice. We applied a Plackett–Burman design and a subsequent full factorial ANOVA to analyze the impact of hyperparameters on the performance of a popular machine learning algorithm (random forest) on a given problem instance.

References

Amrhein, V., Greenland, S., and McShane, B. (2019). "Scientists Rise Up Against Statistical Significance". *Nature*, 567(7748). Springer Nature Limited, pp. 305–307 (cited on p. 102).

Breiman, L. (2001). "Random Forests". *Machine Learning*, 45(1). Kluwer Academic Publishers, pp. 5–32 (cited on p. 122).

Lilja, D. J. (2000). *Measuring Computer Performance: A Practitioner's Guide*. Cambridge University Press: Cambridge, UK (cited on pp. 102, 108, 109, 114).

Noorshams, Q., Bruhn, D., Kounev, S., and Reussner, R. (2013). "Predictive Performance Modeling of Virtualized Storage Systems Using Optimized Statistical Regression Techniques". In: *Proceedings of the 4th ACM/SPEC International*

Conference on Performance Engineering (ICPE 2013). (Prague, Czech Republic). ACM: New York, NY, USA, pp. 283–294 (cited on p. 128).

Pedregosa, F., Varoquaux, G., Gramfort, A., Michel, V., Thirion, B., Grisel, O., Blondel, M., Prettenhofer, P., Weiss, R., Dubourg, V., Vanderplas, J., Passos, A., Cournapeau, D., Brucher, M., Perrot, M., and Duchesnay, É. (2011). "Scikit-learn: Machine Learning in Python". *Journal of Machine Learning Research*, 12, pp. 2825–2830 (cited on p. 122).

Plackett, R. L. and Burman, J. P. (1946). "The Design of Optimum Multifactorial Experiments". *Biometrika*, 33(4). Oxford University Press on behalf of Biometrika Trust: Oxford, UK, pp. 305–325 (cited on p. 118).

Russell, S. and Norvig, P. (2009). *Artificial Intelligence: A Modern Approach*. Third Edition. Prentice Hall Series in Artificial Intelligence. Prentice Hall: Upper Saddle River, New Jersey, USA (cited on pp. 122, 124).

Walpole, R. E., Myers, R. H., Myers, S. L., and Ye, K. E. (2016). *Probability & Statistics for Engineers & Scientists*. Ninth Edition. Pearson Education: London, UK (cited on pp. 102, 108, 109).

Chapter 6
Measurement Techniques

"When you only have a hammer, every problem begins to
resemble a nail."
—*Abraham Maslow*

In the previous chapters, we introduced the most common statistics that can be
used to summarize measurements, that is, indices of central tendency and indices
of dispersion, providing a basis for defining metrics as part of benchmarks. Furthermore, the statistical approaches for quantifying the variability and precision of
measurements were introduced. This chapter looks at the different measurement
techniques that can be used in practice to derive the values of common metrics.
While most presented techniques are useful for performance metrics, some of them
can also be applied generally for other types of metrics.

The chapter starts with a brief introduction to the basic measurement strategies,
including event-driven, tracing, sampling, and indirect measurement. We then look at
interval timers, which are typically used to measure the execution time of a program
or a portion of it. Next, we introduce performance profiling, which provides means
to measure how much time a system spends in different states. A performance profile
provides a high-level summary of the execution behavior of an application or a
system; however, this summary does not provide any information about the order in
which events occur. Thus, at the end of the chapter, event-driven tracing strategies
are introduced, which can be used to capture such information. We focus on call path
tracing—a technique for extracting a control flow graph of an application. Finally, the
chapter is wrapped up with an overview of commercial and open-source monitoring
tools for performance profiling and call path tracing.

6.1 Basic Measurement Strategies

Measurement techniques are typically based on monitoring changes in the system
state. Each change in the system state that is relevant for the measurement of a given

© Springer Nature Switzerland AG 2020

S. Kounev et al., *Systems Benchmarking*, https://doi.org/10.1007/978-3-030-41705-5_6

metric is referred to as an *event*. For example, an event could be a request arrival, a remote procedure call, a processor interrupt, a memory reference, a network access, a failure of a given system component, a rolled back database transaction, a detected denial of service attack, or a security breach. Four fundamental measurement strategies are distinguished: event-driven, tracing, sampling, and indirect measurement (Lilja, 2000).

Event-driven strategies record information required to derive a given metric only when specified events of interest occur. The system may have to be instrumented to monitor the respective events and record relevant information. The term *instrumentation*, in this context, refers to the insertion of the so-called monitoring hooks in the code that observe and record relevant information about the events of interest. For example, counting the number of random disk accesses during the execution of a benchmark can be implemented by incrementing a counter in the respective I/O interrupt handling routine of the operating system and dumping the value of the counter at the end of the benchmark execution.

One important aspect of measurement strategies is how much *overhead* they introduce. The measurement overhead may or may not intrude upon the system behavior, and if it does, such intrusion may lead to a change in the observed behavior, a phenomenon often referred to as *perturbation*. The overhead of an event-driven strategy depends on the frequency of the events being monitored. If the events of interest occur very frequently, the overhead may be significant possibly leading to perturbation. In that case, the behavior of the system under test may change and no longer be representative of the typical or average behavior. Therefore, event-driven strategies are usually considered for events with low to moderate frequency.

Tracing strategies are similar to event-driven strategies; however, in addition to counting how often events of interest occur, they record further information about each event (e.g., information on the system state at the time of the event) required to derive a given metric of interest. For example, in addition to observing each random disk access, one may be interested in the specific files accessed and whether data is read or written. Depending on how much information is stored, tracing may introduce significant overhead. Moreover, the time required to store the additional information may significantly alter the behavior of the system under test.

Sampling strategies record relevant information about the system state in equidistant time intervals. The advantage of such strategies is that the overhead they introduce is independent of the frequency with which the respective events of interest occur. Instead, the overhead depends on the sampling frequency, which can be configured by the user. In contrast to the previous two strategies, sampling strategies do not observe every occurrence of the events of interest. They observe only a statistical sample of the execution behavior, which means that infrequent events may be completely missed. Thus, the sampling frequency should be configured to have the resolution necessary to obtain a representative sample of the events of interest. Given that only a statistical sample of the execution is observed, repetitive sampling-based measurements may produce different results. Sampling strategies are typically used for high frequency events where exact event counts are not required and a statistical summary is enough.

Figure 6.1 illustrates the three measurement strategies considered so far.

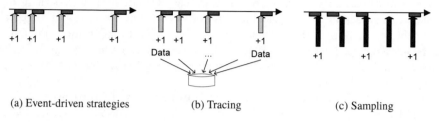

(a) Event-driven strategies   (b) Tracing   (c) Sampling

Fig. 6.1: Measurement techniques and strategies

Indirect measurement strategies are used in cases where the metric of interest cannot be measured directly by observing certain events. In such cases, other metrics that can be measured directly are used to derive or deduce the metric of interest. For example, based on the service demand law (see Chapter 7, Section 7.1.2), the service demand of requests at a given resource can be derived from measured throughput and utilization data.

6.2 Interval Timers

An *interval timer* is a tool for measuring the duration of any activity during the execution of a program. Interval timers are typically used in performance measurements to measure the execution time of a program or a portion of it. Most interval timers are implemented by using a counter variable incremented on each tick of a system clock. Interval timers are based on counting the number of ticks between the beginning and end of the respective activity whose duration needs to be measured. The clock ticks are counted by observing the counter variable at the respective points in the program execution (Figure 6.2).

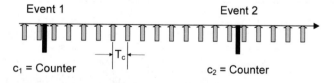

Fig. 6.2: Interval timers

More specifically, based on how an interval timer is implemented, we distinguish between *hardware timers* and *software timers* (Lilja, 2000). In hardware timers, the counter variable is incremented directly by a free-running hardware clock. The counter is typically set to 0 when the system is powered up and its value shows the number of clock ticks that have occurred since then. In software-based timers, the counter variable is not directly incremented; instead, the hardware clock periodically generates a processor interrupt, and the respective interrupt-service routine triggers a process to increment the counter variable accessible to application programs. Depending on the timer implementation, the process of accessing and updating the counter variable may span several software layers (e.g., operating system, virtual machine, middleware).

Denote with T_c the period of time between two updates of the counter variable, referred to as *clock period* or *resolution* of the timer. If c_1 and c_2 are the values of the counter at the beginning and end of the activity whose duration needs to be measured, then the duration reported by the timer is $(c_2 - c_1)T_c$.

6.2.1 Timer Rollover

An important characteristic of an interval timer is the number of bits available for the counting variable, which determines the longest interval that can be measured using the timer. An n bit counter can store values between 0 and $(2^n - 1)$. Table 6.1 shows the longest interval that can be measured for different values of the resolution T_c and the counter size n.

A timer's counter variable is said to "roll over" to zero when its value transitions from the maximum value $(2^n - 1)$ to 0. If a timer's counter rolls over during an activity whose duration is being measured using the timer, then the value $(c_2 - c_1)T_c$ reported by the timer will be negative. Therefore, applications that use a timer must either ensure that roll over can never occur when using the timer or they should detect and correct invalid measurements caused by roll over.

Table 6.1: Length of time until timer rollover (Lilja, 2000)

Resolution (T_c)	Counter size in bits (n)		
	16	32	64
10 ns	655 μs	43 s	58.5 centuries
1 μs	65.5 ms	1.2 h	5,580 centuries
100 μs	6.55 s	5 days	585,000 centuries
1 ms	1.1 min	50 days	5,850,000 centuries

6.2.2 Timer Accuracy

The accuracy of measurements obtained through an interval timer generally depends on two factors: the timer resolution and the timer overhead.

The timer resolution T_c is the smallest time duration that can be detected by the timer. Given that the timer resolution is finite, there is a random *quantization error* in all measurements made using the timer (Lilja, 2000). This is illustrated in Figure 6.3, which shows an example of an interval timer reporting different duration of the same activity (e.g., execution of an operation with a fixed execution time) depending on its exact starting point. Repeated measurements of the same activity duration will lead to values $X \pm \Delta$. This quantization effect was already discussed in Chapter 4 (Section 4.2.1) in the context of random measurement errors.

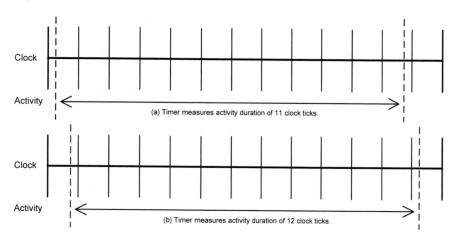

Clock

Activity

(a) Timer measures activity duration of 11 clock ticks.

Clock

Activity

(b) Timer measures activity duration of 12 clock ticks.

Fig. 6.3: Example of random quantization errors in timer measurements

Given that it is unlikely that the actual activity duration T_a is exactly a whole number factor of the timer's clock period, T_a will normally lie within the range $nT_c < T_a < (n + 1)T_c$, where T_c is the timer's clock period. Thus, the measured duration T_m reported by the timer will be the actual duration T_a rounded up or down by one clock period. The rounding is completely unpredictable, introducing random quantization errors into all measurements reported by the timer. The smaller the timer's clock period, the more accurate its measurements will be.

The second factor that affects the accuracy of a timer is its overhead. An interval timer is typically used like a stopwatch to measure the duration of a given activity. For example, the following pseudocode illustrates how a timer can be used within a program to measure the execution time of a critical section in a program:[1]

---

[1] A critical section is a section of code that accesses a shared resource (data structure or device) that must not be concurrently accessed by more than one thread of execution. Critical sections must be executed serially; that is, only one thread can execute a critical section at any given time.

```
time_start = read_timer();
<critical section to be measured>
time_end = read_timer();
elapsed_time = (time_end - time_start) * clock_period;
```

Figure 6.4 shows an exemplary time line of the execution. As we can see from the figure, the time we actually measure includes more than the duration of the critical section of which we are interested. This is because accessing the timer normally requires a minimum of one memory-read operation to read the value of the timer and one memory-write operation to store the read value. These operations must be performed at the beginning and end of the measured activity.

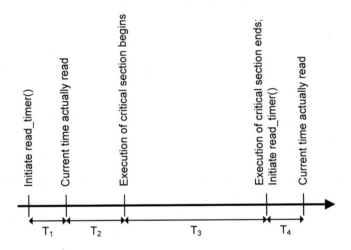

Fig. 6.4: Timer overhead

In Figure 6.4, T_1 and T_4 represent the time required to read the value of the timer's counter variable, whereas T_2 represents the time required to store the value that was obtained. The actual duration of the event we are trying to measure is given by $T_a = T_3$. However, due to the delays accessing the timer, we end up measuring $T_m = T_2 + T_3 + T_4$ instead. Thus, $T_a = T_m - (T_2 + T_4) = T_m - (T_1 + T_2)$, since $T_4 = T_1$. The value of $T_o = T_1 + T_2$ is referred to as *timer overhead* (Lilja, 2000).

If the activity being measured has a duration significantly higher than the timer overhead ($T_a \gg T_o$), then the latter can simply be ignored. Otherwise, the timer overhead should be estimated and subtracted from the measurements. However, estimating the timer overhead may be challenging given that it often exhibits high variability in repeated measurements. We refer the reader to Kuperberg, Krogmann, et al. (2009) for a platform-independent method to quantify the accuracy and overhead of a timer without inspecting its implementation.

Generally, measurements of intervals with duration of the same order of magnitude as the timer overhead are not reliable. A rule of thumb is that for timer measurements to be reliable, the duration of the activity being measured should be 100–1,000 times larger than the timer overhead.

Different timer implementations exhibit different overhead. Evaluating the quality of a given interval timer involves analyzing several properties, such as accuracy, overhead, and timer stability, all of which are platform-dependent. A composite metric, coupled with a benchmarking approach for evaluating the quality of timers, can be found in Kuperberg and Reussner (2011).

6.2.3 Measuring Short Intervals

Given that a timer's clock period T_c is the shortest time interval it can detect, the question arises how a timer can be used to measure the duration of intervals shorter than T_c. More generally, the quantization effect makes it hard to measure intervals that are not significantly larger than the timer's resolution.

In Chapter 4, Section 4.2.3.3, we presented an indirect measurement approach to estimate the execution time of a very short operation (shorter than the clock period of the used interval timer). The idea was to measure the total time for several consecutive repetitions of the operation and divide this time by the number of repetitions to calculate the mean time for one execution. We assume that the number of repetitions is chosen high enough, such that the resolution of the used interval timer can measure the cumulative times. By repeating this procedure n times, we obtain a sample of estimated times for one operation execution and can use this to derive a confidence interval for the mean execution time of the operation. As discussed in Chapter 4, Section 4.2.3.3, while this approach provides a workaround for the issue, the normalization has a penalty. On the one hand, the sample size is reduced, leading to loss of information. On the other hand, we obtain a confidence interval for the mean value of the aggregated operations, as opposed to the individual operations themselves. This leads to reducing the variation and thus the resulting confidence interval might be more narrow than it would have been if applied to the measured duration of single executions.

We now present an alternative approach to measure short intervals (Lilja, 2000). Assume that we would like to measure an interval of size T_a using a timer with a resolution (i.e., clock period) $T_c > T_a$. Short intervals are hard to measure even in cases where $T_a \approx n \times T_c$ for n a small integer.

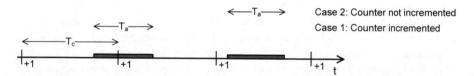

Fig. 6.5: Approximate measures of short intervals

There are two possible cases when measuring an interval of size $T_a < T_c$ (see Figure 6.5): (1) the measured interval begins in one clock period and ends in the next, that is, there is one clock tick during the measurement incrementing the timer's counter variable and (2) the measured interval begins and ends within the same clock period, that is, there is no clock tick during the measurement. Each measurement can thus be seen as a Bernoulli experiment. The outcome of the experiment is 1 with probability $p = T_a/T_c$ corresponding to the first case (counter is incremented during measurement) and 0 with probability $(1-p)$ corresponding to the second case (counter is not incremented during measurement). If we repeat this experiment n times and count the number of times the outcome is 1, the resulting distribution will be approximately Binomial. This is because we cannot assume that the n repetitions are independent, which is required for a true Binomial distribution. The approximation will be more accurate if we introduce a random delay between the successive repetitions of the Bernoulli experiment. If the number of times we get outcome 1 is k, then the ratio $\hat{p} = k/n$ will be a point estimate of p (see Chapter 4, Section 4.2.4). From this, we can derive an estimate for the duration of the measured interval as follows:

$$p \approx \frac{k}{n} \Rightarrow \frac{T_a}{T_c} \approx \frac{k}{n} \Rightarrow T_a \approx \frac{k}{n} T_c \tag{6.1}$$

Furthermore, as shown in Chapter 4, Section 4.2.4, the following approximate confidence interval for p can be derived:

$$P\left(\hat{p} - z_{\alpha/2}\sqrt{\frac{\hat{p}(1-\hat{p})}{n}} \leq p \leq \hat{p} + z_{\alpha/2}\sqrt{\frac{\hat{p}(1-\hat{p})}{n}}\right) \approx 1 - \alpha. \tag{6.2}$$

Multiplying both sides by T_c and considering that $pT_c = T_a$, we obtain the following confidence interval for T_a:

$$P\left(\hat{p}T_c - z_{\alpha/2}T_c\sqrt{\frac{\hat{p}(1-\hat{p})}{n}} \leq T_a \leq \hat{p}T_c + z_{\alpha/2}T_c\sqrt{\frac{\hat{p}(1-\hat{p})}{n}}\right) \approx 1 - \alpha. \tag{6.3}$$

6.3 Performance Profiling

Performance profiling is a process of measuring how much time a system spends in certain states that are of interest for understanding its behavior. A *profile* provides a summary of the execution behavior in terms of the fraction of time spent in different states, for example, the fraction of time spent executing a given function or method, the fraction of time the operating system is running in kernel mode, the fraction of time doing storage or network I/O, or the fraction of time a Java Virtual Machine is running garbage collection. It is often distinguished between *application profiling* and *systems profiling*, where the former stresses that a specific application is being profiled in the case of multiple applications running on the system under test. Application profiling normally aims to identify hotspots in the application code that may be potential performance bottlenecks, whereas systems profiling typically aims to identify system-level performance bottlenecks. A profile may be used as a basis for performance tuning and optimization; for example, heavily loaded application components may be refactored and optimized or system configuration parameters such as buffer sizes, cache sizes, load balancing policies, or resource allocations may be tuned.

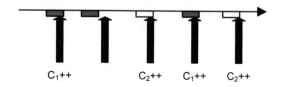

Fig. 6.6: Profiling implemented using sampling-based measurement

Performance profiling is normally implemented using a sampling-based measurement approach. The execution is periodically interrupted to inspect the system state and store relevant information about the states of interest (see Figure 6.6). Assume that there are k states of interest and the goal is to determine the fraction of time spent in each of them. Denote with C_i for $i = 1, 2, ..., k$ the number of times the system was observed to be in state i when interrupted during the profiling experiment. In that case, the interrupt service routine would simply check the current state and increment the respective element of an integer array used to store C_i. At the end of the experiment, a histogram of the number of times each state was observed would be available (see Figure 6.7).

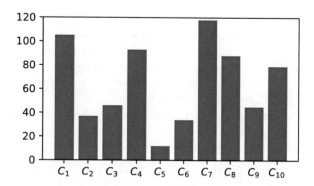

Fig. 6.7: Histogram of state frequencies

Assume that the system is interrupted n times to inspect its state. An estimate of the fraction of time the system spends in state i is given by $\hat{p}_i = C_i/n$. The confidence intervals for proportions that we derived in Chapter 4 (Section 4.2.4) can now be used to obtain an interval estimate of the fraction of time p_i the system spends in state i. Applying Equation (4.31) from Chapter 4, Section 4.2.4, we obtain the following confidence interval for p_i:

$$P\left(\hat{p}_i - z_{\alpha/2}\sqrt{\frac{\hat{p}_i(1 - \hat{p}_i)}{n}} \le p_i \le \hat{p}_i + z_{\alpha/2}\sqrt{\frac{\hat{p}_i(1 - \hat{p}_i)}{n}}\right) \approx 1 - \alpha. \qquad (6.4)$$

We note that the above approach works under the assumption that the interrupts occur asynchronously with respect to any events in the system under test. This is important to ensure that the observations of the system state are independent of each other.

Example A Java program is run for $10\,s$ and interrupted every $40\,\mu s$ for profiling. The program was observed 36,128 times to execute method A. We apply Equation (6.4) to derive a 90% confidence interval for the time spent in method A.

$$m = 36{,}128$$
$$n = 10\,s/40\,\mu s = 250{,}000$$
$$p = m/n = 0.144512 \qquad\qquad\qquad (6.5)$$
$$(c_1, c_2) = 0.144512 \mp 1.645\sqrt{\frac{0.144512(0.855488)}{250{,}000}} = (0.144, 0.146)$$

We conclude with 90% confidence that the program spent 14.4–14.6% of its time in method A.

6.4 Event Tracing

A performance profile provides a high-level summary of the execution behavior of an application or system; however, this summary does not provide any information about the order in which events occur. Event-driven tracing strategies can be used to capture such information. A *trace* is a dynamic list of events generated by the application (or system under study) as it executes (Lilja, 2000). A trace may include any information about the monitored events of interest that is relevant for characterizing the application behavior. In the following, we introduce *call path tracing*, a technique for extracting a control flow graph of an application.

6.4.1 Call Path Tracing

Consider a system that processes transactions requested by clients.[2] An executed system transaction translates into a path through a control flow graph whose edges are basic blocks (Allen, 1970). A *basic block* is a portion of code within an application with only one entry point and only one exit point. A path through the control flow graph can be represented by a sequence of references to basic blocks. It is assumed that the system can be instrumented to monitor the so-called *event records*.

Definition 6.1 (Event Record) An *event record* is defined as a tuple $e = (l, t, s)$, where l refers to the beginning or end of a basic block, t is a timestamp, and s identifies a transaction. The event record indicates that l has been reached by s at time t.

In order to *trace* individual transactions, a set of event records has to be obtained at run time. The set of gathered event records then has to be: (1) partitioned and (2) sorted. The set of event records is partitioned in equivalence classes $[a]_{\mathcal{R}}$ according to the following equivalence relation:

Definition 6.2 $\mathcal{R}$ is a relation on event records: Let $a = (l_1, t_1, s_1)$ and $b = (l_2, t_2, s_2)$ be event records obtained through instrumentation. Then, a relates to b, that is, $a \sim_{\mathcal{R}} b$, if and only if $s_1 = s_2$.

Sorting the event records of an equivalence class in chronological order leads to a sequence of event records that can be used to derive a call path trace. We refer to Briand et al. (2006), Israr et al. (2007), and Anderson et al. (2009) where call path traces are transformed, for example, to UML sequence diagrams.

To reduce the overhead of monitoring system transactions, there exist two orthogonal approaches: (1) *quantitative throttling*—throttling the number of transactions that are actually monitored—and (2) *qualitative throttling*—throttling the level of detail at which transactions are monitored. Existing work on (1) is presented, for example, in Gilly et al. (2009). The authors propose an adaptive time slot scheduling for the monitoring process. The monitoring frequency depends on the load of the system. In phases of high load, the monitoring frequency is throttled. An example of an approach based on (2) is presented in Ehlers and Hasselbring (2011); this approach supports adaptive monitoring of requests; that is, monitoring probes can be enabled or disabled depending on what information about the requests should be monitored.

When extracting call path traces, one is typically interested in obtaining control flow statistics that summarize the most important control flow information in a compact manner. In the rest of this section, we describe the typical control flow statistics of interest by looking at an example.

---

[2] The term *transaction* here is used loosely to refer to any unit of work or processing task executed in the system, for example, an HTTP request, a database transaction, a batch job, a web service request, or a microservice invocation. Transactions, in this context, are also commonly referred to as *requests* or *jobs*.

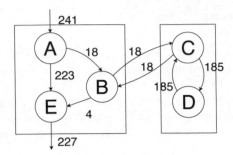

Fig. 6.8: Example call path

Consider the example call path shown in Figure 6.8. We have two different components, depicted as rectangles. The first component contains the basic blocks A, B, and E; the second component contains the remaining basic blocks C and D. An arrow between two basic blocks denotes that the control flow is handed over from one node to another (e.g., by calling a method or service).

The numbers next to the arrows indicate the amount of event records that took the respective explicit call path. The two components could, for example, correspond to two different web servers, communicating over the Internet, while offering certain method interfaces in the form of A, B, C, D, and E. As another example, the components could also correspond to two methods, with A, B, C, D, and E each being a portion of code executed when the methods are called. Here, the first method calls the second method and is then blocked until the second method returns the control flow back to the first method. The granularity of a basic block depends on the specific use case, but also on the capabilities of the tracing tool.

In our example, Figure 6.8 shows 241 event records that enter the first component and trigger execution of basic block A. The latter contains a branch, where 223 of all transactions are directly forwarded to basic block E, and 18 transactions are forwarded to basic block B. For each of those 18 incoming transactions, B is assumed to issue an external call to basic block C in the second component. Basic block C contains a loop that triggers 185 executions of basic block D for each of the 18 transactions. C aggregates the returned information for each of the 18 requests and sends the response back to B. B implements a filtering step based on the information provided by C and therefore again implements a branching, where only four of the 18 received transactions are forwarded to E. Finally, E processes and returns all transactions received by both A and B.

From the described example, we can outline four basic types of information obtainable by call path tracing:

- Call frequencies,
- Branching probabilities,
- Loop iteration counts, and
- Processing times and response times.

We now discuss each of these in more detail.

6.4.1.1 Call Frequencies

By tracing the control flow of transactions between the different basic blocks, it is easy to simply count the frequencies of ingoing and outgoing transactions for each block. Figure 6.8 shows the frequencies at the edges connecting the basic blocks. We usually distinguish between internal and external calls. An *external* call is a call between two different components. In Figure 6.8 components are depicted as rectangles—basic blocks A, B, and E form one component, and basic blocks C and D form another component. Hence, the call from B to C can be seen as an external call.

The calls triggered by a basic block can be easily derived by dividing the number of outgoing edges by the number of incoming edges as measured by call path tracing.

6.4.1.2 Branching Probabilities

Branching probabilities describe the probability of entering each branch transition for every entry of a branch. In Figure 6.8, basic block A represents a branch between forwarding an incoming transaction to block E, or forwarding it to block B. Determining the branching probabilities of a given block is very important for analyzing the performance of a given control flow. For example, Figure 6.8 exhibits very different behavior for transactions forwarded directly to E compared to transactions forwarded to B first. Note that it is also possible to have more than two branch transitions, for example, three, four, or more different actions to take for any specific transaction. In order to extract the respective branching probabilities, one can divide the number of transactions of each particular branch transition by the number of total entries into the branch.

6.4.1.3 Loop Iteration Counts

Similarly to branching probabilities, loop iteration counts are important parameters when analyzing the control flow of an application. Loop iteration counts quantify, how often a specific basic block is entered due to the execution of a loop as part of a transaction. This behavior can be seen at basic block D in Figure 6.8, where basic block C calls basic block D in a loop. The loop iteration counts can be quantified by dividing the number of loop iterations (i.e., sum of loop body repetitions by all transactions) by the number of loop entries (i.e., number of transactions reaching the beginning of the loop).

6.4.1.4 Processing Times and Response Times

The processing time of an individual basic block, as well as of an entire transaction (i.e., the transaction response times), can be easily determined based on the timestamps of the event records corresponding to the beginning and end of the considered basic block and transaction, respectively.

In addition to the above described control flow statistics, tracing tools typically also report transaction throughput and resource utilization data. This allows one to determine further parameters such as *service demands*—also referred to as *resource demands*—of the individual basic blocks or entire transactions. The service/resource demand of a transaction at a given system resource is defined as the average total service time of the transaction at the resource over all visits to the resource. The term resource demand will be introduced more formally in Chapter 7, Section 7.1. Chapter 17 presents a detailed survey and systematization of different approaches to the statistical estimation of resource demands based on easy to measure system-level and application-level metrics. Resource demands can be considered at different levels of granularity, for example, for individual basic blocks or for entire transactions.

6.4.2 Performance Monitoring and Tracing Tools

A number of commercial and open-source monitoring tools exist that support the extraction of call path traces and estimation of the call path parameters discussed above.

Commercial representatives are, for example, Dynatrace,[3] New Relic,[4] AppDynamics,[5] or DX APM.[6] Commercial tools normally have several advantages including product stability, available customer support as well as integrated tooling for analysis and visualization, providing fast and detailed insights into execution behavior.

In addition, many open-source and academic tools are available, such as inspectIT Ocelot,[7] Zipkin,[8] Jaeger,[9] Pinpoint,[10] or Kieker.[11] Open-source tools are often limited in their applicability, supported programming languages, and tooling support; however, they have the advantage of flexibility, extensibility, and low cost. For example, the Kieker framework (Hoorn et al., 2012) has been heavily used and extended

---

[3] https://www.dynatrace.com

[4] https://newrelic.com

[5] https://www.appdynamics.com

[6] https://www.broadcom.com/products/software/aiops/application-performance-management

[7] https://www.inspectit.rocks

[8] https://zipkin.io

[9] https://www.jaegertracing.io

[10] https://naver.github.io/pinpoint

[11] http://kieker-monitoring.net

over the past 10 years by performance engineers both from industry and academia. Some examples of academic works employing Kieker for research purposes include (Brosig et al., 2011; Grohmann et al., 2019; Spinner et al., 2015; Walter, 2018).

6.5 Concluding Remarks

This chapter introduced different measurement techniques that can be used in practice to derive the values of common metrics. While most presented techniques are useful for performance metrics, some of them can also be applied generally for other types of metrics. The chapter started with a brief introduction to the basic measurement strategies, including event-driven, tracing, sampling, and indirect measurement. We then looked at interval timers, which are typically used to measure the execution time of a program or a portion of it. We discussed in detail several issues related to interval timers, that is, timer rollover, timer accuracy, and strategies for measuring short intervals. Next, we looked at performance profiling, which provides means to measure how much time a system spends in different states. A performance profile provides a high-level summary of the execution behavior of an application or a system; however, this summary does not provide any information about the order in which events occur. Thus, at the end of the chapter, event-driven tracing strategies were introduced, which can be used to capture such information. A trace is a dynamic list of events generated by the application (or system under study) as it executes; it may include any information about the monitored events of interest that is relevant for characterizing the application behavior. We focused on call path tracing—a technique for extracting a control flow graph of the application. Finally, the chapter was wrapped up with an overview of commercial and open-source monitoring tools that support the extraction of call path traces and the estimation of call path statistics, such as call frequencies, branching probabilities, loop iteration counts, and response times.

References

Allen, F. E. (1970). "Control Flow Analysis". *ACM SIGPLAN Notices*, 5(7). ACM: New York, NY, USA, pp. 1–19 (cited on p. 141).

Anderson, E., Hoover, C., Li, X., and Tucek, J. (2009). "Efficient Tracing and Performance Analysis for Large Distributed Systems". In: *Proceedings of the 2009 IEEE International Symposium on Modeling, Analysis and Simulation of Computer and Telecommunication Systems (MASCOTS 2009)*. (London, UK). IEEE Computer Society: Washington, DC, USA, pp. 1–10 (cited on p. 141).

Briand, L. C., Labiche, Y., and Leduc, J. (2006). "Toward the Reverse Engineering of UML Sequence Diagrams for Distributed Java Software". *IEEE Transactions on Software Engineering*, 32(9). IEEE Computer Society: Washington, DC, USA, pp. 642–663 (cited on p. 141).

Brosig, F., Huber, N., and Kounev, S. (2011). "Automated Extraction of Architecture-Level Performance Models of Distributed Component-Based Systems". In: *Proceedings of the 26th IEEE/ACM International Conference on Automated Software Engineering (ASE 2011)*. (Oread, Lawrence, Kansas). IEEE Computer Society: Washington, DC, USA, pp. 183–192 (cited on p. 145).

Ehlers, J. and Hasselbring, W. (2011). "Self-Adaptive Software Performance Monitoring". In: *Software Engineering 2011 – Fachtagung des GI-Fachbereichs Softwaretechnik*. Ed. by R. Reussner, M. Grund, A. Oberweis, and W. Tichy. Gesellschaft für Informatik e.V.: Bonn, Germany, pp. 51–62 (cited on p. 141).

Gilly, K., Alcaraz, S., Juiz, C., and Puigjaner, R. (2009). "Analysis of Burstiness Monitoring and Detection in an Adaptive Web System". *Computer Networks*, 53(5). Elsevier North-Holland, Inc.: Amsterdam, The Netherlands, pp. 668–679 (cited on p. 141).

Grohmann, J., Eismann, S., Elflein, S., Kistowski, J. von, Kounev, S., and Mazkatli, M. (2019). "Detecting Parametric Dependencies for Performance Models Using Feature Selection Techniques". In: *Proceedings of the 27th IEEE International Symposium on the Modeling, Analysis, and Simulation of Computer and Telecommunication Systems (MASCOTS 2019)*. (Rennes, France). IEEE Computer Society: Washington, DC, USA (cited on p. 145).

Hoorn, A. van, Waller, J., and Hasselbring, W. (2012). "Kieker: A Framework for Application Performance Monitoring and Dynamic Software Analysis". In: *Proceedings of the 3rd ACM/SPEC International Conference on Performance Engineering (ICPE 2012)*. (Boston, Massachusetts, USA). ACM: New York, NY, USA, pp. 247–248 (cited on p. 144).

Israr, T., Woodside, M., and Franks, G. (2007). "Interaction Tree Algorithms to Extract Effective Architecture and Layered Performance Models from Traces". *Journal of Systems and Software*, 80(4). Elsevier Science Inc.: Amsterdam, The Netherlands, pp. 474–492 (cited on p. 141).

Kuperberg, M., Krogmann, M., and Reussner, R. (2009). "TimerMeter: Quantifying Properties of Software Timers for System Analysis". In: *Proceedings of the 6th International Conference on Quantitative Evaluation of SysTems (QEST 2009)*. (Budapest, Hungary). IEEE: Piscataway, New Jersey, USA, pp. 85–94 (cited on p. 136).

Kuperberg, M. and Reussner, R. (2011). "Analysing the Fidelity of Measurements Performed with Hardware Performance Counters". In: *Proceedings of the 2nd ACM/SPEC International Conference on Performance Engineering (ICPE 2011)*. (Karlsruhe, Germany). ACM: New York, NY, USA, pp. 413–414 (cited on p. 137).

Lilja, D. J. (2000). *Measuring Computer Performance: A Practitioner's Guide.* Cambridge University Press: Cambridge, UK (cited on pp. 132–137, 140).

Spinner, S., Casale, G., Brosig, F., and Kounev, S. (2015). "Evaluating Approaches to Resource Demand Estimation". *Performance Evaluation*, 92. Elsevier Science: Amsterdam, The Netherlands, pp. 51–71 (cited on p. 145).

Walter, J. C. (2018). "Automation in Software Performance Engineering Based on a Declarative Specification of Concerns". PhD thesis. Würzburg, Germany: University of Würzburg (cited on p. 145).

Chapter 7
Operational Analysis and Basic Queueing Models

"All models are wrong, but some are useful."

—*George E. P. Box (1919-2013), British statistician*

In Chapter 1, we introduced the concept of system performance understood in a classical sense as the amount of useful work accomplished by a system compared to the time and resources used. Better performance normally means more work accomplished in shorter time or using less resources. To characterize the performance behavior of a system, performance metrics are used. In Chapter 3 (Section 3.3), we introduced the most common basic performance metrics used in practice: response time, throughput, and utilization.

In this chapter, we start by looking at some basic quantitative relationships, which can be used to evaluate a system's performance based on measured or known data, a process known as operational analysis (Section 7.1). Operational analysis can be seen as part of queueing theory, a discipline of stochastic theory and operations research, which provides general methods to analyze the queueing behavior of one or more service stations. In the second part of the chapter (Section 7.2), we provide a brief introduction to the basic notation and principles of queueing theory. While queueing theory has been applied successfully to different domains, for example, to model manufacturing lines or call center operation, in this chapter, we focus on using queueing theory for performance evaluation of computer systems. Nevertheless, the presented concepts and mathematical models are relevant for any processing system where the generic assumptions described in this chapter are fulfilled. The chapter is wrapped up with a case study, showing in a step-by-step fashion how to build a queueing model of a distributed software system and use it to predict the performance of the system for different workload and configuration scenarios.

S. Kounev et al., *Systems Benchmarking*, https://doi.org/10.1007/978-3-030-41705-5_7

7.1 Operational Analysis

In this section, we introduce a set of basic quantitative relationships between the most common performance metrics. These relationships are commonly known as *operational laws* and can be considered to be consistency requirements (i.e., invariant relations) for the values of performance quantities measured in any particular experiment (Menascé et al., 2004). The process of applying operational laws to derive performance metrics based on measured or known data is known as *operational analysis* (Denning and Buzen, 1978). This section introduces the most important operational laws, which are later revisited in Section 7.2 in the context of queueing theory. We refer the reader to Menascé et al. (2004) for a more detailed treatment of operational analysis.

Consider a system made up of K resources (e.g., servers, processors, storage devices, network links). The system processes requests sent by clients.[1] It is assumed that during the processing of a request, multiple resources can be used, and at each point in time, the request is either being served at a resource or is waiting for a resource to become available. The same resource may be used multiple times during the processing of a request; each time the resource is used, we will refer to this as the request *visiting* the resource. We assume that the system is observed for a finite period of time and that it is in *operational equilibrium* (i.e., steady state) during this period; that is, the number of submitted requests is equal to the number of completed requests.

We will use the notation shown in Table 7.1. Given that the system is assumed to be in operational equilibrium, the following obvious equations hold:

$$S_i = \frac{B_i}{C_i}, \quad U_i = \frac{B_i}{T},$$

$$X_i = \frac{C_i}{T}, \quad \lambda_i = \frac{A_i}{T},$$

$$X_0 = \frac{C_0}{T}, \quad V_i = \frac{C_i}{C_0},$$

$$\lambda_i = X_i.$$

(7.1)

Example During a period of 1 min, 240 requests arrive at a server and 240 requests are completed. The server's CPU is busy for 36 s in this time period. If the server

---

[1] The term *request* here is used loosely to refer to any unit of work or processing task executed in the system, for example, an HTTP request, a database transaction, a batch job, a web service request, or a microservice invocation. Requests in this context are also commonly referred to as *customers*, *jobs*, or *transactions*.

Table 7.1: Notation used in operational analysis (Menascé et al., 2004)

Symbol	Meaning
K	Number of resources in the system
T	Length of time during which the system is observed
B_i	Total length of time during which resource i is busy in the observation period
A_i	Total number of service requests (i.e., arrivals) to resource i
A_0	Total number of requests submitted to the system
C_i	Total number of service completions (i.e., departures) at resource i
C_0	Total number of requests processed by the system
V_i	Average number of times resource i is visited (i.e., used) during the processing of a request, referred to as *visit ratio*
λ_i	Arrival rate at resource i (i.e., average number of service requests that arrive per unit of time)
S_i	Average *service time* of a request at resource i per visit to the resource (i.e., the average time the request spends receiving service from the resource excluding waiting/queueing time)
D_i	Average total service time of a request at resource i over all visits to the resource, referred to as the *service demand* at resource i
U_i	Utilization of resource i (i.e., the fraction of time the resource is busy serving requests)
X_i	Throughput of resource i (i.e., the number of service completions per unit of time)
X_0	System throughput (i.e., the number of requests processed per unit of time)
R	Average request response time (i.e., the average time it takes to process a request including both the waiting and service time in the system)
N	Average number of active requests in the system, either waiting for service or being served

uses no resources apart from the CPU, and it only has a single request class, what is the arrival rate, the CPU utilization, the mean CPU service demand, and the system throughput?

$$K = 1, \quad T = 60 \text{ s}, \quad A_0 = A_1 = 240, \quad C_0 = C_1 = 240, \quad B_1 = 36 \text{ s},$$

$$\lambda_1 = \frac{A_1}{T} = \frac{240}{60 \text{ s}} = 4 \text{ req/s}, \quad U_1 = \frac{B_1}{T} = \frac{36 \text{ s}}{60 \text{ s}} = 0.6 = 60\%, \tag{7.2}$$

$$S_1 = \frac{B_1}{C_1} = \frac{36 \text{ s}}{240} = 0.15 \text{ s}, \quad X_0 = \frac{C_0}{T} = \frac{240}{60 \text{ s}} = 4 \text{ req/s}.$$

In the following, we introduce the five most common operational laws providing the basis for operational analysis.

7.1.1 Utilization Law

The utilization law states that the utilization of resource i is given by the request arrival rate λ_i multiplied by the average service time S_i per visit to the resource; that is,

$$U_i = S_i \times \lambda_i = S_i \times X_i. \tag{7.3}$$

Proof

$$U_i = \frac{B_i}{T} = \frac{\frac{B_i}{C_i}}{\frac{T}{C_i}} = \frac{\frac{B_i}{C_i}}{\frac{1}{\frac{C_i}{T}}} = \frac{S_i}{\frac{1}{X_i}} = S_i \times X_i = S_i \times \lambda_i. \tag{7.4}$$

Example A program computes 190 matrix multiplications per second. If each matrix multiplication requires 1.62 billions of floating point operations, and the underlying CPU can process up to 380 GFLOPS (billions of floating point operations per second), what is the utilization of the CPU?

$$K = 1, \quad X_1 = 190,$$

$$S_1 = \frac{1.62}{360} = 0.0045 \text{ s}, \tag{7.5}$$

$$U_1 = S_1 \times X_1 = 0.0045 \times 190 = 0.855 = 85.5\%.$$

7.1.2 Service Demand Law

The *service demand D_i* (also referred to as *resource demand*) is defined as the average total service time of a request at resource i over all visits to the resource.[2] The service demand law states that the service demand of a request at resource i is given by the utilization of resource i divided by the system throughput X_0, that is,

$$D_i = \frac{U_i}{X_0}. \tag{7.6}$$

Proof

$$D_i = V_i \times S_i = \frac{C_i}{C_0} \times \frac{B_i}{C_i} = \frac{B_i}{C_0} = \frac{U_i \times T}{C_0} = \frac{U_i}{\frac{C_0}{T}} = \frac{U_i}{X_0}. \tag{7.7}$$

---

[2] In this book, we use the terms service demand and resource demand interchangeably.

Example A program that calculates matrix multiplications is run 180 times within 5 min. For this time period, the underlying CPU reports a utilization of 30%. What is the CPU service demand for a single program execution?

$$K = 1, \quad T = 5 \times 60\,\text{s} = 300\,\text{s},$$

$$X_0 = \frac{C_0}{T} = \frac{180}{300\,\text{s}} = 0.6\,\text{runs/s},$$

(7.8)

$$U_1 = 30\% = 0.3,$$

$$D_1 = \frac{U_1}{X_0} = \frac{0.3}{0.6} = 0.5\,\text{s}.$$

7.1.3 Forced Flow Law

By definition of the visit ratio V_i, resource i is visited (i.e., used) V_i times, on average, by each processed request. Therefore, if X_0 requests are processed per unit of time, resource i will be visited $V_i \times X_0$ times per unit of time. So the throughput of resource i, X_i, is given by

$$X_i = V_i \times X_0.$$

(7.9)

This result, known as forced flow law, allows one to compute the system throughput based on knowledge of the visit ratio and the throughput of any one resource in the system. In addition, knowing the visit ratios of all resources and the throughput of just one resource allows for calculation of the throughput of all other resources in the system.

Example A REST-based web service[3] accesses a file server five times and a database two times for every request. If the web service processes 525 requests in a 7 min interval, what is the average throughput of the web service, the file server, and the database?

---

[3] REST (REpresentational State Transfer) is an architectural style for developing web services, which is typically used to build lightweight web and mobile applications. Web services that conform to the REST architectural style provide interoperability between computer systems on the Internet. Nowadays, most public web services provide REST APIs (Application Programming Interfaces) and transfer data in a compact and easy-to-use data-interchange format—the JavaScript Object Notation (JSON).

$$X_{web\_service} = X_0 = \frac{C_0}{T} = \frac{525}{7 \times 60\,\text{s}} = 1.25\,\text{req/s,}$$

$$X_{file\_server} = V_{file\_server} \times X_0 = 5 \times 1.25 = 6.25\,\text{req/s,} \tag{7.10}$$

$$X_{database} = V_{database} \times X_0 = 2 \times 1.25 = 2.5\,\text{req/s.}$$

7.1.4 Little's Law

Little's law states that the average number of active requests N in the system (submitted requests whose processing has not been completed yet) is equal to the average time it takes to process a request (i.e., the request response time R) multiplied by the number of requests processed per unit of time (i.e., the system throughput X_0), that is,

$$N = R \times X_0. \tag{7.11}$$

We consider Little's law in the context of a system processing requests; however, it can generally be applied to any "black box" where some entities arrive, spend some time inside the black box, and then leave. Little's law states that the average number of entities in the black box N is equal to the average residence time R of an entity in the black box multiplied by the average departure rate X (throughput); that is, $N = R \times X$. This is illustrated in Figure 7.1. We refer to Little (1961) for a formal proof. Little's law holds under very general conditions; the only assumption is that the black box does not create nor destroy entities.

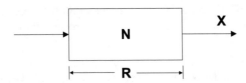

Fig. 7.1: Little's law (Menascé et al., 2004)

Example An enterprise resource planning system is implemented based on a microservice architecture consisting of many individual microservices. What is the average response time of the enterprise resource planning system if it is used by 273 employees at the same time and they execute 9,450 operations per hour?

$$T = 60 \min \times 60 \, s = 3{,}600 \, s,$$

$$X_0 = \frac{C_0}{T} = \frac{9{,}450}{3{,}600 \, s} = 2.625 \, \text{ops/s}, \tag{7.12}$$

$$R = \frac{N}{X_0} = \frac{273}{2.625} = 104 \, s.$$

7.1.5 Interactive Response Time Law

Assume that the system we consider is used by M clients each sitting at their own workstation and interactively accessing the system. This is an example of a *closed workload* scenario (see Chapter 8, Section 8.3.2). Clients send requests that are processed by the system. It is assumed that after a request is processed by the system, the respective client waits some time before sending the next request. We refer to this waiting time as "think time." Thus, clients alternate between "thinking" and waiting for a response from the system. If the average think time is denoted by Z, the interactive response time law (illustrated in Figure 7.2) states that the average response time R is given by

$$R = \frac{M}{X_0} - Z. \tag{7.13}$$

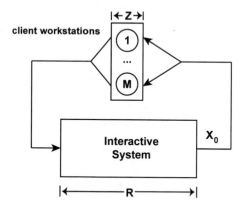

Fig. 7.2: Interactive response time law (Menascé et al., 2004)

Proof To show that the interactive response time law holds, we apply Little's law to the virtual black box composed of the client workstations and the system considered as a whole. We now consider the think time spent at the client workstation before sending a new request as being part of the respective request (e.g., preparation phase). Thus, each time the processing of a request is completed by the system and a response is sent back to the client, we consider this as one entity leaving our virtual black box and at the same time one new entity arriving at the virtual black box (corresponding to the next request). The total number of entities in our virtual black box is equal to the total number of clients M (at each point in time, each request is either at the respective client workstation or it is being processed inside the system). The rate at which requests are completed by the system is given by the system throughput X_0. The total average time a request spends in the virtual black box (i.e., client workstation plus system) is given by $Z + R$. Applying Little's law to the virtual black box, we obtain the following equation, which is equivalent to the interactive response time law:

$$M = X_0(Z + R). \tag{7.14}$$

Example A train booking and reservation system is used by 50 employees. Each of them, on average, issues a request 5 s after receiving the result of the previous request. A request has an average CPU service demand of 0.1 s; a CPU utilization of 32% is observed. How long do employees have to wait on average until a request is completed?

$$X_0 = X_{CPU} = \frac{U_{CPU}}{D_{CPU}} = \frac{0.32}{0.1\,\text{s}} = 3.2\,\text{req/s},$$

$$\tag{7.15}$$

$$R = \frac{M}{X_0} - Z = \frac{50}{3.2} - 5\,\text{s} = 10.6\,\text{s}.$$

In summary, we introduced the following five operational laws:

Utilization law:	
$$U_i = S_i \times X_i$$	(7.16)
Service demand law:	
$$D_i = V_i \times S_i = \frac{U_i}{X_0}$$	(7.17)
Forced flow law:	
$$X_i = V_i \times X_0$$	(7.18)
Little's law:	
$$N = R \times X_0$$	(7.19)
Interactive response time law:	
$$R = \frac{M}{X_0} - Z$$	(7.20)

7.1.6 Multi-Class Versions of Operational Laws

The operational laws can be extended to the case where multiple types of requests are processed by the system. The measured quantities and derived metrics are then considered on a per *request class* basis. An index c is used to distinguish between the respective classes. The following multi-class versions of the operational laws hold (Menascé et al., 2004):

Utilization law:
$$U_{i,c} = S_{i,c} \times X_{i,c} \tag{7.21}$$

Service demand law:
$$D_{i,c} = V_{i,c} \times S_{i,c} = \frac{U_{i,c}}{X_{0,c}} \tag{7.22}$$

Forced flow law:
$$X_{i,c} = V_{i,c} \times X_{0,c} \tag{7.23}$$

Little's law:
$$N_c = R_c \times X_{0,c} \tag{7.24}$$

Interactive response time law:
$$R_c = \frac{M_c}{X_{0,c}} - Z_c \tag{7.25}$$

Most of the quantities in the multi-class versions of the operational laws can normally be easily measured by means of standard system monitoring tools based on the measurement techniques presented in Chapter 6. The only exception is for the utilization $U_{i,c}$ and the service time $S_{i,c}$. For example, monitoring tools can normally provide measurements of the total resource utilization U_i. However, partitioning the total utilization on a per request class basis is not trivial. While performance profiling tools can be used for this purpose (see Section 6.3 in Chapter 6), such tools normally incur instrumentation overhead, which might lead to perturbation impacting the system behavior. Also, suitable profiling tools may not be available for the specific environment. The utilization, broken down on a per request class basis (i.e., $U_{i,c}$), is mainly relevant for obtaining the service demands $D_{i,c}$. In Chapter 17, we look at techniques for estimating service demands (also referred to as resource demands) based on easy to measure high-level metrics.

7.1.7 Performance Bounds

Now that we introduced the basic operational laws, we present some further quantitative relationships between the most common performance metrics, which provide upper and lower bounds on the performance a system can achieve. The bounds can be classified into optimistic and pessimistic bounds and are typically used for bottleneck analysis. The term *bottleneck* is normally used to refer to the resource with the highest utilization. It is assumed that this resource will first be saturated as the load increases. If a bottleneck cannot be removed (e.g., by increasing the capacity of the respective resource), the system is considered non-scalable in terms of performance. In the following two subsections, we present two sets of performance bounds on the system throughput and response time. Optimistic bounds capture the largest possible throughput (X_{opt}) and the lowest possible response time (R_{opt}), while pessimistic bounds capture the lowest possible throughput (X_{pes}) and largest possible response time (R_{pes}):

$$X_{pes} \leq X \leq X_{opt}, \qquad R_{opt} \leq R \leq R_{pes}. \tag{7.26}$$

The optimistic bounds can be derived from the service demands (Menascé et al., 2004). We assume that the service demands are load-independent,[4] which is normally implicitly assumed in the context of operational analysis. The bounding behavior of a system is determined by its bottleneck resource, which is the resource with the largest service demand. Applying the service demand law, we obtain the following upper asymptotic bound on the throughput:

$$X_0 = \frac{U_i}{D_i} \leq \frac{1}{D_i} \leq \frac{1}{\max_{i=1..K}\{D_i\}}. \tag{7.27}$$

Given that a natural lower bound for the response time R is given by the sum of the service demands at all resources, applying Little's law, we obtain another upper asymptotic bound on the throughput:

$$N = R \times X_0 \geq \left(\sum_{i=1}^{K} D_i\right) \times X_0 \Leftrightarrow X_0 \leq \frac{N}{\sum_{i=1}^{K} D_i}. \tag{7.28}$$

In summary, the upper asymptotic bounds on the throughput are given by

$$X_0 \leq \min\left[\frac{1}{\max\{D_i\}}, \frac{N}{\sum_{i=1}^{K} D_i}\right]. \tag{7.29}$$

From Little's law and the upper asymptotic bounds, we obtain the following lower asymptotic bounds on the response time:

$$R = \frac{N}{X_0} \geq \frac{N}{\min\left[\frac{1}{\max\{D_i\}}, \frac{N}{\sum_{i=1}^{K} D_i}\right]} = \max\left[N \times \max\{D_i\}, \sum_{i=1}^{K} D_i\right], \tag{7.30}$$

$$R \geq \max\left[N \times \max\{D_i\}, \sum_{i=1}^{K} D_i\right]. \tag{7.31}$$

---

[4] A service demand is *load-independent* if it does not change as the request arrival rates and the induced utilization of system resources increase or decrease.

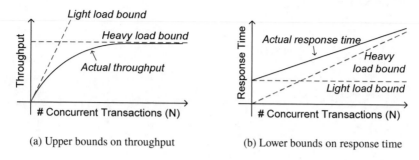

(a) Upper bounds on throughput

(b) Lower bounds on response time

Fig. 7.3: Asymptotic bounds

The asymptotic bounds on throughput and response time are illustrated in Figure 7.3. In addition to the asymptotic bounds, which are normally quite loose, based on a technique known as *balanced job bounds analysis*, the following tighter bounds can be derived (Menascé et al., 1994):

$$\frac{N}{\max\{D_i\}[K + N - 1]} \leq X_0 \leq \frac{N}{\text{avg}\{D_i\}[K + N - 1]}. \tag{7.32}$$

Figure 7.4 illustrates the relationship between the asymptotic bounds and balanced job bounds.

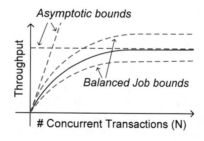

Fig. 7.4: Balanced job bounds (Menascé et al., 1994)

Example Fifty employees use an enterprise resource planning system that is implemented as a three-tier architecture. The web tier has a CPU service demand of 0.2 s, the business logic tier has a CPU service demand of 0.32 s, and the database tier has a CPU service demand of 0.15 s. Calculate the asymptotic and balanced job bounds for the throughput of the enterprise resource planning system under the assumption that all tiers use no resources apart from their CPU.

Asymptotic bounds:

$$X_0 \leq \min\left[\frac{1}{\max\{D_i\}}, \frac{N}{\sum_{i=1}^{K} D_i}\right],$$

$$X_0 \leq \min\left[\frac{1}{\max\{0.2, 0.32, 0.15\}}, \frac{50}{0.2 + 0.32 + 0.15}\right], \tag{7.33}$$

$$X_0 \leq \min[3.1, 74.6] = 3.1.$$

Balanced job bounds:

$$\frac{N}{\max\{D_i\}[K + N - 1]} \leq X_0 \leq \frac{N}{\operatorname{avg}\{D_i\}[K + N - 1]},$$

$$\frac{50}{\max\{0.2, 0.32, 0.15\}[3 + 50 - 1]} \leq X_0 \leq \frac{50}{\operatorname{avg}\{0.2, 0.32, 0.15\}[3 + 50 - 1]}, \tag{7.34}$$

$$3.0 \leq X_0 \leq 4.3.$$

7.2 Basic Queueing Theory

The fundamental operational laws presented in the previous section can be seen as part of *queueing theory*, a discipline of stochastic theory and operations research. It provides general methods to analyze the queueing behavior at one or more service stations and has been successfully applied to different domains in the last decades, for example, to model manufacturing lines or call center operations. When analyzing the performance of a computer system, queueing models are often used to describe the scheduling behavior at hardware resources such as processors, storage, and network devices. In this section, we provide a brief introduction to the basic notation and principles of queueing theory. A detailed treatment of the subject can be found in Lazowska et al. (1984), Bolch, Greiner, et al. (2006), and Harchol-Balter (2013).

7.2.1 Single Queues

The central concept of queueing theory is a *queue*, also referred to as a *service station* or *service center*. A queue (illustrated in Figure 7.5) consists of a waiting line and a server, which serves incoming *requests*.[5] Requests arrive at the queue and are processed immediately unless the server is already occupied. In the latter case, requests are put into the waiting line. After a request has been completely processed by the server, it departs from the queue. A queue can also have several servers, assumed to be identical, in which case we speak of a *multi-server queue*. The semantics are similar; that is, whenever a request arrives, it is processed at one of the servers that is currently free. If all servers are occupied, the request is put into the waiting line.

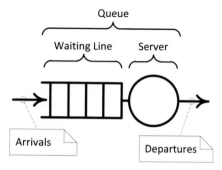

Fig. 7.5: Single queue (service station)

A number of terms are commonly used when describing the timing behavior of a queue. Requests may arrive at a queue at arbitrary points in time. The duration between successive request arrivals is referred to as *inter-arrival time*. The average number of requests that arrive per unit of time is referred to as *arrival rate*, denoted as λ. Each request requires a certain amount of processing at a server. The time a server is occupied by a request is called *service time*. The average number of requests that can be processed per unit of time at a single server is referred to as *service rate*, denoted as μ. The *mean service time* is then defined as $S = 1/\mu$ and specifies the time a server is occupied while processing a request on average. The time a request spends waiting in the waiting line is referred to as *queueing delay* or simply *waiting time*. The *response time* of a request is the total amount of time the request spends at the queue, that is, the sum of waiting time and service time.

When one request is completed, the next request to be served is selected from the requests in the queue according to a *scheduling strategy*. Typical scheduling strate-

---

[5] The term *request* here is used in the same way as in Section 7.1, that is, it refers loosely to any unit of work or processing task executed in the service station. Requests in this context are also commonly referred to as *customers*, *jobs*, or *transactions*.

gies are First-Come-First-Served (FCFS), where jobs are processed in the order of their arrival, Processor-Sharing (PS), where jobs are served concurrently each having an equal share of the total capacity (i.e., round-robin scheduling with infinitesimally small time slices), or Infinite-Server (IS), where all requests in the queue are scheduled immediately as if the queue were to have an infinite number of servers. When modeling computer systems, a FCFS scheduling strategy is typically used for queues representing I/O devices, whereas a PS scheduling strategy is commonly used for queues representing processors (CPUs) and an IS scheduling strategy for queues representing constant delays (e.g., average network delays).

There is a standard notation to describe a queue, known as *Kendall's notation* (Kendall, 1953). A queue is described by means of 6 parameters $A/S/m/B/K/SD$ defined in Table 7.2. The distribution components are characterized using short-hand symbols for the type of distribution, the most common of which are shown in Table 7.3. A deterministic distribution means that the respective times are constant. A general distribution means that the distribution is not known. This is commonly used for empirical distributions obtained from measurements if the underlying shape of the distribution is unknown. Parameters B and K are usually considered infinite and are thus often omitted in queue descriptions.

Table 7.2: Kendall's notation for a queue (A/S/m/B/K/SD)

Symbol	Meaning
A	Arrival process (i.e., distribution of the inter-arrival times)
S	Service process (i.e., distribution of the service times)
m	Number of servers in the service station
B	Maximum number of requests that a queue can hold (if missing, B is assumed to be infinite)
K	Maximum number of requests that can arrive at the queue, referred to as *system population* (if missing, K is assumed to be infinite)
SD	Scheduling strategy (by default FCFS)

Table 7.3: Symbols for types of distributions

Symbol	Meaning
M	Exponential (Markovian) distribution
D	Deterministic distribution (i.e., constant times without variance)
E_k	Erlang distribution with parameter k
G or GI	General (independent) distribution

In practice, many systems serve requests with different arrival and service characteristics (e.g., the service rate of read and write requests to a database may be different). In theory, it would be possible to use multi-modal distributions for such cases; however, this can complicate the parameterization and solution of queueing models (Harchol-Balter, 2013, Chapter 21). Instead, *multi-class queues* are used where multiple types of requests are distinguished, referred to as *request classes* or *workload classes*. Each workload class represents a set of requests with similar characteristics, described by their own arrival rate and service rate parameters.

For a given queue i, performance metrics can be considered for a *transient* point in time t or for the *steady state* (i.e., $t \rightarrow \infty$). Generally, a system is considered to be in a steady state if the variables that define its behavior are unchanging in time (Gagniuc, 2017). In the context of queues, it is normally assumed that after a queue has been in operation for a given amount of time (referred to as *transient phase* or *warm-up period*), it will eventually reach a steady state, in which performance metrics are stable. In the following, we are interested in the steady-state solution of a queue. More details on the transient solution of a queue can be found in Bolch, Greiner, et al. (2006). Typical performance metrics of interest include: the utilization of the queue, the queue length, the request throughput, and the request response time. The *utilization* U_i is the fraction of time in which the queue is busy serving requests. The *queue length* Q_i specifies the number of requests waiting for service (excluding those currently in service). The *throughput* $X_{i,c}$ (where c stands for workload class c) is the number of requests of class c leaving the queue per unit of time. If the maximum number of requests that arrive at a queue is unlimited, the relation $\lambda < \mu$ must hold, so that the queue is stable (i.e., a steady-state solution exists). The *response time* $R_{i,c}$ of requests from workload class c is defined as

$$R_{i,c} = W_{i,c} + S_{i,c}, \tag{7.35}$$

where $W_{i,c}$ is the time a request has to wait in the queue before being served, and $S_{i,c}$ is the service time of the request. The waiting time $W_{i,c}$ depends on a number of parameters including the scheduling strategy and the arrival and service processes (i.e., the request inter-arrival and service time distributions).

7.2.2 Queueing Networks

A queueing network (QN) consists of two or more queues (service stations) that are connected together and serve requests sent by clients. Requests are grouped into classes (workload classes) where each class contains requests that have similar arrival behavior and processing requirements. The routing of requests in the queueing network is specified by a probability matrix. Requests of class c departing from service station i will move to service station j with probability $p_{c,i,j}$ or leave the network with probability $p_{c,i,out} = 1 - \sum_j p_{c,i,j}$. Requests of class c can arrive from outside the network at service station i with a rate $r_{c,i}$.

Figure 7.6 shows an example with three queues, one multi-server queue and two single server queues. The multi-server queue represents a multicore CPU, and the two single server queues represent a disk drive and a network, respectively. The connections between the queues illustrate how requests are routed through the network of queues. An incoming request, after being processed by the CPU, is routed either to the disk or to the network. The routes are labeled with probabilities. With a probability of 0.8, a request coming from the CPU is routed to the disk queue. With a probability of 0.2, a request coming from the CPU is routed to the queue representing the network. If a request is completed at the disk or the network queue, the request either leaves the queueing network with a probability of p_{leave}, or it is immediately routed back to the CPU queue with a probability of $1 - p_{leave}$. A request may visit a queue multiple times while circulating through the queueing network. A request's total amount of service time at a queue, added up over all visits to the queue, is referred to as *service demand* or *resource demand* of the request at the queue.

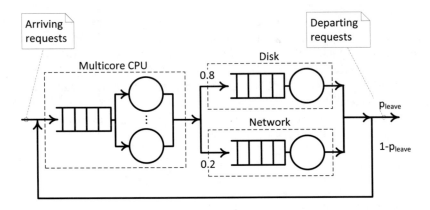

Fig. 7.6: Queueing network

A queueing network where the requests come from a source that is external of the queueing network and leave the network after service completion is referred to as *open*. A queueing network where there is no such external source of requests and there are no departing requests (i.e., the population of requests in the queueing network remains constant and is equal to the initial population) is referred to as *closed*. If a queueing network is open for some workload classes and closed for others, it is referred to as *mixed*.

In the context of queueing networks, the notation shown in Table 7.4 is typically used (similar to the notation we used in Section 7.1 when introducing operational analysis).

Table 7.4: Queueing network notation

Symbol	Meaning
K	Number of queues in the queueing network
C	Number of workload classes
λ_c	Average arrival rate of requests of class c in the queueing network (i.e., average number of requests that arrive per unit of time) (for open queueing networks)
$\lambda_{i,c}$	Average arrival rate of requests of class c at queue i
$\mu_{i,c}$	Service rate of requests of class c at queue i
$S_{i,c}$	Mean service time of requests of class c at queue i per visit to the queue (i.e., average time a request spends receiving service excluding waiting time)
$X_{i,c}$	Throughput of requests of class c at queue i (i.e., average number of service completions for class c per unit of time)
$V_{i,c}$	Average number of times queue i is visited during the processing of a request of class c, referred to as *visit ratio*
$X_{0,c}$	System throughput for class c (i.e., total number of requests of class c processed per unit of time)
U_i	Utilization of queue i (i.e., the fraction of time the queue is busy serving requests of any class)
$U_{i,c}$	Utilization of queue i due to requests of class c (i.e., the fraction of time the queue is busy serving requests of class c)
$D_{i,c}$	Service demand / resource demand (i.e., mean total service time of a request of class c at queue i over all visits to the queue)
$W_{i,c}$	Mean time a request of class c has to wait in the waiting line of queue i before being served
$R_{i,c}$	Mean response time of requests of class c at queue i (i.e., the average time it takes to process a request including both the waiting and service time in the queue)
$N_{i,c}$	Average number of requests of class c at queue i, either waiting for service or being served
$N_{0,c}$	Average number of requests of class c in the queueing network, either waiting for service or being served
Q_i	Average length of queue i (i.e., average number of requests in the queue waiting for service)
$Q_{i,c}$	Average number of requests of class c waiting for service at queue i

Given a queueing network, typical metrics of interest are the response time and throughput for each workload class and the utilization of each queue. In order to analyze a queueing network quantitatively, the queueing network's *workload* needs to be specified. For each workload class, the *workload intensity* and the *resource demands* for each visited queue have to be specified. How the workload intensity is characterized depends on whether it is a closed workload or an open workload. A closed workload is characterized by the number of requests; an open workload is characterized by the inter-arrival time of requests. A queueing network is said to be in *steady state* (or operational equilibrium) if the number of requests arriving at the queueing network per unit of time is equal to the number of requests departing from the queueing network, that is, the arrival rate is equal to the throughput. Closed formulas for the response times of requests are not easy to derive since they depend (among others) on the shape of the involved distributions (i.e., the inter-arrival time and service time distributions for each queue).

The solution of a queueing network with K service stations and C workload classes is based on deriving the steady-state probabilities $\pi(\mathbf{N_1}, \mathbf{N_2}, ..., \mathbf{N_K})$, where $\mathbf{N_i} = (n_1, n_2, ..., n_C)$ is a vector composed of the number of requests of each workload class c at service station i. Calculating the steady-state probabilities for a general queueing network requires construction of the complete state space. This can be a compute and memory-intensive task and suffers from the problem of *state space explosion* with increasing numbers of service stations and requests. However, the construction of the complete state space is not required for a special class of queueing networks called *product-form queueing networks*.

Product-form queueing networks have a special structure that allows one to compute the steady-state probabilities for the queueing network from the respective steady-state probabilities for the individual service stations using the following equation:

$$\pi(\mathbf{N_1}, \mathbf{N_2}, ..., \mathbf{N_K}) = \frac{1}{G} [\pi(\mathbf{N_1}) \cdot \pi(\mathbf{N_2}) \cdot .... \cdot \pi(\mathbf{N_K})], \qquad (7.36)$$

where G is a normalizing constant (Bolch, Greiner, et al., 2006, p. 281). Thus, a solution of the queueing network can be obtained by analyzing the steady-state probabilities of each service station independently. Kelly showed that every queueing network with *quasi-reversible queues* and *Markovian routing* has a product-form solution (Kelly, 1975, 1976). Quasi-reversibility means that "the current state, the past departures, and the future arrivals are mutually independent" (Balsamo, 2000). Markovian routing means that the routing of requests does not depend on the current state of the queueing network.

The BCMP theorem (Baskett et al., 1975) showed that this property holds for the following types of service stations:

1. $M/M/m$ with FCFS scheduling assuming that the service rate does not depend on the workload class,
2. $M/G/1$ with PS scheduling,
3. $M/G/\infty$ with IS scheduling, and
4. $M/G/1$ with LCFS scheduling with preemption.

The service rate distribution in cases (2), (3), and (4) are required to have rational Laplace transforms. In practice, this is no limitation since any exponential, hyperexponential, or hypoexponential distribution fulfills this requirement, and all other types of distributions can be approximated by a combination of these distributions (Cox, 1955).

Furthermore, Baskett et al. (1975) showed that the product-form property holds for these scheduling strategies even with certain forms of state-dependent service rates. Among others, the service rate may depend on the number of requests at a service station. Thus, queues with multiple servers are also allowed for PS and LCFS scheduling.

7.2.3 Operational Laws

The operational laws introduced in Section 7.1 provide a quick and simple way to determine certain average performance metrics of a queue. These laws are independent of the arrival and service processes, or the scheduling strategy. Therefore, they can be applied both to a single queue and to an entire queueing network. The only assumption is that the considered queue (or queueing network) is in steady state (operational equilibrium).

Consider a multi-server queue i with m_i servers. The most fundamental law in queueing theory is *Little's law*, which applied to queue i states that the average number of requests $N_{i,c}$ of workload class c at queue i is equal to the product of the request arrival rate λ_c and the average time $R_{i,c}$ requests spent in the queue (i.e., the response time); that is,

$$N_{i,c} = \lambda_c \cdot R_{i,c}. \tag{7.37}$$

The *utilization law*, applied in the context of queue i, states that

$$U_{i,c} = \frac{X_{i,c} \cdot S_{i,c}}{m_i}, \tag{7.38}$$

where $U_{i,c}$ is the utilization of the queue due to requests of class c, $S_{i,c}$ is the service time, and $X_{i,c}$ is the throughput for requests of class c.

Finally, the *service demand law* relates the service demand $D_{i,c}$ of requests from class c with the utilization $U_{i,c}$ and the system throughput $X_{0,c}$ for class c:

$$D_{i,c} = \frac{m_i \cdot U_{i,c}}{X_{0,c}}. \tag{7.39}$$

7.2.4 Response Time Equations

The response time $R_{i,c}$ for $M/G/m$ queues with PS or preemptive LCFS scheduling, as well as for $M/M/m$ queues with class-independent service rates and FCFS scheduling, is given by

$$R_{i,c} = D_{i,c} \left(1 + \frac{1}{m_i} \cdot \frac{PB_i}{1 - U_i} \right), \tag{7.40}$$

where PB_i is the probability that all m_i servers of the queue are busy and an incoming request has to wait in the waiting line. PB_i can be calculated using the Erlang-C formula:

$$PB_i = \frac{(m_i U_i)^{m_i}}{m_i!(1 - U_i)} \cdot \pi_{i,0}$$

$$\text{with } \pi_{i,0} = \left[\sum_{k=0}^{m_i-1} \frac{(m_i U_i)^k}{k!} + \frac{(m_i U_i)^{m_i}}{m_i!} \frac{1}{1 - U_i} \right]^{-1}. \tag{7.41}$$

If a queue has IS scheduling strategy, a request never has to wait for service and the response time simplifies to

$$R_{i,c} = D_{i,c}. \tag{7.42}$$

For single server queues (i.e., $m_i = 1$), the busy probability PB_i is equal to the utilization U_i. As a result, Equation (7.40) can be simplified to

$$R_{i,c} = \frac{D_{i,c}}{1 - U_i}. \tag{7.43}$$

We refer to Bolch, Greiner, et al. (2006, p. 251) for the derivation and mathematical proof of the above equations.

The previous equations are not valid for $M/M/m$ service stations with FCFS scheduling and service rates depending on the workload class. The response time of such service stations can only be approximated. Franks (2000) compared the accuracy of different approximations and proposed the following one:

$$R_{i,c} = D_{i,c} + \frac{PB_i}{m_i} \sum_{s=1}^{C} Q_{i,c} \cdot D_{i,c}, \tag{7.44}$$

where $Q_{i,c}$ is the queue length of requests of workload class c at service station i.

7.2.5 Solution Techniques for Queueing Networks

Different solution techniques for queueing networks have been developed in the last decades. They can be broadly classified into simulation and analytic techniques. Discrete event simulation can be used to analyze arbitrarily complex queueing networks. However, it often is necessary to simulate a queueing network for a long time in order to obtain sufficiently accurate results.

Analytic techniques can provide exact solutions of a queueing network, avoiding the overhead of simulation. There are state-space and non-state-space techniques (Bolch, Greiner, et al., 2006). State-space techniques rely on the generation of the complete underlying state space of a queueing network, limiting their scalability with increasing numbers of requests, workload classes, and service stations. If certain assumptions are fulfilled, non-state-space techniques can be used instead. Given a product-form queueing network with an open workload, we can apply the equations presented in Section 7.2.4 to directly calculate performance metrics for the individual queues. Given a product-form queueing network with a closed workload, the calculation of the normalizing constant G in Equation (7.36) is nontrivial. Mean Value Analysis (MVA) (Bolch, Greiner, et al., 2006) is a recursive algorithm to calculate the queue lengths in closed product-form queueing networks, avoiding the direct determination of the normalizing constant G.

Techniques to solve queueing networks are supported by various tools, such as SHARPE (Hirel et al., 2000; Sahner and Trivedi, 1987), JMT (Bertoli et al., 2009), JINQS (Field, 2006), SPEED (Smith and Williams, 1997), and queueing-tool (Jordon, 2014).

Queueing networks provide a powerful method for modeling contention due to processing resources, that is, hardware contention and scheduling strategies. For certain classes of queueing networks, there are efficient analysis methods available. However, queueing networks are not suitable for representing blocking behavior, synchronization of processes, simultaneous resource possession, or asynchronous processing (Kounev, 2005). There are extensions of queueing networks such as *Extended Queueing Networks (EQNs)* (Bolch, Greiner, et al., 2006) that provide some support to mitigate the mentioned drawbacks.

7.2.6 Case Study

Now that we have introduced the basics of queueing network models, we present a case study—based on Kounev and Buchmann (2003)—showing how queueing networks can be used to model and predict the performance of a distributed software system. Imagine the following hypothetical scenario: A company is about to automate its internal and external business operations with the help of e-business technology. The company chooses to employ the Java EE platform[6], and it develops an application for supporting its order-inventory, supply-chain, and manufacturing operations. Assume that this application is the one provided by the SPECjAppServer benchmark.[7] SPECjAppServer models businesses using four domains: (1) *customer domain*—dealing with customer orders and interactions; (2) *manufacturing domain*—performing "just-in-time" manufacturing operations; (3) *supplier domain*—handling interactions with external suppliers; and (4) *corporate domain*—managing all customer, product, and supplier information. Figure 7.7 illustrates these domains and gives some examples of typical transactions run in each of them.

---

[6] Java EE platform: https://www.oracle.com/java/technologies/java-ee-glance.html

[7] SPECjAppServer benchmark: https://www.spec.org/jAppServer

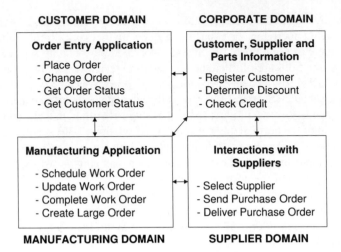

Fig. 7.7: SPECjAppServer business domains

The customer domain models customer interactions using an order-entry application, which provides some typical online ordering functionality. Orders can be placed by individual customers as well as by distributors. Orders placed by distributors are called *large orders*.

The manufacturing domain models the activity of production lines in a manufacturing plant. Products manufactured by the plant are called *widgets*. There are two types of production lines, namely *planned lines* and *large order lines*. Planned lines run on schedule and produce a predefined number of widgets. Large order lines run only when a large order is received in the customer domain. The unit of work in the manufacturing domain is a *work order*. Each work order is for a specific quantity of a particular type of widget. When a work order is created, the bill of materials for the corresponding type of widget is retrieved and the required parts are taken out of inventory. As the widgets move through the assembly line, the work order status is updated to reflect progress. Once the work order is complete, it is marked as completed and the inventory is updated. When the inventory of parts gets depleted, suppliers need to be located and *purchase orders (POs)* need to be sent out. This is done by contacting the supplier domain, which is responsible for interactions with external suppliers.

Assume that the company plans to deploy the application in the deployment environment depicted in Figure 7.8. This environment uses a cluster of WebLogic servers (WLS) as a Java EE container and an Oracle database server (DBS) for persistence. We assume that all machines in the WLS cluster are identical.

Before putting the application into production, the company conducts a capacity planning study in order to come up with an adequate sizing and configuration of the deployment environment. More specifically, the company needs to answer the following questions:

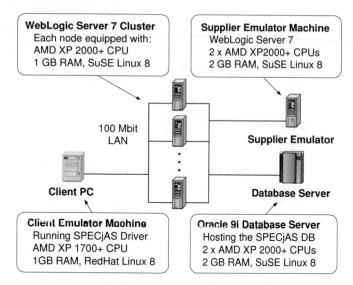

Fig. 7.8: Deployment environment

- How many WebLogic servers would be needed to guarantee adequate performance under the expected workload?
- For a given number of WebLogic servers, what level of performance would the system provide? What would be the average transaction throughput and response time? What would be the utilization (CPU/disk utilization) of the WebLogic servers and the database server?
- Will the capacity of the database server suffice to handle the incoming load?
- Does the system scale or are there any other potential system bottlenecks?

These issues can be approached with the help of queueing network-based performance models.

7.2.6.1 Workload Characterization

The first step in the capacity planning process is to describe the workload of the system under study in a qualitative and quantitative manner. This is called *workload characterization* (Menascé and Almeida, 1998), and it typically includes four steps:

1. Describe the types of requests that are processed by the system (i.e., the *request classes*),
2. Identify the hardware and software resources used by each request class,
3. Measure the total amount of service time for each request class at each resource (i.e., the *service demand*), and
4. Specify the number of requests of each class the system will be exposed to (i.e., the *workload intensity*).

As already discussed, the SPECjAppServer workload is made up of two major components: (1) the *order-entry application* in the customer domain and (2) the *manufacturing application* in the manufacturing domain. Recall that the order-entry application is running the following four transaction types:

1. *NewOrder*: places a new order in the system,
2. *ChangeOrder*: modifies an existing order,
3. *OrderStatus*: retrieves the status of a given order, and
4. *CustStatus*: lists all orders of a given customer.

We map each of them to a separate *request class* in our workload model. The manufacturing application, on the other hand, is running production lines. The main unit of work there is a *work order*. Each work order produces a specific quantity of a particular type of widget. As already mentioned, there are two types of production lines: planned lines and large order lines. While planned lines run on a predefined schedule, large order lines run only when a large order arrives in the customer domain. Each large order results in a separate work order. During the processing of work orders, multiple transactions are executed in the manufacturing domain (i.e., scheduleWorkOrder, updateWorkOrder, and completeWorkOrder). Each work order moves along three virtual stations, which represent distinct operations in the manufacturing flow. In order to simulate activity at the stations, the manufacturing application waits for a designated time at each station. One way to model the manufacturing workload would be to define a separate request class for each transaction run during the processing of work orders. However, this would lead to an overly complex model and would limit the range of analysis techniques that would be applicable for its solution. Second, it would not be of much benefit, since after all, what most interests us is the rate at which work orders are processed and not the performance metrics of the individual work order-related transactions. Therefore, we model the manufacturing workload only at the level of work orders. We define a single request class *WorkOrder*, which represents a request for processing a work order. This keeps our model simple, and as will be seen later, it is enough to provide us with sufficient information about the behavior of the manufacturing application.

Altogether, we end up with five request classes: NewOrder, ChangeOrder, OrderStatus, CustStatus, and WorkOrder. The following resources are used during their processing:

- The CPU of a WebLogic server (WLS-CPU),
- The local area network (LAN),
- The CPUs of the database server (DBS-CPU), and
- The disk drives of the database server (DBS-I/O).

In order to determine the service demands at these resources, we conducted a separate experiment for each of the five request classes. In each case, we deployed the benchmark in a configuration with a single WebLogic server and then injected requests of the respective class into the system. During the experiment, we monitored the system resources and measured the time requests spent at each resource during their processing. For the database server, we used the Oracle 9i Intelligent Agent, which provides exhaustive information about CPU consumption and I/O wait times. For the application server, we monitored the CPU utilization using operating system tools; we then used the *service demand law* $(D = U/X)$ to derive the CPU service demand (see Section 7.2.3).

We decided we could safely ignore network service demands, since all communication was taking place over a 100 MBit LAN, and communication times were negligible. Figure 7.9 reports the service demand measurements for the five request classes in our workload model.

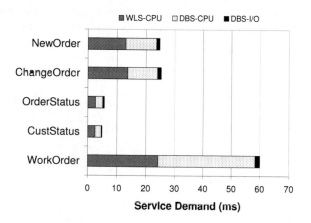

Fig. 7.9: Workload service demands

Database I/O service demands are much lower than CPU service demands. This stems from the fact that data is cached in the database buffer, and disks are usually accessed only when updating or inserting new data. However, even in this case, the I/O overhead is minimal, since the only thing that is done is to flush the database log buffer, which is performed with sequential I/O accesses. Here we would like to point out that the benchmark uses relatively small data volumes for the workload intensities generated. This results in data contention (Kounev and Buchmann, 2002), and as we will see later, it causes some difficulties in predicting transaction response times. Once we know the service demands of the different request classes, we proceed with the last step in workload characterization, which aims to quantify the workload intensity. For each request class, we must specify the rates at which requests arrive. We should also be able to vary these rates, so that we can consider different scenarios. To this end, we modified the SPECjAppServer driver to allow more flexibility in configuring the intensity of the workload generated. Specifically, the new driver allows us to set the number of concurrent order entry clients simulated as well as their average *think time*, that is, the time they "think" after receiving a response from the system, before they send the next request. In addition to this, we can specify the number of planned production lines run in the manufacturing domain and the time they wait after processing a work order before starting a new one. In this way, we can precisely define the workload intensity and transaction mix. We will later study in detail several scenarios under different transaction mixes and workload intensities.

7.2.6.2 Building a Performance Model

We now build a queueing network model of our SPECjAppServer deployment environment. We first define the model in a general fashion and then customize it to our concrete workload scenarios. We use a closed model, which means that for each instance of the model, the number of concurrent clients sending requests to the system is fixed. Figure 7.10 shows a high-level view of our queueing network model.

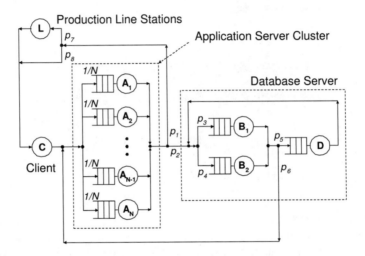

Fig. 7.10: Queueing network model of the system

In the following, we briefly describe the queues used:

C :   Infinite-Server (IS) queue (delay resource) used to model the client machine, which runs the SPECjAppServer driver and emulates virtual clients sending requests to the system. The service time of order entry requests at this queue is equal to the average client think time; the service time of WorkOrder requests is equal to the average time a production line waits after processing a work order before starting a new one. Note that times spent on this queue are not part of system response times.

$A_1..A_N$:   Processor-Sharing (PS) queues used to model the CPUs of the N WebLogic servers.

B_1, B_2 :   Processor-Sharing (PS) queues used to model the two CPUs of the database server.

D :   First-Come-First-Served (FCFS) queue used to model the disk subsystem (made up of a single 100 GB disk drive) of the database server.

L :   Infinite-Server (IS) queue (delay resource) used to model the virtual production line stations in the manufacturing domain. Only WorkOrder requests visit this queue. Their service time at the queue corresponds to the average delay at the production line stations simulated by the manufacturing application during work order processing.

The model is a closed queueing network model with the five classes of requests (jobs) defined in the previous section. The behavior of requests in the model is defined by specifying their respective routing probabilities p_i and service demands at each queue they visit. We discussed the service demands in the previous section. To set the routing probabilities, we examine the life cycle of client requests in the queueing network. Every request is initially at the client queue C, where it waits for a user-specified think time. After the think time elapses, the request is routed to a randomly chosen queue A_i, where it queues to receive service at a WebLogic server CPU.

We assume that requests are evenly distributed among the N WebLogic servers; that is, each server is chosen with probability $1/N$. Processing at the CPU may be interrupted multiple times if the request requires some database accesses. Each time this happens, the request is routed to the database server, where it queues for service at one of the two CPU queues B_1 or B_2 (each chosen equally likely, so that $p_3 = p_4 = 0.5$). Processing at the database CPUs may be interrupted in case I/O accesses are needed. For each I/O access, the request is sent to the disk subsystem queue D; after receiving service there, it is routed back to the database CPUs. This may be repeated multiple times, depending on the routing probabilities p_5 and p_6.

Having completed their service at the database server, requests are sent back to the application server. Requests may visit the database server multiple times during their processing, depending on the routing probabilities p_1 and p_2. After completing service at the application server, requests are sent back to the client queue C. Order entry requests are sent directly to the client queue (for them, $p_8 = 1$ and $p_7 = 0$), while WorkOrder requests are routed through queue L (for them, $p_8 = 0$ and $p_7 = 1$), where they are additionally delayed for 1 s. This delay corresponds to the 1 s delay at the three production line stations imposed by the manufacturing application during work order processing.

In order to set routing probabilities p_1, p_2, p_5, and p_6, we need to know how many times a request visits the database server during its processing and, for each visit, how many times, I/O access is needed. Since we know only the total service demands over all visits to the database, we assume that requests visit the database just once and need a single I/O access during this visit. This allows us to drop routing probabilities p_1, p_2, p_5, and p_6 and leads us to the simplified model depicted in Figure 7.11.

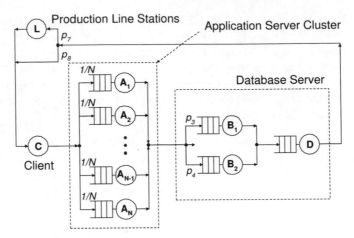

Fig. 7.11: Simplified QN model of the system

The following input parameters need to be supplied before the model can be analyzed:

- Number of order entry clients (NewOrder, ChangeOrder, OrderStatus, and Cust-Status),
- Average think time of order entry clients—*Customer Think Time*,
- Number of planned production lines generating WorkOrder requests,
- Average time production lines wait after processing a work order, before starting a new one—*Manufacturing (Mfg) Think Time*, and
- Service demands of the five request classes at queues A_i, B_j, and D.

In our study, we consider two types of deployment scenarios. In the first one, large order lines in the manufacturing domain are turned off. In the second one, they are running as defined in the benchmark workload. The reason for this separation is that large order lines introduce some asynchronous processing, which is generally hard to model using queueing networks. We start with the simpler case where we do not have such processing, and we then show how large order lines can be integrated into the model.

7.2.6.3 Model Analysis and Validation

We now proceed to analyze several different instances of the model, and we then validate them by comparing results from the analysis with measured data. We first consider the case without large order lines and study the system in three scenarios representing low, moderate, and heavy load, respectively. In each case, we examine deployments with different number of application servers—from one to nine. Table 7.5 summarizes the input parameters for the three scenarios we consider.

Table 7.5: Model input parameters for the three scenarios

Parameter	Low	Moderate	Heavy
NewOrder clients	30	50	100
ChangeOrder clients	10	40	50
OrderStatus clients	50	100	150
CustStatus clients	40	70	50
Planned lines	50	100	200
Customer think time	2 s	2 s	3 s
Mfg think time	3 s	3 s	5 s

We employed the *PEPSY-QNS* tool (Bolch and Kirschnick, 1994), which supports a wide range of solution methods (over 30) for product-form and non-product-form queueing networks. Both exact and approximate methods are provided, which are applicable to models of considerable size and complexity. For the most part, we have applied the *multisum method* (Bolch, 1989) for solution of the queueing network models in this case study. However, to ensure plausibility of the results, we cross verified them with results obtained from other methods such as *bol_aky* and *num_app* (Bolch and Kirschnick, 1994). In all cases, the difference was negligible.

Low Load Scenario Table 7.6 summarizes the results we obtained for our first scenario. We studied two different configurations—the first one with one application server and the second one with two application servers. The table reports throughput (X) and response time (R) for the five request classes as well as CPU utilization (U) of the application server and the database server. Results obtained from the model analysis are compared against results obtained through measurements, and the modeling error is reported.

As we can see from the table, while throughput and utilization results are extremely accurate, this does not hold to this extent for response time results. This is because when we run a transaction mix, as opposed to a single transaction, some additional delays are incurred that are not captured by the model. For example, delays result from contention for data access (database locks, latches), processes, threads, database connections, and so on. The latter is often referred to as *software contention*, in contrast to *hardware contention* (contention for CPU time, disk access, and other hardware resources). Our model captures the hardware contention aspects of system behavior and does not represent software contention aspects. While software contention may not always have a big impact on transaction throughput and CPU utilization, it usually does have a direct impact on transaction response time; therefore, the measured response times are higher than the ones obtained from the model. In Kounev (2006), some techniques were presented for integrating both hardware and software contention aspects into the same model.

Table 7.6: Analysis results for the first scenario—low load

Metric	One application server			Two application servers		
	Model	Measured	Error	Model	Measured	Error
NewOrder throughput	14.59	14.37	1.5%	14.72	14.49	1.6%
ChangeOrder throughput	4.85	4.76	1.9%	4.90	4.82	1.7%
OrderStatus throughput	24.84	24.76	0.3%	24.89	24.88	0.0%
CustStatus throughput	19.89	19.85	0.2%	19.92	19.99	0.4%
WorkOrder throughput	12.11	12.19	0.7%	12.20	12.02	1.5%
NewOrder response time	56 ms	68 ms	17.6%	37 ms	47 ms	21.3%
ChangeOrder resp. time	58 ms	67 ms	13.4%	38 ms	46 ms	17.4%
OrderStatus response time	12 ms	16 ms	25.0%	8 ms	10 ms	20.0%
CustStatus response time	11 ms	17 ms	35.2%	7 ms	10 ms	30.0%
WorkOrder response time	1,127 ms	1,141 ms	1.2%	1,092 ms	1,103 ms	1.0%
WebLogic server CPU util.	66%	70%	5.7%	33%	37%	10.8%
Database server CPU util.	36%	40%	10%	36%	38%	5.2%

From Table 7.6, we see that the response time error for requests with very low service demands (e.g., OrderStatus and CustStatus) is much higher than the average error. This is because the processing times for such requests are very low (around 10 ms) and the additional delays from software contention, while not that high as absolute values, are high relative to the overall response times. The results show that the higher the service demand for a request type, the lower the response time error. Indeed, the requests with the highest service demand (WorkOrder) always have the lowest response time error.

Moderate Load Scenario In this scenario, we have 260 concurrent clients interacting with the system and 100 planned production lines running in the manufacturing domain. This is twice as much compared to the previous scenario. We study two deployments—the first with three application servers and the second with six. Table 7.7 summarizes the results from the model analysis. Again, we obtain very accurate results for throughput and utilization, and we also obtain accurate results for response time. The response time error does not exceed 35%, which is considered acceptable in most capacity planning studies (Menascé et al., 2004).

Heavy Load Scenario In this scenario, we have 350 concurrent clients and 200 planned production lines in total. We consider three configurations—with four, six, and nine application servers, respectively. However, we slightly increase the think times in order to make sure that our single machine database server is able to handle the load. Table 7.8 summarizes the results for this scenario. For models of this size, the available algorithms do not produce reliable results for response time, and therefore, we only consider throughput and utilization in this scenario.

Table 7.7: Analysis results for the second scenario—moderate load

Metric	Three application servers			Six application servers		
	Model	Measured	Error	Model	Measured	Error
NewOrder throughput	24.21	24.08	0.5%	24.29	24.01	1.2%
ChangeOrder throughput	19.36	18.77	3.1%	19.43	19.32	0.6%
OrderStatus throughput	49.63	49.48	0.3%	49.66	49.01	1.3%
CustStatus throughput	34.77	34.24	1.5%	34.80	34.58	0.6%
WorkOrder throughput	23.95	23.99	0.2%	24.02	24.03	0.0%
NewOrder response time	65 ms	75 ms	13.3%	58 ms	68 ms	14.7%
ChangeOrder resp. time	66 ms	73 ms	9.6%	58 ms	70 ms	17.1%
OrderStatus response time	15 ms	20 ms	25.0%	13 ms	18 ms	27.8%
CustStatus response time	13 ms	20 ms	35.0%	11 ms	17 ms	35.3%
WorkOrder response time	1,175 ms	1,164 ms	0.9%	1,163 ms	1,162 ms	0.0%
WebLogic server CPU util.	46%	49%	6.1%	23%	25%	8.0%
Database server CPU util.	74%	76%	2.6%	73%	78%	6.4%

Table 7.8: Analysis results for the third scenario—heavy load

Metric	Four app. servers			Six app. servers			Nine app. servers		
	Model	Msrd.	Error	Model	Msrd.	Error	Model	Msrd.	Error
NewOrder throughput	32.19	32.29	0.3%	32.22	32.66	1.3%	32.24	32.48	0.7%
ChangeOrder throughput	16.10	15.96	0.9%	16.11	16.19	0.5%	16.12	16.18	0.4%
OrderStatus throughput	49.59	48.92	1.4%	49.60	49.21	0.8%	49.61	49.28	0.7%
CustStatus throughput	16.55	16.25	1.8%	16.55	16.24	1.9%	16.55	16.46	0.5%
WorkOrder throughput	31.69	31.64	0.2%	31.72	32.08	1.1%	31.73	32.30	1.8%
WebLogic server CPU util.	40%	42%	4.8%	26%	29%	10.3%	18%	20%	10.0%
Database server CPU util.	87%	89%	2.2%	88%	91%	3.3%	88%	91%	3.3%

Large Order Lines Scenario We now consider the case when large order lines in the manufacturing domain are enabled. The latter are activated upon arrival of large orders in the customer domain. Each large order generates a separate work order, which is processed asynchronously at one of the large order lines. As already mentioned, this poses a difficulty since queueing networks provide limited possibilities for modeling this type of asynchronous processing. As shown in Kounev (2006), other state-space-based models such as *queueing Petri nets (QPNs)* are much more powerful in such situations.

Since large order lines are always triggered by NewOrder transactions (for large orders), we can add the load they produce to the service demands of NewOrder requests. To this end, we rerun the NewOrder experiments with the large order lines turned on. The additional load leads to higher utilization of system resources, and it impacts the measured NewOrder service demands (WLS-CPU: 23.49 ms, DBS-CPU: 21.61 ms, DBS-I/O: 1.87 ms). While this incorporates the large order line activity into our model, it changes the semantics of NewOrder jobs. In addition to the NewOrder transaction load, they now also include the load caused by large order lines. Thus, performance metrics (throughput, response time) for NewOrder requests no longer correspond to the respective metrics of the NewOrder transaction. Therefore, we can no longer quantify the performance of the NewOrder transaction on itself. Nevertheless, we can still analyze the performance of other transactions and gain a picture of the overall system behavior. Table 7.9 summarizes the results for the three scenarios with large order lines enabled. For lack of space, this time we look only at one configuration per scenario—the first one with one application server, the second one with three, and the third one with nine.

Table 7.9: Analysis results for the scenario with large order lines

Metric	Low/1-AS		Moderate/3-AS		Heavy/9-AS	
	Model	Error	Model	Error	Model	Error
ChangeOrder throughput	4.79	6.4%	19.09	3.5%	15.31	4.5%
OrderStatus throughput	24.77	2.9%	49.46	2.3%	48.96	3.1%
CustStatus throughput	19.83	2.4%	34.67	2.1%	16.37	1.9%
WorkOrder throughput	11.96	5.7%	23.43	2.6%	29.19	1.2%
WebLogic server CPU util.	80%	0.0%	53%	1.9%	20%	0.0%
Database server CPU util.	43%	2.4%	84%	2.4%	96%	1.0%

7.2.7 Conclusions from the Analysis

We used a queueing network model to predict the system performance in several different configurations, varying the workload intensity and the number of application servers available. The results enable us to give answers to the initial capacity planning questions. For each configuration, we obtained approximations for the average request throughput, the response time, and the server utilization. Depending on the Service-Level Agreements (SLAs) and the expected workload intensity, we

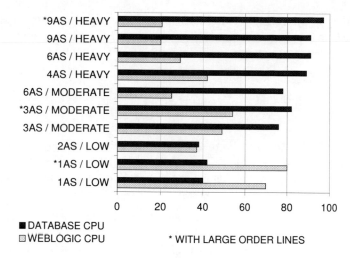

Fig. 7.12: Server utilization in different scenarios

can now determine how many application servers we need in order to guarantee adequate performance. We can also see, for each configuration, which component is mostly utilized and thus could become a potential bottleneck (see Figure 7.12). In the first scenario, we saw that by using a single application server, the latter could easily turn into a bottleneck, since its utilization would be twice as high as that of the database server. The problem is solved by adding an extra application server. In the second and third scenarios, we saw that with more than three application servers, as we increase the load, the database CPU utilization approaches 90%, while the application servers remain less than 50% utilized. This clearly indicates that, in this case, our database server is the bottleneck.

7.3 Concluding Remarks

In this chapter, we introduced some basic quantitative relationships between the most common performance metrics. We showed how these relationships, referred to as operational laws, can be applied to evaluate a system's performance based on measured or known data. This approach, known as operational analysis, can be seen as part of queueing theory, which provides general methods to analyze the queueing behavior at one or more service stations. Having looked at operational analysis, we provided a brief introduction to the basic notation and principles of queueing theory. While queueing theory is used in many different domains, from manufacturing to logistics, in this chapter, we focused on using queueing theory for performance evaluation of computer systems. Nevertheless, the introduced concepts and mathematical models are relevant for any processing system where the assumptions discussed in the beginning of the chapter hold. The chapter was wrapped up with a case study, showing how to build a queueing model of a distributed software system and use it to predict the system performance for different workload and configuration scenarios.

References

Balsamo, S. (2000). "Product Form Queueing Networks". In: *Performance Evaluation: Origins and Directions*. Ed. by G. Haring, C. Lindemann, and M. Reiser. Vol. 1769. Lecture Notes in Computer Science. Springer-Verlag: Berlin, Heidelberg, pp. 377–401 (cited on p. 166).

Baskett, F., Chandy, K. M., Muntz, R. R., and Palacios, F. G. (1975). "Open, Closed, and Mixed Networks of Queues with Different Classes of Customers". *Journal of the ACM*, 22(2). ACM: New York City, NY, USA, pp. 248–260 (cited on pp. 166, 167).

Bertoli, M., Casale, G., and Serazzi, G. (2009). "JMT: Performance Engineering Tools for System Modeling". *SIGMETRICS Performance Evaluation Review*, 36(4). ACM: New York, NY, USA, pp. 10–15 (cited on p. 169).

Bolch, G. (1989). *Performance Evaluation of Computer Systems with the Help of Analytical Queueing Network Models*. Teubner Verlag: Leipzig, Germany (cited on p. 177).

Bolch, G. and Kirschnick, M. (1994). *The Performance Evaluation and Prediction SYstem for Queueing NetworkS—PEPSY-QNS*. Tech. rep. TR-I4-94-18. Germany: University of Erlangen-Nuremberg (cited on p. 177).

Bolch, G., Greiner, S., Meer, H. de, and Trivedi, K. S. (2006). *Queueing Networks and Markov Chains: Modeling and Performance Evaluation with Computer Science Applications*. Second Edition. John Wiley & Sons: Hoboken, New Jersey, USA (cited on pp. 160, 163, 166, 168, 169).

Cox, D. R. (1955). "A Use of Complex Probabilities in the Theory of Stochastic Processes". *Mathematical Proceedings of the Cambridge Philosophical Society*, 51(2). Cambridge University Press: Cambridge, UK, pp. 313–319 (cited on p. 167).

Denning, P. J. and Buzen, J. P. (1978). "The Operational Analysis of Queueing Network Models". *ACM Computing Surveys*, 10(3). ACM: New York, NY, USA, pp. 225–261 (cited on p. 150).

Field, T. (2006). *JINQS: An Extensible Library for Simulating Multiclass Queueing Networks V1.0 User Guide*. Imperial College London. London, UK (cited on p. 169).

Franks, R. G. (2000). "Performance Analysis of Distributed Server Systems". PhD thesis. Ottawa, Canada: Carlton University (cited on p. 168).

Gagniuc, P. A. (2017). *Markov Chains: From Theory to Implementation and Experimentation*. John Wiley & Sons: Hoboken, New Jersey, USA (cited on p. 163).

Harchol-Balter, M. (2013). *Performance Modeling and Design of Computer Systems: Queueing Theory in Action*. Cambridge University Press: Cambridge, UK (cited on pp. 160, 163).

Hirel, C., Sahner, R. A., Zang, X., and Trivedi, K. S. (2000). "Reliability and Performability Modeling Using SHARPE 2000". In: *Proceedings of the 11th International Conference on Modelling Techniques and Tools for Computer Performance Evaluation (TOOLS 2000)*. (Schaumburg, IL, USA). Lecture Notes in Computer Science. Springer-Verlag: Berlin, Heidelberg, pp. 345–349 (cited on p. 169).

Jordon, D. (2014). *Queueing-tool: A network simulator*. https://github.com/djordon/queueing-tool. Accessed: 2019-09-18 (cited on p. 169).

Kelly, F. P. (1975). "Networks of Queues with Customers of Different Types". *Journal of Applied Probability*, 12(3). Applied Probability Trust, pp. 542–554 (cited on p. 166).

– (1976). "Networks of Queues". *Advances in Applied Probability*, 8(2). Applied Probability Trust, pp. 416–432 (cited on p. 166).

Kendall, D. G. (1953). "Stochastic Processes Occurring in the Theory of Queues and their Analysis by the Method of the Imbedded Markov Chain". *The Annals of Mathematical Statistics*, 24(3). The Institute of Mathematical Statistics, pp. 338–354 (cited on p. 162).

Kounev, S. (2005). *Performance Engineering of Distributed Component-Based Systems—Benchmarking, Modeling and Performance Prediction*. Ph.D. Thesis, Technische Universität Darmstadt, Germany. Shaker Verlag: Herzogenrath, Germany (cited on p. 169).

– (2006). "Performance Modeling and Evaluation of Distributed Component-Based Systems using Queueing Petri Nets". *IEEE Transactions on Software Engineering*, 32(7). IEEE Computer Society: Washington, DC, USA, pp. 486–502 (cited on pp. 177, 180).

Kounev, S. and Buchmann, A. (2002). "Improving Data Access of J2EE Applications by Exploiting Asynchronous Processing and Caching Services". In: *Proceedings of the 28th International Conference on Very Large Data Bases (VLDB 2002)*. (Hong Kong, China). VLDB Endowment, pp. 574–585 (cited on p. 173).

– (2003). "Performance Modeling and Evaluation of Large-Scale J2EE Applications". In: *Proceedings of the 29th International Conference of the Computer Measurement Group on Resource Management and Performance Evaluation of Enterprise Computing Systems (CMG 2003)*. (Dallas, TX, USA), pp. 273–283 (cited on p. 169).

Lazowska, E. D., Zahorjan, J., Graham, G. S., and Sevcik, K. C. (1984). *Quantitative System Performance: Computer System Analysis Using Queueing Network Models*. Prentice-Hall: Upper Saddle River, NJ, USA (cited on p. 160).

Little, J. D. C. (1961). "A Proof for the Queuing Formula: $L = \lambda W$". *Operations Research*, 9(3). Institute for Operations Research and the Management Sciences (INFORMS): Linthicum, Maryland, USA, pp. 383–387 (cited on p. 154).

Menascé, D. A. and Almeida, V. A. (1998). *Capacity Planning for Web Performance: Metrics, Models, and Methods*. Prentice Hall: Upper Saddle River, NJ, USA (cited on p. 171).

Menascé, D. A., Almeida, V. A., and Dowdy, L. W. (1994). *Capacity Planning and Performance Modeling: From Mainframes to Client-Server Systems*. Prentice Hall: Upper Saddle River, NJ, USA (cited on p. 159).

– (2004). *Performance by Design: Computer Capacity Planning By Example*. Prentice Hall: Upper Saddle River, NJ, USA (cited on pp. 150, 151, 154, 155, 157, 158, 178).

Sahner, R. A. and Trivedi, K. S. (1987). "Reliability Modeling Using SHARPE". *IEEE Transactions on Reliability*, 36(2). IEEE: Piscataway, New Jersey, USA, pp. 186–193 (cited on p. 169).

Smith, C. U. and Williams, L. G. (1997). "Performance Engineering Evaluation of Object-Oriented Systems with SPE*ED". In: *Proceedings from the International Conference on Modelling Techniques and Tools for Computer Performance Evaluation (TOOLS 1997)*. Ed. by R. Marie, B. Plateau, M. Calzarossa, and G. Rubino. Vol. 1245. Lecture Notes in Computer Science. Springer-Verlag: Berlin, Heidelberg, pp. 135–154 (cited on p. 169).

Chapter 8
Workloads

"It's not so much how busy you are, but why you are busy.
The bee is praised, the mosquito is swatted."
—*Marie O'Conner*

A workload is one of the cornerstones of any benchmark. It is the part that is
actively executed on a system under test (SUT), triggering the system behavior that
is then measured based on a specified *measurement methodology* and quantified
using a set of defined *metrics*. The process by which a benchmark schedules, places,
and executes its workload is referred to as *workload generation*. In this chapter, we
consider workloads in the context of workload generation. To facilitate workload
generation, we must answer questions such as: "What parts of a workload must be
implemented and specified for a benchmark in order to be able to generate it?" and
"What are the primary decision criteria when deciding on the design of a workload?"

The chapter starts with a classification of the different workload facets and artifacts. We introduce the distinction between executable and non-executable parts
of a workload as well as the distinction between natural and artificial workloads.
The executable parts are then discussed in detail, including natural benchmarks,
application workloads, and synthetic workloads. Next, the non-executable parts are
discussed, distinguishing between workload traces and workload descriptions. In the
rest of the chapter, we introduce the different types of workload descriptions that can
be used for batch workloads and transactional workloads, as well as for open and
closed workloads. The challenges of generating steady-state workloads and workloads with varying arrival rates are discussed. Finally, the chapter concludes with a
brief introduction of system-metric-based workload descriptions.

8.1 Workload Facets and Artifacts

In the context of workload generation, we distinguish between executable and non-
executable parts of a workload:

© Springer Nature Switzerland AG 2020
S. Kounev et al., *Systems Benchmarking*, https://doi.org/10.1007/978-3-030-41705-5_8

- **Executable parts**: The executable parts of a workload comprise the actual tasks (i.e., code) being executed on the system, often structured into executable work units. The executable parts can emulate a real-world application or they can be designed synthetically to elicit certain system behavior (e.g., get the system in a certain power-saving state in order to analyze its behavior in that state).
- **Non-executable parts**: The non-executable parts of a workload govern how and when the executable parts are to be run in order to ensure that the workload is executed in a well-defined and reproducible manner. To this end, methods and rules for workload execution are needed. These rules govern the workload's properties and configuration. For example, they define if work units are executed repeatedly and, if yes, how often and in what intervals they should be repeated. They may also define a sequence of different work units or work unit configurations or may be defined in a way as to emulate some user behavior.

Workloads can also be categorized into one of the two categories—*natural workloads* and *artificial workloads* (Menascé, V. A. Almeida, et al., 2004)—sometimes referred to as *workload models* in the literature. Natural workloads are constructed from real workloads of the system under study or from execution traces of real workloads. In the former case, they are called *natural benchmarks*; in the latter case, they are called *workload traces*. A natural benchmark is a set of programs extracted from the real workload such that they represent the major characteristics of the latter. A workload trace is a chronological sequence of records describing specific events that were observed during execution of the real workload. For example, in a three-tier server architecture, the logs collected by the servers at each tier (web servers, application servers, and database servers) can be used as workload traces. While traces usually exhibit good representativeness, they have the drawback that they normally consist of large amounts of data and do not provide a compact representation of the workload.

Unlike natural workloads, artificial workloads are not constructed using basic components of real workloads as building blocks; however, they may try to mimic real workloads. Artificial workloads can be classified into *synthetic workloads*, *application workloads*, and *workload descriptions*. This classification is in line with the classification of benchmark types that we introduced in Chapter 1, Section 1.3. Synthetic workloads are artificial programs designed to execute mixes of operations carefully chosen to elicit certain system behavior and/or to match the relative mix of operations observed in some class of applications. They usually do no real (useful) work. In contrast to this, application workloads are implementations of complete applications that do useful work. They are normally specifically designed to be representative of a given class of real-life applications. Finally, workload descriptions are specifications typically comprised of a set of parameters that specify how the executable parts of the workload are to be executed. Such specifications can be concrete step-by-step instructions with parameters and actions for a specific workload. However, they may also be very generic and abstract based on mathematical models such as Markov chains or other stochastic models (Bolch et al., 2006). Depending on the type of workload, different parameters may be used, such as transaction/request types, times between successive request arrivals (inter-arrival times), transaction execution rates, and so forth. Figure 8.1 illustrates the relationships between the different workload facets and artifacts.

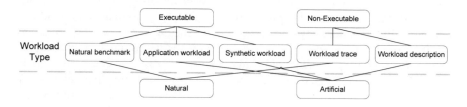

Fig. 8.1: Classification of workload facets and artifacts

In general, taken together, the executable and non-executable parts of a workload must satisfy the quality criteria for benchmarks described in Chapter 1 (Section 1.5): *relevance*, *reproducibility*, *fairness*, and *verifiability* (*usability* being a bit less relevant to the workload itself).

8.2 Executable Parts of a Workload

The executable parts of a workload comprise the tasks (i.e., software components) that are being executed on the SUT. The executable components can be a part of a real-world application, components designed to mimic a real-world application, or completely synthetic components designed to elicit and test certain system behavior.

Common examples for natural executable workload components can be found in compression benchmarks. For example, regular compression libraries and tools, such as *zip* and *tar*, can be run as workloads in larger benchmark suites. Of course, these are not specialized benchmark workloads, but regular compression tools originally created for use by end users. Similarly, in the gaming domain, games are often utilized as natural workloads to test the performance of desktop computers. Again, these workloads have not been created specifically for use in benchmarking, but instead as games to be played by end users.

However, a workload is not completely specified by deciding to run a certain natural benchmark, for example, a *zip* compression tool. In the context of the compression example, the obvious question is: "What data should be compressed?" Similarly, a game or any natural workload usually used interactively by a human user must specify the user input that should be used as part of the benchmarking workload. This is where the non-executable parts of the workload come in. They specify these properties and configurations, which sometimes may be very specific to the executable parts of the workload itself.

Application workloads are specifically created as benchmarking workloads and are thus artificial in nature. Yet, they attempt to mimic real-world applications in terms of the operations they perform. There are multiple reasons why artificial application workloads are often employed instead of simply using natural workloads. The primary reasons usually have to do with the two benchmark quality criteria of *reproducibility* and *fairness*. Natural workloads, or rather real-world applications, are usually not designed with reproducibility regarding performance in mind (nor reproducibility regarding any other property that may be target of benchmarking). Specifying and configuring such applications in a way to be run as a reproducible workload can be very difficult, and it may be easier to simply create an artificial application workload instead. In addition, natural workloads may not be very *fair*. Real-world applications are often heavily optimized towards target hardware and software stacks (e.g., operating system). In-house applications, developed by a company for use on their own devices, have potential for a lot of optimization to achieve the best possible performance on these devices. However, benchmarks are usually designed for comparison of different hardware or software stacks. Running a heavily optimized application as a natural workload within a benchmark might thus be considered *unfair*.

The benchmarks in Part II of this book feature several examples of application workloads. The workload of the SPECpower_ssj2008 energy-efficiency benchmark is an example of such a workload (Lange, 2009) (see Chapter 11). It emulates an online e-business application by introducing a mix of different request types that are run on the emulated application as part of the benchmark. In contrast to natural, real-world applications, SPECpower_ssj2008's work units have been designed for consistent (repeatable) performance. As explained in Chapter 11, energy-efficiency measurements are best performed at stable loads with stable performance and power consumption over the measurement duration (ideally leading to smaller confidence intervals). This can be best achieved with artificial workloads. Using an application workload allows SPECpower_ssj2008 to have this stability while still retaining much of the *relevance* a natural e-business workload would have. TeaStore is an application workload created for similar reasons (Kistowski, Eismann, et al., 2018) (see Chapter 14). TeaStore emulates a microservice application and can be used as a workload in elasticity and cloud resource management benchmarks. Again, reproducibility is one of the major concerns that prompted the development of an artificial application benchmark instead of using a natural real-world microservice workload. Chapter 14 lists several additional reasons for the use of artificial workloads, specific to TeaStore's intended usage scenario.

Finally, synthetic workloads are artificial workloads designed to execute mixes of operations carefully chosen to elicit certain system behavior and/or to match the relative mix of operations observed in some class of applications. In the latter case, the hope is that if the executed instruction mixes are similar, the performance observed when running the benchmark would be similar to the performance obtained when executing an actual application from the respective class. Synthetic workloads, given their flexibility, are especially useful for tailored system analysis allowing one to measure the limits of a system, or a selected part of it, under different configurations and workloads. For example, they can be used to evaluate the performance of a given system operation or a system component under extreme workload conditions stressing that particular operation/component.

Most workloads included in the SPEC SERT (see Chapter 11) serve as examples for synthetic workloads. SERT runs a number of small synthetic workloads, referred to as *worklets*. Each of those is designed to execute a single operation commonly found in server applications, stressing a certain hardware component of the server under consideration. Among other things, the worklets perform matrix decomposition, array sorting, and cryptographic operations. The mix of these *worklets* is intended to provide insight on how the server's energy efficiency reacts to a range of different scenarios.

8.3 Non-executable Parts of a Workload

The non-executable parts of a workload govern how and when the executable parts are to be run. They consist of rules, methods, and/or descriptions that consider, among other things, placement, scheduling, configuration, and potential user inputs for the executable parts. Some non-executable parts of a workload can be very generic, whereas others may be very specific to the workload in question. For example, a web application workload needs to specify the user actions performed on the web application as part of the workload specification. The number of concurrent users is an example of a very generic parameter, as it can be applied to almost any web application benchmark. However, the specific user inputs (e.g., buttons clicked, text entered) are specific to the concrete executable web application used as part of the benchmark.

In general, the non-executable parts of the workload can be split into two categories: *traces* and *workload descriptions*. Traces are records of real-world application runs, whereas workload descriptions describe how to execute a workload based on an abstract mathematical model or specification. For example, workload descriptions may be stochastic models, specifying the probability of certain work units executing next. Traces and workload descriptions may be combined, each describing a different set of parameters. Again, using an executable web application as an example, a trace may be used to define arrival times for the users' requests based on a log from a real-world web server, while user actions may be defined separately using a stochastic model.

8.3.1 Workload Traces

Traces are execution records of real-world applications. They are often, but not exclusively, derived from logs. Traces can be used to define a non-executable part of a workload with the intention of replaying the original behavior. The most intuitive way of using traces is using them in conjunction with a natural benchmark. A trace derived from a real-life execution of a natural benchmark can be used together with its executable counterpart in order to replay a scenario that actually occurred during the run time of the real-life natural application.

However, traces can also be used with artificial workloads. In this case, they can be used to replay a scenario recorded with one application in the context of a different application. Doing so usually requires the traces to be adapted or supplemented with artificial workload descriptions. Sticking with the web application example, when replacing a natural executable web application with an artificial web application, it is likely that the user inputs of the original application may not be directly usable in the context of the new application; for example, the UI may be different. However, more general parameters of the trace may still be applicable. For example, the time between user request arrivals may still be replayed, resulting in replaying the request rate of the original natural application. Table 8.1 shows such an example of a web server trace that might be used for workload generation. When adapting this trace for use with artificial executable workload components, URIs and HTTP-bodies might have to be adjusted to fit the workload. In this case, only the relative timestamps and methods would remain.

Table 8.1: Example web server-based workload trace

Timestamp	Method	URI	Body
1570271839	GET	/api/products	
1570271848	POST	/api/products	{'name':'Pear'}
1570271863	GET	/api/products	
. . .			

Note that traces are also heavily used in the context of instrumentation and monitoring tools as discussed in Chapter 6 (Section 6.4). Such traces overlap a lot with traces used for workload generation. After all, the records used to specify the non-executable parts of a workload are often obtained using instrumentation and monitoring tools. However, the content of traces in the instrumentation and monitoring domain often exceeds the content needed for workload generation. For example, monitoring tools often produce call path traces that detail which method within the code calls which other methods (see Chapter 6, Section 6.4.1). In workload generation, this is left to the executable parts of the workload (which may, of course, have used such information in their design), but is usually not relevant for traces that describe non-executable parts of a workload.

8.3.2 Workload Descriptions

Workload descriptions are specifications typically comprised of a set of parameters that specify how the executable parts of a workload are to be executed. Among other things, they describe how to configure, schedule, and place the executable components during benchmark execution. Workload descriptions can be concrete step-by-step instructions with parameters and actions for specific executable components. These types of descriptions can be very similar to traces, except for their artificial nature. However, workload descriptions may also be very generic and abstract. In the latter case, it is left to the benchmark to derive, at run time, the final concrete set of parameters for its executable components based on the abstract description. For example, an abstract workload description could specify a file of specific length, but containing random data, to be compressed with *zip*. The benchmark would then have to generate a random file according to the description when initializing. Afterwards, it can run the executable component (*zip* tool or library) with this concrete file as input.

Workload descriptions (as well as traces) must consider two major types of executable work units they describe, as the sets of parameters that must be considered by the descriptions differ considerably between these types:

- **Batch Workload:** A batch workload is a workload consisting of a single, usually long-running, executable work unit. A batch workload is run once until it completes or its execution is halted. Batch workloads lend themselves well (but not exclusively) to being used as a basis for building fixed-work benchmarks (see Chapter 1, Section 1.4.1).
- **Transactional Workload:** A transactional workload consists of small work units that are repeated multiple times during the execution of a benchmark. Each execution of such a work unit is referred to as a *transaction*. The workload may consist of multiple transaction types that are interwoven or run in parallel. Transactional workloads lend themselves well (but not exclusively) to being used as a basis for building fixed-time benchmarks (see Chapter 1, Section 1.4.2).

In general, descriptions for batch workload generation are simpler than those for their transactional counterparts. Batch workloads must consider the configuration for their long-running unit of work. This concerns mostly startup configuration and input data. In addition, the descriptions may have to deal with the initial placement of the batch workload on the available computing resources of the SUT.

Descriptions for transactional workloads are more complex. Before explaining this, we provide a definition of a workload transaction in the context of workload generation.

Definition 8.1 (Workload Transaction) A workload transaction is a concrete execution of an executable workload unit. It is characterized by the five properties listed in Table 8.2.

Transactional workload descriptions must specify many of the above properties of their respective workload transactions, although some of them (usually t_{end}) can be

Table 8.2: Properties of workload transactions

Symbol	Meaning
w	An executable unit of work
P	A set of executable workload-specific parameters p_i
V	A set of concrete values c_i for P used to initialize this specific transaction
t_{start}	A concrete point in time when the execution starts
t_{end}	A concrete point in time when the execution ends

a product of the workload's execution. At a minimum, the workload must specify the executable unit of work w and the values V for the workload-specific parameters P. Transaction starting times t_{start} are usually specified in advance, but may also be chosen at benchmark run time. In the latter case, the non-executable workload description must contain some sort of rules on how exactly to derive t_{start} during benchmark execution. t_{end} is usually not specified as part of workload descriptions, but it may be specified in special cases, such as transactional workloads with fixed transaction duration.

Transactional workloads can be classified into two groups (Schroeder et al., 2006):

- **Closed workload:** A closed workload assumes a fixed number of virtual *users* interacting with the system. It describes non-executable parts of a workload in terms of the actions a virtual user takes. Some user actions trigger execution of a transaction, yet other actions are also possible. For example, the user may have to wait for a certain time before triggering the next transaction. For each action, the user waits until the action completes and then performs the next action. The workload is considered *closed*, as all users exist from the beginning and users never leave the system performing a theoretically infinite (usually repeating) sequence of actions until stopped by workload termination (e.g., after a fixed time). In terms of a transaction's properties, closed workloads describe a transaction's start time t_{start} in a manner that depends on the end time t_{end} of some previous transactions (each user's first transaction being an exception).
- **Open workload:** An open workload assumes a varying number of virtual *users* interacting with the system. Users may enter the system at any specified arrival time to perform their actions and execute transactions. The users then exit the system once these actions are completed. In the simplest case, each user executes a single transaction before immediately exiting the system. In this case, the user can be reduced to a concrete set of transaction parameters V and an arrival time, which equals a single transaction's start time t_{start}. In more complex cases, users may perform multiple actions and start multiple transactions. In this case, only the user's arrival time is known in advance. t_{start} for each transaction is derived based on the user specification, as for closed workloads.

In the following, we present several concrete approaches to describe transactional workloads.

8.3.2.1 Closed Workloads

Closed workloads assume a fixed number of virtual *users* performing actions on the system under consideration. Many of these actions trigger the execution of an executable workload transaction. The workload description must cover two aspects: *generic configuration of users* and *description of the user actions*. The former deals with generic questions, such as how many users should be emulated or which resources of the SUT should be allocated to each user? These questions are generic in the sense that they do not consider the specific user actions, but their answers may be very specific to a concrete benchmark setup. For example, allocation of SUT resources to users can only be defined for a specific SUT with a concrete set of resources. Consequently, this configuration is often left to the operator executing the benchmark. It is expected that the operator documents the used parameter values to ensure reproducibility.

Second, a non-executable workload description must specify the user actions performed as part of the transactional workload. User actions are normally specified as a sequence or as a graph. In case of a sequence, users execute a series of (parameterized) transactions and potential wait actions. Considering that users do not leave the system, the sequence is repeated until the benchmark execution terminates. As a result, it can be viewed as a cycle.

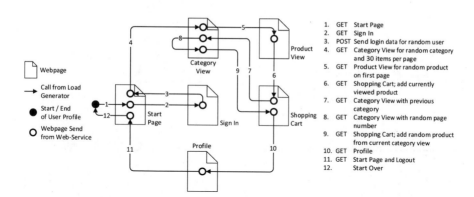

Fig. 8.2: User action sequence for TeaStore's *Browse* workload (see Chapter 14)

Figure 8.2 shows an example user action sequence from TeaStore's *Browse* workload (see Chapter 14). Users navigate the web store's pages. The workload transactions in this case are the web page calls with cookies, query parameters, and so forth, seen as transaction parameters P. The figure also makes it visually intuitive that a closed workload's user action sequence can be viewed as a *non-branching directed cyclic graph*. The directed graph is cyclic, as it connects the last action with the first one (or using a start/stop action connecting those two, as shown in the figure). It is non-branching, as each node has exactly one outgoing edge. In a cycle where every node has exactly one outgoing edge, it follows that each node must also have exactly one incoming edge.

Of course, the next step from a non-branching directed cyclic graph is a *branching directed cyclic graph* where nodes may have multiple outgoing and incoming edges, but all paths return to a defined starting node. Menascé, V. A. F. Almeida, et al. (1999) introduced such a graph for workload description of e-commerce applications, calling it *Customer Behavior Model Graph (CBMG)*. An example for such a graph is shown in Figure 8.3.

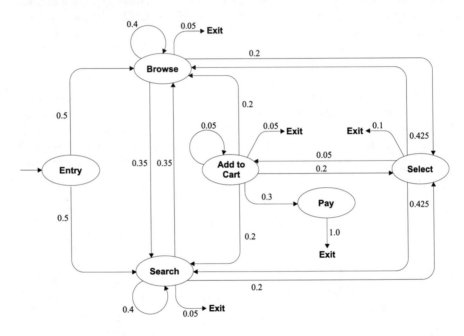

Fig. 8.3: Example of a customer behavior model graph (CBMG) (Menascé, V. A. F. Almeida, et al., 1999)

A CBMG has one node for each possible transaction (e.g., home page, browse (b), search (s), select (t), add to cart (a), and pay (p) in Figure 8.3) and directed edges connecting these transaction nodes. Similar to Markov chains (Bolch et al., 2006), a probability is assigned to each edge. When a virtual user reaches a node with multiple outgoing edges, one of these edges is chosen at random according to the probabilities of those edges. In practice, this choice is usually made using a pseudo-random number generator, which is initialized with a predefined and documented random seed to ensure reproducibility.

CBMGs do not consider wait actions. Instead, they use the concept of *think time* Z_s. Think time is defined as the waiting time between two transactions from the SUT's perspective. Each edge can be labeled with its own think time, indicating the time the workload execution must wait before starting the next transaction. Note that Figure 8.3 does not show think times. Also note that the edges labeled with "Exit" must be reconnected with the "Entry" node for the example to constitute a user example for a closed workload.

A CBMG can be more formally characterized by a pair (P, Z), where $P = [p_{i,j}]$ is an $n \times n$ matrix of transition probabilities between the n states of the CBMG, and $Z = [z_{i,j}]$ is an $n \times n$ matrix that represents the average think times between states of the CBMG.

CBMGs do not distinguish multiple types of virtual users. Instead a separate CBMG is used for each user type and virtual users are assigned a type and a corresponding CBMG according to a separately specified distribution.

If an application is deployed in a production environment, CBMGs can be automatically extracted from monitoring data collected during operation. An exemplary approach in this area, based on the techniques described in Chapter 6 (Section 6.4), is described by Vögele et al. (2018). The approach, called WESSBAS, enables the automatic extraction of workload descriptions similar to CBMGs from recorded execution logs of session-based web applications. The extracted workload descriptions can be used for workload generation (using load testing tools) or for building a performance model of the application (e.g., based on the queueing modeling techniques described in Chapter 7).

8.3.2.2 Open Workloads

Open workloads are workloads where virtual users may enter the system at any time to perform actions and execute transactions. The users then exit the system once these actions are completed. In other words, in open workloads, new jobs arrive independent of previous job completions. Open workloads are common in Web applications, as human users interacting with Web services are usually unaware of each other. In contrast to closed workloads, open workloads must specify how to determine when new users arrive. The *arrival time* of a user is the time at which a new user starts executing actions on the SUT. In the simplest case, a user simply executes a single transaction before immediately exiting the system. In this case, the user can be reduced to a concrete set of transaction parameters V and its arrival time equals a single transaction's start time t_{start}.

With users entering the system at different times and then leaving after completion of their activities, *load intensity* becomes a major workload property to consider. In the context of benchmark workloads, Kistowski, Herbst, et al. (2017) define *load intensity* as the *arrival rate* of abstract workload units (usually virtual users or single transactions) at a given point in time.

A *load intensity profile* is a function that describes the load intensity over time. Real-life examples of such profiles can be found for many applications. As an example, Figure 8.4 shows a load profile of HTTP requests to the NASA Kennedy Space Center web server starting July 1, 1995 at 00:00. This example profile is a *varying* profile, as the arrival rate changes over time, which is common in real-life applications.

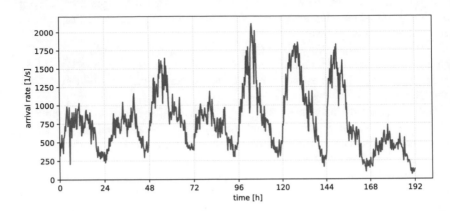

Fig. 8.4: Load intensity profile of the NASA Kennedy Space Center web server

Steady State   In order to improve the ability to compute statistical measures for measurements taken during a benchmark run, many open workloads are designed to be executed in *steady state*, also referred to as *operational equilibrium* (see Chapter 7, Section 7.1). This implies that for a given measurement interval, the number of work units present in the system at the beginning of the interval should equal the number of units at the end of the interval. The intended effect of this state is that, for multiple intervals, the number of work units completed per interval (i.e., the throughput) should remain constant. In practice, it is hard to achieve a true steady state for workloads executed on real-world computing devices. After all, the rate of work unit completion is a product of the SUT and not necessarily known in advance. In addition, it is reasonable to expect the SUT to exhibit at least some performance variability.

The quality (i.e., steadiness) of a steady-state workload can be measured by considering the throughput variability, where a lower variability indicates a higher workload stability. The indices of dispersion introduced in Chapter 4 (Section 4.1) can be used to quantify the throughput variability. The sample *variance* and *standard deviation* are generally applicable in this context. However, they have the drawback of being workload dependent; that is, a workload with a higher mean throughput (e.g., due to smaller, less computationally expensive work units) is likely to have higher absolute throughput variance and standard deviation. To account for this, the coefficient of variation (COV), which is a dimensionless quantity, is normally used.

Based on the throughput COV, a benchmark can report the quality of its generated steady-state workload. In addition, industry-standard and regulatory benchmarks can define upper bounds for this metric for steady-state workloads. Benchmark runs where the workload exceeds these bounds are considered invalid. For example, the Power and Performance Benchmark Methodology (SPECpower Committee, 2014) defines an upper bound of 5% on the throughput COV for steady-state workloads.

Generating Steady-State Workloads The generation of any open workload requires definition of the *arrival times* of the work units (i.e., transactions, virtual users) under consideration. For steady-state workloads, it is intuitive that the (mean) arrival time should be evenly distributed. The obvious way of achieving this is to use a constant inter-arrival time, resulting in equidistant arrival times. Doing this would result in an equal amount of work arriving in each interval. The workload's throughput variation should be small as long as the SUT is able to handle the given load intensity.

However, equidistant arrival times have some drawbacks. First, they only allow testing of a very specific scenario where the SUT has a guaranteed pause after the arrival of each request until the arrival of the next. A benchmarker might want to have more variation in order to test the SUT's behavior when dealing with varying inter-arrival times. Second, equidistant arrival times are not representative of the behavior of real-world system users. Especially, human users send requests independently and are generally unaware of each other.

Instead of using equidistant arrival times, we assume that request arrivals follow a *Poisson process*. In general, a Poisson process describes random arrivals that arrive at a mean arrival rate of λ, but are otherwise independent of each other. This is useful for generating steady-state open workloads. We do want each workload to have a stable mean arrival rate, but also want it to exhibit some variation. The Poisson assumption of independent users matches our perception of real-world users for many types of open workloads. The inter-arrival times needed to generate such workloads can be modeled using an *exponential distribution*. Equation (8.1) shows the probability density function (PDF) for the exponential distribution with a mean arrival rate λ.

$$f_\lambda(x) = \begin{cases} \lambda e^{-\lambda x} & x \geq 0 \\ 0 & x < 0 \end{cases} \tag{8.1}$$

To generate an open workload with exponentially distributed inter-arrival times, we dispatch a work unit (i.e., create a virtual user or start a transaction) and then draw a waiting time from an exponential distribution. This exponential distribution must be parameterized with our target mean arrival rate as its parameter λ.

A practical concern when generating load with varying inter-arrival times (usually exponentially distributed) is the amount of computational work that must be performed by the load driver. The load driver must perform computations in order to draw from the exponential distribution for every single request. If run on the SUT, the load on the benchmark harness might influence the measurement results. If run on a separate machine sending requests over a network, the hardware requirements for the load generator machine might prevent some users from being able to execute the benchmark. A practical solution to this is to perform some work unit batching as done in the SPEC Power benchmarks (SPECpower Committee, 2014). To reduce the computational load on the load driver, work units are aggregated into work unit batches of a fixed size. All work units within these batches are sent out at once and the waiting times are only used to derive inter-batch waiting times.

Open Workloads with Varying Arrival Rates Steady-state measurements are usually preferred when working with open workloads as they allow for calculation of statistically significant measures on the set of obtained results. However, some benchmarking use cases require arrival rates to vary and change over time resulting in non-steady-state measurements. Examples include stress tests that steadily increase the load intensity in order to determine the maximum load that can be handled by the SUT. A more complex example of varying arrival rates can be found in the context of the cloud elasticity benchmarks described in Chapter 15. These benchmarks are designed to evaluate the resource management behavior of cloud systems when the load intensity varies.

A workload description for an open workload with a varying arrival rate profile must specify the arrival rates and how they change over time. Concrete inter-arrival times for the user (or transaction) arrivals can then be derived from this profile. This can be achieved by specifying the target arrival rate for each measurement interval and then drawing concrete inter-arrival times from stochastic distributions (e.g., exponential distribution) in the same way that is done for steady-state workloads.

A varying arrival rate profile can be modeled as a *time series*. It can be reduced to a single scalar data point (i.e., arrival rate) defined for a series of points in time. Kistowski, Herbst, et al. (2017) extract workloads from real-world arrival rate time series by decomposing them into different workload-relevant parts: *seasonal*, *trend*, *burst*, and *noise* (inspired by regular time series decomposition schemes such as the ones by Verbesselt et al. (2010) and Cleveland et al. (1990)). Figure 8.5 shows an example of such a decomposition (without the optional burst part).

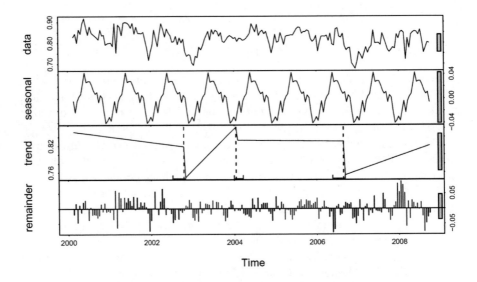

Fig. 8.5: Example decomposition of a time series into *season*, *trend*, and *noise* (Verbesselt et al., 2010)

The *seasonal* part of a load intensity profile is its repeating part. It repeats indefinitely until the profile ends or until a major break in the profile replaces it with a new seasonal pattern. Seasonal patterns are often sinusoidal in appearance and may be described or approximated using sinusoidal functions. The seasonal part has an inherent period (i.e., the duration of a single season). In a real-life profile, seasonal patterns would constitute things such as daily or weekly usage patterns.

The *trend* part of the load intensity profile is a piecewise function that models the workload changes over longer time frames. It spans one or more seasonal periods and is normally added to or multiplied with the seasonal base function. Trends show overarching developments over time, for example, an increasing number of users of an online shop each day in December up to the holiday season. In this example, the base night–day seasonal pattern remains stable, but the number of users per day increases.

The *burst* part is an optional part that describes planned or unplanned single events that significantly affect the profile for a short time span. Bursts are not considered in generic time series decomposition methods, as they are somewhat specific to workload intensity profiles. However, they are of relevance for benchmark engineers as they may want to test a system's response to a sudden unexpected increase in load. An example for a planned burst would be the sudden increase in hits to a manufacturer's site after a big product announcement. An example for an unplanned burst could be the increase in load to a social media site after a natural disaster.

Finally, the *noise* part constitutes the remainder that is not captured as part of the season, trend, and burst parts. It can be modeled as a stochastic distribution parameterized with the parameters specific to the distribution of choice.

8.3.3 System-Metric-Based Workload Descriptions

In this book, we consider workload descriptions to describe non-executable parts of a workload in terms of its relevant parameters and elements. Workload descriptions typically cover transactions, transaction parameters, request arrival times, user profiles, and user actions. This is the primary way of describing workloads for benchmark designers whose goal normally is to evaluate the system behavior when executing the respective workloads.

However, some areas of research also require the reverse way of workload specification, that is, specifying a workload that elicits a certain target behavior on the SUT, characterized by a specified system metric. For example, a researcher or a system designer might want a workload to cause a CPU utilization of 80% on the SUT in order to conduct some specific SUT analysis. This would result in a workload specification based on targeted system metrics instead of workload metrics. Generating a workload based on a system metric specification is usually done using one of the two approaches: (1) a priori workload analysis and calibration or (2) run-time control loops.

A priori workload analysis and calibration runs one or more separate experiments to measure the SUT-specific workload characteristics. The benchmark then derives a regular non-executable workload description with the target SUT metrics based on these calibration and analysis results. An example of such a priori calibration runs can be found in the BUNGEE Cloud Elasticity Benchmark (Herbst et al., 2015) described in Chapter 15. Note that such workload analysis and calibration experiments also have many uses outside of benchmarking. Among other things, they can be used by software developers for bottleneck detection or by system operators for evaluation of resource management strategies.

As an alternative to a priori calibration, a workload can use a *run-time control loop*. This loop is configured with the observed system metrics during execution and controls the parameters of the workload in order to achieve a target metric result. Some care must be taken when designing such a loop, as control loops are generally prone to oscillation.

8.4 Concluding Remarks

In this chapter, we focused on benchmark workloads considering their characteristics in the context of workload generation. We started by introducing the distinction between executable and non-executable parts of a workload as well as the distinction between natural and artificial workloads. The executable parts were then discussed in detail, including natural benchmarks, application workloads, and synthetic workloads. Next, the non-executable parts were discussed, distinguishing between workload traces and workload descriptions. In the rest of the chapter, we introduced the different types of workload descriptions that can be used for batch workloads and transactional workloads as well as for open and closed workloads. The challenges of generating steady-state workloads and workloads with varying arrival rates were discussed. Finally, the chapter concluded with a brief introduction of system-metric-based workload descriptions.

References

Bolch, G., Greiner, S., Meer, H. de, and Trivedi, K. S. (2006). *Queueing Networks and Markov Chains: Modeling and Performance Evaluation with Computer Science Applications*. Second Edition. John Wiley & Sons: Hoboken, New Jersey, USA (cited on pp. 186, 194).

Cleveland, R. B., Cleveland, W. S., McRae, J. E., and Terpenning, I. (1990). "STL: A Seasonal-Trend Decomposition Procedure Based on Loess". *Journal of Official Statistics*, 6(1). Statistics Sweden (SCB): Stockholm, Sweden, pp. 3–73 (cited on p. 198).

Herbst, N. R., Kounev, S., Weber, A., and Groenda, H. (2015). "BUNGEE: An Elasticity Benchmark for Self-adaptive IaaS Cloud Environments". In: *Proceedings of the 10th International Symposium on Software Engineering for Adaptive and Self-Managing Systems (SEAMS 2015)*. (Florence, Italy). IEEE: Piscataway, NJ, USA, pp. 46–56 (cited on p. 200).

Kistowski, J. von, Eismann, S., Schmitt, N., Bauer, A., Grohmann, J., and Kounev, S. (2018). "TeaStore: A Micro-Service Reference Application for Benchmarking, Modeling and Resource Management Research". In: *Proceedings of the 26th IEEE International Symposium on the Modelling, Analysis, and Simulation of Computer and Telecommunication Systems (MASCOTS 2018)*. (Milwaukee, WI, USA). IEEE Computer Society: Washington, DC, USA (cited on p. 188).

Kistowski, J. von, Herbst, N. R., Kounev, S., Groenda, H., Stier, C., and Lehrig, S. (2017). "Modeling and Extracting Load Intensity Profiles". *ACM Transactions on Autonomous and Adaptive Systems*, 11(4). ACM: New York, NY, USA, 23:1–23:28 (cited on pp. 195, 198).

Lange, K.-D. (2009). "Identifying Shades of Green: The SPECpower Benchmarks". *Computer*, 42(3). IEEE: Piscataway, NJ, USA, pp. 95–97 (cited on p. 188).

Menascé, D. A., Almeida, V. A. F., Fonseca, R. C., and Mendes, M. A. (1999). "A Methodology for Workload Characterization of E-Commerce Sites". In: *Proceedings of the 1st ACM Conference on Electronic Commerce (EC'99)*. (Denver, Colorado, USA). ACM: New York, NY, USA, pp. 119–128 (cited on p. 194).

Menascé, D. A., Almeida, V. A., and Dowdy, L. W. (2004). *Performance by Design: Computer Capacity Planning By Example*. Prentice Hall: Upper Saddle River, NJ, USA (cited on p. 186).

Schroeder, B., Wierman, A., and Harchol-Balter, M. (2006). "Open Versus Closed: A Cautionary Tale". In: *Proceedings of the 3rd Conference on Networked Systems Design & Implementation - Volume 3 (NSDI 2006)*. (San Jose, CA). USENIX Association: Berkeley, CA, USA, pp. 18–18 (cited on p. 192).

SPECpower Committee (2014). *Power and Performance Benchmark Methodology V2.2*. Gainesville, VA, USA: Standard Performance Evaluation Corporation (SPEC) (cited on pp. 196, 197).

Verbesselt, J., Hyndman, R., Newnham, G., and Culvenor, D. (2010). "Detecting Trend and Seasonal Changes in Satellite Image Time Series". *Remote Sensing of Environment*, 114(1). Elsevier Science: Amsterdam, The Netherlands, pp. 106–115 (cited on p. 198).

Vögele, C., Hoorn, A. van, Schulz, E., Hasselbring, W., and Krcmar, H. (2018). "WESSBAS: Extraction of Probabilistic Workload Specifications for Load Testing and Performance Prediction—A Model-Driven Approach for Session-Based Application Systems". *Software & Systems Modeling*, 17(2). Springer-Verlag: Berlin, Heidelberg, pp. 443–477 (cited on p. 195).

Chapter 9
Standardization

> "The reputation of current 'benchmarketing' claims regarding system performance is on par with the promises made by politicians during elections." (1993)
> —*Kaivalya M. Dixit (1942-2004), Long-time SPEC President*

In order to maintain the usefulness of a good benchmark, it needs a continuous development cycle to keep up with emerging technologies. For example, in order to accurately measure the performance gain of a new computer microarchitecture, a compiled version of the benchmark code (including its libraries, if applicable) supporting this new microarchitecture would be required. Performance gains of less than 3.0% from microarchitecture optimizations are quite common. In an effort to provide and maintain fair industry standards for measuring system-level and component-level performance of computer systems, industry-standard consortia such as the Standard Performance Evaluation Corporation (SPEC)[1] and the Transaction Processing Performance Council (TPC)[2] were established in 1988. In 1998, the Storage Performance Council (SPC)[3] was founded with a focus on standardizing industry-standard storage benchmarks. In this chapter, we provide an overview of benchmark standardization efforts in the area of computer systems benchmarking. We focus on SPEC and TPC, the two most prominent benchmark standardization bodies in the area of computer systems and information technology (IT). A brief overview of SPC can be found in Chapter 13.

9.1 Historical Perspective on Computer Systems Benchmarking

Since the earliest days of digital computer systems, the goal of quantifying, improving, and optimizing computer performance has been a subject of great interest. The

---

[1] Standard Performance Evaluation Corporation (SPEC): https://www.spec.org

[2] Transaction Processing Performance Council (TPC): http://www.tpc.org

[3] Storage Performance Council (SPC): https://spcresults.org

© Springer Nature Switzerland AG 2020

S. Kounev et al., *Systems Benchmarking*, https://doi.org/10.1007/978-3-030-41705-5_9

earliest performance benchmarks were based on comparisons of low-level instruction execution times. A mix of several of these execution times would be combined to produce an overall rating that could be compared between systems. The most well-known of these early benchmarks was the Gibson Mix, devised by Jack Gibson of IBM (Gibson, 1970). As high-level computer languages were developed, more complex applications were created to develop additional rigorous methods of measuring a system's performance. Whetstone (Longbottom, 2004) and Dhrystone (Weiss, 2002) are both early examples of high-level language benchmarks.

One of the first benchmarks to attempt to standardize the measurement of floating-point performance of CPUs was Whetstone. Developed in 1972 by Harold Curnow of the UK Central Computer and Telecommunications Agency,[4] the benchmark workload was a representation of a set of 124 simple Whetstone ALGOL 60 compiler instructions translated into FORTRAN. The benchmark result was measured in thousands of Whetstone instructions per second (KWIPS), and later in millions of Whetstone instructions per second (MWIPS). The benchmark was updated over the years and ported to C, C++, Basic, and Java. It has frequently been included in component benchmark suites.

The synthetic benchmark program Dhrystone (a pun on the benchmark name Whetstone) was developed by Reinhold P. Weicker in 1984 to measure integer-based processing performance. It utilized metadata from several applications written in different programming languages with frequency of high-level language constructs similar to that of real applications studied. For many years, Dhrystone was considered the representative benchmark for general processor performance. Originally written in Ada, it was translated into C and ported to UNIX, and it is still often used as part of component benchmark suites. In later years, Weicker joined SPEC to develop industry-standard benchmarks that focus on compute performance and advised that people should rely on the SPEC CPU benchmarks (see Chapter 10) in place of Dhrystone.

As computer systems became more complex, benchmarks were developed to measure the performance of the individual system components such as memory, floating-point arithmetic coprocessors, data I/O, etc. Most of these early benchmarks utilized synthetic workloads and were usually provided to users as source code that needed to be compiled on the system under test (SUT). This allowed such benchmarks to be used on multiple platforms, but there were generally no run rules on how to compile such benchmarks or how to compare results between different architectures, which limited the scope of their use.

The LINPACK[5] benchmark (Dongarra et al., 2003) uses the LINPACK software library to solve a set of n-by-n linear algebra equations in order to measure a system's floating-point computing performance using *floating-point operations per second (FLOPS)* as a metric. The benchmark workload is almost exclusively floating-point based, so it is an excellent stressor of the processors' math and vector instruction sets. There have been several versions of LINPACK benchmarks since their creation

---

[4] Whetstone benchmark history and results: http://www.roylongbottom.org.uk/whetstone.htm

[5] LINPACK benchmark programs and reports: http://www.netlib.org/benchmark/index.html

in 1979, which include LINPACK 100 (n=100), LINPACK 1000 (n=1000), and HPLinpack (a highly parallelized version that can run across multiple systems). HPL is a portable implementation of the HPLinpack benchmark written in C. Precompiled LINPACK and HPL are available for a number of system architectures.

The STREAM[6] benchmark (McCalpin, 1995) is a simple synthetic benchmark that measures sustainable memory bandwidth, reported in MB/s. It requires that the dataset must be much larger than the available processor cache on any given system so that the results are more indicative of the performance of a very large vector-style application. The benchmark yields four metrics representing different memory operations: Copy, Add, Scale, and Triad. The benchmark is available in C and FORTRAN, which can run either in a single-threaded or distributed fashion. A precompiled version of this benchmark is often included in component benchmark suites.

lmbench[7] measures the memory and network data bandwidth performance, as well as the latency of operating system primitive operations, such as system calls and process creation. It was originally developed by Larry McVoy during his work at Sun Microsystems. He continued its development after his move to Silicon Graphics and was joined by Carl Staelin from the Hewlett-Packard Laboratories.

Netperf[8] performs bandwidth testing between two hosts on a network. It measures the performance of bulk data transfer and request/response network traffic, using either TCP or UDP via BSD sockets. There are optional tests that measure the performance of DLPI, UnixDomainSockets, the Fore ATM API, and the HP HiPPI LLa interface. Originally developed by Hewlett-Packard, it is now available on GitHub. Netperf has been ported to run on numerous distributions of UNIX, Linux, Windows, and VMware.

These benchmarks are useful tools to analyze IT equipment and troubleshoot performance bottlenecks. They utilize standard applications (or their core routines that focus on a particular access pattern) in order to measure the performance of a primary server or storage component, such as CPU computations, memory accesses, storage I/O, or network I/O. By limiting their scope, component benchmarks enable deeper analysis of the targeted subsystem. At the same time, component benchmarks are often less complex and easier to develop than benchmarks that stress the complete system environment. Therefore, component benchmarks are typically less expensive to run because they require less equipment and engineering resources.

Single component benchmarks are generally not directly useful for evaluating complete IT environments, as they only evaluate a specific system aspect or component. A suite of component benchmarks like the SERT suite (Lange and Tricker, 2011) can be a key method for measuring the behavior of the primary server and storage components. Nonetheless, they are not measuring the interaction and possible performance bottlenecks between those components. The real usefulness of component benchmarks is their role in simplifying performance analysis and pinpointing

---

[6] STREAM benchmark: https://www.cs.virginia.edu/stream/

[7] lmbench benchmark: http://www.bitmover.com/lmbench

[8] Netperf benchmark: https://github.com/HewlettPackard/netperf

the actual performance bottlenecks within a component. The primary application of component benchmarks is their usage during system development and the design/deployment phases of new IT environments. In general, the first step is to run one of the component suites (or a series of hand-picked component benchmarks) in order to determine if one subsystem exhibits lower-than-expected performance. Next, an analysis of the subsystem is conducted to further pinpoint the root causes. For example, suppose that the performance results from the SERT suite show lower-than-expected CPU subsystem performance. The next step would include running the SPEC CPU2017 benchmark suite (cf. Chapter 10) to further investigate the root cause. Finally, after a possible resolution of the issues is implemented, the original component suite should be run again in order to verify that the resolution satisfactorily fixed the bottleneck. Note that it is the nature of performance bottlenecks to switch from one component to another once the root cause of the original bottleneck is resolved.

9.2 Standard Performance Evaluation Corporation (SPEC)

The global non-profit consortium, SPEC, was formed in 1988 with the goal to establish, maintain, and endorse a standardized set of relevant benchmarks that can be applied to the newest generation of compute equipment. SPEC fostered the collaboration of hardware and software vendors, as well as academia, to advance the practice of computer performance and server efficiency measurement. Over 20 benchmarks and tools were developed by SPEC to ensure that the marketplace has an industry-standard set of metrics to differentiate computing systems in a fair and useful manner. For the last 30+ years, its benchmarks have been well-studied in academia (Hennessy and Patterson, 1990) and influenced industry designs of computer architecture and software. SPEC became an influential example for other groups, both in methodology and organization.

9.2.1 SPEC's Origin

In the late 1980s, UNIX and C had become widespread, which increased software portability and eased creations of new microprocessor architectures. There was tremendous interest in which of the many new processor designs would enable computer workstations to break out and bring the promise of high-performance computing directly to the individual engineers and designers in a myriad of offices around the world. These microprocessor wars were fierce and their marketing was confusing, often invoking ill-defined ratings in millions of instructions per second (MIPS) or millions of floating-point operations per second (MFLOPS). The existing benchmarks were weakly defined, and their ambiguities allowed vendors to increase their scores in ways that impeded fair comparisons. Nonetheless, performance results were republished or created by magazines, for example, Byte, Digital Review, UNIX Review, or Electronic Engineering Times (EE Times).

The idea that started SPEC and changed the ways in which computers were measured and compared arose from a small group of industry's leading performance-minded computer architects sharing a round of drinks in a local bar. The engineers were frustrated at the quality of information being used to try to evaluate their new designs, and even worse, being used to make decisions that determined which designs were funded and which were ignored.

Key to this conversation was the host of this gathering, the respected journalist Stan Baker from EE Times magazine. At a recent trade event, Baker had again fielded complaints from architects about the news coverage of their new designs and the "microkernel" benchmark based comparisons. In particular, John Mashey from MIPS Computer Systems complained about an article ranking systems based on Dhrystone MIPS. He pointed out that his testing of actual customer applications, as published in the MIPS Performance Brief, showed a completely different story, and no vendor liked the Dhrystone-based rankings. Baker threw the challenge back at these architects suggesting "If you don't like it, give me something better!" More importantly, Baker initiated the next step and offered his bar in Campbell, California as a neutral meeting ground for Mashey and the representatives from his major competitors, Hewlett-Packard, Apollo Computer, and Sun Microsystems, in order to listen to each other's complaints. In spite of the intense company rivalries and massive corporate expenditures on competitive marketing, key designers and other principals knew each other well enough to be comfortable "talking shop" with each other, mostly because the community of leading processor and system architects was relatively small.

Baker began a series of meetings to discuss what they should do to provide useful benchmarks that produce well-documented, repeatable, and reliable results. They were all using a copy of the popular GCC compiler[9] as a test for basic computations as well as workloads based on the common SPICE tool[10] to simulate calculation-intensive circuits and stress the processor's floating-point unit (FPU). There were more than a dozen of these tests in common usage across the internal tests; unfortunately, everybody was using a different GCC version and different input data. They quickly reached agreement on an overall methodology that included the need for multiple sub-benchmarks with a metric that reported performance ratios using the geometric mean for composite summaries as discussed in detail in Chapter 3 (Section 3.5.3.2).

Earnest work began to create a single copy of these codes, with the same set of input files, and all producing the same outputs across each system tested. This code could not be under the control of a single vendor and therefore the group convinced their respective companies to support this effort by creating a workable organizational structure and by recruiting additional vendors. In November 1988, EE Times, Apollo Computer, Hewlett-Packard, MIPS, and Sun Microsystem decided to form

---

[9] GNU website: https://gcc.gnu.org

[10] SPICE website: http://bwrcs.eecs.berkeley.edu/Classes/IcBook/SPICE

the non-profit Standard Performance Evaluation Cooperative (SPEC)—later changed
to Standard Performance Evaluation Corporation. Thus, what started as a series of
informal meetings became a formal cooperative, established to develop standard
benchmarks for comparing systems. Stan Baker served as the first President when
SPEC was incorporated, and he was later succeeded by Kaivalya Dixit, Walter Bays,
and David Reiner.

9.2.2 Membership

SPEC has grown over the last 30 years from a single benchmark development group
into the largest organization in its field. Its diverse membership[11] is comprised
of interested computer hardware and software vendors, educational and research
institutions, government agencies, and supporting individuals who commit to support
SPEC's common goals. Their reasons for joining and contributing to SPEC include:

- Access to cutting-edge benchmark development,
- Access to all benchmarks of a specific group,
- Influence on the development of new benchmarks and tools,
- Participation in development meetings,
- Getting information on the latest thinking in commercial engineering,
- Publication of benchmark results,
- Gaining real-world experience for graduate students to aid in dissertation research
  and job searches,
- Connecting with many leading universities globally for research collaboration,
- Utilizing collaboration opportunities for participation in the ACM/SPEC International Conference on Performance Engineering (ICPE).

9.2.3 Structure and Organization

SPEC has established four groups (see Figure 9.1), each with its own governing
bodies, subcommittees, project groups, and working groups. These groups report to
SPEC's Board of Directors, which acts on behalf of SPEC's membership to make
overall policy decisions, provide oversight, and perform SPEC's financial and legal
fiduciary responsibilities.

---

[11] SPEC membership: https://www.spec.org/consortium

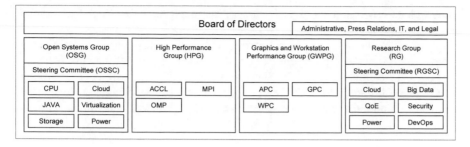

Fig. 9.1: SPEC's organizational structure

9.2.4 Open Systems Group (OSG)

The OSG, the original SPEC group, focuses on component- and system-level benchmarks for desktop systems, high-end workstations, and servers running open systems operating environments. It is governed by the Open System Steering Committee (OSSC), which helps with overarching issues and supports the collaboration between its large number of subcommittees, benchmarks, and members. In 2020, the OSG has six subcommittees and one working group, each focusing on a different computing area.

The OSG CPU Subcommittee created the first SPEC benchmark SPECmark, later known as SPEC CPU 89, and subsequently released new versions over the years. For the full history and details on their benchmark releases, we refer the reader to Chapter 10.

The first storage benchmark from SPEC was released in 1993 by the SFS Subcommittee, now called the OSG Storage Subcommittee. The latest version, SFS2014, measures file server throughput and response time of end-to-end storage solutions for specific applications and its details can be found in Chapter 13.

The OSG Java Subcommittee develops client- and server-side Java benchmarks. Their current benchmarks are JVM2008, JBB2015, the SPECjEnterprise (Java EE) Enterprise Application Server benchmarks, and the Java Message Service benchmark SPECjms2007 (Sachs et al., 2009).

In 2006, the new OSG Power Subcommittee was founded and developed SPECpower_ssj2008, the first industry-standard benchmark for evaluating the energy efficiency for server class computers (Lange, 2009). Additionally, they released the SPEC PTDaemon, the Server Efficiency Rating Tool (SERT) (Lange and Tricker, 2011), and the Chauffeur Worklet Development Kit (WDK). More details about this subcommittee and its work can be found in Chapter 11.

The OSG Virtualization Subcommittee's SPEC VIRT_SC 2013 benchmark measures the end-to-end performance of data center servers used in virtualized server consolidation. Details about their development can be found in Chapter 12.

The SPEC Cloud IaaS 2016 Benchmark, developed by the OSG Cloud Subcommittee, provides metrics and workloads for performance evaluation of public and private cloud environments, focusing on Infrastructure-as-a-Service (IaaS) cloud platforms.

In late 2018, the OSG Machine Learning (ML) working group was established in order to explore the requirements for benchmarks in the area of machine learning and possible creation of a new OSG Subcommittee. At the conclusion of the working group's feasibility study, the OSSC may either terminate the working group or charter it as a subcommittee to continue its work to develop a standard benchmark.

9.2.5 Graphics and Workstation Performance Group (GWPG)

Initially, SPEC was focused only on CPU benchmarks. Administrative functions were contracted to the National Computer Graphics Association (NCGA), which had an analogous mission for graphics performance benchmarks. NCGA had grown out of an effort in ACM's SIGGRAPH to create application standards. Financial difficulties forced NCGA to the brink of dissolution, which would have eliminated the standard graphics performance benchmark efforts as well as SPEC's administrative contract. Both sides shared common principles of openness, repeatability, and representative measures and in 1996, SPEC not only hired NCGA's administrative staff but moved the Graphics Performance Council (GPC), now called the Graphics and Workstation Performance Group (GWPG), under its umbrella. GWPG's focus is on the development of benchmarks that measure the performance of professional-level workstations and graphics subsystems. Over the years, the group expanded to three project groups in order to create a stronger focus in each of their development teams.

The Graphics Performance Characterization (SPECgpc) group[12] establishes graphics performance benchmarks for systems running under OpenGL and other application programming interfaces (APIs). Its SPECviewperf benchmark is the most popular standardized software worldwide for evaluating performance based on professional-level CAD/CAM, digital content creation, and visualization applications.

The Application Performance Characterization (SPECapc) group[13] provides a broad-ranging set of standardized benchmarks spanning popular CAD/CAM, digital content creation, and visualization applications.

The Workstation Performance Characterization (SPECwpc) group[14] has created a benchmark that measures the performance of workstations running algorithms used in popular professional applications, but without requiring the full application and associated licensing to be installed on the system under test.

---

[12] SPECgpc project group: https://www.spec.org/gwpg/gpc.static/overview.html

[13] SPECapc project group: https://www.spec.org/gwpg/apc.static/apc_overview.html

[14] SPECwpc project group: https://www.spec.org/gwpg/wpc.static/wpc_overview.html

9.2.6 High Performance Group (HPG)

The Perfect Club was an academic organization dedicated to the creation of a set of benchmarks suitable for evaluating performance of high performance and parallel systems. The professors involved wanted to focus on performance issues and had little time and interest in the ancillary work of managing the organization. Reassured by the successful integration of the GPC, the Perfect Club came into SPEC as the High Performance Group in 1994. Their goal is to develop benchmarks that target high-performance system architectures such as symmetric multi-processor systems, workstation clusters, distributed memory parallel systems, and traditional vector and vector parallel supercomputers. SPEC's HPG developed and maintained three distinguished benchmarks:

- SPEC ACCEL[15] focuses on the performance of highly parallel compute-intensive applications using hardware acceleration based on the OpenCL and OpenACC standards.
- SPEC MPI[16] is SPEC's benchmark suite for measuring the performance of compute-intensive applications using the Message-Passing Interface (MPI) across a wide range of cluster and SMP hardware.
- SPEC OMP[17] is designed for measuring the performance of applications based on the OpenMP standard for shared-memory parallel processing. The benchmark also includes an optional metric for measuring energy consumption.

9.2.7 Research Group (RG)

SPEC had a semi-regular tradition of benchmark workshops spurred on by European members like Reinhold Weicker, as the European industry had more of an academic orientation than the US industry. Some academics participated, attracted by the potential benefits to their research and by the existence of the HPG. But there was not a good structure for academics to participate in subcommittees, given that they are oriented towards relatively short-term deliverables relevant to the current market, whereas researchers are often oriented towards the evaluation of future architectures. Moreover, the SPEC workshops, which were not refereed, did not count towards university publications, and so it was difficult for professors and students to get funding to travel to these workshops to present their work or to hear about work of others in their field.

In 2011, SPEC's Research Group (RG)[18] was formed with the mission to promote innovative research in the area of quantitative system evaluation and analysis by

---

[15] SPEC ACCEL: https://www.spec.org/accel

[16] SPEC MPI: https://www.spec.org/mpi2007

[17] SPEC OMP: https://www.spec.org/omp2012

[18] SPEC RG: https://research.spec.org

serving as a platform for collaborative research efforts and to foster interactions between industry and academia in the field.

The scope of this group includes computer benchmarking, performance evaluation, and experimental system analysis in general, considering both classical performance metrics such as response time, throughput, scalability, and efficiency as well as other non-functional system properties included under the term dependability, for example, availability, reliability, and security (cf. Section 1.2 in Chapter 1).

The conducted research efforts span the design of metrics for system evaluation as well as the development of methodologies, techniques, and tools for measurement, load testing, profiling, workload characterization, dependability, and efficiency evaluation of computing systems.

The RG started off with two working groups covering the areas of cloud performance and security benchmarking, and it subsequently established four additional working groups expanding into the areas of Big Data, DevOps, Power, and Quality-of-Experience (QoE). Besides guiding its working groups, the Research Group Steering Committee (RGSC) publishes the regular SPEC RG Newsletter, determines the annual winner of the SPEC Kaivalya Dixit Distinguished Dissertation Award, and coordinates with the ICPE Steering Committee on its upcoming conferences.

The RG also maintains a peer-reviewed tools repository[19] for quantitative system evaluation and analysis. Tools published in this repository have undergone a thorough review process by multiple independent experts to ensure high quality and relevance to the community. The review process covers important quality factors, including maturity, availability, and usability. Most tools include ready-to-use binaries, documentation, usage rules (including licenses), and source code. Figure 9.2 illustrates the interaction of SPEC RG with other groups within SPEC as well as with external entities.

9.2.8 Benchmark Development Cycle

Over the years, SPEC has implemented and fine-tuned its development processes in order to guide its membership to produce fair benchmarks. In the following, we briefly describe the general SPEC benchmark development cycle (see Figure 9.3). Individual subcommittees have customized this process in order to accommodate their specific target workload and performance domain.

For each benchmark, the workload and benchmark harness code is developed and ported to a variety of platforms by members of a subcommittee that focuses on a specific compute area or subsystem, for example, CPU, storage, energy efficiency. This ensures that the timing of the workload and the execution of the actual stress on the subsystem(s) are equally challenging on each platform and therefore rendering the results from different architectures comparable. A number of different harnesses

---

[19] SPEC RG tool repository: https://research.spec.org/tools

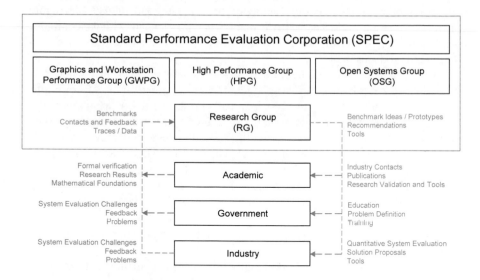

Fig. 9.2: SPEC RG's interaction within SPEC and with external entities

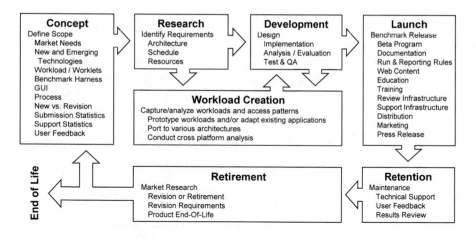

Fig. 9.3: SPEC's benchmark development cycle

are in use at SPEC, developed for the requirements of particular workloads. However, it is quite common that a new benchmark can reuse a harness developed by another group as-is, or with minor alterations.

The members of the subcommittee are also responsible for writing the *Run and Reporting Rules (R&RR)* for each of their benchmarks, which must be followed in order to create a valid benchmark result in the form of a *Full Disclosure Report (FDR)*. In order to help the benchmark user to measure a compliant result, the subcommittee creates a corresponding report generator and validation program, which combines and validates the performance (and power) data with the configuration details, flags any invalid or inconsistent information, calculates the benchmark metric, and produces the FDR.

Results produced with the benchmark can be submitted to SPEC, where they will undergo a 2-week review cycle conducted by the members of the subcommittee which rejects results that are not in compliance with the R&RR. During this review period the subcommittee may question the submitter concerning details of the measurement and the tested equipment, and the submitter responses may alleviate the subcommittee's concerns regarding run rule compliance. The FDR of a compliant result that passed the review will be published on SPEC's website.

SPEC has published *Fair Use Rules*[20] for the use of each SPEC benchmark result in order to guide fair public comparisons. The benchmark support for each benchmark is also handled by the corresponding subcommittee, further encouraging members to put the highest quality in their products in order to minimize their support burden.

SPEC has reviewed over 64,000 results and turned them into a large public repository of well-documented, peer-reviewed benchmark results.

9.3 Transaction Processing Performance Council (TPC)

In the 1980s, commercial computing came into its own. No longer was computing the realm of government, academia, and very large corporations. Virtually every business of reasonable size was looking to computer technology for "run your business" applications. This generated a large demand for computing products, which a wide range of hardware and software manufacturers were happy to fulfill.

These "run your business" applications were typified by individual units of work referred to as *transactions*. As an example, you go to a bank to withdraw some cash, the teller reduces the balance in your account, and delivers the cash to you—a complete transaction. As another example, you bring groceries to the counter, check them out, and pay—a complete transaction. In each case, it is important that the entire transaction completes (you would not be happy if the bank teller reduced your balance but did not deliver the cash; nor would the store be happy if you collected your groceries without paying).

Given the extensive opportunities in the area of transaction processing, the competition among computer vendors was intense. A key aspect of this competition was to demonstrate superiority in the ability to perform these business transactions. Beginning in the mid-1980s, computer system and database vendors began to make performance claims based upon the TP1 benchmark, a benchmark originally developed within IBM that then found its way into the public domain. However, being in the public domain without regulation allowed each vendor to implement the "benchmark" in

---

[20] SPEC fair use rules: https://www.spec.org/fairuse.html

ways that highlighted their strengths and avoided their weaknesses—miraculously, EVERYONE was best! As a result and not surprisingly, the TP1 marketing claims, had little credibility with the press, market researchers (among them Omri Serlin, the founder of TPC), or users. The situation also deeply frustrated vendors who believed their competitors' marketing claims, based upon flawed benchmark implementations, were ruining every vendor's credibility.

Early Attempts at Civilized Competition, as stated by Kim Shanley, TPC's first consortium administrator (Shanley, 1998):

In the April 1, 1985 issue of Datamation, Jim Gray in collaboration with 24 others from academia and industry published (anonymously) an article titled: "A Measure of Transaction Processing Power." This article outlined a test for online transaction processing, which was given the title of "DebitCredit." Unlike the TP1 benchmark, Gray's DebitCredit benchmark specified a true system-level benchmark where the network and user interaction components of the workload were included. In addition, it outlined several other key features of the benchmarking process that were later incorporated into the TPC process:

- **Total system cost published with the performance rating.** Total system cost included all hardware and software used to successfully run the benchmark, including 5 years of maintenance costs. Until this concept became law in the TPC process, vendors often quoted only part of the overall system cost that generated a given performance rating.
- **Test specified in terms of high-level functional requirements** rather than specifying any given hardware or software platform or code-level requirements. This allowed any company to run the benchmark if it could meet its functional requirements.
- **The benchmark workload scale up rules**—the number of users and size of the database tables—increased proportionally with the increasing power of the system to produce higher transaction rates. The scaling prevented the workload from being overwhelmed by the rapidly increasing power of online transaction processing (OLTP) systems.
- **The overall transaction rate would be constrained by a response time requirement.** In DebitCredit, 95% of all transactions had to be completed in less than one second.

While having a "standard benchmark" was a noteworthy endeavor, the industry soon discovered that having an "unregulated standard benchmark" was not the least bit "standard." There was a need for both the standardization of a benchmark definition and a validation (and subsequent certification) that rules of the benchmark were appropriately met.

9.3.1 The Beginning of TPC

In 1988, the Transaction Processing Performance Council (TPC) was formed by representatives across the industry with the specific purposes of defining and regulating computer benchmarks that were transactional in nature and exercised a broad range of the components that make up a commercial computing environment. Early TPC benchmarks featured several characteristics:

- A focus on data processing (as opposed to "compute intensive").
- Language-based rather than code-based specifications: The data processing industry was and continues to be rapidly evolving. Because consumers and vendors have quite different methods for satisfying the same business requirements, early TPC benchmarks were defined in a technology-agnostic way as functional specifications that included descriptions of the data to be processed, necessary input, necessary output, and a set of required "robustness" functions, without requiring a specific technology to be used for the implementation.
- The inclusion of system price and a price/performance metric (to encourage being realistic in the configuration of systems measured). Initially, a "system" included not only the computer, but all of the storage, networking, and end-user terminals required to deliver the entire business computing solution.
- Specific rules for scaling data and the number of users as the capacity of a computer grows.
- The inclusion of ACID (Atomicity, Consistency, Isolation, and Durability) properties intended to ensure that transactions are either fully completed or rolled back as if they never started.
- The inclusion of a Quality-of-Service (QoS) requirement (such as 90% of transactions completing within 2 s, as was the case for the first TPC benchmark).
- A requirement to demonstrate sustained performance over a period of time.
- A requirement for public disclosure of the benchmark implementation at a level that would both demonstrate compliance with the benchmark rules and allow others to reproduce the results.
- Publication of results from validated implementations on an official TPC database (initially in hardcopy, eventually online).

9.3.2 From Engineering to Marketing, From Benchmarking to Benchmarketing

With the level of presumed integrity that the rigor of TPC's benchmark definition and implementation processes provided, the use of TPC benchmark results rapidly gained popularity as tools for helping to sell computing solutions to the end consumer. However, consider the following familiar progression:

- Engineer: "We've measured 190 active users with TPC Benchmark A."
- Manager: "We can drive almost 200 active users in a TPC benchmark."

- Marketing: "This system delivers the work of 200 active users, as verified by the TPC."
- Sales: "You can be confident that your application will support over 200 active users on this system. We proved that with TPC benchmarks."

Not only were there challenges associated with the proper portrayal of TPC results, there was also intense pressure at the engineering level to improve upon those results. Many of these improvements delivered real and tangible benefits to the end consumer. However, some of them took advantage of the necessarily simplistic nature of the benchmark to deliver an improved benchmark value without delivering an improvement for a more general application.

It became clear to the members of TPC that additional regulation was needed to ensure the integrity of TPC benchmark results and their use in public. Within the first few years of TPC's formation, the processes were enhanced with:

- A requirement that benchmark implementations be reviewed and attested as valid prior to publication.
- A requirement that the TPC benchmark identifiers could not be used for any result that was not deemed to be official within TPC.
- The formation of a Technical Advisory Board populated by members of TPC who served as the "grand jury" (making recommendations to the full council) when someone felt that a benchmark implementation did not follow the requirements of the benchmark specification.
- Requirements for the window of time between when a result is published and when a customer can order and install the benchmarked configuration and software.
- Fair use requirements on the use of TPC-related information, including requirements associated with

  - Fidelity: Adherence to facts, accuracy,
  - Candor: Above-board; needful completeness,
  - Due Diligence: Care for integrity of TPC results.

9.3.3 A Progression of Benchmarks

TPC, like other benchmark development groups, has seen a need to continue to develop new benchmarks for a variety of reasons:

- To exercise important functions that have not been well stressed in prior benchmarks.
- To correct or adapt existing benchmarks where the functions stressed are not as representative as one would hope or where the benchmark definition allowed for implementations that do not reflect customer reality.
- To keep pace with technology growth and the explosion of new functions and new techniques that this has allowed.
- To adapt to trends in the industry for the delivery of data processing solutions.

Thus, in the area of traditional data processing on a single system, the TPC developed:

- TPC-A (Gray, 1993), which added TPC's rigor to the DebitCredit benchmark. It was TPC's first benchmark to measure the performance of online transaction processing (OLTP) applications.
- This was followed by the addition of TPC-B (Gray, 1993), which focused on the central computer of an OLTP application by providing the primary data processing transaction in a batch mode that did not require networking or a user interface.
- TPC-C (Raab, 1993) shifted from a single, simple transaction to a mixture of multiple transaction types and included added complexity for storage I/O and end-user display I/O, thereby mimicking a more complex OLTP application. The weight of the end-user display I/O demonstrated the need (in both the benchmark and the industry in general) to develop three-tier environments where the end-user interface is handled by a middle-tier application server, leaving the primary server to focus specifically on the data processing.
- While the above benchmarks were developed at a period where free-form application development was still required due to lack of standards or de-facto standards, the TPC-E (Hogan, 2009) benchmark was able to rely on SQL standards to more rigidly define portions of the implementation as well as adding some of the complexity reflective of more modern applications, additional integrity requirements, and an application design that fit naturally with either a two-tier or a three-tier environment.

TPC-C and TPC-E continue to be active benchmarks, while TPC-A and TPC-B have been retired as being too simplistic to adequately measure today's systems.

Although the word "transaction" is a part of TPC's name, a more appropriate (but wordy) description might be the "Business Information Data Processing Performance Council," because there are other important areas to information processing that do not fit the mold of an interactive online application. In particular, TPC recognized a need to develop benchmarks associated with queries that might run for some period of time (termed "decision support" or "data warehouse" or "business intelligence").

The first of these was TPC-D (both because it was the fourth benchmark in TPC's development series and perhaps "D" for decision support). TPC-D was designed to be a series of moderate and complex queries that would be executed against a database of information. The complexity of mapping the queries to the data precluded a smooth scaling mechanism as had been used for the transactional benchmarks and required TPC-D to be split into a series of non-comparable database sizes.

A challenge with any benchmark definition, but particularly with one that is specification-based, is that sometimes optimization techniques can be employed that deliver results in ways that are far faster than originally expected. "The development of aggregate/summary structures (e.g., join indices, summary tables, materialized views) that are automatically maintained and transparently used by the query optimizer via query rewrite was spurred by TPC-D because this technology decreased query elapsed times resulting in an over proportional increase in the main performance metric" (Nambiar and Poess, 2006). These new optimization technologies provided results much like what one might expect from a regularly run report program and very unlike what one would expect from a unique new query. As a result, TPC divided the benchmark into TPC-R (for "report") which allowed these new functions, and TPC-H (Poess and Floyd, 2000) (for "ad hoc") which did not.

The TPC-DS (Nambiar and Poess, 2006) (for "decision support") benchmark reflected the inclusion of many SQL features that were not standardized at the time TPC-D/R/H were developed. It differs from TPC-H in the overall database design, the constraints defined between tables, the number and complexity of queries executed, and the method for computing the overall QoS metric. It resembles TPC-H in a requirement for specific query language and execution over a selection of non-comparable database sizes. Version 2 of TPC-DS, a significant rewrite of the specification, targets the performance measurement of Big Data implementations (Poess, 2017; Poess, Rabl, and Jacobsen, 2017).

In addition to the importance of the actual business intelligence functions in today's data processing environments, there is a growing need to efficiently move data from an online transaction processing system to a system that is dedicated to the business intelligence functions. The TPC developed the TPC-DI (Poess, Rabl, Jacobsen, and Caufield, 2014) (for "data integration") benchmark to simulate the functions in Extract, Transform, and Load (ETL) environments that might migrate information from a variety of transactional systems into a data warehouse environment.

Finally, the TPC-W (for "web") benchmark is a benchmark for business-oriented transactional web servers. The workload is based on a controlled Internet commerce environment and simulates a bookshop. The benchmark simulates multiple online browser sessions by accessing dynamically generated pages. The performance metric reported by TPC-W is the number of web interactions processed per second. The benchmark simulates three profiles that differ by the browse-to-buy request ratio: (1) primarily shopping, (2) browsing, and (3) web-based ordering. Although discontinued, TPC-W has often been employed as a reference web application by researchers evaluating their work.

While TPC-D, TPC-R, and TPC-W have been retired, the TPC-H, TPC-DS, and TPC-DI benchmarks are actively in use today.

9.3.4 Evolution of the TPC Model Over Time

The computing industry has changed radically over recent decades, and so it is natural that the TPC benchmark model would change, too.

The workload in OLTP applications is mostly driven by interface devices that enable end users to input and display application output. In real life, these devices are referred to as workstations. The pricing of individual workstations as a part of the overall system cost was eliminated from the specifications, both because optimal benchmark implementations generated work of an overwhelming number of simulated workstations and because of the transition to multi-purpose personal computers in place of the character mode displays that were common when TPC was formed.

It also became practical to manage pricing rules at a "corporate" level, rather than benchmark by benchmark, so a TPC Pricing standard was created, providing a consistent set of rules for all benchmarks.

As the millennium turned, another substantial component of the cost of computing became important: the amount of energy required to provide a computing solution. TPC developed and published a TPC Energy specification (Poess, Nambiar, et al., 2018), which detailed methods to quantify the power/work required to deliver a TPC benchmark result.

Both the TPC Pricing and the TPC Energy specifications are common specifications across all benchmarks. They augment all TPC benchmarks by adding methodologies and requirements for including and reporting pricing and energy metrics.

The requirement for benchmark publications to be reviewed and attested as compliant with specifications required the formal introduction of auditors into the TPC policies. They define the role, responsibilities as well as the process of becoming a TPC certified auditor.

As industry-standard benchmarking matured, so too did techniques for stretching the limits where marketing claims were concerned. The TPC tightened rules for fair use of TPC-related information, including a documented penalty progression for those who violated these rules. In order to help ensure fair comparisons, TPC also reclassified older results that were perfectly valid for their time but might not be representative of the current time. A new "Historical Result" category allowed the results to stay on the books, but not to be unfairly compared to a brand new result.

> While the TPC-C specification has changed over time, the base application requirements of the benchmark have remained the same. When introduced in 1992, the highest TPC-C published throughput result was 54 tpmC with price/performance of $188,562/tpmC (IBM AS/400 Model E35, Historical Result, online reference not available). By the end of 2002, the highest result was 709,220 tpmC with price/performance of $14.96/tpmC (HP Pro-Liant DL760-900-256P Historical Result http://www.tpc.org/tpcc/results/tpcc_result_detail.asp?id=101091903). This result was not comparable to the prior one listed because the rules for pricing changed in the interim. As of 2012, the highest throughput result was 30,249,688 tpmC with a price/performance of $1.01/tpmC (SPARC SuperCluster with T3-4 servers).

The advances in computing technology (raw compute power of processors, dramatic improvements in memory and storage technologies, and impressive advances in software capabilities) that allowed the growth in a score from just over 50, to over 700,000 a decade later, to over 30,000,000 a decade after that, have spurred developments that have altered the way TPC benchmarks are defined and managed:

- The massive amount of compute power has enabled the work that was once contained on a single system to now be hosted as a "virtual system" using only a fraction of the resources on a larger system. This has prompted the creation of a number of virtualization support products from computing hardware and software manufacturers and has led TPC to the clear need to provide tools to demonstrate performance in these environments, with regard to the data processing environments that are the focus of TPC.

- The massive amount of compute power has also enabled the development of a broad range of information processing applications that were unheard of in the first two decades of TPC's existence. With TPC's interest in business information processing, this opened an opportunity for a broader spectrum of functions to be covered by TPC benchmarks.

The complexity of modern information processing applications and the size of modern computing solutions make it extremely expensive to generate and optimize an application (including an application that implements a benchmark specification) from scratch. Fortunately, the industry has also matured enough that there are sufficient standards and pseudo-standards for application implementations that some information processing benchmarks can be defined as executable code. A custom application from a functional specification is no longer a requirement to ensure fairness.

9.3.5 The Need and Opportunity for Kit-Based Benchmarks

When TPC was formed, the variety of implementation methods in use for solving business data processing problems was widespread. This necessitated the creation of functional specifications that did not dictate a specific implementation. This, in turn, prompted the creation of a rigorous set of tests to ensure the specification was met, and the requirement for a third-party attestation as to the probable validity of the benchmark implementation.

These aspects are some of the true strengths of TPC benchmarks. However, they can also be perceived as detractors for benchmark implementers (Huppler and Johnson, 2014):

- The fact that TPC specifications are technology agnostic enables the use of a wide range of technologies to be benchmarked. It also encourages the development of new technologies to improve the performance of computer systems for the type of application TPC benchmarks mimic. However, it also requires extensive resources to implement and maintain a TPC benchmark implementation.
- The requirement for an audit and a set of tests (including crashing the system and proving appropriate recovery) adds expense and complexity, especially if the purpose of running the benchmark is an academic study.
- In addition, the TPC benchmarks discussed thus far tend to require fairly robust system configurations in terms of processor, memory, and storage—adding yet another expense that can be discouraging for both computer manufacturers and academia.

- Furthermore, TPC's pricing requirement (another perceived strength with the first several TPC benchmarks) makes it difficult to move from a traditional in-house, capitalized single-server environment to one of the many virtual options (in-house virtualization, shared resource solutions, cloud solutions, and more) that are available today.
- Finally, the time required to create a new TPC benchmark precluded the delivery of benchmarks that exercised new advances in technology while they were still actually new.

In 2012–2013, a proposal for a revised benchmark development approach was presented to TPC. The net of the proposal was that TPC should follow two tracks. The first one, called the *enterprise track*, would focus on the style of existing TPC benchmarks, retaining their inherent qualities and value. The second one, called the *express track*, would focus on developing ready-to-run benchmark kits, trading more rigid requirements on benchmark implementation for greater ease and cost of measuring.

Kit-based benchmarks have a proven record of success in SPEC, which has typically focused on a variety of areas where it was more reasonable to define specific executable applications. While TPC continues to find strength in technology-agnostic specifications, this is no longer a requirement for TPC benchmarks, both because of the maturity of database and related standards and because of the reduction of likely hardware and operating environments that are common today.

Table 9.1, updated from its original proposal by Huppler and Johnson (2014), summarizes some of the current aspects in the dual methodology approach:

Table 9.1: Dual methodology approach of Huppler and Johnson (2014)

Enterprise model	Express model
Functional benchmark specification; perhaps with some required TPC-provided code	Executable benchmark kit, enhanced by documentation such as a user guide
Custom implementation	Only system tuning for the fixed implementation
Audit by TPC certified auditor	Much self-validation
Price required	Price optional (Note: price was "eliminated" in the original proposal, but shifted to "optional" as implemented)
Full system configuration (including servers, storage, and intra-server networking)	Limited configuration focused on stressing key components of the benchmark
Substantial implementation costs	Reduced implementation costs

Another key aspect of Express benchmark specifications is that they are restricted to specific platforms. If a TPC member makes modifications to the benchmark specification to allow for an expansion to another platform and those changes are reviewed and found compliant with the current specification, the potential audience for the benchmark is expanded. This aspect can help accelerate the time between when a benchmark is proposed and when it can be used by the general public.

The inclusion of the Express model for benchmark development has had a very positive impact on TPC. New members have joined to work on benchmarks in new areas of data processing. Several new benchmarks have been released. In fact, in the 5 years since the proposal was formalized, there have been five new TPC benchmarks that are based on the Express model—a substantial change from prior years! When coupled with the TPC-DI benchmark discussed earlier and the TPC-VMS benchmark discussed in the following section, it is clear that TPC has greatly broadened the areas of data processing that can be evaluated with its benchmarks and taken steps to ensure that this process is available broadly to both industry and academia.

The current Express benchmarks are TPCx-BB (big data benchmark) (Cao et al., 2016; Wang et al., 2017), TPCx-HCI (benchmark for hyper-converged infrastructure) (Taheri et al., 2018), TPCx-HS (big data system benchmark) (Nambiar, Poess, et al., 2014), TPCx-IoT (benchmark for IoT gateway systems) (Poess, Nambiar, et al., 2018), and TPCx-V (virtualization benchmark for database workloads) (Sethuraman and Taheri, 2010).

9.3.6 The Virtual World of Computing

Advances in hardware, software, storage, and networking technologies have allowed customers to share resources in a highly protected way, where each customer can act as if they have dedicated systems, but in fact they are using resources that are shared among many. This can be done using virtualization techniques on a single server, or it can be extended by what is commonly called the Cloud, where a specific amount of compute resources (particularly processor and storage, often network bandwidth and capacity, and sometimes other logical components) are contracted to be available, without any specific understanding of the physical system(s) where those resources reside. In the case of cloud systems, not only are compute resources shared among many users, but systems management (back-up, disaster protection, software updates, etc.) can also be a part of the contract.

Early TPC benchmarks were written with the single, dedicated server in mind. There is still a strong need for this level of information, as there is still a strong use of this compute paradigm. However, there is a growing need to measure the performance of applications running in cloud environments.

To enable the existing TPC benchmarks to be run in cloud environments, TPC has updated most benchmarks and the pricing specification to include cloud wording. Specifically, TPC has updated the pricing specification to allow for cloud-based pricing. If a benchmark standard does not specify a pricing model, a default pricing methodology, as defined in the pricing specification applies. The price of the entire priced configuration of a benchmark publication, that is, prices for all hardware and software components including their maintenance, must be used. For cloud publications this wording was amended to include licensed compute services. TPC defines licensed compute services as "...publicly offered processing, storage, network, and software services that are hosted on remote computer servers accessed via a wide area network (e.g., the Internet). A customer pays a license fee to the Licensed Compute Services vendor for the use of the processing, storage, network, and software services. The Licensed Compute Services are not located or installed on a customer's premises."

Because cloud providers offer short term and even "pay as you go" licensed compute services, TPC added support for those pricing models. The wording accommodates most vendors. For instance, if a vendor's pricing does not include a 1-year price, the pricing of a benchmark publication may multiply the price of the licensed compute services 1-month price by 12 to satisfy the above requirement.

At the same time, TPC has incorporated licensed compute services into benchmark specifications to allow for publication in clouds. To publish in public clouds there remains one challenge: ACID. Many enterprise class benchmark specifications such as TPC-C, TPC-E, and TPC-H mandate proof of ACID (Atomicity, Consistency, Isolation, and Durability) compliance. To prove ACID compliance, each benchmark publication must run an ACID test. This test, among others, requires failing a durable media. Failing a durable media in a public cloud is inherently difficult, unless a vendor isolates the test environment from other customers of its cloud. TPC is currently discussing approaches to solving this issue.

More recent TPC benchmarks focus specifically on the expanding areas of virtualization and cloud computing. All of the benchmarks mentioned above that were developed under the Express model relate to these environments. In addition, TPC has developed and delivered the TPC-VMS benchmark using the Enterprise model.

9.4 Concluding Remarks

In an effort to provide and maintain fair industry standards for measuring system-level and component-level performance of computer systems, industry-standard consortia such as the Standard Performance Evaluation Corporation (SPEC)[21] and the Transaction Processing Performance Council (TPC)[22] have established themselves in the computer industry. We provided an overview of benchmark standardization efforts in the area of computer systems. We focused on SPEC and TPC, the two most prominent benchmark standardization bodies in the area of computer systems and information technology (IT). One of their next big challenges is to tackle artificial intelligence (AI) and machine learning (ML). While there exist benchmarks

---

[21] Standard Performance Evaluation Corporation (SPEC): https://www.spec.org

[22] Transaction Processing Performance Council (TPC): http://www.tpc.org

for evaluating AI capabilities, these benchmarks focus mainly on the performance of a single application that fits in a server or a set of servers. However, many of today's commercial AI systems run very large, complex applications. Measuring the performance of such systems calls for a benchmark framework that can encapsulate the complexity of such systems. It must include multiple servers running in multiple data centers, user interfaces, high availability, network communication, and storage I/O. Beyond a training and inference component, it must include mechanisms that enable high concurrent access and load balancing capabilities to measure latency and throughput.

References

Cao, P., Gowda, B., Lakshmi, S., Narasimhadevara, C., Nguyen, P., Poelman, J., Poess, M., and Rabl, T. (2016). "From BigBench to TPCx-BB: Standardization of a Big Data Benchmark". In: *Performance Evaluation and Benchmarking: Traditional—Big Data—Internet of Things. 8th TPC Technology Conference (TPCTC 2016), Revised Selected Papers*. Ed. by R. O. Nambiar and M. Poess. Vol. 10080. Lecture Notes in Computer Science. Springer-Verlag: Berlin, Heidelberg, pp. 24–44 (cited on p. 223).

Dongarra, J. J., Luszczek, P., and Petitet, A. (2003). "The LINPACK Benchmark: Past, Present and Future". *Concurrency and Computation: Practice and Experience*, 15(9). John Wiley & Sons: Hoboken, New Jersey, USA, pp. 803–820 (cited on p. 204).

Gibson, J. C. (1970). *The Gibson Mix*. Tech. rep. TR 00.2043. Poughkeepsie, NY, USA: IBM Corp., Systems Development Division (cited on p. 204).

Gray, J., ed. (1993). *The Benchmark Handbook: For Database and Transaction Systems*. Second Edition. The Morgan Kaufmann Series in Data Management Systems. Morgan Kaufmann: Burlington, Massachusetts, USA (cited on p. 218).

Hennessy, J. L. and Patterson, D. A. (1990). *Computer Architecture: A Quantitative Approach*. The Morgan Kaufmann Series in Computer Architecture and Design. Morgan Kaufmann: Burlington, Massachusetts, USA (cited on p. 206).

Hogan, T. (2009). "Overview of TPC Benchmark E: The Next Generation of OLTP Benchmarks". In: *Performance Evaluation and Benchmarking—First TPC Technology Conference (TPCTC 2009), Revised Selected Papers*. Ed. by R. O. Nambiar and M. Poess. Vol. 5895. Lecture Notes in Computer Science. Springer-Verlag: Berlin, Heidelberg, pp. 84–98 (cited on p. 218).

Huppler, K. and Johnson, D. (2014). "TPC Express - A New Path for TPC Benchmarks". In: *Performance Characterization and Benchmarking—5th TPC Technology Conference (TPCTC 2013), Revised Selected Papers*. Ed. by R. O. Nambiar and M. Poess. Vol. 8391. Lecture Notes in Computer Science. Springer-Verlag: Berlin, Heidelberg, pp. 48–60 (cited on pp. 221, 222).

Lange, K.-D. (2009). "Identifying Shades of Green: The SPECpower Benchmarks". *Computer*, 42(3). IEEE: Piscataway, NJ, USA, pp. 95–97 (cited on p. 209).

Lange, K.-D. and Tricker, M. G. (2011). "The Design and Development of the Server Efficiency Rating Tool (SERT)". In: *Proceedings of the 2nd ACM/SPEC International Conference on Performance Engineering (ICPE 2011)*. (Karlsruhe, Germany). ACM: New York, NY, USA, pp. 145–150 (cited on pp. 205, 209).

Longbottom, R. (2004). *Whetstone Benchmark History and Results*. http://www. roylongbottom.org.uk/whetstone.htm (cited on p. 204).

McCalpin, J. D. (1995). "Memory Bandwidth and Machine Balance in Current High Performance Computers". *IEEE Computer Society Technical Committee on Computer Architecture (TCCA) Newsletter*, pp. 19–25 (cited on p. 205).

Nambiar, R. O. and Poess, M. (2006). "The Making of TPC-DS". In: *Proceedings of the 32nd International Conference on Very Large Data Bases (VLDB 2006)*. (Seoul, Korea). VLDB Endowment, pp. 1049–1058 (cited on pp. 218, 219).

Nambiar, R. O., Poess, M., Dey, A., Cao, P., Magdon-Ismail, T., Ren, D. Q., and Bond, A. (2014). "Introducing TPCx-HS: The First Industry Standard for Benchmarking Big Data Systems". In: *Performance Characterization and Benchmarking: Traditional to Big Data—6th TPC Technology Conference (TPCTC 2014), Revised Selected Papers*. Ed. by R. O. Nambiar and M. Poess. Vol. 8904. Lecture Notes in Computer Science. Springer-Verlag: Berlin, Heidelberg, pp. 1–12 (cited on p. 223).

Poess, M. (2017). "Methodologies for a Comprehensive Approach to Measuring the Performance of Decision Support Systems". Dissertation. Munich, Germany: Technische Universität München (cited on p. 219).

Poess, M. and Floyd, C. (2000). "New TPC Benchmarks for Decision Support and Web Commerce". *ACM SIGMOD Record*, 29(4). ACM: New York, NY, USA, pp. 64–71 (cited on p. 219).

Poess, M., Nambiar, R. O., Kulkarni, K., Narasimhadevara, C., Rabl, T., and Jacobsen, H. (2018). "Analysis of TPCx-IoT: The First Industry Standard Benchmark for IoT Gateway Systems". In: *Proceedings of the 34th IEEE International Conference on Data Engineering (ICDE 2018)*. (Paris, France). IEEE: Piscataway, New Jersey, USA, pp. 1519–1530 (cited on pp. 220, 223).

Poess, M., Rabl, T., and Jacobsen, H.-A. (2017). "Analysis of TPC-DS: The First Standard Benchmark for SQL-based Big Data Systems". In: *Proceedings of the 2017 Symposium on Cloud Computing (SoCC 2017)*. (Santa Clara, CA, USA). ACM: New York, NY, USA, pp. 573–585 (cited on p. 219).

Poess, M., Rabl, T., Jacobsen, H.-A., and Caufield, B. (2014). "TPC-DI: The First Industry Benchmark for Data Integration". *Proceedings of the VLDB Endowment (PVLDB)*, 7(13). VLDB Endowment, pp. 1367–1378 (cited on p. 219).

Raab, F. (1993). "TPC-C: The Standard Benchmark for Online Transaction Processing (OLTP)". In: *The Benchmark Handbook: For Database and Transaction Systems*. Ed. by J. Gray. Second Edition. The Morgan Kaufmann Series in Data Management Systems. Morgan Kaufmann: Burlington, Massachusetts, USA (cited on p. 218).

Sachs, K., Kounev, S., Bacon, J., and Buchmann, A. (2009). "Performance Evaluation of Message-Oriented Middleware using the SPECjms2007 Benchmark". *Performance Evaluation*, 66(8). Elsevier Science: Amsterdam, The Netherlands, pp. 410–434 (cited on p. 209).

Sethuraman, P. and Taheri, H. R. (2010). "TPC-V: A Benchmark for Evaluating the Performance of Database Applications in Virtual Environments". In: *Performance Evaluation, Measurement and Characterization of Complex Systems—Second TPC Technology Conference (TPCTC 2010), Revised Selected Papers*. Ed. by R. O. Nambiar and M. Poess. Vol. 6417. Lecture Notes in Computer Science. Springer-Verlag: Berlin, Heidelberg, pp. 121–135 (cited on p. 223).

Shanley, K. (1998). *History and Overview of the TPC*. http://www.tpc.org/information/about/history.asp (cited on p. 215).

Taheri, H. R., Little, G., Desai, B., Bond, A., Johnson, D., and Kopczynski, G. (2018). "Characterizing the Performance and Resilience of HCI Clusters with the TPCx-HCI Benchmark". In: *Performance Evaluation and Benchmarking for the Era of Artificial Intelligence—10th TPC Technology Conference (TPCTC 2018), Revised Selected Papers*. Ed. by R. O. Nambiar and M. Poess. Vol. 11135. Lecture Notes in Computer Science. Springer-Verlag: Berlin, Heidelberg, pp. 58–70 (cited on p. 223).

Wang, K., Bian, B., Cao, P., and Riess, M. (2017). "Experiences and Lessons in Practice Using TPCx-BB Benchmarks". In: *Performance Evaluation and Benchmarking for the Analytics Era—9th TPC Technology Conference (TPCTC 2017), Revised Selected Papers*. Ed. by R. O. Nambiar and M. Poess. Vol. 10661. Lecture Notes in Computer Science. Springer-Verlag: Berlin, Heidelberg, pp. 93–102 (cited on p. 223).

Weiss, A. R. (2002). *Dhrystone Benchmark: History, Analysis, "Scores" and Recommendations*. www.eembc.org/techlit/datasheets/dhrystone_wp.pdf (cited on p. 204).

Part II
Applications

Chapter 10
The SPEC CPU Benchmark Suite

Klaus-Dieter Lange, James Bucek, and Alexander Carlton

This chapter presents an overview and retrospective on the emergence, development, and evolution of one of the industry's most popular standard benchmarks for computing systems, the SPEC CPU benchmark suite by the Standard Performance Evaluation Corporation (SPEC). SPEC CPU is designed to stress a system's processor, memory subsystem, and compiler. The original version of this benchmark SPEC CPU89 was released in 1989 as SPEC's first benchmark. Since then, five new generations of the SPEC CPU benchmark have been released: CPU92, CPU95, CPU2000, CPU2006, and CPU2017. In the following, we describe each of these benchmarks and show how they have influenced the computer industry over the years, helping to boost computing performance by several orders of magnitude. For CPU2017, we provide details on the benchmark architecture, workloads, metrics, and full disclosure report.

10.1 SPEC CPU89

SPEC's goal with CPU89 was to shift the focus of the marketplace away from the existing problematic microkernel implementations for MIPS and MFLOPS tests. With the release of CPU89, SPEC was driving two major changes. First, to become far more rigorous in the definition of the benchmarks and thus make comparisons more meaningful. Second, to upscale the benchmarks dramatically so that current and upcoming systems had to work hard to provide good performance and scalability.

While the old microkernels were typically only a few dozen lines of code each, which may or may not be written equivalently for all systems, the SPEC CPU benchmark included 214,000 lines (including white space and comments) of explicitly defined portable source code (Henning, 2007).

CPU89 consisted of ten workloads that all met the necessary criteria (cf. Chapter 1, Section 1.5). These criteria included requirements that the workloads be based on useful applications with code and inputs taken from real-world usage in order to exercise new processor designs in a realistic manner. Each workload used a single set of source code that compiled on all systems of interest without changes, used a single set of input files, and had one set of reference output files against which results

© Springer Nature Switzerland AG 2020

S. Kounev et al., *Systems Benchmarking*, https://doi.org/10.1007/978-3-030-41705-5_10

were compared to validate correct operation. Also all code and inputs had to be either freely available or licensed to SPEC so that they could be easily redistributed in this standardized form. All workloads had to run long enough that measurement timings were robust and not greatly impacted by startup effects. In the first release, four of these workloads were primarily integer-based workloads of varying complexity written in C, while the rest were FORTRAN programs dominated by their floating-point calculations.

The new benchmark generated considerable traction when it was announced. By the time of CPU89, the original group of the EE Times magazine and the four founding vendors of SPEC had grown to a full dozen member companies, including the big names in computing, and the rapid growth had drawn notable attention. The presence of the EE Times magazine in a leadership role of the SPEC organization added to the degree of coverage in the press.

The public reception of the new benchmark was further aided when Reinhold Weicker, the author of the then popular Dhrystone benchmark commonly used (against his advice) to measure MIPS, publicly supported the new CPU89 benchmark. Weicker's 10 page article, "An Overview of Common Benchmarks" in IEEE Computer of December 1990 (Weicker, 1990) included a deep technical review of the popular Dhrystone, Whetstone, and LINPACK benchmarks as well as touching on several of the other known public tests including the new SPEC benchmark, which he described as "probably the most important current benchmarking effort." Weicker eventually became a key participant in the SPEC CPU Subcommittee helping to develop four generations of its benchmarks. His insight gleaned from the work to define some of industry's first run rules for Dhrystone later influenced many sections of the SPEC CPU rules that are described below.

One of the notable aspects of SPEC's new benchmark was the amount of information published with a result (cf. Chapter 1, Section 1.5.2). In addition to the top-level *SPECmark score* (the main metric summarizing the measured CPU performance), every result disclosure listed the runtime for each of the ten individual workloads along with each resulting performance score, calculated so that everyone could see which workloads did especially well and which workloads showed less performance. Hence, each result disclosure showed a sort of fingerprint from which an astute reader could begin to determine which of the ten benchmarks matched their own use cases and therefore which aspects of a system design were the likely performance bottlenecks. Furthermore, complete information about the system tested, including a full listing of every compiler switch used, made it much easier for others to replicate the experiment and prove to themselves the results were sound. Companies and academics were free to try and estimate their SPECmark scores, but all results published in the SPEC Newsletter underwent a review by the members of SPEC that would check for errors, question the compliance of compilers and other performance techniques, and serve as a significant hurdle for those who might want to overstate their capabilities. Before too long many parts of the computer marketplace, from the tech press to the purchasing manager dealing with vendor sales materials, learned there was value in a proper SPEC result that included all the details.

After the initial release of SPEC's CPU89 benchmark, it quickly became clear that changes and enhancements were needed. A little over a year later, the benchmark was on its second update. The most significant change was the definition of the developer-favored *SPECint* and *SPECfp* metrics in order to replace the press-favored combined metric. This addressed the problem of attempting to have a single SPECmark metric to try to cover both integer performance and the very rapidly evolving arena of floating-point performance.

The update also included the first attempt to define throughput metrics and testing methodology to enable comparisons against multi-processing capable systems where even more performance could be realized with multiple processes executing simultaneously.

10.2 SPEC CPU92

Within another year, SPEC released the CPU92 benchmark.[1] This release was an upgrade to the original CPU89 benchmark. The developers started with the existing workloads and all that had been learned from them, and then looked at many new suggested workloads as well as ways to improve all of the existing workloads.

As released, CPU92 expanded the set of workloads to 6 integer-centric workloads and 14 floating-point intensive workloads including two that reflected the changes happening in computer languages where some interesting new work was being done in C rather than FORTRAN. The new workloads expanded the application space to include file compression, ray tracing and analysis of sound, neural networks, and a variety of simulation and modeling applications from electromagnetic plasma through atomic structures up to shallow water models from weather forecasting.

While the application space was expanded, overall the practical scope of the workload source codes remained largely similar. The lines of code expanded slightly, to about 240,000. Several of the existing individual workloads were replaced with updated code and larger inputs that increased the complexity of those workloads in order to better stay ahead of the current state of the art in processor and compiler techniques. And, in a sign of what would happen to any static benchmark facing rapidly evolving technology, one workload, `030.matrix300`, was dropped entirely from the benchmark because that workload had been rendered too simplistic by the sophisticated optimizations and advances of compiler technology.

SPEC benchmark developers improved their checking of assumptions with analytic data. Workload candidates were analyzed not just for their portability and scope, but also for their micro-level statistics (e.g., instruction mix or cache behavior), and evaluated on their behavior and their stability as well as their usefulness and applicability.

Many initially interesting workload candidates suffered from being too tightly coupled to their target architecture, relying on non-portable compiler features unique

---

[1] SPEC CPU92: https://www.spec.org/cpu92

to a specific environment. Other popular workloads proved to suffer from numerical stability issues, for example, executing notably different iteration counts because of details such as architecture specific underflows. Some applications produced similar but inconsistent results across different systems, variations which application experts considered to be equally valid but rendered comparisons unmanageable. Some applications could not be set up to run for long enough times without inordinate amounts of input, while some others only reached a long runtime from high degrees of repetitive behavior. With each passing meeting more promising workload candidates would prove to suffer from unsolvable forms of this kind of problem and hence were dropped from the lists along the way towards the final release.

By this time, the development for the SPEC benchmarks was punctuated by a series of what were called *benchathons*. These were week-long meetings where engineers would leave their respective company offices and travel to one location where everyone set up workstations in some large room and work together side-by-side, fixing the benchmarks. Often groups of different experts would be standing over some engineer at the keyboard, everyone throwing out ideas for the issues that were causing one workload or another to misbehave. Good work could get done via email and phone calls during all the other weeks, but key to the quality of the SPEC benchmarks was getting all this talent away from their day jobs and then having them work together for days on end just to make each benchmark as good as it could be.

Soon after the release of CPU92, SPEC announced the definition of *SPECrates*, an improvement to the multi-processing metric that remained the basis for the measurement methodology for the next several releases. The original throughput methodology was somewhat cumbersome and because the metric was explicitly tied to the number of simultaneous processes it worked against making any comparisons across different configurations (which was becoming a problem as there were starting to be some single-processor systems that could run two or more copies of a workload almost as fast as some of the multi-processor systems). The new SPECrate metrics offered a way to compare the total throughput achieved regardless of the level of concurrency used to reach those levels. These new metrics also enabled an easier way to look at a multi-processor system's ability to scale total throughput as the count of processes was increased, revealing in some cases systems which struggled to supply all that their processors would demand when fully utilized.

During CPU92's time as a popular benchmark, performance (and especially compiler technology) advanced rapidly. Soon, SPEC was faced with a problem of how carefully crafted compiler tools could lead to notably higher scores than common compilers. Smart compiler writers could target specific compiler techniques at specific issues in specific codes which then could be turned into opportunities for dramatic increases in performance, but perhaps only for relatively narrow use cases, and this could be a problem if the narrow uses were only a bit wider than necessary to validate the results of a CPU92 benchmark.

SPEC already had rules in place against the use of compiler tricks—or any other technique—if such tricks were effective only for a specific benchmark. However, sometimes legitimate improvements in optimization techniques caused existing benchmarks to be obsoleted. For example, the 300×300 matrix multiplication benchmark, 030.matrix300, had long been considered useful, but then compilers added valuable cache-aware optimizations for vector and matrix algorithms. These were not gimmicky benchmark specials, but they boosted performance on that benchmark far more than they did on larger, more realistic codes, so 030.matrix300 became unrepresentative and it was dropped.

In 1994, SPEC announced a distinction between *base results* and *peak results*. This enabled the separation of SPEC CPU results by the kinds of compiler features that could be utilized. The base rules emphasized safety (could not lead to unexpected behavior) and broad applicability (would lead to performance improvements across a wide variety of types of code). Under the base rules, all compiler flags used had to be endorsed as good for general use, only a limited number of flags (four) could be passed to the compiler, and the same set of compiler flags would be used for all of the workloads in the set. Additionally, base flags could not specify an assertion (for example, assert that in this application no data structures ever overlapped in memory), nor could a flag name any specific routine or variable in the sources (hence could not specify what functions to inline or which variables to promote), nor enable feedback-directed optimization.[2]

In the other category, the peak rules allowed some room for compiler features that could have benefits on some types of code but that might suffer problems when applied to other types of code. Here the list of compiler flags, or even the compiler itself, was allowed to be unique to each specific test, so that one could enable compiler features only for the particular workloads that would benefit. Further, there was no limit on the length of the list of compiler flags, so that it was possible to enable yet another feature to get that last percentage of extra performance. However, the rules stated that if a result utilized the peak rules, then one is also required to publish the same configuration as measured under the base rules; and the benchmark tools were set up to generate both sets of scores and test information on the same page.

The base rules about safety set the tone for what was expected by these rules which made it more likely that the techniques and tools used would be a more reasonable match for average customers. However, in practice two aspects of the new base rules accounted for much of the differences in vendor measurements. The simple limit on the count of flags in base results meant that vendors had to focus on the effective use of only a few switches, which kept the lists of options from overwhelming customers reading the results. But also the base rules pushed compilers to focus on successfully generalizing their key techniques to be safe and effective across almost all code simply because of the variety of wildly different applications in the benchmark set, and that each of these different applications needed to have all their results pass explicitly defined output validation.

Also worthy of noting about CPU92, this was the release where SPEC learned a lot about what happens when the world at large is motivated to improve their SPEC scores. CPU92 included 072.sc as one of the workloads, which was derived from an ASCII spreadsheet application which was considered to be a workload of common

---

[2] Two-pass compilers where the executable built by the first pass of the compiler was then exercised to generate run-time profile data that would be used to guide the compiler's second pass in order to generate code optimized for the profiled behavior.

interest. Unfortunately, SPEC underestimated the value that vendors could squeeze out by reimplementing the "curses" library that was integral to the design of the original application and was still involved in a notable percentage of the workload's execution profile.

During the years when CPU92 was in high use, several vendors shipped increasingly clever implementations of this "curses" library, implementations that adapted their behavior to the run-time conditions in ways that greatly reduced the amount of work performed in several situations including how this library was used in the CPU92 benchmark. Late in the life cycle of CPU92, SPEC addressed this problem by releasing a SPEC-specific version of this library and updated the rules to require all new measurements to be based on this specific version of the library. Still, the SPEC developers learned to be very careful to avoid making assumptions about the behavior of any code not provided by the benchmark itself. From this point onwards, SPEC added a more robust analysis of all execution times to the candidate workload evaluation criteria, and since then most SPEC CPU workloads spend 95% or more of their instructions in code explicitly compiled from sources provided by the SPEC benchmark.

Related to the learning experience with the 072.sc workload, the CPU92 benchmark was the first benchmark where SPEC provided support for Microsoft Windows. Taking advantage of Windows NT support for the POSIX API, the Unix-based workloads could now be compiled on a Windows system. SPEC's efforts to produce clean single source implementations of the applications in the suite pushed the SPEC developers to avoid code that relied on proprietary extensions either in the compiler namespace or in the library namespace. It was a relatively straightforward task to port the resulting code to any system that provided complete support for the POSIX interface definitions, including the new POSIX feature in Windows NT. This enabled the SPEC CPU benchmarks to be run on a whole new category of systems, which became especially interesting to those seeking to compare the RISC designs in Unix-based systems to Intel's CISC designs that were primarily available in Windows-based systems.

10.3 SPEC CPU95

Barely 3 years later, the evolution of computer performance already demanded a new set of benchmarks. For the CPU95 release the SPEC CPU team threw aside just about everything and started from scratch to create a new benchmark suite that was several times larger and far more robust.[3]

Most of the workloads in the CPU95 suite were entirely new. A few cases used the same base application, but the CPU95 workload was significantly changed from the similar workload in CPU92, usually based on a newer release of the application code, and in all cases with much larger and usually much more complex input sets.

---

[3] SPEC CPU95: https://www.spec.org/cpu95

For example, in CPU95 the benchmark based on the "li" Xlisp interpreter now evaluated an entire suite of Lisp stress tests rather than CPU92's one implementation of a 9-Queens chessboard puzzle. And instead of this chessboard puzzle, CPU95 entered the area of artificial intelligence in computer gaming with a full version of an internationally ranked "Go" playing program. Similar leaps in scope happened across the entire suite of workloads. Overall, the total lines of code across all the workloads in the suite had more than doubled from CPU92 to 426,000 lines.

SPEC also developed an entirely new benchmark harness to manage both the building and the execution of the benchmarks as well as the production of all result files. For SPEC CPU95 and later suites, whoever runs the benchmark edits a single configuration file with all of the desired settings including specifying any benchmark-specific compiler switches or flags, and once this configuration file is set one script invocation does everything: build or rebuild any of the benchmarks as necessary, set up the execution environment, execute each benchmark as defined, verify that correct answers are obtained, and produce a formatted PostScript report including a graph of the results. This new harness enabled the automation of CPU95 measurements and removed the opportunity for manual interventions that might affect the integrity of a benchmark during execution.

10.4 SPEC CPU2000

CPU2000 was the fourth generation of the SPEC CPU benchmark suite.[4] And much like its predecessors, CPU2000 carried most of the same basic approaches to measuring processor and system performance, just scaled up with more modern applications and workloads to meet the needs of better comparative testing of the latest processors and systems.

It took 5 years to develop this next generation of the SPEC CPU benchmark. This was partially due to difficulties in finding applications that can satisfy the ever-increasing requirements for a candidate workload to be relevant. Faster systems implied the need for longer computations for a benchmark to remain doing interesting work for enough time to enable robust measurements, and the source code was not available for many interesting applications designed to remain compute bound for long periods of time. And not all of those applications had readily available workloads to use as inputs that fit within reasonable storage and memory limitations and also produce stable results that can be validated by automated methods.

For CPU2000, SPEC openly solicited candidate codes from the general public in exchange for a small award to offset the costs of working with SPEC to get a candidate code through the benchmark development process. In the end, 17 of the 26 workloads in the CPU2000 suite came to SPEC through this public solicitation, which enabled the benchmark to provide a much richer set of performance challenges.

---

[4] SPEC CPU2000: https://www.spec.org/cpu2000

The resulting benchmark had an integer suite, called CINT2000, with 12 work-loads in C and C++, as well as a floating point suite, CFP2000, with another 14 work-loads in FORTRAN 77 and FORTRAN 90. The total lines of code to be compiled across the entire benchmark has again about doubled to be 811,000 lines.

With the increasing size of the workloads, SPEC paid closer attention to the memory usage patterns of the workloads. Workloads that are too small will readily have their working set living in cache and hence potentially lead to overoptimistic performance expectations. However, workloads that are too large risk driving common configurations into significant paging behavior making them unstable and also uninteresting to most of the performance community. The target for most workloads in CPU2000 was preferably 100 MB or more, but no more than 200 MB so that the workload can run comfortably on a system with a 256 MB memory configuration. This memory requirement becomes potentially significant when running the benchmark on the larger server systems with 32, 64, 128, and even more processors, each of which may have a process eagerly consuming 200 MB of memory.

10.5 SPEC CPU2006

The fifth generation of the SPEC CPU benchmark suite, CPU2006 was released in August 2006 after another 5+ years of development, again using a public *Search Program* to solicit candidate codes from a wider range of sources. To keep up with the increases in system performance and capabilities, the new workloads were again several times larger than was common for CPU2000, the target memory sizes were now 1 GB rather than 200 MB, and again the overall lines of code had more than tripled to three million lines of code.

The benchmark harness was also significantly upgraded. A large change was the much improved support for replicating workloads across the potentially large number of processors in the bigger system. However, there were also a slew of new features that made it easier to manage large-scale testing, including a new sysinfo capability to automatically extract information from the system being tested avoiding the need to tailor the benchmark configuration file for each and every system tested.

This focus on improvements to the benchmark harness was a reflection of the growth in the usage of SPEC CPU measurements. Back in the days of CPU89 there were ~200 results submitted to SPEC for publication. CPU92 had ~1,200 result submissions published by SPEC. For CPU95 that count had jumped to ~2,000. With CPU2000 the count leapt again up to over 7,500 results. By the end of CPU2006, there had been nearly 50,000 results submitted to SPEC for publication. This data, along with SPEC CPU2017 data, can be seen in Table 10.1.

Table 10.2 briefly details the changes between all of the SPEC CPU benchmark suites throughout the years (Henning, 2007).

Table 10.1: Growth of SPEC CPU benchmark result publications on www.spec.org as of June 24, 2020

	CPU89	CPU92	CPU95	CPU2000	CPU2006	CPU2017
Number of results	191	1,292	2,574	7,654	48,381	19,648

Table 10.2: Growth of SPEC CPU benchmarks (KLOC, thousands of lines of code)

	CPU89	CPU92	CPU95	CPU2000	CPU2006	CPU2017
			Integer			
Workloads	4	6	8	12	12	10
KLOC	182	163	394	583	1,612	2,484
Languages	C	C	C	C, C++	C, C++	C, C++, FORTRAN 95
			Floating point			
Workloads	6	14	10	14	17	14
KLOC	32	77	32	236	1,719	4,684
Languages	FORTRAN 77	C, FORTRAN 77	C, FORTRAN 77	C, FORTRAN 77 + 90	C, C++, FORTRAN 77 + 90	C, C++ FORTRAN 77 + 90 + 95 + 2003

10.6 SPEC CPU2017

The most recent industry-standard compute-intensive benchmark from SPEC is SPEC CPU2017.[5] Similar to its five predecessor benchmarks, SPEC CPU2017 is designed to stress a computing system's processor, memory subsystem, and compiler (Bucek et al., 2018). The benchmark consists of four suites, containing 43 distinct workloads, capable of producing 16 different metrics, which one can use to measure and compare computing performance.

SPEC CPU2017 is delivered to those that hold a license for the benchmark suite in an ISO image that contains source code files. Since SPEC CPU2017 is a collection of source code and pre-compiled tools, the suite is portable to many operating environments. Since there are pre-built tools that come with the overall suite, the user typically does not need to build the main harness tools as part of the installation process. SPEC CPU2017 is ported to various architectures (such as AMD64, ARMv8, AArch64, Intel IA32, Power ISA, SPARC, and more) and various

---

[5] SPEC CPU2017: https://www.spec.org/cpu2017

Unix-based (AIX, Linux, Mac OS X, and Solaris) and Windows operating systems.[6] The install scripts that are provided with the SPEC CPU2017 image recognize supported systems. If a user is installing SPEC CPU2017 on an unsupported, or a not fully supported environment, the user will likely have to build some tools manually. Documentation provides some guidance on how to accomplish this feat.

Since SPEC CPU2017 is delivered as source code, the individual workloads within the suite need to be compiled in order to create an executable binary. To build these binaries a user will need compilers that can build C99, C++2003, and Fortran-2003. Through building executable binaries with compiler options that fit with the SPEC CPU2017 *Run and Reporting Rules*, the suite is able to stress a system's compiler. Results can vary greatly from a very basic compilation without optimizations to results that have a high base optimization level and specialized peak optimization for various workloads. Alternatively, if you are a license holder that routinely publishes SPEC CPU2017 results for comparison purposes, you may be able to obtain a set of pre-compiled binaries bundled together and distributed from various OEMs (typically processor or compiler manufacturers).

During the development of SPEC CPU2017, the SPEC CPU committee conducted a *Search Program* in order to find acceptable candidate workloads to include in the suite.[7] Some workloads from the previous and now retired suite, SPEC CPU2006, were updated to newer versions of their respective source codes and/or workloads for SPEC CPU2017. The SPEC CPU committee continued its tradition of preferring to adapt real-world applications into benchmarks, instead of using synthetic programs.

In the rest of the chapter, we present SPEC CPU2017 in detail describing its architecture, workloads, metrics, and full disclosure report.

10.6.1 SPEC CPU2017 Suites

As previously mentioned, SPEC CPU2017 has four suites.[8] These suites are as follows:

- SPECspeed 2017 Integer
- SPECspeed 2017 Floating Point
- SPECrate 2017 Integer
- SPECrate 2017 Floating Point

Each of the four SPEC CPU2017 suites contains at least ten workloads and produces an overall base metric, with an optional peak metric. These metrics are allowed

---

[6] SPEC CPU2017 system requirements:
https://www.spec.org/cpu2017/Docs/system-requirements.html

[7] SPEC CPU benchmark *search program*: https://www.spec.org/cpu/cpuv6

[8] SPEC CPU2017 suites: https://www.spec.org/cpu2017/Docs/overview.html#suites

to be used for any purpose that fits within the *Fair Use Rules* for SPEC CPU2017, including comparisons to other systems.[9]

A SPECspeed suite and a SPECrate suite differ in terms of what type of metric is being measured, the number of copies of a given workload that may be run, whether parallelism can be used during the benchmark, how much memory is required by the benchmark (due to different workload sizes), and how much disk space is required. In a SPECrate suite, the user determines the number of copies of a given workload to run at a given time. For a SPECspeed suite, only one copy of a given workload will be run at a given time. This single copy does not mean that the workloads are single threaded. SPECspeed can have multiple threads run due to the use of OpenMP and/or compiler auto-parallelization. In contrast, SPECrate suites explicitly disallow the use of parallelization by the run rules.[10] In order to properly fit the workload size of SPECrate suites into a system, SPEC CPU2017 requires 1 GB (if compiled in 32-bit) to 2 GB (if compiled in 64-bit) of physical memory per copy. SPECspeed suites require a minimum of 16 GB of physical memory due to the workload size.[11] All SPEC CPU2017 suites are recommended to have at least 250 GB of disk space available. SPECrate suites require up to an extra 1.2 GB of disk space per copy of an active benchmark.[12]

The difference between an integer or floating point suite is based on the amount of floating-point operations performed by each workload. The SPEC CPU subcommittee measured candidate workloads and found that (depending on the system and compiler) the integer suites typically issue 1% or fewer floating-point instructions, whereas the floating point suites typically issue 10–35% floating-point instructions.

10.6.2 SPEC CPU2017 Workloads

As previously mentioned, SPEC CPU2017 contains 43 workloads, which can be seen as separate benchmarks (sub-benchmarks) within the four suites. The integer-based suites (SPECspeed 2017 Integer and SPECrate 2017 Integer), as well as the SPECspeed 2017 Floating Point suite, each contain ten benchmarks. The SPECrate 2017 Floating Point suite contains 13 benchmarks. These benchmarks are listed in Figure 10.1.[13]

For the integer suites, each benchmark has a SPECspeed and SPECrate benchmark pair that are similar to each other (except for the differences noted in the last section) and have very similar benchmark names—5xx.something_r for SPECrate

---

[9] Fair use rules for SPEC CPU2017:
https://www.spec.org/fairuse.html and https://www.spec.org/fairuse.html#CPU2017

[10] Compiler parallelization: https://www.spec.org/cpu2017/Docs/runrules.html#compilerParallel

[11] SPEC CPU2017 physical memory system requirements:
https://www.spec.org/cpu2017/Docs/system-requirements.html#memory

[12] SPEC CPU2017 disk space system requirements:
https://www.spec.org/cpu2017/Docs/system-requirements.html#disk

[13] SPEC CPU2017 benchmarks: https://www.spec.org/cpu2017/Docs/#benchmarks

The Benchmarks

SPEC CPU2017 has 43 benchmarks, organized into 4 suites:

```
SPECrate 2017 Integer          SPECspeed 2017 Integer
SPECrate 2017 Floating Point   SPECspeed 2017 Floating Point
```

Benchmark pairs shown as:

```
5nn.benchmark_r / 6nn.benchmark_s
```

are similar to each other. Differences include: compile flags; workload sizes; and run rules. See: [OpenMP] [memory] [rules]

SPECrate 2017 Integer	SPECspeed 2017 Integer	Language [1]	KLOC [2]	Application Area
500.perlbench_r	600.perlbench_s	C	362	Perl interpreter
502.gcc_r	602.gcc_s	C	1,304	GNU C compiler
505.mcf_r	605.mcf_s	C	3	Route planning
520.omnetpp_r	620.omnetpp_s	C++	134	Discrete Event simulation - computer network
523.xalancbmk_r	623.xalancbmk_s	C++	520	XML to HTML conversion via XSLT
525.x264_r	625.x264_s	C	96	Video compression
531.deepsjeng_r	631.deepsjeng_s	C++	10	Artificial Intelligence: alpha-beta tree search (Chess)
541.leela_r	641.leela_s	C++	21	Artificial Intelligence: Monte Carlo tree search (Go)
548.exchange2_r	648.exchange2_s	Fortran	1	Artificial Intelligence: recursive solution generator (Sudoku)
557.xz_r	657.xz_s	C	33	General data compression

SPECrate 2017 Floating Point	SPECspeed 2017 Floating Point	Language [1]	KLOC [2]	Application Area
503.bwaves_r	603.bwaves_s	Fortran	1	Explosion modeling
507.cactuBSSN_r	607.cactuBSSN_s	C++, C, Fortran	257	Physics: relativity
508.namd_r		C++	8	Molecular dynamics
510.parest_r		C++	427	Biomedical imaging: optical tomography with finite elements
511.povray_r		C++, C	170	Ray tracing
519.lbm_r	619.lbm_s	C	1	Fluid dynamics
521.wrf_r	621.wrf_s	Fortran, C	991	Weather forecasting
526.blender_r		C++, C	1,577	3D rendering and animation
527.cam4_r	627.cam4_s	Fortran, C	407	Atmosphere modeling
	628.pop2_s	Fortran, C	338	Wide-scale ocean modeling (climate level)
538.imagick_r	638.imagick_s	C	259	Image manipulation
544.nab_r	644.nab_s	C	24	Molecular dynamics
549.fotonik3d_r	649.fotonik3d_s	Fortran	14	Computational Electromagnetics
554.roms_r	654.roms_s	Fortran	210	Regional ocean modeling

[1] For multi-language benchmarks, the first one listed determines library and link options (details)

[2] KLOC = line count (including comments/whitespace) for source files used in a build / 1000

Some individual benchmark in the suite have additional documents, found in the benchmark "Docs" subdirectory on your installed benchmark tree, or on the SPEC CPU2017 distribution media. For example, additional information about 554.roms_r may be found in your installed copy of SPEC CPU2017 at:

```
$SPEC/benchspec/CPU/554.roms_r/Docs/ (Unix)
```
or
```
%SPEC%\benchspec\CPU\554.roms_r\Docs\ (Windows)
```

Fig. 10.1: SPEC CPU2017 benchmark suite

benchmarks and `6xx.something_s` for SPECspeed benchmarks. Among the floating point suites, there are only nine SPECspeed and SPECrate benchmark pairs. The SPECrate 2017 Floating Point suite contains four benchmarks that are not in the SPECspeed 2017 Floating Point suite. There were various reasons for this case, but most commonly the benchmark either did not have OpenMP support or the workload was deemed too similar to another benchmark. There is one benchmark in the SPECspeed2017 Floating Point suite that is not in the SPECrate 2017 Floating Point suite. This was due to not being able to obtain a workload that fits within the size requirements for SPECrate benchmarks.

The SPEC CPU2017 benchmarks are written in C, C++, Fortran, or some combination of those programming languages. The benchmarks come from a wide range of application areas such as (but not limited to) programming languages, route planning, discrete event simulation, XML to HTML conversion, video compression, artificial intelligence, data compression, molecular dynamics, fluid dynamics, explosion modeling, various imaging applications, various weather forecasting/modeling applications, physics and electromagnetics applications. The applications in the integer suites are all written in one of the three aforementioned languages (five written in C, four written in C++, and one written in Fortran). The floating point suite applications are written in one or more languages of C, C++, Fortran (three in C only, two in C++ only, three in Fortran only, two in C++ and C, three in Fortran and C, and one in C++, C, and Fortran). All of this shows that the benchmarks in SPEC CPU2017 are derived from a diverse spectrum of computing domains and are well representative of many applications that users care about or interact with on a regular basis.

Of the 43 benchmarks in SPEC CPU2017, 13 benchmarks were updated and share similar names to SPEC CPU2006 benchmarks. However, during the update process new source code and workloads were provided or modified such that SPEC CPU2006 and SPEC CPU2017 benchmarks with similar names may not perform the same. The other 30 benchmarks were new applications that were included via the SPEC CPU Benchmark *Search Program*. The *Search Program* was designed to encourage individuals or teams to submit their real-world, compute bound, portable applications with various problem sizes for consideration. Not every submission successfully entered the *Search Program*, and not all submissions that did enter the *Search Program* successfully completed all six steps. Along the path to completing each step, it was expected that the submitter of an application will be able to work with the SPEC CPU Subcommittee to port the application to the SPEC CPU harness, provide workloads as necessary demonstrating the application's profile, and assist in porting the application to various environments.

10.6.3 SPEC CPU2017 Metrics

Of the 16 different metrics SPEC CPU2017 can measure, four per suite, the most important differentiation occurs between SPECspeed and SPECrate metrics. A SPECspeed metric answers the common question of how fast a computing system can complete a given set of workloads; in other words, it is a time-based metric (cf. Chapter 3, Section 3.3). A SPECrate metric answers the common question of how much work a computing system can complete in a measured amount of time; in other words, it is a throughput metric.

Given that a SPECspeed and a SPECrate metric measure different aspects of a computing system's performance, the values that are used as a basis to derive these types of metrics are also computed differently. After a single copy of a SPECspeed benchmark is completed on a given system under test (SUT), the runtime of that copy is recorded and divided into the runtime of the same benchmark on a reference machine. This produces a ratio that is then shown in results disclosures. This ratio can be increased either through optimizations (compiler, BIOS, OS, hardware configuration) or through running a multi-threaded versus a single-threaded copy of a given SPECspeed benchmark. A SPECrate metric shares the same basis for computing a metric as a SPECspeed benchmark (SPECrate benchmark runtime on a SUT divided into the runtime of the same SPECrate benchmark on a reference machine), but it has an extra multiplier. The multiplier for the SPECrate benchmark comes from the number of copies a user chooses to run on a SUT. A SPECrate metric is not comparable or convertible to a SPECspeed metric. This is due to run rules, system requirements, and implementation of the benchmarks within SPEC CPU2017. A summary of the differences between SPECspeed and SPECrate metrics is provided in Table 10.3.[14] For both SPECspeed and SPECrate metrics, in order to provide some assurance that results are repeatable, the entire process is repeated. The tester may choose: (1) to run the suite of benchmarks three times, in which case the tools select the medians of the ratios or (2) to run twice, in which case the tools select the lower ratios (i.e., slower).

The second differentiation for SPEC CPU2017 metrics are base and peak metrics. Each result must have one base metric and optionally can have one peak metric. The difference between a base and peak metric primarily comes from the compilation environment used for the metrics. Base metrics are intended to represent a simpler build process and environment. In a base metric, all benchmarks of a given language (C, C++, Fortran) must use the same compiler flags in the same order. On the other hand, a peak metric is intended to represent a more complex environment where more consideration may be given to optimizing performance of individual applications. In a peak metric, benchmarks of the same language may have different compiler optimizations applied. Peak metrics also allow for feedback-directed optimization, whereas base metrics do not.[15]

Although SPEC CPU2017 metrics are calculated to many decimal points in the raw file (.rsf files produced by runs) and logs of an individual run, SPEC CPU2017 metrics are always reported to a maximum of three significant digits. SPEC CPU2017 results report the overall metrics (e.g., SPECrate2017_fp_peak) shown in Full Disclosure Reports using a geometric mean of the computed performance ratios for the individual benchmarks.

[14] SPECspeed and SPECrate metrics: https://www.spec.org/cpu2017/Docs/overview.html#Q15
[15] SPEC CPU2017 base and peak metrics:
https://www.spec.org/cpu2017/Docs/overview.html#Q16

Table 10.3: SPECspeed and SPECrate metrics

Calculating SPECspeed Metrics	Calculating SPECrate Metrics
One copy of each benchmark in a suite is run	One can choose how many concurrent copies to run
One can choose how many OpenMP threads to use	OpenMP is disabled
For each benchmark, a performance ratio is calculated: $$\frac{\text{time on a reference machine}}{\text{time on the SUT}}$$	For each benchmark, a performance ratio is calculated: $$\text{number of copies} \times \frac{\text{time on a reference machine}}{\text{time on the SUT}}$$
Example: • The reference machine ran `600.perlbench_s` in 1,775 s • A particular SUT took about 1/5 the time, scoring about 5 • More precisely: 1775/354.329738 = 5.009458	Example: • The reference machine ran one copy of `500.perlbench_r` in 1,592 s • A particular SUT ran 8 copies in about 1/3 the time, scoring 24 • More precisely: 8 × (1592/541.52471) = 23.518776

For both SPECspeed and SPECrate, the selected ratios are averaged using the *geometric mean*, which is reported as the overall metric

The motivation to use normalized metrics (i.e., performance ratios with respect to a reference machine) aggregated using a geometric mean is that each of the benchmarks should be treated as equally important; that is, the workloads modeled by the different benchmarks are assumed to be equally important for customer applications without weighting them in any way. The geometric mean is used to compute the overall metric, so that the results are independent of the reference machine used by SPEC. The intent is that improvements in each benchmark are encouraged and rewarded equally. In other words, a 20% improvement in one benchmark should have the same effect on the overall mean as a 20% improvement on any of the other benchmarks, and another 20% improvement on that benchmark should have the same effect as the last 20% improvement. This ensures that no single benchmark in the suite becomes more important than any of the others in the suite. The properties of the geometric mean that ensure this behavior were discussed in detail in Chapter 3 (Section 3.5.3.2).

10.6.4 SPEC CPU2017 Energy Metrics

Experimental power statistics were introduced with V1.0 in order to gain a better understanding on how much power is consumed by the SUT and how much of this consumption is influenced by the workloads (Lange, 2009). The energy metrics matured over time and became officially supported with the release of SPEC CPU2017 V1.1.[16] Now, vendors may choose to publish and make public comparisons based on any or all of the eight additional metrics. To conduct such SPEC CPU2017 energy metric measurements, the following additional hardware is required:

- a power analyzer,
- a temperature sensor,
- a separate Linux or Windows controller system, in order for the SPEC PTDaemon (Huppler et al., 2012) to gather power data without interfering with the SUT.

When measuring the energy metrics (e.g., SPECrate2017_int_energy_base), in addition to obtaining geometric mean performance and geometric mean energy metrics, the user can obtain data on the energy (in kilojoules), average power, and maximum power for each benchmark within a suite (e.g., 500.perlbench_r in the SPECrate2017_int suite). The Energy Ratios for each benchmark are based on the collected energy data and calculated as follows:

---

[16] https://www.spec.org/cpu2017/Docs/changes-in-v1.1.html

Energy Ratio (SPECspeed_benchmark) =

$$= \frac{\text{Energy (SPECspeed\_benchmark) of the reference machine}}{\text{Energy (SPECspeed\_benchmark) of the SUT}},$$

Energy Ratio (SPECrate_benchmark) =

$$= \frac{\text{Energy (SPECrate\_benchmark) of the reference machine}}{\text{Energy (SPECrate\_benchmark) of the SUT}} \times \text{number of copies.}$$

$$(10.1)$$

These Energy Ratios are used to compute the geometric mean Energy Ratios, which are seen as the SPEC CPU2017 energy metrics.[17] As an example, the first non-reference system result that published a SPEC CPU 2017 energy metric produced a SPECrate2017_int_energy_base result of 1,080.[18]

The SPEC CPU2017 energy metrics were incorporated as part of the *SPEC Power and Performance Benchmark Methodology* (SPECpower Committee, 2014), the methodology used when designing the SPECpower_ssj2008 benchmark (Lange et al., 2012). The SPECpower_ssj2008 benchmark and the SPEC Power and Performance Benchmark Methodology are presented in detail in Chapter 11.

10.6.5 SPEC CPU2017 Full Disclosure Report

In addition to containing measured performance data (graphs and tables to display runtimes, ratios, statistics, and metrics), the *Full Disclosure Report (FDR)* for a SPEC CPU2017 result contains information that is essential to understanding the result. To understand a SPEC CPU2017 FDR, it is best to look at one. Let us consider the first result from the reference system, a SPECrate2017_fp result gathered on a Sun Fire V490 system.[19]

Looking at the top of the first page, the user can see information about the system, hardware vendor, test sponsor/tester, test and availability dates as well as the geometric means reported as the SPECrate2017_fp metrics for the result. Notice, there is only a SPECrate2017_fp_base metric and the SPECrate2017_fp_peak metric is shown as "Not Run." SPEC CPU2017 requires all results to produce a base metric, but the peak metrics are optional. Below the top sections of the result, there is a graph area. This graph is meant to be a summary and visual representation of information found in the results table at the bottom of the second page of the result.

Also included in the FDR are required sections to fully and accurately describe the SUT hardware and software, notes fields (for the operating system, platform, and other general notes), compiler invocation details and portability flags used,

---

[17] https://www.spec.org/cpu2017/Docs/runrules.html#rule_4.10.3

[18] https://spec.org/cpu2017/results/res2019q3/cpu2017-20190903-17792.html

[19] SPEC CPU2017 reference system result:
https://spec.org/cpu2017/results/res2017q2/cpu2017-20161026-00001.pdf

optimization flags and other compiler flags used, and user supplied flag files that explain compiler and systems settings in more details.

The result table (see Figure 10.2) in any SPEC CPU2017 result shows all of the performance data measured and computed during a run. Besides the runtime of an individual benchmark, all of the data in this table have been rounded to three significant digits. To understand the result table, it is best to break it down into sections.

Base Results Table

Benchmark	Copies	Seconds	Ratio	Energy (kJ)	Energy Ratio	Average Power	Maximum Power	Seconds	Ratio	Energy (kJ)	Energy Ratio	Average Power	Maximum Power	Seconds	Ratio	Energy (kJ)	Energy Ratio	Average Power	Maximum Power
503.bwaves_r	1	10027	1.00	10900	1.00	1090	1120	10026	1.00	10900	1.00	1090	1120						
507.cactuBSSN_r	1	1264	1.00	1390	1.00	1100	1120	1266	1.00	1390	1.00	1100	1120						
508.namd_r	1	949	1.00	1030	1.00	1090	1100	949	1.00	1030	1.00	1090	1100						
510.parest_r	1	2616	1.00	2840	1.00	1090	1100	2615	1.00	2850	1.00	1090	1100						
511.povray_r	1	2335	1.00	2530	1.00	1080	1090	2334	1.00	2530	1.00	1080	1090						
519.lbm_r	1	1026	1.03	1170	1.03	1140	1140	1053	1.00	1200	1.00	1140	1140						
521.wrf_r	1	2239	1.00	2440	1.00	1090	1100	2239	1.00	2440	1.00	1090	1100						
526.blender_r	1	1521	1.00	1650	1.00	1080	1090	1523	1.00	1650	1.00	1080	1100						
527.cam4_r	1	1748	1.00	1900	1.00	1090	1120	1748	1.00	1900	1.00	1090	1110						
538.imagick_r	1	2486	1.00	2690	1.00	1080	1090	2486	1.00	2690	1.00	1080	1090						
544.nab_r	1	1683	1.00	1820	1.00	1080	1090	1682	1.00	1820	1.00	1080	1090						
549.fotonik3d_r	1	3897	1.00	4340	1.00	1110	1130	3897	1.00	4340	1.00	1110	1120						
554.roms_r	1	1589	1.00	1750	1.00	1100	1120	1588	1.00	1750	0.999	1100	1120						
SPECrate2017_fp_base =	1.00																		
exp_SPECrate2017_fp_energy_base =			1.00																

Results appear in the order in which they were run. Bold underlined text indicates a median measurement.

Fig. 10.2: SPEC CPU2017 results table

The base table (there would be a peak table if the result ran the peak metric) in the FDR previously referenced can be defined by four groups of columns. The first group of columns are the two leftmost columns that show the name of the benchmark and the number of copies. If this were a SPECspeed result, the copies column would be replaced by a threads column. The next group of columns is from the first column labeled "seconds" to the first column labeled "maximum power." These six columns represent the first iteration of the benchmarks for the SPECrate2017_fp_base metric. The next six columns represent the second iteration, and the blank last six columns represent the third iteration (if it had been run).

In the case of the SPECrate2017_fp_base result being studied, each value in each "seconds" column for all benchmarks is the number of seconds it took for the individual copy to run rounded to the nearest second. In the event that a SPECrate2017 result is a multi-copy result, the results in each "seconds" column for each benchmark would represent the time the slowest copy took to complete. Moving to the right, a "ratio" column displays the ratio for the benchmark run as described in Section 10.6.3 (Table 10.3). The next four columns display power statistics as well as one Energy Ratio.

Each benchmark in a result table for a given SPEC CPU2017 result will have one set of information displayed in bold text for a given iteration. This bold text shows which iteration is used to calculate geometric mean ratios. In the event of a two iteration run, such as the referenced SPECrate2017_fp_base result, the slower of the two iterations will be used to calculate geometric mean ratios. If a result has all three base or peak iterations run, then the median runtime of all three iterations for a benchmark (based on the full runtime calculated to multiple decimal points) would be used to calculate geometric means. The geometric means can be seen below all the values in the results table, near the metric or geometric mean values gathered during the run.

10.6.6 Concluding Remarks

This chapter presented an overview and retrospective on the emergence, development, and evolution of the SPEC CPU benchmark suite, which is designed to stress a system's processor, memory subsystem, and compiler. We looked at the six generations of this benchmark starting from 1989 with the release of SPEC CPU89 until the latest release in 2017 (SPEC CPU2017).

Moving forward with the next suite, the SPEC CPU committee is already exploring internal workload candidates for the next SPEC CPU suite (in collaboration with the SPEC High Performance Group and the SPEC Research Group), discussing how to organize a new *Search Program*, and trying to proactively determine some rules and requirements that were previously very contentiously debated. It is hard to say with any certainty what exact changes may be introduced; nonetheless, new applications and workloads, updated source codes to stay relevant with the status of programming languages, and ever-evolving tools seem like good bets. The general hope is to have a much shorter development period for the next benchmark suite.

References

Bucek, J., Lange, K.-D., and Kistowski, J. v. (2018). "SPEC CPU2017: Next-Generation Compute Benchmark". In: *Companion of the 2018 ACM/SPEC International Conference on Performance Engineering (ICPE 2018)*. (Berlin, Germany). ACM: New York, NY, USA, pp. 41–42 (cited on p. 239).

Henning, J. L. (2007). "SPEC CPU Suite Growth: An Historical Perspective". *ACM SIGARCH Computer Architecture News*, 35(1). ACM: New York, NY, USA, pp. 65–68 (cited on pp. 231, 238).

Huppler, K., Lange, K.-D., and Beckett, J. (2012). "SPEC: Enabling Efficiency Measurement". In: *Proceedings of the 3rd ACM/SPEC International Conference on Performance Engineering (ICPE 2012)*. (Boston, Massachusetts, USA). ACM: New York, NY, USA, pp. 257–258 (cited on p. 246).

Lange, K.-D. (2009). "The Next Frontier for Power/Performance Benchmarking: Energy Efficiency of Storage Subsystems". In: *Computer Performance Evaluation and Benchmarking—SPEC Benchmark Workshop 2009—Proceedings*. Ed. by D. Kaeli and K. Sachs. Vol. 5419. Lecture Notes in Computer Science. Springer-Verlag: Berlin, Heidelberg, pp. 97–101 (cited on p. 246).

Lange, K.-D., Tricker, M. G., Arnold, J. A., Block, H., and Sharma, S. (2012). "SPECpower_ssj2008: Driving Server Energy Efficiency". In: *Proceedings of the 3rd ACM/SPEC International Conference on Performance Engineering (ICPE 2012)*. (Boston, MA, USA). ACM: New York, NY, USA, pp. 253–254 (cited on p. 247).

SPECpower Committee (2014). *Power and Performance Benchmark Methodology V2.2*. Gainesville, VA, USA: Standard Performance Evaluation Corporation (SPEC) (cited on p. 247).

Weicker, R. P. (1990). "An Overview of Common Benchmarks". *Computer*, 23(12). IEEE Computer Society Press: Los Alamitos, CA, USA, pp. 65–75 (cited on p. 232).

Chapter 11
Benchmarking the Energy Efficiency of Servers

Jóakim von Kistowski, Klaus-Dieter Lange, and Jeremy A. Arnold

The measurement and benchmarking of computing server energy efficiency has become an ever more important issue over the last decades. In addition to mobile and other end-user devices, the energy efficiency of data centers and servers has gained attention as power consumption increases and is expected to continue increasing in the future. In 2010, the U.S. Environmental Protection Agency (U.S. EPA) estimated that 3% of the entire energy consumption in the USA is caused by data center power draw (Lange and Tricker, 2011). According to a New York Times study from 2012, data centers worldwide consume about 30 billion watts, which is equivalent to the approximate output of 30 nuclear power plants (Glanz, 2012).

Improving the energy efficiency of data centers and servers requires the ability to measure and rate that efficiency. A comprehensive rating method can enable data center owners to purchase more efficient devices. It can also help service providers to select the most efficient servers for their specific applications. Finally, a reliable rating method makes it possible for regulators to define standards and regulations specifying which devices are considered energy efficient and which are not. To achieve these goals, a rating method must meet a number of criteria based on the generic benchmark quality criteria we discussed in Chapter 1, that is, it must be relevant, reproducible, fair, and verifiable.

Relevance in the context of energy efficiency is challenging, as most servers in modern day data centers are not being utilized to their full capacity. Instead, servers are used to serve requests that arrive over time and are provisioned with additional capacity in order to be able to cope with variations in load such as unexpected bursts. This leads to an average load somewhere between 10% and 50% (Barroso and Hölzle, 2007). However, servers consume a different amount of power depending on the load level. An energy-efficiency benchmark must account for this and measure these states to obtain a complete picture of the server's energy efficiency. Older server efficiency benchmarks did not consider this issue of low load power consumption. While some benchmarks used for power and efficiency testing, such as JouleSort by Rivoire et al. (2007), run multiple workloads in a suite, these benchmarks are executed only at full load.

This chapter describes a rating methodology developed by the SPEC OSG Power Subcommittee for commodity servers. It is designed to characterize and rate the energy efficiency of a SUT for multiple load levels, showcasing load level differ-

© Springer Nature Switzerland AG 2020
S. Kounev et al., *Systems Benchmarking*, https://doi.org/10.1007/978-3-030-41705-5_11

ences in system behavior regarding energy efficiency. The methodology was first implemented in the SPECpower_ssj2008 benchmark and later extended with more workloads, metrics, and other application areas for the SPEC Server Efficiency Rating Tool (SERT). The SERT suite was developed to fill the need for a rating tool that can be utilized by government agencies in their regulatory programs, for example, the U.S. Environmental Protection Agency (EPA) for the use in the Energy Star program for servers.

11.1 SPEC Power and Performance Benchmark Methodology

All SPEC Power benchmarks and rating tools share the underlying *SPEC Power and Performance Benchmark Methodology* (SPECpower Committee, 2014) as their basis. The methodology has been developed by the SPEC OSG Power Committee as a tool for the analysis and evaluation of the energy efficiency of server systems. It was first implemented in SPECpower_ssj2008 (Lange, 2009) and later in the SPEC SERT (Lange and Tricker, 2011) and SPEC Chauffeur Worklet Development Kit (SPECpower Committee, 2017a). In the following, we discuss the measurement methodology and its general building blocks.

11.1.1 Device Setup

The SUT is at the center of the methodology's power measurement setup. It is a physical system that runs the workloads used for evaluation. The SUT's power consumption and its performance during testing are used to derive the energy-efficiency score. Performance metrics are gathered from the SUT using a testing software harness. The actual test execution software on the SUT is referred to as the *host* software. The host spawns separate on-SUT processes, referred to as *clients*, for each logical CPU core (hardware thread). These client processes execute the executable part of the workload. Spawning multiple clients allows for easy parallelization, as workloads can simply be executed in parallel within different isolated client environments. Alternatively, a client may also be configured to span multiple logical CPUs, in which case the executable workload is expected to run in a multi-threaded environment, utilizing all available CPU resources. The overarching goal of this parallelization scheme is to ensure scalability, which, in this case, is considered to be a subset of the *relevance* criterion from Chapter 1.

In most cases, a transactional workload (see Chapter 8) is executed on the clients. The clients collect the performance metrics for their workload and forward this information to the host. The workload is controlled by the *controller* system. It coordinates which workload to run at which load level. It also collects all measurements both from the SUT, as well as from external measurement devices, and it calculates the metrics and scores. The *director* manages all software instances as well as all measurement devices. The setup is illustrated in Figure 11.1.

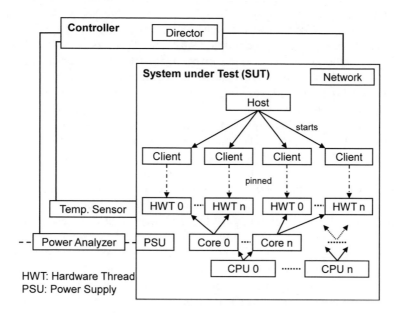

Fig. 11.1: Typical server power measurement device setup

The power methodology requires at least one external power analyzer and one temperature sensor. The power analyzer measures the power consumption of the entire SUT, whereas the temperature sensor verifies the validity of measurements, ensuring that all experiments are conducted under similar environmental conditions. External power and temperature instrumentation are used, as opposed to potential internal instrumentation, as the methodology makes no assumptions about the internal structure of the SUT, allowing for maximum portability. Reliance on external power measurement devices also enables the definition of tight constraints on the accuracy of the power measurement devices. Specifically, power measurement devices must feature a maximum measurement error of 1% or better.

The use of internal instrumentation may be adequate and appropriate for research purposes when working with a specific hardware model and when the researcher understands exactly what the sensors are measuring. Nonetheless, making comparisons across different models or architectures based on internal sensors is likely to result in inaccurate comparisons.

11.1.2 Load Levels

According to Barroso and Hölzle (2007), servers spend most of their time in a CPU utilization range between 10% and 50%. To account for this, workloads within the *SPEC Power and Performance Benchmark Methodology* are designed to measure system energy efficiency at multiple load levels. This sets benchmarks implementing the methodology apart from conventional performance benchmarks, such as SPEC CPU (cf. Chapter 10), or other energy-efficiency benchmarks, such as JouleSort (Rivoire et al., 2007) or the TPC-Energy benchmarks (Poess et al., 2010). To achieve workload execution at different load levels, a methodology-compliant benchmark calibrates the load by first determining the maximum transaction rate for the given workload on the SUT. The maximum transaction rate is measured by running concurrently on each client as many workload transactions as possible. For the calibration, the executable workload is executed according to the *closed workload* scheme (cf. Chapter 8, Section 8.3.2.1); that is, a new transaction is scheduled after the previous transaction in the respective thread (client) terminates.

This calibrated rate is then set as a 100% load level for all consecutive runs. For each target load level (e.g., 100%, 75%, 50%, 25%), the benchmark calculates the target transaction rate and derives the corresponding mean time from the start of one transaction to the start of the next transaction. During the measurement interval, these delays are randomized using an exponential distribution that statistically converges to the desired transaction rate. As a result, lower target loads consist of short bursts of activity separated by periods of inactivity. It follows that these load levels are executed according to the *open workload* scheme (cf. Chapter 8, Section 8.3.2.2), as the point in time when a transaction terminates has no bearing on the time at which the next transaction is dispatched.

Figure 11.2 shows how calibration and the following measurement intervals would run using intervals at 100%, 67%, and 33% as an example. Note that the load levels are defined as percentage of target throughput and do not indicate CPU utilization, which is a common misconception.

11.1.3 Phases and Intervals

The transactional executable workload is executed in three phases to achieve reproducible calibration and measurement results: a warm-up phase, a calibration phase, and a measurement phase. The warm-up phase runs the executable workload at full load for a short period of time discarding any measurements to account for transient side-effects. After warm up, the workload enters the calibration phase. During calibration, transactions are executed as fast as possible to determine the maximum transaction rate on the specific SUT. Finally, the measurement phase takes place. In the measurement phase, transactions are scheduled according to the targeted load level.

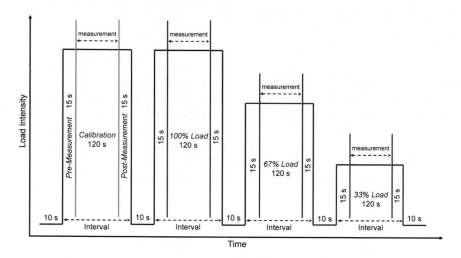

Fig. 11.2: Example intervals for the calibration and measurement phase (Kistowski, Beckett, et al., 2015)

Each phase is split into a configurable number of intervals, which serve different purposes depending on the phase in question. Each interval is the period in time, during which the actual work of the phase is being executed.

The executable workload is put to sleep for 10 s between each interval, allowing external power analyzers to adjust their range settings for the next interval. Each interval is also split into a pre-measurement, measurement, and post-measurement period. The pre-measurement period allows the interval to reach a steady state, whereas the post-measurement period ensures that the workload and hardware do not begin shutdown during measurement. The measurement period performs the phase-specific work. It measures the maximum throughput during calibration and the current throughput and power consumption during the measurement phase. In this time, all transactions are logged and power measurements are reported at 1 s intervals.

Each phase runs its intervals in sequence. The type of sequence depends on the phase in question. The warm-up phase runs multiple intervals of varying length, and the calibration phase runs multiple identical calibration intervals in sequence. The calibration result is the average throughput of those intervals. The measurement phase runs its intervals in a *graduated measurement sequence* executing workloads at gradually diminishing target transaction rates. Running multiple warm-up intervals provides higher visibility as to whether the warm-up time was sufficient to reach steady state.

11.1.4 Basic Energy-Efficiency Metric

The power methodology computes efficiency based on performance and power measurements. In addition to defining how power is measured, it must also define a performance measure and measurement method. This performance measure is intended to be used in conjunction with the power measurements in order to derive an efficiency metric. For this context, throughput (see Chapter 3, Section 3.3.2) has established itself as the commonly used metric.

As the size and execution duration may vary between different workloads, throughput is often normalized by comparing it to the throughput of a reference system—see Equation (11.1). This results in a speedup metric (see Chapter 3, Section 3.3.1).

$$normalized\_throughput = \frac{measured\_throughput}{reference\_throughput} \qquad (11.1)$$

The basic energy-efficiency metric for a single point in time or single measurement interval is computed as a ratio of performance to power consumption—see Equation (11.2)—where performance is either throughput or normalized throughput.

$$efficiency = \frac{performance}{power\_consumption} \qquad (11.2)$$

Alternatively, efficiency can be calculated as the ratio of work performed—see Equation (11.3)—to the energy expended, which is mathematically equivalent to performance per power consumption in the case of throughput being the primary performance metric.

$$efficiency = \frac{work\_performed}{energy\_expended} \qquad (11.3)$$

Using throughput as performance metric, energy efficiency is the ratio of throughput to power consumption in Watts. This is mathematically equivalent to the alternative efficiency ratio, as work units per time divided by power equals work units divided by energy—see Equation (11.4).

$$efficiency = \frac{throughput}{power\_consumption} \left[\frac{s^{-1}}{W} \right] = \frac{work\_units}{energy\_expended} \left[\frac{1}{J} \right] \qquad (11.4)$$

Both SPECpower_ssj2008 and the SPEC SERT use this base metric for each measurement interval. For each specific executable workload and each concrete load level, average throughput is normalized and then divided by average power consumption—see Equation (11.5).

$$load\_level\_efficiency = \frac{normalized\_throughput}{power\_consumption} \left[\frac{1}{J} \right] \qquad (11.5)$$

11.2 SPECpower_ssj2008

The SPECpower_ssj2008 benchmark was developed by the SPEC OSG Power Committee and was the first industry-standard benchmark to measure the energy efficiency of servers. It was developed in conjunction with the initial version of the SPEC Power and Performance Benchmark Methodology and served both as the basis for developing the first draft of the methodology and as its first implementation. The lessons learned during the development of the benchmark were incorporated into the methodology. The benchmark was based on the earlier SPECjbb2005 benchmark, which was a Java implementation of a simple OLTP workload. In SPECpower_ssj2008 the workload was modified to run at ten different load levels (100%, 90%, ..., 10%) as well as an active idle measurement, rather than only measuring performance at full utilization like its predecessor.

The order of the load levels, from 100% down to 10% and then Idle, was chosen intentionally in order to eliminate a sudden change in load between calibration and the first measurement interval. Jumping directly from 100% utilization during calibration to a 10% load is both unrealistic (for most server environments) and difficult to measure accurately, since it may take time for the server to adjust to the new load.

The benchmark is implemented in Java for portability to different operating systems and processor architectures, and it makes use of multiple threads and Java Virtual Machines to scale to different size systems. While the initial version of the benchmark only included support for measuring the energy efficiency of a single server, later updates allowed the benchmark to test multiple servers together. This capability is important for measuring the energy efficiency of blades and similar servers that utilize a shared power infrastructure.

11.2.1 Metric Calculation

The SPECpower_ssj2008 report[1] shows the throughput (ssj_ops) and power consumption as well as a load level efficiency score ("Performance to Power Ratio") for each load level. The load level efficiency score is calculated as in Equation (11.5), but in this case the throughput is not normalized. It was not necessary to normalize the performance in SPECpower_ssj2008 since there was only a single workload and the scores did not need to be combined.

The overall metric is calculated as the sum of the throughput for each load level divided by the sum of the power consumption in each load level (including active idle). This metric weights each of the load levels equally, and making improvements to either the performance score or the power consumption at any load level will result in an improvement to the score.

---

[1] https://www.spec.org/power_ssj2008/results/res2007q4/power_ssj2008-20071129-00015.html

One drawback of using an energy-efficiency ratio as the only primary metric of SPECpower_ssj2008 results is that it does not account for the capacity of the servers when comparing results. So while System A may be more efficient than System B, this may be irrelevant if System A does not have high enough performance to meet the needs of a particular application when System B does. So the reader of the results should be considering the maximum performance as well as the efficiency.

11.2.2 System Configuration

Another innovation in SPECpower_ssj2008 was the detailed reporting of the system configuration required in the Full Disclosure Report (FDR) for published results. While SPEC benchmarks have historically required documentation of any hardware, software, and other configuration details required to reproduce the result (in support of the reproducible and verifiable benchmark quality criteria described in Chapter 1), the SPEC OSG Power Committee recognized that many components of the system could influence the power consumption even if they did not affect performance.

As a result, the SPECpower_ssj2008 full disclosure report has more detail than most benchmarks regarding specific vendors, power supply details, and the presence of extra hardware such as additional network cards, keyboard, and optical drives which will not affect the reported performance but may influence the power consumption of the server. The run rules also require detailed disclosure of non-default firmware settings, which can often be used to influence power consumption, even if such settings are not often adjusted by most users.

11.3 SPEC Server Efficiency Rating Tool (SERT)

The SPEC Server Efficiency Rating Tool (SERT) has been developed by the SPEC OSG Power Committee as a tool for the analysis and evaluation of the energy efficiency of server systems. In contrast to energy-efficiency benchmarks such as JouleSort (Rivoire et al., 2007), the TPC-Energy benchmarks (Poess et al., 2010), and SPECpower_ssj2008, SERT does not execute an application from a specific domain. It does not aim to emulate real-world end-user workloads, but instead provides a set of focused synthetic micro-workloads called *worklets* that exercise selected aspects of the SUT. The worklets have been developed to exercise the processor, memory, and storage I/O subsystems.

For each of the server components to be stressed, SERT offers a range of worklets designed to exercise the targeted component in a different manner. This allows for thorough analysis of system energy behavior under different workload types designed to target the same component. As an example, the CryptoAES worklet profits from both specialized instruction sets, as well as better CPU to memory connectivity, whereas the SOR worklet primarily scales with processor frequency.

11.3.1 Workload and Worklets

SERT's goal is the execution of different mini-workloads at multiple load levels. Those mini-workloads are referred to as *worklets* and are grouped into worklet collections, referred to as *workloads*. Specifically, a workload is a collection of worklets with a common testing goal. All worklets within a workload are designed to test a common resource by utilizing it in a specific fashion. They execute work units, referred to as *transactions*. The SERT v2.0 suite features three separate workloads: CPU, Memory, and Storage. Each of these workloads consists of multiple worklets, which are executed at several load levels.

Each worklet's performance and power consumption are measured separately for each load level, and the energy efficiency, as well as the normalized energy efficiency, is calculated from the measurement results. The workload score is an aggregate of all the separate worklet scores. It provides a workload efficiency score, which signifies how well the tested system performed for all the worklets in the specified category (for details, see Section 11.3.2).

In the following, we describe each of the workloads in detail. Each workload was designed so that it primarily stresses the server subsystem after which it was named (the CPU workload stresses CPU, the Memory workload stresses memory, the Storage workload stresses internal storage devices). However, it is important to keep in mind that workloads do not exclusively stress that subsystem. Workloads also measure and characterize the energy efficiency of interactions between multiple subsystems. To this end, the CPU workload also utilizes some memory, the memory workload utilizes some CPU, and the storage workload utilizes some CPU and memory. All following descriptions are consistent with the SERT design document (SPECpower Committee, 2017b).

11.3.1.1 CPU Workload

The CPU workload is defined as a collection of seven CPU worklets:

1. **Compress**: De-/compresses data using a modified Lempel–Ziv–Welch (LZW) method (Welch, 1984).
2. **CryptoAES**: Encrypts/decrypts data using the AES or DES block cipher algorithms.
3. **LU**: Computes the LU factorization of a dense matrix using partial pivoting.
4. **SHA256**: Performs SHA-256 hashing transformations on a byte array.
5. **SOR** (Jacobi Successive Over-Relaxation): Exercises typical access patterns in finite difference applications.
6. **SORT**: Sorts a randomized 64-bit integer array during each transaction.
7. **Hybrid / SSJ**: The hybrid SSJ worklet stresses both CPU and memory, with either serving as the primary bottleneck, depending on the system configuration. SSJ performs multiple different simultaneous transactions, simulating an enterprise application.

11.3.1.2 Memory Workload

The memory workload consists of worklets designed to scale with installed memory. Specifically, this means that the worklets are designed to measure a higher (better) performance score with improved memory characteristics (e.g., higher bandwidth, lower latency, total memory size). The primary memory characteristics being tested are bandwidth and capacity.

The memory worklets serve as the major exception to the load level and interval specification in Section 11.1.2. In contrast to other worklets, they do not scale via transaction rate, but instead scale with memory capacity. In addition, they do not use throughput as their performance metric, but they modify it to include bandwidth and/or capacity.

1. **Flood**: A sequential memory bandwidth test that exercises memory using arithmetic operations and copy instructions. Flood is multi-threaded to reward servers that can utilize more memory concurrently with multiple CPUs and DIMMs. It automatically adjusts to use all available system RAM. It runs at two load levels called "Full" and "Half," utilizing all and half of the system memory, respectively. Flood's performance score is a function of both the memory capacity and the bandwidth measured during testing.
2. **Capacity**: A memory capacity test that performs XML operations on a minimum and maximum dataset. Capacity scales with capacity over its load levels. If the worklet's memory set exceeds the amount of physically available memory, it incurs a performance penalty for each transaction that attempts to read data not stored within physical memory. The final metric is a function of transaction rate and physical memory size including performance penalties.

11.3.1.3 Storage Workload

The developers of the SERT suite have included a workload for testing storage in order to enable a well-rounded system test. Storage worklets test the server's internal storage devices.

1. **Random**: Reads and writes data to/from random file locations.
2. **Sequential**: Reads and writes data to/from file locations picked sequentially.

11.3.1.4 Idle Workload

Idle keeps the system in an idle state in order to measure the idle power consumption. It does not measure any efficiency metric (only consumption).

11.3.2 Energy-Efficiency Metrics

SERT calculates separate intermediate energy-efficiency metrics, where each step aggregates the efficiency of the previous step. The calculation is illustrated in Figure 11.3 and consists of the following intermediate metrics:

1. Interval efficiency,
2. Worklet efficiency (over all load levels),
3. Workload efficiency (for all worklets),
4. Total efficiency.

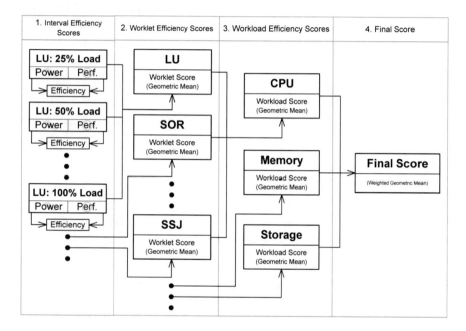

Fig. 11.3: Calculation of energy-efficiency metrics (Kistowski, Lange, et al., 2019)

11.3.2.1 Interval Energy Efficiency

Energy efficiency is calculated separately for each interval using the metric described in Section 11.1.4. As a small change, interval efficiency is multiplied by a constant factor of 1000—Equation (11.6). This is a cosmetic factor used to move the resulting score into a number range easier to read for a human reader.

$$\text{interval\_efficiency} = \frac{\text{normalized\_throughput}}{\text{power\_consumption}} \left[\frac{1}{J}\right] \times 1000 \qquad (11.6)$$

11.3.2.2 Worklet Energy Efficiency

The worklet energy-efficiency score is calculated using the geometric mean of each worklet's separate interval scores as follows:

$$\text{worklet\_efficiency} = \left(\prod_{i=1}^{n} (\text{interval\_efficiency}_i) \right)^{\frac{1}{n}}, \quad (11.7)$$

where n represents the number of load levels per worklet, and interval_efficiency$_i$ represents the energy efficiency for load level i.

SERT uses the geometric mean over the arithmetic mean as it is known to preserve ratios (such as energy efficiency and the normalized throughput, see Chapter 3, Section 3.5.3.2).

11.3.2.3 Workload Energy Efficiency

The workload energy-efficiency score is calculated by aggregating the efficiency scores of all worklets within the workload using the geometric mean as follows:

$$\text{workload\_efficiency} = \left(\prod_{i=1}^{n} (\text{worklet\_efficiency}_i) \right)^{\frac{1}{n}}, \quad (11.8)$$

where n represents the number of worklets per workload, and worklet_efficiency$_i$ is the energy efficiency for each specific worklet, calculated using Equation (11.7).

11.3.2.4 Final Aggregate Energy Efficiency

The server energy-efficiency score is the final aggregate of the workload scores. It is also derived using the geometric mean. In contrast to the other geometric mean aggregates, the final score does not consider all workloads equally. Instead, it uses a weighted mean, putting a different focus on each of the workload scores. For specific use cases, weights may be chosen according to the use case. The U.S. EPA has adopted SERT v2.0 for regulatory purposes. They use the following workload weights:

- **High** CPU weight: 65%,
- **Medium** Memory weight: 30%,
- **Low** Storage weight: 5%.

With these weights, the final score would be calculated as follows:

$$server\_efficiency = exp(0.65 \times ln(\text{CPU\_workload\_efficiency})$$
$$+ 0.3 \times ln(\text{memory\_workload\_efficiency}) \qquad (11.9)$$
$$+ 0.05 \times ln(\text{storage\_workload\_efficiency})).$$

This specific weighting is targeted at regular data center compute nodes, resulting in a high CPU and medium memory weight that is intended to mirror a typical real-world compute workload's resource profile. Storage is weighted with a low 5% weight, as storage servers are not the target devices for this weighting.

11.4 Concluding Remarks

This chapter introduced the SPEC Power and Performance Benchmark Methodology, which is designed to facilitate the measurement and rating of server energy efficiency. Taking into account that servers are usually not fully utilized, the methodology is built to ensure workload execution at multiple load levels to obtain a thorough and relevant view of the server in question. The chapter described two implementations of the methodology in detail: SPECpower_ssj2008 and the SPEC SERT suite.

SPECpower_ssj2008, the first benchmark to implement this methodology, has been successfully applied to measure the energy efficiency of servers since its release in 2007, and it has driven the development of new, energy efficient servers since then. In contrast, the SERT suite is not a benchmark, but a rating tool intended for use by regulatory programs such as the U.S. EPA Energy Star Version 3.0 Enterprise Servers Program,[2] and the EU Commission Regulation 2019/424.[3] Also, the International Organization for Standardization (ISO), in collaboration with the International Electrotechnical Commission (EIC), adopted the SERT suite in their server energy standard (ISO/IEC 21836),[4] which will foster the usage of the SERT suite globally. SERT implements the methodology, running multiple executable mini-workloads, each at multiple load levels. It aggregates its partial results in a single metric using multiple intermediate geometric means.

The SPEC Power and Performance Benchmark Methodology has had a significant impact on the development of new benchmarks and on the energy efficiency of servers. It has been applied in many benchmarks, including some TPC and VMware benchmarks, and it has helped drive and measure a significant improvement in the energy efficiency of servers since 2007.

Energy-efficient servers are one part of the combination necessary to provide services. The second part, the software itself, can still be wasting energy, either through deficient configuration, suboptimal deployment, unnecessary computations, or a combination of those. Several initiatives are underway to extend the scope of server efficiency, for example, the SPEC Power Research Working Group started

---

[2] https://www.energystar.gov/products/data_center_equipment/enterprise_servers

[3] https://eur-lex.europa.eu/legal-content/EN/TXT/PDF/?uri=CELEX:32019R0424&from=EN

[4] https://www.iso.org/standard/71926.html

to identify what programming languages are more sensitive to compiler optimizations (Schmitt et al., 2020), and ISO/IEC is drafting a new standard energy efficiency of middleware (ISO/IEC JTC 1/SC 39, 2020). These will help to consider how to benchmark and rate the energy efficiency of software in standardized benchmarks.

References

Barroso, L. A. and Hölzle, U. (2007). "The Case for Energy-Proportional Computing". *Computer*, 40(12). IEEE Computer Society: Washington, DC, USA, pp. 33–37 (cited on pp. 251, 254).

Glanz, J. (2012). *Power, Pollution and the Internet*. New York Times, Sept. 22, 2012. New York, USA (cited on p. 251).

ISO/IEC JTC 1/SC 39 (2020). *ISO/IEC DIS 23544: Information Technology—Data Centres—Application Platform Energy Effectiveness (APEE)*. https://www.iso. org/standard/76000.html, last accessed July 2020. Geneva, Switzerland (cited on p. 264).

Kistowski, J. von, Beckett, J., Lange, K.-D., Block, H., Arnold, J. A., and Kounev, S. (2015). "Energy Efficiency of Hierarchical Server Load Distribution Strategies". In: *Proceedings of the 23rd IEEE International Symposium on Modeling, Analysis, and Simulation of Computer and Telecommunication Systems (MASCOTS 2015)*. (Atlanta, GA, USA). IEEE Computer Society: Washington, DC, USA (cited on p. 255).

Kistowski, J. von, Lange, K.-D., Arnold, J. A., Beckett, J., Block, H., Tricker, M., Sharma, S., Pais, J., and Kounev, S. (2019). "Measuring and Rating the Energy-Efficiency of Servers". *Future Generation Computer Systems*, 100. Elsevier Science: Amsterdam, The Netherlands, pp. 579–589 (cited on p. 261).

Lange, K.-D. (2009). "Identifying Shades of Green: The SPECpower Benchmarks". *Computer*, 42(3). IEEE: Piscataway, NJ, USA, pp. 95–97 (cited on p. 252).

Lange, K.-D. and Tricker, M. G. (2011). "The Design and Development of the Server Efficiency Rating Tool (SERT)". In: *Proceedings of the 2nd ACM/SPEC International Conference on Performance Engineering (ICPE 2011)*. (Karlsruhe, Germany). ACM: New York, NY, USA, pp. 145–150 (cited on pp. 251, 252).

Poess, M., Nambiar, R. O., Vaid, K., Stephens, J. M., Huppler, K., and Haines, E. (2010). "Energy Benchmarks: A Detailed Analysis". In: *Proceedings of the 1st International Conference on Energy-Efficient Computing and Networking (e-Energy 2010)*. (Passau, Germany). ACM: New York, NY, USA, pp. 131–140 (cited on pp. 254, 258).

Rivoire, S., Shah, M. A., Ranganathan, P., and Kozyrakis, C. (2007). "JouleSort: A Balanced Energy-Efficiency Benchmark". In: *Proceedings of the 2007 ACM*

SIGMOD International Conference on Management of Data. (Beijing, China). ACM: New York, NY, USA, pp. 365–376 (cited on pp. 251, 254, 258).

Schmitt, N., Bucek, J., Lange, K.-D., and Kounev, S. (2020). "Energy Efficiency Analysis of Compiler Optimizations on the SPEC CPU 2017 Benchmark Suite". In: *Companion of the 11th ACM/SPEC International Conference on Performance Engineering (ICPE 2020)*. (Edmonton, Canada). ACM: New York, NY, USA, pp. 38–41 (cited on p. 264).

SPECpower Committee (2014). *Power and Performance Benchmark Methodology V2.2*. Gainesville, VA, USA: Standard Performance Evaluation Corporation (SPEC) (cited on p. 252).

– (2017a). *Chauffeur Worklet Development Kit (WDK) User Guide 2.0.0.* Gainesville, VA, USA (cited on p. 252).

– (2017b). *Server Efficiency Rating Tool (SERT) Design Document 2.0.0.* Gainesville, VA, USA (cited on p. 259).

Welch, T. A. (1984). "A Technique for High-Performance Data Compression". *Computer*, 17(6). IEEE Computer Society: Los Alamitos, CA, USA, pp. 8–19 (cited on p. 259).

Chapter 12
Virtualization Benchmarks

Klaus-Dieter Lange, David Schmidt, and David Morse

The concept of partitioning a computer's physical resources to create virtualized user environments has been around for decades. From the mainframes of the 1960s and 1970s through the current era of x86 servers, the goal of maximizing the utilization and efficiency of business IT resources has driven the ongoing development of server virtualization technologies. The fundamental component of server virtualization is the hypervisor, which is computer software, firmware, or hardware that creates and runs virtual machines. Hypervisors can run directly on a host's hardware, or can run as an application within a traditional OS, to manage and control virtual machines (VMs) on the host.

At the end of the twentieth century and the beginning of the twenty-first century, a new wave of hypervisors, led by VMware's VMware Workstation and VMware ESX Server, ushered in a renaissance of server virtualization in the computer industry. These new hypervisors ran on newer x86 servers which were increasing in popularity with businesses. In less than 10 years, many hardware and software vendors such as HP, Sun, Microsoft, Citrix, Oracle, and Red Hat introduced competing virtualization solutions. Additionally, the open-source community developed hypervisors like Xen.

One of the early uses of these hypervisors was to take advantage of improved performance of newer generations of server hardware products to consolidate the business applications running on older servers onto fewer new ones. This consolidation increased the utilization of servers in a data center and because fewer servers were needed it led to reduced space, cooling, and energy costs.

Further development of hypervisors introduced redundancy capabilities allowing VMs to be moved between physical servers and storage pools within a cluster of hypervisors while still being fully active. This capability allowed IT departments to perform maintenance on the hardware, add new hardware to a given cluster, and balance the resource utilization across multiple servers, all with no downtime for the end users. New VMs can be provisioned from predefined templates for rapid deployment. These hypervisor capabilities provide the infrastructure for what is now known as "The Cloud."

With the introduction and rise in popularity of new server virtualization products in the early 2000s, the inevitable question arose: Which solution performs better? The question is not a simple one, as virtualization environments consist of hypervisors, server platforms, storage, and networking. No common workload was devel-

© Springer Nature Switzerland AG 2020
S. Kounev et al., *Systems Benchmarking*, https://doi.org/10.1007/978-3-030-41705-5_12

oped to measure head-to-head performance of different hypervisors, as traditional benchmarks were intended to run on bare-metal servers, not within a virtualized environment. The traditional benchmark would be constrained by the resources provided to the VM rather than the entire virtualization solution. Likewise, running a traditional benchmark on the bare-metal server with the hypervisor present, even if possible, would not provide a meaningful measure of the hypervisor's performance.

In this chapter, we provide an overview of established benchmarks for evaluating the performance of virtualization platforms. We focus on the SPEC VIRT series of industry-standard benchmarks released by SPEC (SPEC VIRT_SC 2010, SPEC VIRT_SC 2013, and SPECvirt Datacenter 2020) while also considering the VMmark benchmark released by VMware.

12.1 SPEC Virtualization Benchmarks

In October 2006, SPEC established the OSG Virtualization Working Group to explore the possibility of developing an industry-standard benchmark to measure virtualization performance. The initial members of the working group were representatives from AMD, Dell, Fujitsu Siemens, Hewlett-Packard, Intel, IBM, Sun Microsystems, and VMware. In March 2007, the working group became a full subcommittee with its initial charter: *"The goal of the subcommittee is to develop a standard method for comparing virtualization performance of data center servers. The subcommittee's deliverable will be a benchmark that will model server consolidation of commonly virtualized systems including mail servers, database servers, application servers, web servers, and file servers. The benchmark will support hardware virtualization, operating system virtualization, and hardware partitioning schemes for server consolidation scenarios."*

12.1.1 SPEC VIRT_SC 2010

The first SPEC virtualization benchmark was SPEC VIRT_SC 2010 (Lange et al., 2012), released on July 14, 2010. It was designed to be a standard method for measuring a virtualization platform's ability to manage a server consolidation scenario and for comparing performance between virtualized environments. SPEC VIRT_SC 2010 measures the performance of the hardware, software, and application layers within a virtualized environment with a single hypervisor host. It uses three modified SPEC benchmarks as a workload to stress the system under test (SUT). Each of these three applications, SPECweb2005, SPECjAppServer2004, and SPECmail2008, drives predefined loads against the SUT. The benchmark requires the use of a set of clients to support the benchmark harness and drive the workloads on the SUT. SPEC VIRT_SC 2010 also supports the use of the SPECpower methodology to measure power usage during the benchmark. Results can be submitted in three categories: performance only (SPECvirt_sc2010), performance/power for the SUT (SPECvirt_sc2010_PPW), and performance/power for server only (SPECvirt_sc2010_ServerPPW).

12.1.1.1 Design

The benchmark suite consists of several SPEC workloads that represent applications that, at the time, industry surveys reported to be common targets of virtualization and server consolidation. The workloads were modified to match a typical server consolidation scenario's resource requirements for CPU, memory, disk I/O, and network utilization for each workload. The SPEC workloads used were:

- SPECweb2005: This workload represents a web server, a file server, and an infrastructure server. The SPECweb workload is partitioned into two virtual machines (VMs): a web server and a combined file server and backend server (BeSim). SPEC VIRT_SC 2010 uses the support workload from the original benchmark with a modified dataset.
- SPECjAppserver2004: This workload represents an application server and backend database server. Specifically, SPECjAppServer2004 was modified such that it created a dynamic load, increased the database scale, and decreased the session lengths. Additionally, the injection rate for queries varied significantly during the course of the benchmark. A sequence of different injection rates are cycled through during the course of a run, where each tile starts at a different injection rate in this sequence in order to create a "bursty" utilization pattern for the workload.
- SPECmail2008: This workload represents a mail server. Specifically, the harness employs the SPECmail IMAP component with new transactions.

SPEC VIRT_SC 2010 employs a fourth workload called SPECpoll developed explicitly for the benchmark. SPECpoll serves two functions: It sends and acknowledges network pings against an idle server VM in the 100% load phase to measure its responsiveness, and to all VMs in the 0% load phase (active idle) during power-enabled runs. SPECpoll ensures that sufficient resources are allocated to the idle server to function during the benchmark.

The four workloads described above run across 6 VMs in a set known as a "tile." Figure 12.1 shows the structure of the tile and its interaction with the SUT and client harness. A tile will deliver a specific amount of stress to the SUT and each workload must achieve a minimum level of Quality-of-Service (QoS). Scaling the benchmark on the SUT entails running an increasing number of tiles. Peak performance is reached at the point in which the addition of another tile fails to achieve the QoS criteria. The final benchmark result is the sum of the score achieved for each tile. The VMs of the same type were required to be configured identically across all tiles; only items like VM, IP, and NFS share names could be unique.

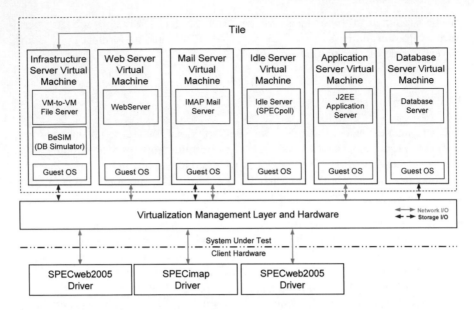

Fig. 12.1: SPEC VIRT_SC 2010 single-tile layout

To allow for fine tuning of the workload scaling, the final tile employed can be a "partial tile." This partial tile throttles down the workload drivers so that less stress is delivered to the SUT. The partial tile's score is proportionally scaled down.

12.1.1.2 The Need for a New Benchmark

SPEC VIRT_SC 2010 was released in July 2010 and several vendors published results on server configurations with 2–16 CPUs. Within a year of its release, a few trends became clear:

- As the number of tiles used by the benchmark increased, each injection rate used by the application server workload was exercised simultaneously by one of the tiles. In this case, the overall utilization across all tiles became more constant, removing the desired variability (i.e., burstiness) during the course of a run. As a result, the overall SUT CPU utilization could be driven to near 100%, which was not representative of real-world use cases.
- The workload levels for the tiles were too low. The initial utilization levels for the workloads within a tile were intended to be representative. However, as time went on, the amount of virtual resources needed for each VM decreased significantly. Within a year of the release, no VM needed more than a single vCPU, and the memory footprints for several VMs were less than 1 GB. This was significantly less than intended for the benchmark.

- A result of the reduced virtual resources needed per tile led to an increase in the number of tiles a SUT could support. Results that supported more than 17 tiles (102 VMs) on a 2P server became quite common. Feedback from customers expressed the large number of VMs reported in the results were unrealistic. Additionally, the benchmark harness struggled with the number of tiles being run on 8P and 16P configurations, topping over 100 tiles in some cases.

These concerns drove the SPEC Virtualization Subcommittee to develop a replacement benchmark.

12.1.2 SPEC VIRT_SC 2013

SPEC VIRT_SC 2013, released in May 2013, represents a significant update to its predecessor SPEC VIRT_SC 2010 which retired in February 2014. While still employing the concept of a tile for its basic unit of work, the design of the tile itself changed, with a set of tiles sharing a single database VM. Each workload was overhauled to increase its stress level and the idle server VM was replaced with a batch server VM with a new workload. Workload injection rates were made variable on the mail server in addition to the application server. Lastly, the web server introduced encryption in its web requests. All of the above updates are made for a much more robust tile.

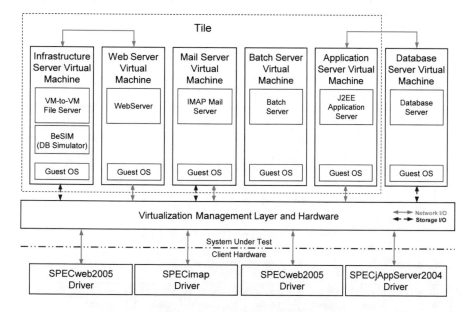

Fig. 12.2: SPEC VIRT_SC 2013 single-tile layout

Figure 12.2 shows the updated tile layout for SPEC VIRT_SC 2013. Notable enhancements for the new benchmark over its predecessor are as follows:

- **Shared database VM.** To ensure the presence of multi-vCPU VMs in the benchmark, the application server workload's database VM was pulled out of the tile. With SPEC VIRT_SC 2013, the application server VMs for every four tiles share the same database server VM, each with its own data within the database. This configuration requires the database VM to consume more resources to handle the increased database activity. Figure 12.3 shows a multi-tile configuration with the shared database VMs.
- **Web-server workload implemented SSL encryption.** To increase the utilization on the web-server VM, SSL encryption was introduced into the web-server workload. With the latest version of SPEC VIRT_SC 2013, SSLv3 and TLS 1.x encryptions are supported.
- **New batch workload.** To introduce more burstiness in the benchmark's workload profile, the new batch server VM replaces the idle server VM in the tile. The batch workload is based on one of the SPEC CPU 2006 training workloads, which runs 10 copies of the workload every hour and is idle for the rest of the hour. The 10 "jobs" must complete within 15 min, necessitating resource allocation from the SUT sufficient to satisfy this requirement. The batch jobs are staggered from one tile to another to avoid an unreasonable spike in server utilization at the beginning of the benchmark.
- **Mail server workload profile is now bursty.** Again, to add workload variation, the mail server workload now has a bursty profile akin to the application server's workload profile.

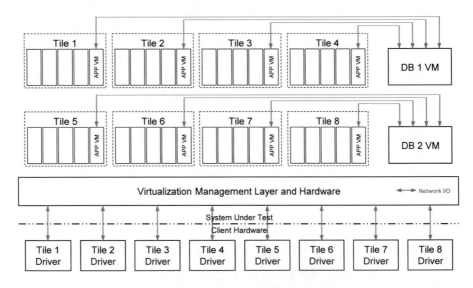

Fig. 12.3: SPEC VIRT_SC 2013 multi-tile layout

The operation of SPEC VIRT_SC 2013 is the same as SPEC VIRT_SC 2010. Scaling the workload is identical with the exception that only one database VM is added for every four tiles. All VMs of the same type must be identical across tiles. Partial tiles are allowed in SPEC VIRT_SC 2013. As with SPEC VIRT_SC 2010, SPEC VIRT_SC 2013 also supports measuring power performance.

SPEC VIRT_SC 2013 achieved its goal of a more intensive tile. At the time of the release, a 2P server that would require 28 tiles (168 VMs) to saturate it with SPEC VIRT_SC 2010 would need only 6.6 tiles (37 VMs) with SPEC VIRT_SC 2013. The benchmark continues to be active with new publications on the latest generations of hardware.

12.1.3 SPECvirt Datacenter 2020: The Next Generation

As the virtualization industry evolved, more complex environments became common. Configurations with multiple hypervisor hosts, shared networking, and common storage, all controlled by a central management application, are prevalent in modern data centers. Simple server consolidation is no longer the most interesting use case for businesses. The need for an industry-standard, multi-host virtualization benchmark became more urgent. Such a benchmark is needed to factor in common data center operations such as dynamic provisioning of VMs, automatically balancing resource utilization across multiple hosts, and introducing new physical resources into an environment. The subcommittee's charter was expanded to reflect this goal: *"The goal of the subcommittee is to develop standard methods for comparing virtualization performance of data centers. The subcommittee will develop and maintain benchmarks that represent typical virtualized infrastructure for various enterprise customer scenarios, such as server consolidation and multi-host virtualized environments."*

With this goal in mind, the first SPEC virtualization multi-host benchmark, SPECvirt Datacenter 2020, is planned to be released in 2020. It is a completely new virtualization benchmark designed to measure the performance of a different use case than SPEC VIRT_SC 2013, a multi-host virtualized data center. In addition to measuring traditional host capacity performance like SPEC VIRT_SC 2013, SPECvirt Datacenter 2020 also measures the virtual data center's ability to dynamically deploy VMs, balance workload levels across a cluster of hosts, and utilize new host resources that come online during run time. SPECvirt Datacenter 2020 also introduces preconfigured template VMs to simplify its setup and use.

12.1.3.1 Design

SPECvirt Datacenter 2020 uses five workloads contained within a 12-VM tile as its unit of work; see Figure 12.4 for the tile layout. Some of the VMs within a tile are deployed from a template during the course of the benchmark, while others

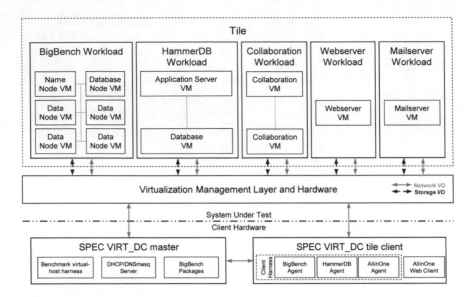

Fig. 12.4: SPECvirt Datacenter 2020 single-tile layout

are brought online from a powered off state. This behavior models the dynamic nature of a real-world virtualized data center environment. The workloads used in SPECvirt Datacenter 2020 are:

- a synthetic workload that simulates the stress of a pair of collaboration servers interacting with each other, modeled from real-world data. Two Collaboration Server VMs interact with each other to run this workload.
- a synthetic workload that simulates the stress of a web-server environment based on the SPEC VIRT_SC 2013 web-server workload. A Web Server VM runs on the SUT and interacts with a remote process that runs on the client.
- a synthetic workload that simulates the stress of an IMAP mail server application environment based on the SPEC VIRT_SC 2013 mail server workload. A standalone Mail Server VM runs this workload.
- a transactional database workload based on the HammerDB load testing and benchmarking tool.[1] The workload utilizes two VMs running on the SUT: an Application Server VM and a Database Server VM.
- a big data workload based on a modified version of BigBench that utilizes an Apache/Hadoop environment to execute complex database queries. The workload runs across six VMs on the SUT: a Name Node VM, a Database VM, and four Data Node VMs.

Unlike SPEC VIRT_SC 2013 where all of the tiles were started at the beginning of the benchmark and began their measurement intervals at the same time,

---

[1] https://www.hammerdb.com

SPECvirt Datacenter 2020 employs a more complex run profile as shown in Figure 12.5. During the first phase of the measurement interval, 1/4 of the hosts within the SUT are in maintenance mode. The benchmark will then bring the tiles' workloads online, starting or deploying the VMs used for each tile as needed. The ability of the SUT environment to deploy more rapidly and start a tile's workloads will be reflected as a longer active duration for that tile's measurement intervals. Once the target number of tiles for Phase 1 have been deployed, the SUT will remain at steady state until the end of the phase. Phase 2 begins with the activation of all of the hosts that were in maintenance mode during Phase 1. The SUT then will be able to take advantage of the newly available resources to balance the load on the systems. Phase 3 then sees the deployment of additional tiles to fully saturate the entire SUT environment.

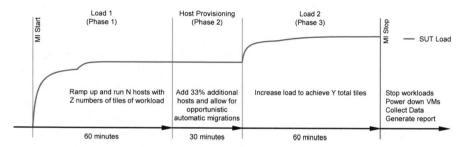

Fig. 12.5: SPECvirt Datacenter 2020 measurement interval (MI) profile

The performance score for each tile uses the aggregate throughput for each workload across all phases during which it was active. These throughput scores are normalized to reference values and then combined using a weighted geometric mean. The final score is the sum of the weighted means for all tiles. SPECvirt Datacenter 2020 also permits the use of a partial tile to allow for finer tuning of the saturation of a SUT. However, unlike SPEC VIRT_SC 2013, a partial tile for SPECvirt Datacenter 2020 consists of a subset of the workloads within a single tile; the partial tile will contain only the VMs needed to run the subset of workloads. The order of adding the workloads to a partial tile is fixed to ensure reproducibility of the benchmark results.

12.1.3.2 SPECvirt Datacenter 2020 Template VMs

SPECvirt Datacenter 2020 is a highly complex benchmark, even more so than the SPEC VIRT_SC benchmarks. In an effort to focus more attention on tuning the virtualization solution rather than tuning the application stacks within the tiles' VMs, SPECvirt Datacenter 2020 utilizes pre-built template VMs provided with the benchmark kit to create and deploy all of the VMs needed to build the benchmark harness (master controller and clients) and all of the tile's workloads. No modifications are needed—or allowed—within the VMs beyond the provided configuration and control scripts. This frees up the focus of performance tuning to be solely at the hypervisor and host level. At the time of the initial release, the template provides scripts for VMware's vSphere and Red Hat's RHV virtualization products. Other toolkits for different or newer versions of hypervisors are allowed but must be reviewed and approved by the SPEC Virtualization Subcommittee.

12.2 VMware's Virtualization Benchmarks

VMmark is a virtualization benchmark developed and maintained by VMware. It is intended for hardware vendors aiming to showcase the performance of their products using the VMware ESXi hypervisor. The first VMmark multi-workload server consolidation benchmark was released in August 2007 and measured the single-host performance in virtualized environments. Its successor, VMmark 2, was enhanced with multi-host virtual machine capabilities that addressed the increasing virtualization of bursty and heavy workloads, dynamic virtual machine and data store relocation, and the automation of many provisioning and administrative tasks across large-scale multi-host environments. In this new paradigm, some of the stress on the CPU, network, disk, and memory subsystems is generated by the underlying infrastructure operations. While still focusing on user-centric application performance, this benchmark also accounted for the effects of infrastructure activities on the overall platform performance.

12.2.1 The VMmark 3 Benchmark

Over the years, virtualization has become more common and end users are now considering highly scalable workloads and more complex online transaction processing (OLTP) workloads. VMmark 3 was developed to address this evolution as well as the additional challenges resulting from the increased load, frequency, and complexity of infrastructure operations.

The unit of work for a benchmark targeted at evaluating virtualized consolidation environments is generally defined as a collection of virtual machines executing a set of diverse workloads and the VMmark 3 benchmark follows the convention of its predecessor and refers to it as a tile. The total number of VMmark tiles (see Figure 12.6) a multi-host platform can accommodate provides a coarse-grained measure of that platform's consolidation capacity. This concept is similar to some server benchmarks, such as TPC-C (see Chapter 9, Section 9.3), that scale the workload in a stepwise fashion to increase the system load.

Tiles are relatively heavyweight objects that cannot capture small variations in platform performance. To address this, both the number of tiles and the performance of each individual workload determine the overall benchmark score. Each workload

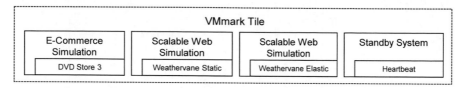

Fig. 12.6: VMmark tile

within a tile is constrained to execute at less than full utilization of its virtual machine. However, the performance of each workload can vary to a degree with the speed and capabilities of the underlying platform, for example, the addition of a fast disk array might result in disk-centric workloads producing a more favorable score. These variations can capture system improvements that do not warrant the addition of another tile. However, the workload throttling forces the use of additional tiles for large jumps in platform performance.

When a tile is added, the performance of the workloads in existing tiles might decrease. However, the aggregate score should increase if the system has not been overcommitted and the minimum Quality-of-Service (QoS) requirements are met. This results in a flexible benchmark metric that provides a measure of the total number of workloads that can be supported by a particular multi-host platform as well as the overall performance level within the workload virtual machines.

12.2.1.1 Workloads

A meaningful consolidation benchmark should be based on a set of relevant data center workloads. A survey of data center applications led to the inclusion of the workloads shown in Table 12.1 representing popular applications commonly run by VMware customers and a series of common infrastructure activities described later in this section. Rather than developing workloads from scratch, existing workloads and benchmarks were used where possible in order to reduce the implementation effort and to provide a well-understood foundation upon which to build.

Table 12.1: VMmark 3 workloads

Workload	Application	Virtual Machine Platform (CentOS 7.2 64-bit—16 GB disk)			
			vCPU	Memory [GB]	Data Drive(s) [GB]
		Auction Web (2)	2	8	–
		Auction App (2)	4	14	–
Scalable Web	Weathervane	Auction LB	2	4	–
Simulation	Auction Static	Auction MSQ	2	4	–
		Auction DB	2	8	20
		Auction NoSQL	2	16	100
		Elastic Web (2)	2	4	–
Scalable Web	Weathervane	Elastic App (2)	2	8	–
Simulation	Auction Elastic	Elastic LB	1	4	–
		Elastic DB	2	8	–
E-Commerce	DVD Store 3	Database	8	32	100 + 250
Simulation		Web (3)	1	4	–
Standby System	None	Idle	1	2	–
Deploy	None	Infrastructure	4	8	100

Scalable Web Simulation Scalable web applications are used to provide a wide variety of services such as social networking and online auction websites. These applications typically will have a core application that implements the business logic, surrounded by a variety of support services such as load balancers, web servers, message servers, and databases. The application logic may be distributed among multiple independently deployed services. Each tier in a scalable web application deployment might stress different infrastructure resources. For example, the application servers might have high CPU demands, while the data services might place high demands on storage or memory.

Weathervane[2] is an application-level benchmark for virtual infrastructure and cloud performance tests. The Weathervane application, named Auction, is a scalable web application that implements a website for hosting real-time auctions. The Auction application uses a scalable architecture that allows deployments to be easily sized for a large range of user loads. A deployment of the application involves a wide variety of support services such as caching, messaging, NoSQL data store, and relational database tiers.

In VMmark 3, the Weathervane workload uses two independent instances of the Weathervane Auction application, a static instance and an elastic instance. The virtual machine configuration used in these application instances are shown in Table 12.1. Each instance includes:

- a load balancer running HAproxy 1.5.18,
- web servers running Nginx 1.12.0,
- application servers running Tomcat 8.5.13 and Java 1.8.0.121,
- a message server running RabbitMQ 3.5.3,
- a database running PostgreSQL 9.3, and
- a NoSQL data service running MongoDB 3.0.14.

In the static application instance, all of these services run on their own virtual machines. In the elastic application instance, the message server, load balancer, and NoSQL data service share a single virtual machine.

The static application instance, as its name implies, injects a relatively consistent load on the SUT. The elastic application instance, on the other hand, is both elastic and bursty. As in today's data centers it is increasingly common to have self-scaling applications that dynamically add and remove resources to meet demands, VMmark 3 takes advantage of Weathervane's elasticity-related capabilities to add and remove an application server and a web server throughout the benchmark run. This elastic component (along with the cyclical application profile generated by DVD Store 3 described below) allows VMmark 3 to represent more accurately today's bursty environments. The load for Weathervane is generated by a workload driver that simulates users interacting with the Weathervane Auction application. The load generated by each user is constant as long as the application can satisfy its quality-of-service (QoS) requirements. These QoS requirements specify the 99th-percentile response time for each operation as well as the required mix of operations performed

---

[2] Weathervane: https://github.com/vmware/weathervane

by all users. The performance metrics from Weathervane include the operation throughput, the average response time for each operation, and the percentage of each operation that completes within the response-time limits.

E-Commerce Simulation Databases running transactional workloads support a wide array of applications, typically as part of a multi-tier architecture. Databases tend to be resource-intensive and exercise most server and infrastructure components. In many cases, database systems also face strict response-time demands. Transaction processing often exhibits bursty behavior, resulting in widely varying resource demands over time. The ability of the underlying platform to support usage spikes is critical to maintaining acceptable performance.

DVD Store Version 3 (DS3)[3] is a complete online e-commerce test application with a back-end database component, a web application layer, and driver programs. The DS3 driver simulates users logging into a web server and browsing a catalog of products using basic queries. Users may select items for purchase, and then proceed to check out or continue shopping. Each web server communicates with a database server that maintains user accounts and inventory data.

The DS3 workload used in VMmark 3 utilizes four virtual machines in each tile, three web servers and one database server. The three virtual machines in the DS3 web tier (DS3WebA, DS3WebB, and DS3WebC) each run the Apache 2.4.6 web server, and the DS3 database tier runs the MySQL database. One of the web servers delivers a constant load to the database throughout each benchmark interval. The other two web servers deliver periodic load to the database during the benchmark interval to create a bursty overall load profile and varying resource demands. For VMmark 3, each web server is driven by 24 driver threads when active. The performance metric for this workload is the total number of transactions per minute. Minimum QoS metrics must also be met.

Virtual Machine Cloning and Deployment Creating a new virtual machine and installing a guest operating system and applications can be time-consuming. Using virtual machine cloning technology, administrators can make many copies of a virtual machine using a single installation and configuration process. Cloning, configuration, and deployment operations create bursty loads on platform resources, particularly the storage subsystem as the virtual machine files are copied.

The infrastructure workload: (1) clones the VMmark template virtual machine, (2) powers-on and pings the clone, (3) takes a snapshot, (4) performs a hot add of CPU and memory, (5) takes another snapshot, (6) creates a small MySQL database, (7) then reverts the snapshots, (8) pings the clone again, and (9) finally deletes the clone.

The benchmark then waits 40 s and repeats this process, continuing for the duration of the benchmark period. The number of concurrent clone and deploy operations increases with the number of tiles and the number of hosts in the benchmark cluster. The performance metric used is the number of clone and deploy operations per hour.

---

[3] DVD Store Version 3: http://github.com/dvdstore/ds3

Dynamic Virtual Machine Relocation Between Servers Live migration technology such as VMware vMotion leverages the complete virtualization of servers, storage, and networking to move an entire running virtual machine seamlessly from one server to another. During a vMotion operation, the active memory and precise execution state of a virtual machine are rapidly transmitted over a high-speed network from one physical server to another and access to the virtual machine's disk storage is instantly switched to the new physical host. This transition can result in bursty loads on platform resources, particularly the networking subsystem. VMmark mimics the manual relocation of a virtual machine, which can be a common task performed by an administrator.

This infrastructure workload acts on one of the AuctionMSQ virtual machines selected in a round-robin fashion from among all the tiles. A destination host is selected at random from among all hosts in the benchmark cluster (other than the virtual machine's current host). The virtual machine is moved to the destination host, left there for 2 min, and then returned to its original host. VMmark then waits another 2 min and repeats this process, continuing for the duration of the benchmark period. The number of concurrent relocation operations increases with the number of tiles and the number of hosts in the benchmark cluster. The performance metric used is the number of relocations per hour.

Dynamic Virtual Machine Relocation Across Storage Live migration of virtual machine disk files across or within storage arrays enables enormous flexibility for storage maintenance, upgrades, and load balancing. Storage relocations can create bursty loads on platform resources, particularly the storage subsystem.

In this infrastructure workload, VMmark relocates a virtual machine's disk files to a maintenance partition, then returns them to their original location. This round-trip approach models an administrator temporarily evacuating a disk partition, performing maintenance on the storage system, and then returning the system to its initial state.

This infrastructure workload acts on one of the standby server virtual machines selected in a round-robin fashion from among all the tiles. The virtual machine's files are moved to the maintenance partition, left there for 2 min, and then moved back to their original location. VMmark then waits another 2 min and repeats this process, continuing for the duration of the benchmark period. The number of concurrent storage relocation operations increases with the number of tiles and the number of hosts in the benchmark cluster. The performance metric used is the number of relocations per hour.

Simultaneous Server and Storage Virtual Machine Relocation The live migration of virtual machines simultaneously across both servers and storage (vMotion without shared storage) allows even more flexibility than either capability alone. This infrastructure workload produces a combination of the infrastructure loads created by the individual operations.

In this infrastructure workload, VMmark uses vMotion to relocate a virtual machine while simultaneously invoking the storage relocation of the same virtual machine's disk files to a maintenance partition. After two and a half minutes, the virtual machine is returned to its original host and the files are returned to their original location. VMmark then waits another two and a half minutes and repeats the process. This workload models an administrator temporarily evacuating a host and disk partition, performing maintenance on the host and/or storage system, and then returning the system to its initial state.

This infrastructure workload acts on one of the DS3WebA virtual machines selected in a round-robin fashion from among all the tiles. The number of concurrent relocation operations increases with the number of tiles and the number of hosts in the benchmark cluster. The performance metric used is the number of relocations per hour.

Automated Load Balancing Automatically balancing resource demands among multiple physical servers using technology such as VMware's Distributed Resource Scheduler (DRS) has become a fundamental part of modern virtualized data centers. Intelligently allocating and balancing resources allow the underlying platform to respond effectively to bursty-load conditions even when utilizations are high.

VMmark requires DRS to be enabled and running at (or above) a specific level to ensure that rebalancing occurs in a timely manner when utilizations are high. This should improve overall performance by addressing load imbalances occurring during the benchmark interval.

12.2.1.2 Scoring Methodology

VMmark 3 aggregates the throughput metrics of all application and infrastructure workloads to create a single overall benchmark metric that can be used to quickly compare different platform configurations. If any of the workloads within any tile fails to run, produces errors during a run, or fails its minimum QoS requirement, the entire VMmark run is considered to be incompliant. After the completion of a compliant VMmark benchmark run, each individual application and infrastructure workload reports its relevant performance score (see Table 12.2). These scores were collected every 60 s during the standard 3 h run resulting in a series of meaningful numbers for each of the workloads. VMmark 3 automatically generates graphs of key performance metrics for each workload as shown in Figure 12.7.

The scores of the application and infrastructure workloads are computed and aggregated separately based on the geometric mean, and the final benchmark metric is the weighted arithmetic mean of the scores (geometric means) for the application-workload component (80%) and the infrastructure-workload component (20%). These weights were chosen to reflect the relative contribution of infrastructure and application workloads to overall resource demands.

The VMmark 3 metric shows the virtualization overheads of the individual workloads as well as the scalability of the entire system. Therefore, results for multi-tile runs are reported as the aggregate score for all tiles, the individual scores for each of the tiles, and the scores for the workloads within the tiles as well as the individual scores for each infrastructure workload. If two different virtualization platforms

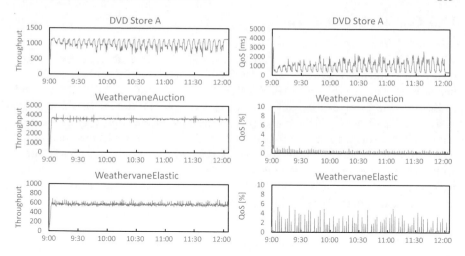

Fig. 12.7: Throughput and Quality-of-Service (QoS)

Table 12.2: Individual VMmark workload scores

Workload name	Applications(s)	Scores
Weathervane static	Auction	Operations/s
Weathervane elastic	Auction	Operations/s
DS3WebA	Apache, MySQL	Transactions/min
DS3WebB	Apache, MySQL	Transactions/min
DS3WebC	Apache, MySQL	Transactions/min
Standby server	None	None
Clone and deploy	Infrastructure	Deployed VMs/h
vMotion	Infrastructure	VM migrations/h
Storage vMotion	Infrastructure	VM migrations/h
XvMotion	Infrastructure	VM migrations/h
Distributed Resource Scheduler (DSR)	Infrastructure	None

achieve similar VMmark scores with a different number of tiles, the score with the lower tile count is generally preferred. The higher tile count could be a sign that the underlying hardware resources were not properly balanced. Studying the individual workload metrics is suggested in these cases.

12.3 Concluding Remarks

We provided an overview of established benchmarks for evaluating the performance of virtualization platforms. We focused on the SPEC VIRT series of industry-standard benchmarks (SPEC VIRT_SC 2010, SPEC VIRT_SC 2013, and SPECvirt Datacenter 2020) while also considering the VMmark benchmark by VMware. The discussed benchmarks provide users with the capability of measuring different virtualization solutions on either single-host or multi-host platforms, using workloads and methodologies that are designed for fair comparisons. Great effort was taken to ensure a wide range of virtualization solutions can utilize the benchmarks and they have been used by hardware and software vendors to showcase, analyze, and design the latest generations of virtualization products.

References

Lange, K.-D., Schmidt, D., Bond, A., and Roderick, L. (2012). "SPECvirt_sc2010—Driving Virtualization Innovation". In: *Proceedings of the 3rd ACM/SPEC International Conference on Performance Engineering (ICPE 2012)*. (Boston, MA, USA). ACM: New York, NY, USA, pp. 251–252 (cited on p. 268).

Chapter 13
Storage Benchmarks

Klaus-Dieter Lange, Don Capps, Sitsofe Wheeler, Sorin Faibish, Nick Principe, Mary Marquez, John Beckett, and Ken Cantrell

Many operating systems (OS) and information technology (IT) solutions have been tested and tuned for the storage subsystems to work well with frequently used applications. This accelerates the storage input/output (I/O) for the respective subsets of workloads. Nonetheless, the application operation mix will likely change over time as applications evolve, for example, the system administrator decides to allocate the same server/storage solution for additional office automation tasks.

Several benchmarks are available to evaluate the storage performance of a specific storage system or storage component. They can be used by system administrators to evaluate and compare different products and ensure high performance for their particular environment. This chapter presents a brief history of the SPEC System File Server (SFS) benchmarks and takes a closer look at SPEC SFS 2014. It then introduces the benchmarks from the Storage Performance Council (SPC) and the IOzone file system benchmark. Finally, the Flexible I/O Tester (fio) is presented, showing some examples of how it can be used to measure I/O performance.

13.1 Historical Perspective on System File Server Benchmarks

In the 1990s, commercial Network File System (NFS) storage server arrays started to become mainstream. No longer was storage the realm of government, academia, and large corporations. This increase of storage solution choices created a need for a benchmark to enable users of NFS servers to select the solution with the highest performance. NFS server vendors joined forces with academics and government to build an NFS benchmark with relevant and meaningful performance metrics. In October 1992, the synthetic benchmark LADDIS (Wittle and Keith, 1993), named using the initials of the involved organizations (Legato, Auspex, Data General, Digital Equipment, Interphase, and Sun Microsystems), was released. It was based on the *nhfsstone* workload and measured guaranteed performance, that is, performance achieved for a given latency target. A higher LADDIS score indicates higher I/O performance at a lower latency.

© Springer Nature Switzerland AG 2020

S. Kounev et al., *Systems Benchmarking*, https://doi.org/10.1007/978-3-030-41705-5_13

In 1993, the LADDIS group joined the Standard Performance Evaluation Corporation (SPEC) and became its System File Server (SFS) Subcommittee. There, the NFS benchmark was enhanced for the NFSv2 protocol and released under its new name SPEC SFS 93. The SPEC SFS 97 benchmark, released in December 1997, was further enhanced with new functionality and support for the NFSv3 protocol.[1] It became one of the most popular storage performance benchmarks during that time.

In June 2001, a series of bug fixes were released via SPEC SFS 97 V2.0. Later in 2001, SPEC released SPEC SFS 97_R1 V3.0 with additional bug fixes and support for Linux and FreeBSD as well as initial support for various UNIX operating systems. The benchmark remained an NFS benchmark; nonetheless, the need for a new benchmark that supports the Server Message Block (SMB) protocol, in particular the Common Internet File System (CIFS), was increasing as most storage vendors started to support both NFSv3 and SMB protocols. At this point, the members of the SFS Subcommittee started to develop a new benchmark for Windows servers using the SMB protocol. In 2008, the work on this benchmark was completed and the first dual protocol storage benchmark—SPEC SFS 2008—was published.[2] In addition to the introduction of the SMB protocol, several enhancements were made to the NFSv3 benchmark, including operation mix change and adding new metadata operations, aligned with the evolving requirements of the storage industry.

During the lifetime of SPEC SFS 2008, its user base started asking for support for measuring the performance of the clients and servers in a single unified benchmark. Coincidentally, in December 2010, Don Capps was finishing his development of *Netmist*—the first benchmark and framework designed as a system benchmark that runs at the system call level instead of the protocol level. He granted SPEC the permission to use it as the basis for the next generation file server benchmark. Netmist combines benchmark ideas from both the SFS benchmarks and the IOzone benchmark (see Section 13.4), and it was designed as a multi-client, multi-server benchmark.

13.2 SPEC SFS 2014

After 4 years of joint development, SPEC SFS 2014 was released in November 2014.[3] It introduced many novel benchmark ideas inspired by the established file server benchmarks and included support for cluster file systems (e.g., Lustre and GPFS) as well as network file servers (e.g., based on NFSv3, NFSv4, and SMB). The SFS Subcommittee also implemented the support for local POSIX file systems created on block storage device benchmarks via any POSIX file systems on the raw block devices and supporting any type of client host OSes including SOLARIS, Linux, Windows, SGI, AIX, etc., and any client local POSIX file systems.

---

[1] NFS v3 protocol; IETF 1995: https://tools.ietf.org/html/rfc1813

[2] SPEC SFS 2008 benchmark: https://www.spec.org/sfs2008

[3] SPEC SFS 2014 benchmark: https://www.spec.org/sfs2014

The SPEC SFS 2014 benchmark introduced the concept of *business metrics (BMs)*, inspired from real storage applications, and added the capability to easily modify existing BMs and to create new BMs for research purposes. The five included BMs (see Table 13.1) measure guaranteed performance based on the same request–response principles of the five most popular types of storage application characteristics (e.g., mixes for metadata and data, read and write, and for different I/O sizes). With the new capability to saturate all physical resources, including CPU, disk, pipes (FC and IP), BUSes, and memory, the SFS benchmark evolved into an application benchmark. This enabled the different storage vendors to showcase their storage solutions for the BM that matched their customers' usage for either protocol.

Table 13.1: Workloads and their business metric names

Workload	Business metric name
Electronic design automation (EDA)	Job sets
Database (DATABASE)	Databases
Software build (SWBUILD)	Builds
Video data acquisition (VDA)	Streams
Virtual desktop infrastructure (VDI)	Desktops

In 2016, the SPEC SFS 2014 benchmark was enhanced to also serve as a load generator used for measuring the power consumption of storage servers as defined by the Storage Networking Industry Association (SNIA)—a feature used by SNIA in the Emerald specification as well as by the U.S. Environmental Protection Agency's (EPA) Energy Star program for storage certification.

All previous SFS benchmark results were presenting only two performance metrics, the NFS/CIFS I/O operations (IOPS) and overall response time (ORT), as well as a result table and a graph (see Table 13.2 and Figure 13.1[4]), showing the guaranteed performance achieved for each requested I/O load. Starting with SPEC SFS 2014, the new performance variables, Business Metric (workload specific) and Bandwidth in MB/sec, were added to the result (see Table 13.3 and Figure 13.2[5]).

With the continuous evolution of storage applications and technology, including new storage media like solid-state drives (SSD) and non-volatile memory (NVM), additional workloads become of interest and the current workloads need to be modified or replaced to reflect new users' needs and usage models of new application areas like machine learning, Genomics, and others. The SPEC OSG Storage Subcommittee, the new name of the SFS Subcommittee, is working to deliver the next generation of SFS benchmarks, addressing the need for new features and representative workloads for the storage industry.

---

[4] Corresp. result: https://www.spec.org/sfs2008/results/res2008q1/sfs2008-20080218-00083.html

[5] Corresp. result: https://www.spec.org/sfs2014/results/res2014q4/sfs2014-20141029-00002.html

Table 13.2: Exemplary SPEC SFS 2008 publication table

Throughput (ops/sec)	Response time (ms)
320	1.5
642	1.8
961	2.0
1,285	2.3
1,607	2.6
1,924	3.2
2,244	4.0
2,579	5.6
2,897	8.5
3,088	10.6

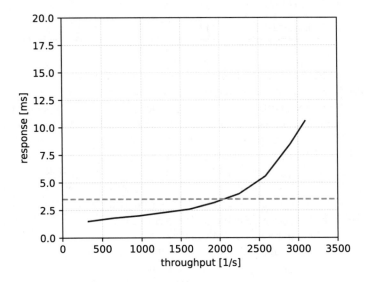

Fig. 13.1: Exemplary SPEC SFS 2008 publication graph

Table 13.3: Exemplary SPEC SFS 2014 publication table

Business metric (builds)	Average latency (ms)	Builds (ops/sec)	Builds (MB/sec)
2	0.6	1,000	12
4	0.7	2,000	25
6	0.7	3,000	38
8	0.7	4,000	51
10	1.0	5,000	64
12	1.1	6,000	77
14	1.1	7,000	90
16	1.0	8,001	103
18	0.9	9,000	116
20	1.0	10,001	128
22	1.1	11,001	141
24	1.3	12,001	154

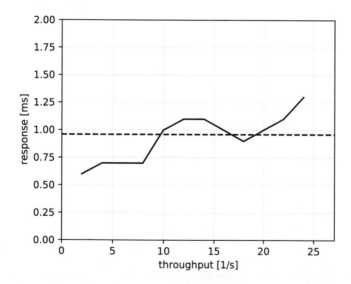

Fig. 13.2: Exemplary SPEC SFS 2014 publication graph

13.3 Storage Performance Council (SPC)

The vendor-neutral SPC was founded in 1998 with the goal to develop industry-standard benchmarks focusing on storage subsystems and to publish third-party audited benchmark results that include performance and pricing information. Their core benchmarks—SPC-1 and SPC-2—measure the performance of storage systems, and they utilize a common SPC framework for benchmark components.

13.3.1 SPC-1

Introduced in 2001, SPC-1 had a single workload and targeted storage performance of business-critical applications with a high random I/O mix and a series of performance hotspots. The benchmark includes query and update operations, and it covers a broad range of business functions, system configurations, and user profiles.

The SPC-1 benchmark uses the concept of *stimulus scaling units (SSUs)* to scale the I/O load while maintaining the operation mix and constraints. The balance between application I/O and logging I/O is maintained as the SSUs are scaled to the desired I/O load. Application storage units (ASUs) form the abstracted storage configuration, which provides the environment in which the workload (represented by SSUs) is executed. Each ASU is considered the source or destination of data that requires persistence beyond the benchmark run itself. Figure 13.3 shows an example of the distribution of the average response time for the first repeatability test run at the 100% load level.

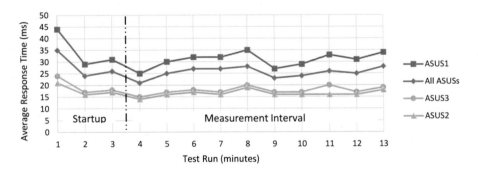

Fig. 13.3: SPC-1 average response time distribution

SPC-1 has several workload components scaled from smallest to largest:

- I/O REQUEST: A single unit of work,
- I/O STREAM: A single sequence of I/O REQUESTS,
- ASU STREAM: A collection of I/O STREAMs,
- WORKLOAD: A collection of ASU STREAMs.

The performance results and response time are part of the benchmark final report, which includes detailed system and storage subsystem configuration details as well as pricing information.

13.3.2 SPC-2

SPC-2, introduced in 2005, has three different workloads to stress the storage system with large-scale sequential data movement, which is one of several differences to the random I/O nature of the SPC-1 standard. The modeled I/O operations include large file processing, large database queries, and video on demand.

The SPC-2 benchmark leverages structured patterns of I/O requests referred to as *streams*; the number of concurrent streams varies during benchmark execution. Three or more of these streams are executed for each workload; the maximum and intermediate number of streams are defined by the benchmark tester. Figure 13.4 shows an example of the average data rate per stream for a load of 60,000 streams.

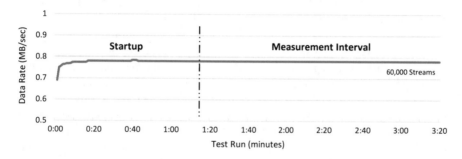

Fig. 13.4: SPC-2 average data rate per stream

13.3.3 Component and Energy Extension

The derived SPC-1C and SPC-2C benchmarks target specific storage components like storage devices and controllers, storage enclosures, and storage software. SPC-1C and SPC-2C retain the essential random or sequential nature, respectively, of their benchmark progenitors. These two benchmarks are intended to provide performance data for individual storage components as opposed to a larger storage configuration.

Each SPC benchmark has an optional energy extension (SPC-1/E, SPC-2/E, SPC-1C/E, and SPC-2C/E), which adds a mode of execution in which also the power consumption is measured. Power consumption is measured at three load intervals (idle, moderate, and heavy) and reported with the performance results and pricing of the regular benchmark run. SPC benchmark results with energy extension include the following additional metrics:

- Nominal Operating Power (W): The average power consumption across the three intervals,
- Nominal Traffic in IOPS: The average I/O measured across the three intervals,
- Operating IOPS/watt: The computed power metric representing the overall efficiency for I/O traffic,
- Annual Energy Use (kWh): The estimated annual energy usage.

13.4 The IOzone Benchmark

IOzone was initially designed and written by William Norcott and released in the early 1980s. The initial version, a fairly simple C-code, measured the time for opening a file, write/read data, and close the file.

Don Capps started his work on extending IOzone's functionality in 1985; he fundamentally redefined IOzone for more accurate performance measurements of file systems. He added support for large-scale NUMA supercomputers in 1991 and expanded IOzone's capability to cover multiple file servers running in parallel.

In 2000, the IOzone.org site was created and the IOzone development continued under a freeware licensing model with Don Capps as the benchmark maintainer. This license model allows the users to compile and use the benchmark for free on any platform and OS. The IOzone benchmark continues to be a living project with contributions from developers worldwide (e.g., Android support for the use of IoT devices). Nonetheless, developers are not allowed to distribute changes by themselves, as it is maintained by a single entity to preserve the integrity of code contributions and their proper integration.

Similar to fio,[6] Iometer,[7] and IOR,[8] the IOzone benchmark has evolved to one of the more sophisticated file system performance benchmark utilities, generating and measuring a variety of file operations (see Table 13.4).

Table 13.4: IOzone's file operations

read	re-read	fread	random read	aio read	pread variants
write	re-write	fwrite	random write	aio write	pwrite variants
read backwards	read strided	mmap			

IOzone has been ported to many platforms and is available on most OSes including AIX, BSDI, HP-UX, IRIX, FreeBSD, Linux, OpenBSD, NetBSD, OSFV3, OSFV4,

---

[6] Flexible I/O Tester (fio): https://fio.readthedocs.io

[7] Iometer Project: http://www.iometer.org

[8] IOR Benchmark: https://media.readthedocs.org/pdf/ior/latest/ior.pdf

OSFV5, SCO OpenServer, Solaris, Mac OS X, and Windows (via the Cygwin runtime application[9]). Its results can be exported into useful graphs (e.g., Figure 13.5 depicts the fwrite performance under Windows), which can be leveraged to show performance characteristics and bottlenecks of the disk I/O subsystem, enabling users to optimize their applications to achieve the best performance for their platform and OS. This is one of the reasons why the benchmark is widely used to evaluate HPC storage for supercomputers and computer clusters.

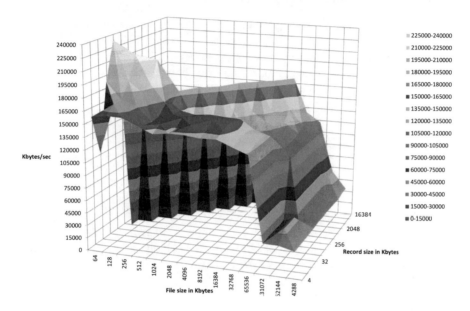

Fig. 13.5: IOzone fwrite performance

13.5 Flexible I/O Tester (fio)

The Flexible I/O Tester (fio) was designed by Jens Axboe in 2005, filling the void for a flexible method to simulate customizable I/O workloads and to gain meaningful I/O statistics on the Linux I/O subsystem and its schedulers.

The fio architecture is comprised of three major parts: (1) *front-end* that parses a job description file; (2) *back-end layer* that performs common work like managing parallel workers, collecting I/O statistics, and generating/validating I/O patterns; and (3) implementation of pluggable *ioengines* that send I/O in different ways over the network via library calls.

---

[9] Cygwin: http://www.cygwin.com

The small and portable fio code is pre-packaged by major Linux distributions because of its versatile nature of exploring various aspects of storage subsystems:

- Investigation of storage performance and root-cause analysis of bottlenecks,
- Modeling of workloads with a balanced read/write access mix across multiple workers,
- Replay of recorded and hand-built workload patterns,
- Analysis of the effectiveness of different caching algorithms, and
- Reproduction of hardware and software issues.

Fio has been ported to many platforms; nonetheless, its capabilities on other platforms might not be the same as on Linux, because some features might not have been ported, or different platforms may not implement the same functionality in the same way. The latest version can be found at the fio Git repository.[10] In the following, we present a series of examples illustrating fio's capabilities on Linux.

13.5.1 Running a Simple Job

A fio job file contains a set of statements describing what I/O workload should be executed. The following example describes a new job called `simple` that creates a file at the path `/tmp/fio.tmp` with a size of two megabytes (by default, all single- and three-letter storage units in fio are powers of two, for example, 2 M is 2,097,152 bytes). It then performs read I/O using the default ioengine (on Linux, this is psync) and the default block size (4,096 bytes).

```
[simple]
filename=/tmp/fio.tmp
size=2M
rw=read
```

If the above was saved to the file `simple.fio`, it can be run via:

```
fio simple.fio
```

Running this job will create an output similar to the following (lines 1–31):

```
1   simple: (g=0): rw=read, bs=(R) 4096B-4096B, (W) 4096B-4096B,
        (T) 4096B-4096B, ioengine=psync, iodepth=1
2   fio-3.16
3   Starting 1 process
4   simple: Laying out IO file (1 file / 2MiB)
5
6   simple: (groupid=0, jobs=1): err= 0: pid=19566: Sat Nov 9
        11:39:05 2019
7     read: IOPS=56.9k, BW=222MiB/s (233MB/s)(2048KiB/9msec)
8       clat (nsec): min=896, max=944834, avg=16216.53,
            stdev=101996.63
```

---

[10] Flexible I/O Tester (fio) Git repository: https://github.com/axboe/fio.git

```
 9        lat (nsec): min=934, max=944898, avg=16284.52,
               stdev=102006.39
10      clat percentiles (nsec):
11       |  1.00th=[   940],  5.00th=[   1032], 10.00th=[   1064],
               20.00th=[  1688],
12       | 30.00th=[  1784], 40.00th=[   1800], 50.00th=[   1816],
               60.00th=[  1832],
13       | 70.00th=[  1848], 80.00th=[   1880], 90.00th=[   1960],
               95.00th=[  2160],
14       | 99.00th=[716800], 99.50th=[872448], 99.90th=[946176],
               99.95th=[946176],
15       | 99.99th=[]
16    lat (nsec)   : 1000=2.15%
17    lat (usec)   : 2=90.23%, 4=4.88%, 20=0.39%, 50=0.20%,
          250=0.20%
18    lat (usec)   : 500=0.39%, 750=0.78%, 1000=0.78%
19    cpu          : usr=0.00%, sys=25.00%, ctx=13, majf=0, minf=10
20    IO depths    : 1=100.0%, 2=0.0%, 4=0.0%, 8=0.0%, 16=0.0%,
          32=0.0%, >=64=0.0%
21      submit     : 0=0.0%, 4=100.0%, 8=0.0%, 16=0.0%, 32=0.0%,
               64=0.0%, >=64=0.0%
22      complete   : 0=0.0%, 4=100.0%, 8=0.0%, 16=0.0%, 32=0.0%,
               64=0.0%, >=64=0.0%
23      issued rwts: total=512,0,0,0 short=0,0,0,0 dropped=0,0,0,0
24      latency    : target=0, window=0, percentile=100.00%, depth=1
25
26  Run status group 0 (all jobs):
27     READ: bw=222MiB/s (233MB/s), 222MiB/s-222MiB/s
            (233MB/s-233MB/s), io=2048KiB (2097kB), run=9-9msec
28
29  Disk stats (read/write):
30      dm-0: ios=0/0, merge=0/0, ticks=0/0, in_queue=0,
               util=0.00%, aggrios=12/0, aggrmerge=0/0, aggrticks=8/0,
               aggrin_queue=8, aggrutil=3.31%
31     sda: ios=12/0, merge=0/0, ticks=8/0, in_queue=8, util=3.31%
```

The output is comprised of the following parts:

Line 1:   A summary of some of the parameters within the job
Line 2:   The fio version
Lines 3–4:   Information about the job starting
Lines 5–6:   Process identification
Line 7:   Average IOPS and bandwidth information
Lines 8–15:   Latency break down per I/Os
Lines 16–24: Further breakdown of the I/O information
Lines 25–27: Summary of I/O by group
Lines 28–31: Information about how the kernel performed disk I/O

The key information on how the job performed (lines 7–15) is depicted in Figure 13.6; detailed guidelines on the interpretation of the different parts of the output can be found in the fio documentation.[11]

---

[11] https://fio.readthedocs.io/en/latest/fio_doc.html#interpreting-the-output

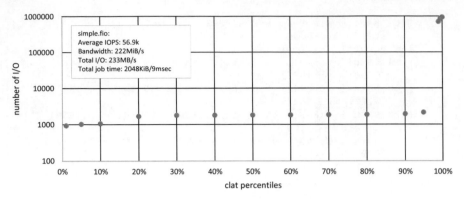

Fig. 13.6: Completion latency (clat) per I/O

A job can also be specified using command line options; for example, the previous job can be written as:

```
fio --name=simple --filename=/tmp/fio.tmp --size=2M --rw=read
```

A section is started by using the -name option followed by a value, and parameters become double-dashed options followed by their value. Although job files are useful for repeatability and sharing, the remaining jobs shown in this chapter are specified as command line options for the sake of brevity.

In the read job above, fio actually wrote the data to the file semi-randomly before reading it back. This is done to prevent special-case optimizations (which may be applied within the storage stack) from distorting the results of a particular run. An in-depth explanation on how the random data is generated can be found in the fio documentation.[12]

13.5.2 More Complex Workloads

It is easy to change the simple workload from performing read access to write access by basically changing the -rw command from read to write. It should be pointed out that using write workloads will destroy the data in the files specified. The following example shows a job that performs sequential writes with an increased block size of 64 kilobytes (64×1024^2 bytes):

```
fio --name=simplewrite --filename=/tmp/fio.tmp --size=2M
    --rw=write --bs=64k
```

Fio has the capability to work with block devices directly, allowing one to measure performance without the overhead of the file system. In the following examples,

---

[12] https://fio.readthedocs.io/en/latest/fio_doc.html#buffers-and-memory

/dev/sdd represents such a block device, and fio will try to write to 64 kilobyte sized blocks in a random order (-rw=randwrite), but it will cover each block exactly once:

```
fio --name=simplewrite --filename=/dev/sdd --rw=randwrite
    --bs=64k
```

Additionally, while fio will try and flush kernel caches on supported platforms before starting a job, by default, no flushing takes place when the job finishes; thus, data may still be in kernel RAM caches (and non-volatile disk caches). The end_fsync=1 option can be used to ensure that write data has reached the disk by the time the job finishes.

```
fio --name=simplewrite --filename=/dev/sdd --rw=randwrite
    --bs=64k --end_fsync=1
```

Fio jobs can be run in parallel in order to model real-life environments with multiple concurrent workloads. The following simple example runs two read workloads accessing different files in parallel:

```
fio --name=simple1 --filename=/tmp/fio1.tmp --size=2M --rw=read
    --name=simple2 \
    --filename=/tmp/fio2.tmp --size=2M --rw=read
```

A global section can be utilized to share common parameters between the jobs, eliminating duplications.

```
fio --size=2M --rw=read --name=simple1 --filename=/tmp/fio1.tmp
    --name=simple2 \
    --filename=/tmp/fio2.tmp
```

By default, all jobs are part of the same group, which allows fio to provide a way of summarizing some of the results of multiple jobs (see lines 26–27 in the previous output example). Note that this summary information may be inaccurate if the jobs do not actually start at the same time.

Fio provides a number of options for modeling simultaneous reads and writes. For cases where reads and writes are independent of each other, the following method can be applied:

```
fio --size=2M --filename=/tmp/fio1.tmp --name=writes --rw=write
    --name=read --rw=read
```

If they are somehow dependent on each other, the reads and writes can be handled by the same job via the -rw=readwrite option, and the mix can be specified via the -rwmixread parameter. The following example requests four reads for every write:

```
fio --size=2M --filename=/tmp/fio1.tmp --name=mix --rw=readwrite
    --rwmixread=80
```

13.5.3 Unusual I/O Patterns

The previous job examples perform uniformly distributed random I/O across the area being accessed. In some cases, for example, when analyzing the effectiveness of caching, it might be helpful to access different parts of the targeted area with different frequency. Fio has multiple ways to define such a distribution; Figure 13.7 shows an example `cache_test` that utilizes the `-random_distribution=zoned` option:

```
fio --name=cache_test --filename=/tmp/fio1.tmp --size=20G
    --rw=randread \
    --random_distribution=zoned:30/15:14/15:40/5:14/20:2/45
```

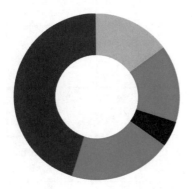

■ 30% of accesses in the first 15%

■ 14% of accesses in the next 15%

■ 40% of accesses in the next 5%

■ 14% of accesses in the next 20%

■ 2% of accesses in the next 45%

Fig. 13.7: Randomly distributed I/O via zones

Many unusual I/O patterns can be created via the vast possibilities of combining different fio options. The last two examples in this chapter might be helpful in order to recreate I/O patterns to root-cause hardware and software issues of extent-based storage.

The `gappy` job writes every other 8 kilobytes of `/tmp/fio1.tmp`:

```
fio --name=gappy --filename=/tmp/fio1.tmp --size=2M
    --rw=write:8k --bs=8k
```

The `backwards` job seeks 16 kilobytes backwards after every 8 kilobyte writes are done, before writing the next 8 kilobytes.

```
fio --name=backwards --filename=/tmp/fio1.tmp --size=2M
    --rw=write:-16k --bs=8k
```

13.5.4 ioengines

The ioengine used in the above examples has been synchronous, which means that fio will wait for an I/O operation to complete before sending another I/O operation. However, modern disks and disk controllers have multiple queues that achieve maximum performance when many I/O operations are submitted in parallel. In cases where a kernel cache is being used, the kernel's buffering can help synthesize that parallelism at a small cost. However, some I/O engines can create that asynchrony themselves with lower overhead.

On Linux, the `libaio` ioengine is typically used for this purpose, but it comes with strict requirements to prevent blocked submissions:

- I/O must be sent using the O_DIRECT option.
- The amount of I/O backlog should be kept limited.

It is important to adhere to these rules and avoid blocking submissions, because fio will not be able to queue any more I/O until submissions return.

The following example job utilizes the `libaio` engine and sets the `iodepth`, which controls the maximum amount of I/O operations to be sent simultaneously and queued. There is no guarantee that, at any given point, the `iodepth` amount of I/O operations will be queued up, as I/O operations are queued one at a time, and if their completion is fast enough, there will not be much outstanding work at any given time.

```
fio --ioengine=libaio --iodepth=32 --name=parallelwrite
    --filename=/dev/sdd \
    --rw=randwrite --bs=64k
```

It is quite common to run a workload for a fixed amount of time in order to reproduce hardware or software issues. This can be achieved by utilizing the `time_based` and `runtime` options. The following fio job will continue to loop the pattern until `runtime` has expired:

```
fio --name=one-minute --filename=/tmp/fio1.tmp --size=2M
    --rw=write --time_based \
    --runtime=1m
```

In order to measure the maximum performance of very fast storage subsystems, it might be necessary to minimize fio's overhead. The `io_uring`[13] interface was introduced with the 5.1 Linux kernel, and it is supported by fio version 3.13 and higher. It has a lower overhead and can therefore push higher bandwidths than the previous libaio/KAIO interface. Using it is just a matter of changing the ioengine:

```
fio --ioengine=io_uring --iodepth=32 --name=parallelwrite
    --filename=/dev/sdd \
    --rw=randwrite --bs=64k
```

---

[13] https://kernel.dk/io_uring.pdf

13.5.5 Future Challenges

Driven by an active development community, fio has grown to be a popular tool, continuously offering new features, bug fixes, ioengines, and support for new platforms. In this chapter, we touched upon some of the many capabilities of fio, which should help guide investigation in storage performance, root-cause analysis of bottlenecks, and the reproduction of hardware and software issues. A future area to explore would be the ability to create generative models based on the analysis of previously recorded I/O traces. This would enable the portability of realistic workload replays.

13.6 Concluding Remarks

Several benchmarks have emerged in the last decades specifically designed to evaluate the performance of storage systems and storage components. This chapter presented a brief history of the SPEC System File Server (SFS) benchmarks and took a closer look at SPEC SFS 2014. It then introduced the benchmarks from the Storage Performance Council (SPC) and the IOzone file system benchmark. Finally, the Flexible I/O Tester (fio) was presented, showing some examples of how it can be used to measure I/O performance.

With the continuous evolution of storage applications and technology, including new storage media like solid-state drives (SSD) and non-volatile memory (NVM), additional storage workloads become of interest and the current workloads need to be modified or replaced to reflect new users' needs and usage models of new application areas like machine learning, Genomics, and others.

References

Wittle, M. and Keith, B. E. (1993). "LADDIS: The Next Generation in NFS File Server Benchmarking". In: *Proceedings of the 1993 Summer USENIX Technical Conference*. (Cincinnati, Ohio). USENIX Association: Berkeley, CA, USA, pp. 111–128 (cited on p. 285).

Chapter 14
TeaStore: A Microservice Reference Application

Jóakim von Kistowski, Simon Eismann, Norbert Schmitt, André Bauer, Johannes Grohmann, and Samuel Kounev

Modern distributed applications have complex performance characteristics, as their constituent components and services feature different bottlenecks that may change over time. However, these applications also offer many degrees of freedom, which are intended to help deal with this challenge. For example, they can be deployed in various ways and configured using different settings and software stacks. These degrees of freedom can be used at design time, deployment time, and at run time for continuous system optimization. Current research employs many methods of modeling, analysis, and optimization that utilize these degrees of freedom at different points of the software life cycle to tackle the challenging performance behavior (Becker et al., 2009; Brunnert et al., 2015; Ilyushkin et al., 2017). More generally, the goal of such research is the improvement of a system's quality attributes such as performance, availability, reliability, or energy efficiency (see Section 1.2 in Chapter 1).

Verifying, comparing, and evaluating the results of such research is difficult. To enable practical evaluation, researchers need a distributed application that can be deployed as a reference and that offers realistic degrees of freedom. The reference application must also feature sufficient complexity regarding performance behavior. Finding such an application and performing the necessary experiments are often difficult. The software in question should be open-source, lend itself to instrumentation, and should produce results that enable analysis and comparison of research findings, all while being indicative of how the evaluated research would affect applications in production use. In the context of this book, such a reference application shares many of the requirements and properties for a benchmarking workload. Thus, it must address many of the issues discussed in Chapter 8 in the context of workloads.

Among others, a reference application workload should lend itself to instrumentation, and it should generally meet the workload quality criteria described in Chapter 8 including *reproducibility* and *relevance*. Many older test and reference applications in the research community lack *relevance*, as they are usually created for specific testing scenarios (Happe et al., 2011). Such applications are often designed specifically for evaluating a single contribution, making comparisons difficult. Other existing and broadly used test software does not offer the necessary degrees of freedom and often is manually customized, reducing comparability (Willnecker et al., 2015).

© Springer Nature Switzerland AG 2020

S. Kounev et al., *Systems Benchmarking*, https://doi.org/10.1007/978-3-030-41705-5_14

Some of the most widely used test and reference applications, such as RUBiS or Dell DVD Store, are outdated and therefore not representative of modern real-world applications.

In this chapter, we introduce TeaStore[1] (Kistowski, Eismann, et al., 2018), a microservice-based test and reference application that can be used as a benchmarking framework by researchers. It is designed to provide multiple degrees of freedom that users can vary depending on their target use case. TeaStore consists of five different services, each featuring unique performance characteristics. Due to its varying performance characteristics and its distributed nature, TeaStore may also be used as a software for testing and evaluation of software performance models and model extraction techniques. It is designed to be scalable and to support both distributed and centralized deployments. In addition, its architecture supports run-time scalability, as services and service instances can be added, removed, and replicated at run time. The services' different resource usage profiles enable performance and efficiency optimization with nontrivial service placement and resource provisioning decisions.

TeaStore was originally designed with the following research areas in mind:

1. Evaluation of software performance modeling approaches and model extraction (learning) techniques,
2. Evaluation of run-time performance management techniques (e.g., service placement and autoscaling),
3. Evaluation of server energy efficiency, power consumption modeling techniques, and optimization techniques.

This chapter demonstrates the application of TeaStore as a test and benchmarking workload by using it as a reference application showing its use in an energy-efficiency benchmarking context to evaluate the energy efficiency of service placements. To keep the example simple, we evaluate several specific placement options for TeaStore and show how placement decisions lead to different power consumption and energy efficiency.

14.1 Requirements on TeaStore

When designing a workload, one must ensure that the workload's design meets the criteria for workloads described in Chapter 8. The TeaStore application itself is an *executable application workload*. It is an *artificial workload*, as it is an application specifically designed to be used as part of a benchmark. TeaStore was developed because *natural workloads* (i.e., existing real-world, microservice applications) do not meet all requirements on a microservice workload for research use. Broadly, these requirements boil down to *reproducibility* and *relevance*. In the concrete context of a microservice workload for researchers, they can be formulated as more specific requirements.

---

[1] TeaStore on GitHub: https://github.com/DescartesResearch/TeaStore
TeaStore on Docker Hub: https://hub.docker.com/u/descartesresearch

Table 14.1: Microservice benchmark requirements (Aderaldo et al., 2017) and our research benchmark requirements on TeaStore in comparison to ACME Air, Spring Cloud Demo Apps, Sock Shop, and MusicStore

Microservice benchmark requirement	TeaStore	ACME Air	Spring Cloud Demo	Sock Shop	MusicStore
R1 Explicit topological view	✓		✓	✓	
R2 Pattern-based architecture	✓	✓	✓	✓	✓
R3 Easy access from a version control repository	✓	✓	✓	✓	✓
R4 Support for continuous integration	✓		✓	✓	
R5 Support for automated testing	✓		✓	✓	
R6 Support for dependency management	✓	✓	✓	✓	✓
R7 Support for reusable container images	✓	✓	✓	✓	
R8 Support for automated deployment	✓			✓	
R9 Support for container orchestration	✓	✓		✓	
R10 Independence of automation technology	✓			✓	
R11 Alternate versions	✓	✓		✓	✓
R12 Community usage and interest	✓	✓			
B1 Benchmark must stress the system under test (SUT)	✓	✓	(Unknown)		✓
B2 Support for exercising different system components	✓	✓	✓		
B3 Support for different load generators	✓	✓	✓	✓	✓
B4 Load profiles publicly available	✓				

Aderaldo et al. (2017) identify 15 requirements for microservice research bench-marks. Table 14.1 lists 12 of these requirements (relevant for our work) and checks common benchmark applications for compliance. These 12 criteria suit microservice benchmarks, yet they do not cover the ability of an application to be used as a refer-ence research benchmark application in performance modeling and resource man-agement. Kistowski, Eismann, et al. (2018) therefore extended the requirements by four additional research benchmark requirements shown in Table 14.1. A benchmark must stress the system under test (B1) and should not be focused only on a single-server component like memory or CPU (B2). The benchmark should lend itself to be exercised by different load generators in order to fit a wide variety of benchmarking environments and non-executable workload descriptions (B3). Finally, the used load profiles should be made publicly available to ensure reproducibility (B4).

In terms of compliance to these requirements, TeaStore satisfies all require-ments except for the requirement *Alternate Versions* (R11), which requires al-ternate implementations of at least some services to be provided. ACME Air,[2] Spring Cloud Demo,[3] Sock Shop,[4] and MusicStore,[5] also compared in Table 14.1, satisfy fewer requirements. In addition, TeaStore satisfies all of the research bench-mark requirements, whereas the next best application (ACME Air) does not satisfy the requirement for publicly available load profiles.

14.2 Workload

TeaStore's executable application workload is an online store for tea and tea-related utilities. Being a web store, it offers and displays products on web pages. The general usage scenario for TeaStore is that virtual users, described by the *non-executable workload description*, access these pages and perform actions on them. This, in turn, causes TeaStore's different microservices to perform computational work, which puts the system under test (SUT) under load.

TeaStore offers tea-related products, which are sorted into categories. For online shopping, the store supports an overview of products including preview images for each category and featuring a configurable number of products per page. All pages of TeaStore show an overview header bar and include the category menu and page footer. As main content, it shows the products for the selected category including short product information and the preview image. Depending on the number of products shown per page, users have the option to navigate through multiple pages of the category view.

Each product can be viewed on a separate product page containing detailed information, a large image, and advertisements for other store items. Besides the

---

[2] ACME Air: https://github.com/acmeair/acmeair

[3] Spring Cloud Demo: https://github.com/kbastani/spring-cloud-microservice-example

[4] Sock Shop: https://github.com/microservices-demo/microservices-demo

[5] MusicStore: https://github.com/aspnet/MusicStore

regular header, footer, and category list, this page includes a detailed image of the product (provided by the *Image Provider* service), a description, and a price. The page also contains an advertisement panel suggesting three products the user might be interested in. The advertised products are provided by the *Recommender* service and are selected depending on the viewed product.

All products can be placed in a shopping cart and users can proceed to order the current contents of the shopping cart. The user can choose to modify the shopping cart at any time. The shopping cart page lists all products currently included in the cart together with some product information and the quantity. The shopping cart view also displays product advertisements provided by the *Recommender* service and selected depending on the shopping cart's contents.

To order, a user must supply personal information about the billing address and payment details. After confirmation by the user, the current shopping cart is stored in the order history database utilizing the *Persistence* service. The store also supports user authentication and login. Registered users can view their order history after login.

In addition to regular operations, TeaStore's user interface provides some administrative functions for the benchmark operator. These functions are not part of the executable workload but are necessary for running the workload. For example, they provide an overview of all running service instances and an option to regenerate the database. In case a specific database setup or size is necessary, the database can be regenerated with user-defined parameters, such as the number of categories, the number of products per category, the number of users, and the maximum number of orders per user history.

14.3 Architecture

TeaStore consists of five distinct services and a Registry service as shown in Figure 14.1. All services communicate with the Registry. Additionally, the WebUI service issues calls to the Image Provider, Authentication (Auth), Persistence, and Recommender services.

The Image Provider and Recommender both connect to an interface provided by the Persistence service. However, this is only necessary on startup (dashed lines). The Image Provider must generate an image for each product, whereas the Recommender needs the current order history as training data. Once running, only the Authentication and the WebUI services access, modify, and create data using the Persistence service.

All services communicate via representational state transfer (REST) calls, as REST has established itself as the de-facto industry standard in the microservice domain. The services are deployed as web services on the Apache Tomcat Java Servlet container. Yet, the services can be deployed on any Java application server able to run web services packaged as war files. As an alternative to deploying the war files, TeaStore can also be deployed using Docker container images containing the entire Tomcat stack. Each service is packaged in its own war file or Docker image.

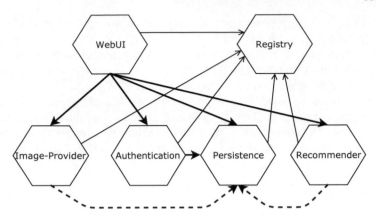

Fig. 14.1: TeaStore's architecture

TeaStore uses the client-side load balancer Ribbon[6] to support replication of service instances. Ribbon distributes REST calls among running instances of a service. Instead of using the popular Netflix Eureka[7] registry, TeaStore uses its own registry that supplies service instances with target instances of a specified target-specific service type. To enable this, all running instances register and unregister at the registry, which can be queried for all running instances of a service. This allows for dynamic addition and removal of service instances at run time. Each service also sends heartbeats to the registry. In case a service is overloaded or crashed and therefore fails to send heartbeat messages, it is removed from the list of available instances. This mechanism ensures good error recovery and minimizes the amount of requests sent to unavailable service instances that would otherwise generate timeouts.

TeaStore is open-source and lends itself to instrumentation using available monitoring solutions. These solutions are not part of the workload itself, but they are necessary to facilitate detailed measurements depending on the benchmark built around TeaStore. Pre-instrumented Docker images for each service that include the Kieker[8] monitoring application (Hoorn, Rohr, et al., 2009; Hoorn, Waller, et al., 2012), as well as a central trace repository service, are already available.

Generally, all requests to the WebUI by a user or load generator are handled in a similar fashion. The WebUI always retrieves information from the Persistence service. If all information is available, images for presentation are fetched from the Image Provider and embedded into the page. Finally, a Java Server Page (JSP) is compiled and returned. This behavior ensures that even non-graphical browsers and simple load generators that otherwise would not fetch images from a regular site cause image I/O in TeaStore, which ensures comparability regardless of the load generation method.

---

[6] Netflix Ribbon: https://github.com/Netflix/ribbon

[7] Netflix Eureka: https://github.com/Netflix/eureka

[8] Kieker APM: http://kieker-monitoring.net

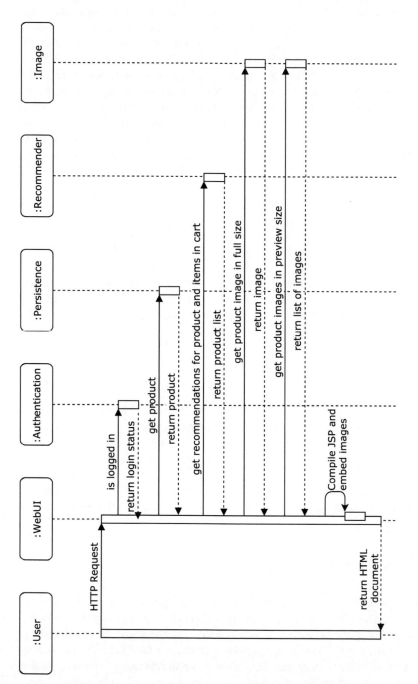

Fig. 14.2: Service calls when requesting product page

Figure 14.2 shows the service calls for a user request to open a product information page. After receiving the HTTP request, the WebUI checks the user's login status by calling the Authentication service. Next, it queries the Persistence service for the corresponding product information based on a unique identifier. Afterwards, the WebUI requests advertisement options for the current product from the Recommender service, which generates a recommendation based on the learned historical order data. The call to the Recommender service takes the current login status into account. Specifically, a logged-in user receives personalized recommendations, whereas an anonymous user is served recommendations based on general item popularity. Having received all product information, the WebUI queries the Image Provider to supply a full-size image of the product shown in detail and preview images for the recommendations. The image data is embedded in the HTML response represented in the form of base-64 encoded strings.

14.4 Services

TeaStore's executable workload consists of five services in addition to a registry necessary for service discovery and load balancing. In case monitoring is enabled, a trace repository service can be used to collect the monitoring traces centrally.

14.4.1 WebUI

The WebUI service provides the user interface, compiling and serving Java Server Pages (JSPs). All data, available categories, their products, product recommendations and images, are retrieved from the Image Provider and Persistence service instances. The WebUI service performs preliminary validity checks on user inputs before passing inputs to the Persistence service. It focuses purely on presentation and web front-end operations. However, the performance of WebUI depends on the page that has to be rendered, as each page contains at least one picture in different formats.

14.4.2 Image Provider

The Image Provider serves images of different image sizes to the WebUI service when being queried. It optimizes image sizes depending on the target size in the presentation view. The Image Provider uses an internal cache and returns the image with the target size from the cache if available. If an image of this size is not available, the Image Provider uses the largest available image for the category or product, scales it to the target size, and loads it into the cache. It uses a least frequently used cache, which optimizes performance for frequently accessed data. The response time for an image depends on whether the image is in the cache or not. This service queries the Persistence service once on startup to generate all product images with a fixed random seed.

14.4.3 Authentication

This service is responsible for the verification of both the login and the session data of a user. The session data is validated using SHA-512 hashes. For login verification, the BCrypt algorithm is used. The session data includes information about the current shopping cart contents, the user's login status, and previous orders. Thus, the performance of the hashing for the session data depends on the number of articles in the cart and the number of previous orders. Furthermore, as all session data is passed to the client, the Authentication service itself remains stateless and does not need additional information on startup.

14.4.4 Recommender

The Recommender service uses a rating algorithm to recommend products for the user to purchase. The recommendations are based on items other customers bought, on the products in a user's current shopping cart, and on the product the user is currently viewing. The initial Recommender instance uses an automatically generated dataset for training, which is provided by the Persistence service at initial startup. Further Recommender instances query existing instances for their training dataset and they use only that data for training. This way, all Recommender instances stay coherent, recommending identical products for the same input. In addition, using identical training input also ensures that different instances of the Recommender service exhibit the same performance characteristics, which is important for many benchmarking and modeling contexts. The Recommender service queries the Persistence service only once on startup.

Different recommendation algorithms exhibiting different performance are available. In addition to a fallback algorithm based on overall item popularity, two variants of Slope One (Lemire and Maclachlan, 2005) and one order-based nearest-neighbor approach are currently implemented. One variant of Slope One calculates the predicted rating matrix beforehand and keeps it in memory (memory-intensive), whereas the other one calculates every row if needed but discards all results after each recommendation step (CPU-intensive).

14.4.5 Persistence

The Persistence service provides access and caching for the store's database. Products, their categories, purchases, and registered store users are stored in a relational SQL database. The Persistence service uses caching to improve response times and to reduce the load on the database itself for improved scalability. The cache is kept coherent across multiple Persistence service instances. The service uses the EclipseLink JPA implementation as a black-box cache. All data inside the database itself is generated at the launching of the initial persistence instance. Using a persistence service separated from the actual database improves scalability by providing a caching service. However, the performance of database access operations depends on the content in the database that can change during the operation of the store.

14.4.6 Registry

The Registry service is not part of the TeaStore application under test but is a necessary support service. It keeps track of all running service instances, their IP addresses or host names, and port numbers under which the services are accessible. All service instances send heartbeat messages to the registry after registration. If a service unregisters or no heartbeat message is received within a fixed time frame, the service is removed from the list of available service instances. All services can query the list of service instances for a specified service type in order to distribute their outgoing requests (on a round-robin basis) between running target instances.

14.5 Workload Descriptions for TeaStore

TeaStore itself is an *executable application workload*. It thus covers only one part of a workload and needs a fully specified non-executable workload description to be used in a benchmark. TeaStore ships two types of *non-executable workload descriptions* (which may be combined with one another): *user profiles* and *load-intensity specifications*. The content of requests arriving at TeaStore (i.e., the user actions) are defined using a stateful user profile. TeaStore uses a cyclical user profile, in which users browse the store. Figure 14.3 shows this profile. Users log in, browse the store for products, add these products to the shopping cart, and then log out. This profile can be used both in closed or open workloads. To use it in closed workloads, one only needs to specify the number of concurrent users. For use in open workloads, a load-intensity specification is required.

TeaStore ships load-intensity specifications and an HTTP load generator, first introduced by Kistowski, Deffner, et al. (2018), which can utilize these specifications to send requests based on an open workload model. The load-intensity specifications (load profiles) can be defined such that request rates may vary over time.

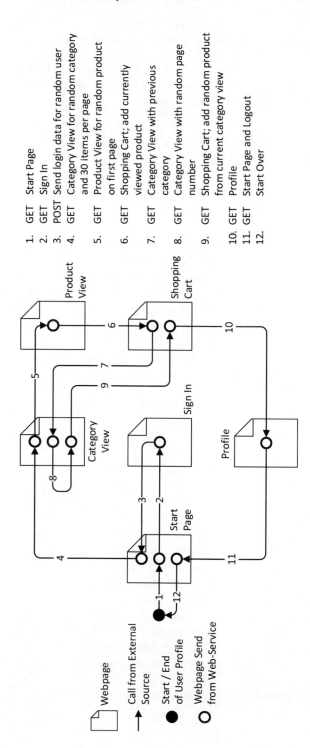

1. GET Start Page
2. GET Sign In
3. POST Send login data for random user
4. GET Category View for random category and 30 items per page
5. GET Product View for random product on first page
6. GET Shopping Cart; add currently viewed product
7. GET Category View with previous category
8. GET Category View with random page number
9. GET Shopping Cart; add random product from current category view
10. GET Profile
11. GET Start Page and Logout
12. Start Over

Fig. 14.3: "Browse" user profile including delivered web pages and HTTP request type (unused web pages omitted for clarity)

Load profiles can be combined with the user profiles. In this case, each time a request should be sent, the load generator picks an idle user from the pool of users. This user then executes a single action on the store. It performs this action and returns to the pool. This means that the user state and actions are chosen as described in Chapter 8 for a closed workload model, whereas the arrival times of the individual requests are chosen according to an open workload model.

14.6 Case Study: TeaStore in Action

This section presents a case study showing how TeaStore can be used as a workload in an energy-efficiency benchmarking context. Specifically, it demonstrates TeaStore's use for testing the energy efficiency of service placements. To keep the example simple, it tests multiple different placement options for TeaStore and shows that placement decisions lead to different power consumption and energy efficiency.

Energy efficiency of placements is a research area focusing on predicting and optimizing the power consumption and energy efficiency of service instances running on different servers in distributed systems, for example, Beloglazov et al. (2012) and Basmadjian et al. (2011). The underlying challenge is that different distributions of application services among physical hosts may result not only in different performance behavior but also in differences in the overall power consumption. The case study we present in the following demonstrates this effect using TeaStore. It shows that different placements of TeaStore's services can result in different performance and in different power consumption both on homogeneous and heterogeneous systems. Thus, we demonstrate that TeaStore can be used as a workload to compare and test the quality of placement methods aiming to minimize power consumption or maximize energy efficiency.

The presented experiments use an increasing load intensity profile as part of the workload description discussed in the previous section. The load profile starts at eight requests per second and increases to 2,000 requests per second over the time of 4 min. The request content is specified using the user browse profile for the 128 users accessing the store. Depending on the current SUT configuration, some of the 4 min are spent in a state in which the load intensity exceeds the capacity of the SUT. The power consumption of the physical servers and the throughput of TeaStore are measured during the entire run. However, only measurements made during the time in which workload arrives at the system are taken into account. Each measurement is taken on a per-second basis and thus tightly coupled to the current load intensity.

In this case study, TeaStore's primary services are placed on several HPE ProLiant DL160 servers, each equipped with a Xeon E5-2640 v3 processor with 16 logical cores at 2.6 GHz and 32 GB RAM. The Registry service is deployed on a separate physical host.

The following metrics are computed based on the measured throughput and power consumption:

1. **Energy Efficiency**: In line with SPEC's Power Methodology (SPECpower Committee, 2014) and Chapter 11, energy efficiency is defined as the ratio of throughput and power consumption:

$$Efficiency[J^{-1}] = \frac{Throughput[s^{-1}]}{Power[W]}.$$

Multiple energy-efficiency scores can be aggregated using a geometric mean.

2. **Estimated Capacity**: The throughput capacity of each configuration is estimated by averaging the last 50 s of the executed load profile; note that all configurations are operating at maximum load (capacity) at this time.

3. **Maximum Power Consumption**: The maximum measured power consumption (in Watts) indicates the power load that the configuration can put on the SUT.

14.6.1 Energy Efficiency on Homogeneous Systems

In the first set of experiments, TeaStore is run in Docker containers on up to two servers. Table 14.2 shows the estimated capacity (with confidence intervals), maximum power, and mean energy efficiency for different TeaStore deployments (service names in the table are abbreviated to their first letters). The table confirms our previous assertion that TeaStore performs differently depending on the service placement. Capacity (maximum throughput) varies significantly for the different deployments, with some two-server deployments barely exceeding the capacity of the single-server deployment and others, almost doubling it.

Table 14.2: Energy efficiency on homogeneous servers

#	Server 1	Server 2	Capacity	Max. power	Energy efficiency
1	Web., Auth., Rec., Img., Per.	–	779.7 ±[29.7]	**114.4 W**	**5.3**
2	Web., Img.	Auth., Rec., Per.	1,177.5 ±[31.5]	193.6 W	4.2
3	Web., Auth., Img.	Rec., Per.	883.4 ±[39.4]	175.8 W	3.8
4	Web., Auth., Rec., Img., Per.	Img., Per.	863.0 ±[40.5]	173.5 W	3.9
5	Web., Auth., Rec., Img., Per.	Auth., Img., Per.	1,228.7 ±[18.9]	208.4 W	4.2
6	Web., Auth., Img., Per.	Web., Auth., Rec., Per.	1,231.8 ±[18.7]	203.7 W	4.3
7	Web., Auth., Rec., Img., Per.	Web., Auth., Img., Per.	1,404.1 ±[14.5]	217.9 W	4.3
8	Web., Auth., Rec., Img., Per.	Web., Auth., Rec., Img., Per.	**1,413.2** ±[14.7]	217.7 W	4.3

The single-server deployment (deployment #1) exhibits the lowest performance, but also the lowest power consumption resulting in the highest energy efficiency among all tested configurations. This is mostly due to the increasing stress test profile. At low load, as the load increases, the single system is still capable of handling all requests while consuming less power. At high load, it operates at full capacity but still consumes less power than the two-server setups. Figure 14.4 visualizes the energy efficiency over time for the single-server and two selected two-server deployments. The figure shows that an efficient two-server deployment can reach a similar energy efficiency as the single-server deployment at maximum load. However, some low performance deployments are incapable of reaching this efficiency and are overall less efficient due to the power overhead of the second server.

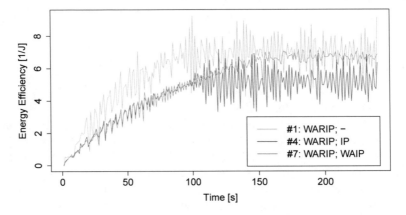

Fig. 14.4: Energy efficiency for linearly increasing loads (services are abbreviated to their first letters)

Among the two-server deployments, the maximum power consumption is usually greater for those deployments with greater capacity, but some notable differences exist. This indicates that there is room for power and efficiency optimization even on homogeneous systems. Comparing deployments #2 and #3 shows that deployment #2 (which deploys the WebUI and Image Provider services on one server and the Authentication, Recommender, and Persistence services on the other server) exhibits both better performance and smaller power footprint than deployment #3 (which deploys the WebUI, Authentication, and Image Provider services on one server and the Recommender and Persistence services on the other server). Consequently, deployment #2 features better energy efficiency. In this example, one deployment is obviously better than the others, and TeaStore can be used to evaluate if a prediction method or a management mechanism actually selects the better option. However, in some cases, power does not scale in the same way as performance. An example of this can be seen when comparing deployment #5 and #6. Both deliver equal performance, but deployment #6 consumes slightly less power and is therefore a bit more efficient.

14.6.2 Energy Efficiency on Heterogeneous Systems

For the measurements on heterogeneous systems, the second server is replaced with an HP ProLiant DL20 system featuring an Intel Xeon E3-1230 v5 processor with four cores at 3.5 GHz and 16 GB RAM. This second server does not offer as much performance and consumes less power compared to its eight-core counterpart. Naturally, when deploying on this heterogeneous system, the order of deployment matters, as servers differ in power and performance.

Table 14.3 presents the measurement results for the heterogeneous system. It shows the performance capacity (with confidence intervals), power, and energy efficiency for selected deployments. It illustrates the effect the deployment order has on the heterogeneous system especially regarding deployments #2 and #3, which are equivalent with exception that they deploy each respective stack on a different server. Deployment #2 deploys the full stack on the smaller server and replicates some components on the larger machine, whereas deployment #3 does the reverse. Although deployment #3 consumes more power than #2, it has far better performance and greater overall efficiency. It should also be noted that deployments with fewer services on the smaller machine seem to be more efficient in the heterogeneous environment compared to the respective deployments in the homogeneous environment. Deployment #5 corresponds to deployment #7 on the homogeneous system (see Table 14.2), which is the most efficient system in that context. However, on the heterogeneous system, it is exceeded in performance and efficiency by deployment #3, which places fewer services on the smaller machine.

Table 14.3: Energy efficiency on heterogeneous servers

#	8-Core server	4-Core server	Capacity	Max. power	Energy efficiency
1	Web., Auth., Rec., Img., Per.	–	779.7 ±[29.7]	114.4 W	5.3
2	Auth., Img., Per.	Web., Auth., Rec., Img., Per.	781.1 ±[11.1]	**163.1 W**	3.9
3	Web., Auth., Rec., Img., Per.	Auth., Img., Per.	**1,207.3** ±[23.4]	189.5 W	**4.6**
4	Web., Auth., Img., Per.	Web., Auth., Rec., Img., Per.	1,011.9 ±[24.7]	179.6 W	4.4
5	Web., Auth., Rec., Img., Per.	Web., Auth., Img., Per.	1,067.7 ±[26.7]	187.0 W	4.3
6	Web., Auth., Rec., Img., Per.	Web., Auth., Rec., Img., Per.	1,003.9 ±[24.9]	179.7 W	4.1

In addition, the heterogeneous system demonstrates a trade-off between energy efficiency and performance when compared to the homogeneous system. The most efficient heterogeneous deployment has a slightly lower performance capacity than the best homogeneous one, yet consumes less power and has a better energy efficiency.

Overall, the experiments show that TeaStore exhibits different performance and power behavior depending on the service placement, both on heterogeneous and homogeneous systems. Thus, TeaStore can be used as a basis for evaluating the prediction accuracy of performance and power modeling techniques. In addition, some of the considered configurations feature a performance versus energy-efficiency trade-off, which demonstrates TeaStore's suitability for evaluating run-time performance and power management techniques.

14.7 Concluding Remarks

This chapter introduced TeaStore, a test and reference application intended to serve as a benchmarking framework for researchers evaluating their work.[9] TeaStore is designed to offer the degrees of freedom and performance characteristics required by software performance modeling and management research. Specifically, TeaStore is designed to be used in one of the three target domains: (1) evaluation of software performance modeling approaches and model extraction techniques; (2) evaluation of run-time performance management techniques such as autoscalers; and (3) evaluation of server energy efficiency, power models, and optimization techniques.

TeaStore is designed as a distributed microservice-based application, consisting of five separate services, each of which can be replicated, added, and removed at run time. TeaStore's services are available both as Docker containers and as manually deployable components. TeaStore's use was demonstrated by analyzing the energy efficiency of different deployments for TeaStore showing the nontrivial power and performance effects that placement decisions can have. In addition, the presented case study showed that some TeaStore configurations offer a trade-off between energy efficiency and performance, which provides a basis for evaluating run-time performance and power management mechanisms.

References

Aderaldo, C. M., Mendonça, N. C., Pahl, C., and Jamshidi, P. (2017). "Benchmark Requirements for Microservices Architecture Research". In: *Proceedings of the 1st International Workshop on Establishing the Community-Wide Infrastructure for Architecture-Based Software Engineering*. (Buenos Aires, Argentina). IEEE: Piscataway, New Jersey, USA, pp. 8–13 (cited on pp. 303, 304).

---

[9] TeaStore setup:
https://github.com/DescartesResearch/TeaStore/wiki/Testing-and-Benchmarking

Basmadjian, R., Ali, N., Niedermeier, F., Meer, H. de, and Giuliani, G. (2011). "A Methodology to Predict the Power Consumption of Servers in Data Centres". In: *Proceedings of the 2nd International Conference on Energy-Efficient Computing and Networking (e-Energy'11)*. (New York, NY, USA). ACM: New York, NY, USA, pp. 1–10 (cited on p. 312).

Becker, S., Koziolek, H., and Reussner, R. (2009). "The Palladio Component Model for Model-driven Performance Prediction". *Journal of Systems and Software*, 82(1). Elsevier Science: Amsterdam, The Netherlands, pp. 3–22 (cited on p. 301).

Beloglazov, A., Abawajy, J., and Buyya, R. (2012). "Energy-aware Resource Allocation Heuristics for Efficient Management of Data Centers for Cloud Computing". *Future Generation Computer Systems*, 28(5). Elsevier Science: Amsterdam, The Netherlands, pp. 755–768 (cited on p. 312).

Brunnert, A., Hoorn, A. van, Willnecker, F., Danciu, A., Hasselbring, W., Heger, C., Herbst, N. R., Jamshidi, P., Jung, R., Kistowski, J. von, Koziolek, A., Kroß, J., Spinner, S., Vögele, C., Walter, J. C., and Wert, A. (2015). *Performance-oriented DevOps: A Research Agenda*. Tech. rep. SPEC-RG-2015-01. Gainesville, VA, USA: SPEC RG—DevOps Performance Working Group, Standard Performance Evaluation Corporation (SPEC) (cited on p. 301).

Happe, J., Koziolek, H., and Reussner, R. (2011). "Facilitating Performance Predictions Using Software Components". *IEEE Software*, 28(3). IEEE: Piscataway, New Jersey, USA, pp. 27–33 (cited on p. 301).

Hoorn, A. van, Rohr, M., Hasselbring, W., Waller, J., Ehlers, J., Frey, S., and Kieselhorst, D. (2009). *Continuous Monitoring of Software Services: Design and Application of the Kieker Framework*. Tech. rep. TR-0921. Department of Computer Science, Kiel University, Germany (cited on p. 306).

Hoorn, A. van, Waller, J., and Hasselbring, W. (2012). "Kieker: A Framework for Application Performance Monitoring and Dynamic Software Analysis". In: *Proceedings of the 3rd ACM/SPEC International Conference on Performance Engineering (ICPE 2012)*. (Boston, Massachusetts, USA). ACM: New York, NY, USA, pp. 247–248 (cited on p. 306).

Ilyushkin, A., Ali-Eldin, A., Herbst, N. R., Papadopoulos, A. V., Ghit, B., Epema, D., and Iosup, A. (2017). "An Experimental Performance Evaluation of Autoscaling Policies for Complex Workflows". In: *Proceedings of the 8th ACM/SPEC International Conference on Performance Engineering (ICPE 2017)*. (L'Aquila, Italy). ACM: New York, NY, USA, pp. 75–86 (cited on p. 301).

Kistowski, J. von, Deffner, M., and Kounev, S. (2018). "Run-time Prediction of Power Consumption for Component Deployments". In: *Proceedings of the 15th IEEE International Conference on Autonomic Computing (ICAC 2018)*. (Trento, Italy). IEEE: Piscataway, New Jersey, USA (cited on p. 310).

Kistowski, J. von, Eismann, S., Schmitt, N., Bauer, A., Grohmann, J., and Kounev, S. (2018). "TeaStore: A Micro-Service Reference Application for Benchmarking,

Modeling and Resource Management Research". In: *Proceedings of the 26th IEEE International Symposium on the Modelling, Analysis, and Simulation of Computer and Telecommunication Systems (MASCOTS 2018)*. (Milwaukee, WI, USA). IEEE Computer Society: Washington, DC, USA (cited on pp. 302, 304).

Lemire, D. and Maclachlan, A. (2005). "Slope One Predictors for Online Rating-Based Collaborative Filtering". In: *Proceedings of the 2005 SIAM International Conference on Data Mining (SDM 2005)*. (Newport Beach, CA, USA). Society for Industrial and Applied Mathematics (SIAM): Philadelphia, USA, pp. 471–475 (cited on p. 309).

SPECpower Committee (2014). *Power and Performance Benchmark Methodology V2.2*. Gainesville, VA, USA: Standard Performance Evaluation Corporation (SPEC) (cited on p. 313).

Willnecker, F., Dlugi, M., Brunnert, A., Spinner, S., Kounev, S., and Krcmar, H. (2015). "Comparing the Accuracy of Resource Demand Measurement and Estimation Techniques". In: *Computer Performance Engineering—Proceedings of the 12th European Performance Engineering Workshop (EPEW 2015)*. (Madrid, Spain). Ed. by M. Beltrán, W. Knottenbelt, and J. Bradley. Vol. 9272. Lecture Notes in Computer Science. Springer-Verlag: Berlin, Heidelberg, pp. 115–129 (cited on p. 301).

Chapter 15
Elasticity of Cloud Platforms

Nikolas R. Herbst, André Bauer, and Samuel Kounev

Infrastructure-as-a-Service (IaaS) cloud platforms provide the benefit of utility computing and pay-per-use. Accordingly, many providers offer tools that allow customers to configure automated adaptation processes and thus benefit from the increased flexibility and the ability to react on variations in the load intensity. Predicting and managing the performance impact of such adaptation processes is a challenging task. However, customers require that performance-related Service-Level-Objectives (SLOs) for their applications are continuously met.

As defined in Chapter 1 (Section 1.2), the ability of a system to automatically adapt to workload changes by provisioning and deprovisioning resources at run time to continuously match the actual demand is captured by the system attribute of *elasticity*. The elasticity of cloud platforms is influenced by the employed adaptation processes, as well as by other factors, such as the underlying hardware, the virtualization technology, or the cloud management software. These factors vary across providers and often remain unknown to the cloud customer. Even if they were known, the effect of specific configurations on the performance of an application is hard to quantify and compare. Furthermore, the available adaptation processes are quite different in their methods and complexity as shown in the surveys by Lorido-Botran et al. (2014), by Galante and Bona (2012), and by Jennings and Stadler (2015).

Traditional approaches to designing elasticity metrics and benchmarks evaluate this quality attribute only indirectly and to a limited extent. The focus of early metrics lies either on the technical provisioning time (e.g., in the work of Chandler et al. (2012)), on the response time variability (e.g., in the work of Almeida et al. (2013)), or on the impact on business costs (e.g., in the work of Islam et al. (2012)). Traditional evaluation approaches do not account for differences in the efficiency of the underlying physical resources, and they employ load profiles that are rarely representative of modern real-life workloads with variable load intensities over time. However, the quality of an adaptation mechanism, in terms of its ability to maintain SLOs, depends both on the specific deployment scenario and on the workload characteristics.

In this chapter, we present a set of intuitively understandable metrics for characterizing the elasticity of a cloud platform including ways to aggregate them. The focus is on IaaS clouds; however, the presented approach can also be applied in the context of other types of cloud platforms. The metrics support evaluating both the

© Springer Nature Switzerland AG 2020

S. Kounev et al., *Systems Benchmarking*, https://doi.org/10.1007/978-3-030-41705-5_15

accuracy and the timing aspects of elastic behavior. We discuss how the metrics can be aggregated and used to compare the elasticity of cloud platforms. The metrics are designed to support human interpretation and to ease decision making by comparing resource supply and demand curves. Furthermore, the chapter outlines an elasticity benchmarking approach—called Bungee[1]—that explicitly takes into account the performance of the underlying hardware infrastructure and its influence on the elastic behavior. In combination with the proposed metrics, this enables an independent quantitative evaluation of the actual achieved system elasticity.

15.1 Defining Elasticity

Elasticity has been originally defined in physics as a material property capturing the capability of returning to its original state after a deformation. In economic theory, informally, elasticity denotes the sensitivity of a dependent variable to changes in one or more other variables. In both cases, elasticity is an intuitive concept that can be precisely described using mathematical formulas.

The concept of elasticity has been transferred to the context of cloud computing, and it is commonly considered to be one of the central attributes of the cloud paradigm. In this book, we use the following widely adopted definition of elasticity in the context of cloud computing:[2]

Definition 15.1 (Elasticity in Cloud Computing) Elasticity is the degree to which a system is able to adapt to *workload changes* by provisioning and deprovisioning resources in an *autonomic* manner, such that, at each point in time, the available *resources match* the current *demand* as closely as possible (Herbst, Kounev, and Reussner, 2013).

In the following, we first describe some important prerequisites in order to be able to speak of elasticity, and then we analyze its core aspects and dimensions. Finally, we discuss the difference between elasticity and its related terms, scalability and efficiency.

The scalability of a system, including all hardware, virtualization, and software layers within its boundaries, is a prerequisite for elasticity. Scalability is the ability of a system to sustain increasing workloads with adequate performance, provided that hardware resources are added. In the context of distributed systems, it has been defined in the work of Jogalekar and Woodside (2000), as well as in the works of Duboc et al. (2007), where also a measurement methodology is proposed.

Given that elasticity is related to the ability of a system to adapt to changes in workloads and demanded resource units, the existence of at least one adaptation process is typically assumed. The process is normally automated, but it may contain manual steps. Without a defined adaptation process, a scalable system cannot scale

---

[1] Bungee cloud elasticity benchmark: http://descartes.tools/bungee

[2] https://en.wikipedia.org/wiki/Elasticity_(cloud_computing)

in an elastic manner, as scalability on its own does not include temporal aspects. For assessing the quality of elasticity, the following points need to be checked beforehand:

- **Automated Scaling:** What adaptation process is used for automated scaling?
- **Elasticity Dimensions:** What is the set of resource types scaled as part of the adaptation process?
- **Resource Scaling Units:** For each resource type, in what unit is the amount of allocated resources varied?
- **Scalability Bounds:** For each resource type, what is the upper bound on the resources that can be allocated?

Any given adaptation process is defined in the context of at least one or possibly multiple types of resources that can be scaled up or down as part of the adaptation. Each resource type can be seen as a separate dimension of the adaptation process with its own elasticity properties. If a resource type comprises other resource types, like in the case of a virtual machine (VM) having assigned CPU cores and memory, elasticity can be considered at multiple levels. Normally, resources of a given resource type can only be provisioned in discrete units like CPU cores, VMs, or physical nodes. For each dimension of the adaptation process with respect to a specific resource type, elasticity captures the following core aspects of the adaptation:

- **Timing:** The timing aspect reflects the time shares in which a system is in an underprovisioned, overprovisioned, or optimal state as well as the stability of adaptations (including the presence of oscillations).
- **Accuracy:** The accuracy aspect reflects the relative deviation of the amount of allocated resources from the actual resource demand, on average.

A direct comparison between two systems in terms of elasticity is only possible if the same resource types, measured in identical units, are scaled. To evaluate the actual elasticity in a given scenario, one must define the criterion based on which the amount of provisioned resources is considered to *match* the actual demand needed to satisfy the application SLOs. Based on such a matching criterion, specific metrics that quantify the above mentioned core aspects, as discussed in more detail in Section 15.2, can be defined, enabling comparison of the practically achieved elasticity with the hypothetical *optimal elasticity*. The latter corresponds to the hypothetical case where the system is scalable with respect to all considered elasticity dimensions (without any upper bounds on the amount of resources that can be provisioned) and where resources are provisioned and deprovisioned immediately as needed while exactly matching the actual demand at any point in time. *Optimal elasticity*, as defined here, would be limited only by the granularity of the resource scaling units.

The conceptual differences between elasticity and the related terms scalability and efficiency can be summarized as follows:

Scalability is a prerequisite for elasticity, but it does not consider the temporal aspects of how fast, how often, and at what granularity scaling actions can be performed. Scalability is the ability of the system to sustain increasing workloads by making use of additional resources, and therefore, in contrast to elasticity, it is not directly related to how well the actual resource demands are matched by the provisioned resources at any point in time.

Efficiency expresses the amount of resources consumed for processing a given amount of work. In contrast to elasticity, efficiency is directly linked to the resource types that are scaled as part of the system's adaptation mechanisms. Normally, better elasticity results in higher efficiency. This implication does not apply in the other direction, as efficiency can be influenced by other factors (e.g., different implementations of the same operation).

15.2 Elasticity Metrics

In order to compare and quantify the performance of different mechanisms for elastic scaling, commonly referred to as *autoscalers*, we use a set of system-level and user-oriented metrics (Herbst, Bauer, et al., 2018). The set of metrics we present in this section has been endorsed by the Research Group of the Standard Performance Evaluation Corporation (SPEC) as documented in Herbst, Krebs, et al. (2016). The metrics have been designed in a way oriented around the generic metric quality criteria discussed in Chapter 3, Section 3.4.2. They have been successfully applied to evaluate and compare the elasticity of modern autoscaling mechanisms on a level playing field (Bauer et al., 2019).

We distinguish between three different types of elasticity metrics:

- *Provisioning accuracy metrics* that explicitly distinguish between overprovisioning and underprovisioning states and quantify the (relative) amount of resources supplied in excess or below the actual demand, on average,
- *Wrong provisioning time share metrics* that again explicitly distinguish between overprovisioning and underprovisioning states and quantify the percentage of time spent in each of these states, and
- *Instability and jitter metrics* that quantify the degree of convergence of the demand and supply. Instability captures the percentage of time in which the demand and supply change in opposite directions; jitter accounts for the relative amount of superfluous (positive) or missed (negative) adaptations in the supply.

Since underprovisioning results in violating SLOs, a customer might want to use a system that minimizes underprovisioning while at the same time minimizing the amount of overprovisioned resources. The accuracy and time share metrics that we present in this section enable providers to better communicate their autoscaling capabilities, and they enable customers to select an autoscaler that best matches their needs.

In addition to system-oriented metrics, we highlight the importance of user-oriented metrics in this context. We consider important indicators to be: the frequency of adaptations, the average number of virtual machine (VM) instances, the accounted instance minutes, and the average and median service response time, in combination with the percentage of SLO violations. When considering cost-based metrics, one should keep in mind that they normally depend directly on the employed cost model of the provider and are thus inherently biased.

When using only individual metrics to evaluate the performance of autoscalers, the results can be ambiguous. Therefore, we consider different approaches to derive aggregate metrics (cf. Sections 3.5.2 and 3.5.3 in Chapter 3) from the individual metrics: (1) metrics based on the deviation of each autoscaler from the theoretically optimal autoscaler, (2) metrics based on pairwise comparisons among the autoscalers, and (3) metrics based on quantifying the gain from using an autoscaler via an elastic speedup metric.

We will use the following notation to introduce the various metrics in the rest of this section:

- T denotes the experiment duration with the time t varying in the interval $[0, T]$,
- s_t denotes the resource supply at time t, and
- d_t denotes the resource demand at time t.

For illustration, we will assume that the type of resource scaled is virtual machines (VMs) and the unit of scaling is defined as the number of running VMs.

The resource demand d_t is the minimum amount of resources (i.e., number of VMs) required to meet a predefined SLO under the load at time t. The demand curve is derived based on systematic load measurements as part of the Bungee elasticity measurement methodology, which we present in Section 15.4. The resource supply s_t is the monitored number of running VMs at time t.

Figure 15.1 illustrates the time spans in under-/overprovisioned states as A_i, B_i and respective areas U_i, O_i derived by comparing the supply curve s_t with the demand curve d_t.

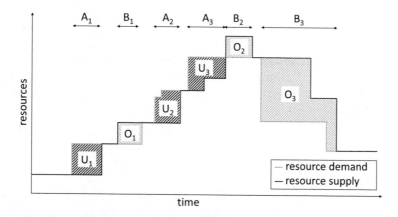

Fig. 15.1: Exemplary supply and demand curves illustrating the intention of the accuracy metrics (see U_i, O_i areas) and time share metrics (see A_i, B_i intervals)—red/orange areas indicate under-/overprovisioning

15.2.1 Provisioning Accuracy

The *provisioning accuracy metrics* θ_U and θ_O capture the (relative) amount of resources that are underprovisioned and overprovisioned, respectively, during the measurement interval. The *underprovisioning accuracy* θ_U is the amount of missing resources required to meet the SLOs in relation to the current demand, normalized by the length of the experiment. Similarly, the *overprovisioning accuracy* θ_O is the amount of resources that the autoscaler supplies in excess of the current demand, normalized by the length of the experiment. The values of these metrics lie in the interval $[0, \infty)$, where 0 is the best value indicating that there is no underprovisioning or overprovisioning during the entire measurement interval. The two metrics θ_U and θ_O are formally defined as follows:

$$\theta_U[\%] := \frac{100}{T} \cdot \int_{t=0}^{T} \frac{\max(d_t - s_t, 0)}{\max(d_t, \varepsilon)} dt, \tag{15.1}$$

$$\theta_O[\%] := \frac{100}{T} \cdot \int_{t=0}^{T} \frac{\max(s_t - d_t, 0)}{\max(d_t, \varepsilon)} dt, \tag{15.2}$$

with $\varepsilon > 0$; we selected $\varepsilon = 1$. The role of ε in the above equations is to avoid division by zero in intervals where the actual resource demand is zero.

These normalized accuracy metrics are particularly useful when the resource demand varies significantly over time and it can assume both large and small values. Indeed, underprovisioning one resource unit when two resource units are required is much more harmful than in the case when hundreds of resource units are required. Therefore, this type of normalization allows a more fair evaluation of the achievable performance.

For an intuitive interpretation when comparing results in experiments with low variation in the resource demand, we define the *unscaled provisioning accuracy metrics* a_U and a_O as the average amount of resource units by which the demand exceeds the supply for a_U, and analogously, the average amount of excessive resources during overprovisioned periods for a_O. The two metrics a_U and a_O are formally defined as follows:

$$a_U[\#res] := \frac{1}{T} \cdot \int_{t=0}^{T} \max(d_t - s_t, 0) dt, \tag{15.3}$$

$$a_O[\#res] := \frac{1}{T} \cdot \int_{t=0}^{T} \max(s_t - d_t, 0) dt. \tag{15.4}$$

Figure 15.1 illustrates the meaning of the accuracy metrics. The underprovisioning accuracy a_U is equivalent to summing up the areas U where the resource demand exceeds the supply, normalized by the duration of the measurement period T. Similarly, the overprovisioning accuracy metric a_O is based on the sum of the areas O where the resource supply exceeds the demand.

15.2.2 Wrong Provisioning Time Share

The *wrong provisioning time share metrics* τ_U and τ_O capture the (relative) portion of time in which the system is underprovisioned and overprovisioned, respectively, during the measurement interval. The *underprovisioning time share* τ_U is the portion of time relative to the measurement duration, in which the system has insufficient resources. Similarly, the *overprovisioning time share* τ_O is the portion of time relative to the measurement duration, in which the system has more resources than required. The values of these metrics lie in the interval [0, 100]. The best values (i.e., $\tau_U = 0$ and $\tau_O = 0$) are achieved when no underprovisioning and no overprovisioning, respectively, is detected within the measurement period. The two metrics τ_U and τ_O are formally defined as follows:

$$\tau_U[\%] := \frac{100}{T} \cdot \int_{t=0}^{T} \max\left(sgn(d_t - s_t), 0\right) dt, \tag{15.5}$$

$$\tau_O[\%] := \frac{100}{T} \cdot \int_{t=0}^{T} \max\left(sgn(s_t - d_t), 0\right) dt. \tag{15.6}$$

Figure 15.1 illustrates the meaning of the wrong provisioning time share metrics. The underprovisioning time share τ_U is equivalent to summing up the lengths of the intervals A where the resource demand exceeds the supply, normalized by the duration of the measurement period T. Similarly, the overprovisioning time share τ_O is based on the sum of the lengths of the intervals B where the resource supply exceeds the demand.

15.2.3 Instability

The *accuracy* and *time share* metrics quantify the core aspects of elasticity. Still, systems can behave differently while exhibiting the same metric values for the *accuracy* and *time share* metrics. An example of such a situation is shown in Figure 15.2. System A and System B exhibit the same accuracy and spend the same amount of time in the underprovisioned and overprovisioned states. However, System A triggers four resource supply adaptations, whereas System B triggers eight. This results in a different fraction of time in which the system is in stable phases. To take this into account, we introduce a further metric called *instability*, which aims to capture basic unstable behavior (e.g., oscillations) as typically considered in the context of control theory (Janert, 2013).

We define the *instability* metric v as the fraction of time in which the supply curve and the demand curve change in opposite directions. As a requirement for the calculation of this metric, the average provisioning and deprovisioning time per resource unit have to be determined experimentally before or during the measurement period. The step functions of demanded and supplied resource units are transformed

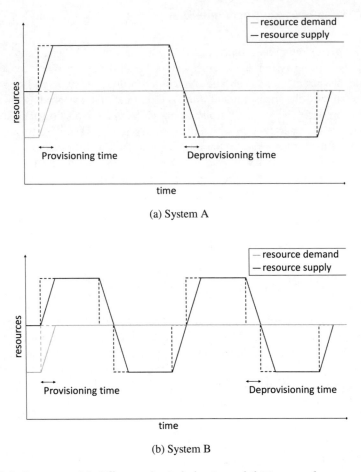

(a) System A

(b) System B

Fig. 15.2: Systems with different elastic behavior exhibiting equal *accuracy* and *timeshare* metrics

to ramps based on the average provisioning and deprovisioning time as depicted in Figure 15.2a. Without this transformation, the resulting value would either become zero or it would depend on the sampling granularity of the demand and supply curves d_t and s_t. In summary, υ captures the fraction of time in which the demanded resource units and the supplied units change in different directions. The metric υ is formally defined as follows:

$$\upsilon[\%] = \frac{100}{T} \cdot \int_{t=0}^{T} \min\left(\left|sgn\left(\frac{d}{dt}s_t\right) - sgn\left(\frac{d}{dt}d_t\right)\right|, 1\right) dt. \qquad (15.7)$$

An *instability* value close to zero indicates that the system adapts closely to changes in the demand. A high value indicates that the system oscillates heavily and does not converge to the demand. In contrast to the accuracy and time share metrics, a v value of zero is a necessary but not sufficient requirement for a perfectly elastic system. For example, continuously allocating too few resources in parallel to the demand curve would result in a value of zero. Instability is a useful indicator for reasoning about the cost overhead of instance-time-based pricing models as well as for assessing the resource adaptation overhead from the cloud operator's perspective.

Although the *instability* metric v comes with a complex computation process, it has the benefit of having a finite positive value range [0, 100]. As will be seen later, this is an important aspect for integration into an aggregated metric.

15.2.4 Jitter

The *jitter* metric j compares the number of adaptations in the supply curve E_S with the number of adaptations in the demand curve E_D. The difference is normalized by the length of the measurement period T. If a system de-/allocates more than one resource unit at a time, the adaptations are counted individually per resource unit. The jitter metric is formally defined as follows:

$$j \left[\frac{\#}{t} \right] = \frac{E_S - E_D}{T}. \tag{15.8}$$

A negative j value indicates that the system adapts rather sluggishly to changes in the demand. A positive j value means that the system tends to oscillate like System A (slightly) and B (heavily) as illustrated in Figure 15.2. In general, high absolute values of the jitter metric indicate that the system is not able to react to demand changes appropriately. In other words, the jitter metric denotes the average amount of missed (negative) or superfluous (positive) adaptations per time unit. In contrast to the accuracy and time share metrics, and as for the instability metric v, a jitter value of zero is a necessary but not sufficient requirement for a perfect elastic system. The *jitter* metric j is easier to compute compared to the instability metric and also comes with an intuitive interpretation. It has a theoretically unbounded value range, but it is capable of distinguishing between oscillating/instable elasticity and elasticity with inertia to adapt timely to the workload changes.

15.3 Aggregating Elasticity Metrics

In this section, we present three different ways to aggregate the introduced elasticity metrics into a single composite metric providing a consistent ranking of autoscaling mechanisms.

15.3.1 Autoscaling Deviation

One approach to evaluate the performance of a set of autoscalers and rank them is to compute the *autoscaling deviation* σ of each autoscaler compared to the theoretically optimal autoscaler. For computing the deviation σ between two autoscalers, we use the *Minkowski distance* d_p:

Let x, y $\in \mathbb{R}^n$ and $1 \leq p \leq \infty$:

$$d_p(x, y) = \|x - y\|_p := \left(\sum_{i=1}^{n} |x_i - y_i|^p\right)^{\frac{1}{p}}. \tag{15.9}$$

Here, the vectors consist of a subset of the aforementioned system-oriented evaluation metrics. We take the provisioning accuracy metric θ, the wrong provisioning time share metric τ, and the instability metric υ. The metrics are specified as percentages. The closer the value of a metric is to zero, the better the autoscaler performs with respect to the aspect characterized by the given metric. Therefore, the closer the autoscaling deviation is to zero, the closer the behavior of the autoscaler would be compared to the theoretically optimal autoscaler.

The first step is to calculate the elasticity metrics. Then, we calculate the *overall provisioning accuracy* θ and the *overall wrong provisioning time share* τ. Hereby, we use a weighted sum for both metrics consisting of their components weighted based on a penalty factor $0 < \gamma < 1$. This penalty can be set individually to reflect custom requirements, with $\gamma > 0.5$ indicating that underprovisioning is worse than overprovisioning, $\gamma = 0.5$ indicating that underprovisioning and overprovisioning are equally bad, and $\gamma < 0.5$ indicating that overprovisioning is worse than underprovisioning. In the case study presented later in this chapter, we always set γ to 0.5. The metrics θ and τ are formally defined as follows:

$$\theta[\%] := \gamma \cdot \theta_U + (1 - \gamma) \cdot \theta_O, \tag{15.10}$$
$$\tau[\%] := \gamma \cdot \tau_U + (1 - \gamma) \cdot \tau_O. \tag{15.11}$$

In the next step, the Minkowski distance d_p between the autoscaler and the theoretically optimal autoscaler is calculated. As the theoretically optimal autoscaler is assumed to know when and how much the demanded resources change, the values for the provisioning accuracy θ, the wrong provisioning time share τ, and the instability υ are equal to zero. In other words, if an autoscaler is compared to the theoretically optimal autoscaler, the L_p-norm can be used as $\|x - 0\|_p = \|x\|_p$ with $x = (\theta, \tau, \upsilon)$. In our case, the *autoscaling deviation* σ between a given autoscaler and the theoretically optimal autoscaler is defined as follows:

$$\sigma[\%] := \|x\|_3 = \left(\theta^3 + \tau^3 + \upsilon^3\right)^{\frac{1}{3}} \tag{15.12}$$

given that we have three dimensions: the overall provisioning accuracy, the overall wrong provisioning time share, and the instability.

The smaller the value of the autoscaling deviation σ, the better the autoscaler is rated in the given context.

15.3.2 Pairwise Comparison

Another approach to ranking—given a fixed set of autoscaler experiments—is to use the *pairwise comparison method* (David, 1987). Here, for every autoscaler, the value of each metric is pairwise compared with the value of the same metric for all other autoscalers. As values closer to zero are better, an autoscaler is given one point for every metric where it manages to achieve the lowest value compared to the other considered autoscalers. If a metric has equal value for two autoscalers, the autoscalers each get half a point. In addition, we divide the achieved score of each autoscaler by the maximum achievable score. The *pairwise comparison metric* κ shows the fraction of the achievable points an autoscaler manages to collect. For the comparison, we take the metrics $x = (\theta, \tau, \upsilon)$ into account. Mathematically, the metric κ for an autoscaler $a \in [1, n]$, where n is the number of autoscalers, can be expressed as:

$$\kappa_a[\%] := \frac{100}{(n-1) \cdot |x|} \cdot \sum_{i=1; i \neq a}^{n} \sum_{j=1}^{|x|} \omega(i,j), \quad \text{where} \quad \omega(i,j) := \begin{cases} 0, & x_a(j) > x_i(j) \\ 0.5, & x_a(j) = x_i(j) \\ 1, & x_a(j) < x_i(j) \end{cases}$$

(15.13)

The closer the value of the pairwise comparison metric κ is to 100%, the better the autoscaler is rated in the given context compared to the other autoscalers in competition.

15.3.3 Elastic Speedup Score

The *elastic speedup score* ϵ is computed in a way similar to the aggregation and ranking of results in established benchmarks, for example, SPEC CPU2017 (cf. Chapter 10, Section 10.6.3). Here, the use of the geometric mean to aggregate speedups in relation to a defined baseline scenario is a common approach.

As discussed in Chapter 3 (Section 3.5.3.2), the geometric mean produces consistent rankings, and it is suitable for normalized measurements. The resulting *elastic speedup score* allows one to compare autoscaler elasticity without having to compare each elasticity metric separately. It is also possible to add a new result to the ranking at a later point in time (in contrast to using a fixed set as in the pairwise comparison).

A drawback of the elastic speedup score is its high sensitivity to values close to zero and the fact that it is undefined if one or more of the metrics are zero. To minimize the probability of zero-valued metrics, we aggregate the normalized accuracy and time share metrics into an overall accuracy θ and an overall wrong provisioning time share τ, respectively; see Section 15.3.1, Equations (15.10) and (15.11). This way, θ and τ become zero only for the theoretical optimal autoscaler.

We compute the *elastic speedup score* ϵ based on the accuracy, time share, and instability metrics for an elasticity measurement k and the respective values from a shared baseline scenario *base* as follows:

$$\epsilon_k = \left(\frac{\theta_{base}}{\theta_k}\right)^{w_\theta} \cdot \left(\frac{\tau_{base}}{\tau_k}\right)^{w_\tau} \cdot \left(\frac{\upsilon_{base}}{\upsilon_k}\right)^{w_\upsilon},$$
(15.14)

where $w_\theta, w_\tau, w_\upsilon \in [0, 1]$, $w_\theta + w_\tau + w_\upsilon = 1$.

The weights can be used to implement user-defined preferences, for example, to increase the influence of the accuracy and time share aspects compared to the instability aspect if desired. We assume here that a baseline measurement is available with the same application and workload profile executed within the same predefined range of resource units. The higher the value of the *elastic speedup score* ϵ_k, the better the autoscaler is rated in the given context compared to the baseline scenario.

15.4 Elasticity Benchmarking Framework

The elasticity of a cloud platform is influenced by many factors including the underlying hardware, the used virtualization technology, and the cloud management software. These factors vary across providers and often remain unknown to the cloud customer. Even if they were known, the effect of specific configurations on the performance of an application is hard to quantify and compare. In this section, we present an elasticity benchmarking framework, called Bungee,[3] that takes these factors into account and addresses generic and cloud-specific benchmark requirements (cf. Chapter 1, Section 1.5).

15.4.1 Overview of Bungee

We provide a brief overview of the benchmark components and the benchmarking workflow. An implementation of Bungee is available as an open-source tool. More details on the design of Bungee can be found in Herbst, Kounev, Weber, et al. (2015).

---

[3] Bungee cloud elasticity benchmark: http://descartes.tools/bungee

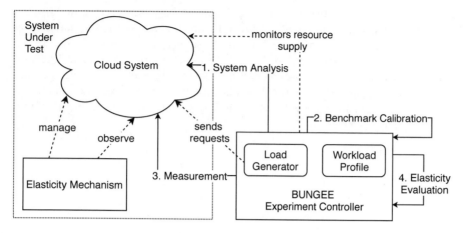

Fig. 15.3: Bungee experimental environment

Figure 15.3 illustrates a Bungee experimental environment comprised of the system under test (SUT)—the elastic IaaS cloud platform—and the *Bungee Benchmark Controller*, which runs the benchmark. Bungee automates the process of benchmarking resource elasticity in four sequential steps:

1. **System Analysis:** The cloud platform is analyzed with respect to the performance of its underlying resources and its scaling behavior. A discrete mapping function is generated that determines for each load-intensity level the associated minimum amount of resources required to meet the Service-Level Objectives (SLOs).
2. **Benchmark Calibration:** The results of the analysis are used to adjust the varying load profile injected on the system in a way to induce the same resource demand on all compared systems.
3. **Measurement:** The load generator exposes the cloud platform to a varying workload according to the adjusted load profile. The benchmark controller monitors the amount of supplied resources at each point in time during the measurement interval as well as the performance of the system with respect to the SLOs.
4. **Elasticity Evaluation:** The elasticity metrics introduced in the previous two sections are computed and used to compare the resource demand and resource supply curves with respect to different elasticity aspects.

In the following, we will use the term *resource demand*[4] to refer to the minimum resource amount that is necessary to handle the load intensity without violating the SLOs (e.g., response times). The resource demand of a platform for a given load intensity depends on two factors: (1) the efficiency of a single underlying resource unit and (2) the overhead caused by combining multiple resource units.

---

[4] Note that this notion of resource demand, in the context of elasticity benchmarking, is different than the more general concept of resource demand (also referred to as service demand) discussed in Chapter 17.

Both aspects can vary from platform to platform, and they correspond to two distinct properties, namely efficiency and scalability. Figure 15.4 shows an example of three platforms with different resource demand for the same load intensity. The difference in the resource demand is due to different scaling behaviors and different levels of efficiency of the underlying resources. When comparing elasticity, it is important to consider workloads that induce the same resource demand variations on each compared platform. To this end, the load intensity profile executed on each platform is calibrated as described below.

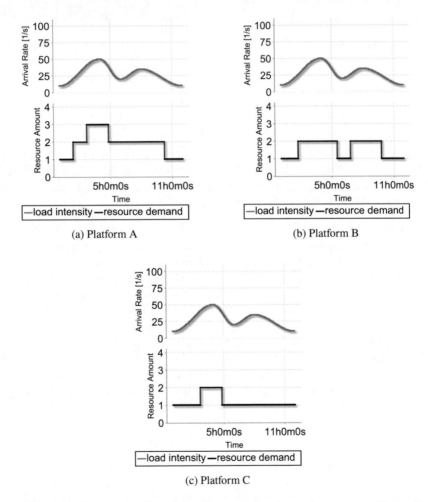

Fig. 15.4: Platforms with different resource demands for the same load intensity

The first step (system analysis) is to derive a function for each platform that maps a given load intensity to the corresponding resource demand. The analysis works by exposing the system to a specific load intensity and checking whether the SLOs are fulfilled. For each amount of allocated resources, the maximum sustainable load intensity for which the SLOs are fulfilled is measured. The search starts with one resource unit and increases the number of resources, until the maximum sustainable load stops to increase or until the maximum number of available resources is reached.

In the second step (benchmark calibration), the load profile injected on each tested platform is adjusted in a way to induce the same resource demand at each point in time during the measurement period. The target resource demand is derived by considering the scaling behavior of a baseline system serving as a reference for comparisons. To achieve this, Bungee adapts the load intensity curve for every platform to compensate for different levels of efficiency of the underlying resources and for different scaling behavior. The calibration uses the mapping function from the system analysis step, which is specific for every platform. Figure 15.5 shows the induced load demand for the three example platforms using the adjusted load profiles. Although the platforms have underlying resources with different levels of efficiency and different scaling behavior (see Figure 15.4), the induced resource demand variations are now equal for all compared platforms. With this adjustment, it is now possible to directly compare the quality of the adaptation process and thus evaluate the platform elasticity in a fair manner.

15.5 Case Study

In this section, we present a case study showing that the scaling behavior (i.e., elasticity) of a standard, reactive, CPU utilization-rule-based autoscaler depends on the specific environment (cloud platform) in which it is deployed and used. The presented experiment results adhere to the established principles and best practices for conducting reproducible experiments in cloud computing environments as described in Papadopoulos et al. (2019a,b).

The case study evaluates the scaling behavior of the autoscaler when scaling a CPU-intensive application—an implementation of the LU worklet (lower–upper decomposition of an $n \times n$ matrix) from the SPEC SERT 2 suite (cf. Chapter 11, Section 11.3)—in three different deployment environments:

- a CloudStack-based private cloud (CSPC),
- Amazon Elastic Compute Cloud (AWS EC2), and
- the DAS-4 IaaS cloud of a medium-scale, multi-cluster experimental environment (MMEE) used for computer science research.

The implemented autoscaler and experiment data are available online.[5] We use a real-life trace from the FIFA championship 1998.[6] We apply the analysis of variance (ANOVA) technique (cf. Chapter 5, Section 5.1) to determine the impact of the deployment environment on the scaling behavior (i.e., elasticity) of the autoscaler.

---

[5] Autoscaler and experiment data: https://doi.org/10.5281/zenodo.1169900

[6] FIFA Source: ftp://ita.ee.lbl.gov/html/contrib/WorldCup.html

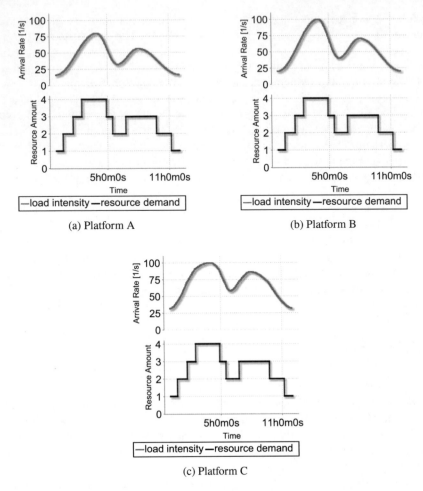

Fig. 15.5: Resource demands for adjusted, platform-specific load profiles

Using the Bungee measurement methodology, the ideal resource supply is derived based on repeated and systematic load tests for each scaling level in the considered three environments.

We extract a sub-trace containing three similar days for internal repetitions, and we run each trace in each environment. To cover setups with background noise, the application is deployed both in the public AWS EC2 IaaS cloud and in an OpenNebula-based[7] IaaS cloud of a medium-scale multi-cluster experimental environment (MMEE) used exclusively for these experiments. Each experiment was run for 9.5 h—a duration that covers seasonal patterns, for example, the daily peaks.

---

[7] OpenNebula: https://opennebula.org

For compactness of the presentation, we skip the analysis of further application workloads including other load traces.

Table 15.1: Specification of the VMs

Component	CSPC	EC2 (m4.large)	MMEE
Operating system	CentOS 6.5	CentOS 6.5	Debian 8
vCPU	2 cores	2 cores	2 cores
Memory	4 GB	8 GB	2 GB

In the CSPC scenario, the application is deployed in a private Apache CloudStack[8] cloud that manages 8 identical virtualized Xen-Server (v6.5) hosts (HP DL160 Gen9 with eight physical cores @2.4 Ghz Intel E5-2630 v3). We deactivate hyperthreading to limit VM overbooking and rely on a constantly stable performance per VM. Dynamic frequency scaling is enabled by default and also further CPU-oriented features are not changed. The hosts each have 2×16 GB RAM (DIMM DDR4 RAM operated @ 1866 MHz). The specification of each VM in all setups is listed in Table 15.1. For all scenarios, Tomcat 7 is used as an application server. As the LU worklet of the SERT 2 suite is CPU-bound, there is no disk I/O during the experiments and only low utilization of the Gigabit Ethernet of the hosts is observed. In all three deployments, the autoscaler is configured identically to scale up VMs when an average CPU utilization threshold of 90% is exceeded for 1 min and to scale down VMs when the average CPU utilization falls below 60% for 1 min. CPU utilization is measured inside the VMs using the top[9] command and averaged across all concurrently running VMs.

Figure 15.6 shows the scaling behavior of the reactive autoscaler in each environment. The horizontal axis shows the time of the measurement (in minutes) since the beginning of the experiment; the vertical axis shows the number of concurrently running VMs. The blue line shows the ideal number of supplied VMs; the green dashed line represents the supplied VMs in MMEE; the red line shows the supplied VMs in EC2; and the black dashed line shows the supplied VMs in CSPC.

---

[8] Apache CloudStack: https://cloudstack.apache.org

[9] top command manual: http://man7.org/linux/man-pages/man1/top.1.html

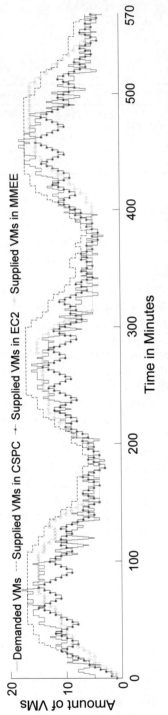

Fig. 15.6: VMs allocated by the reactive autoscaler in the private, EC2, and MMEE IaaS cloud environments

Figures 15.7 and 15.8 show the distributions of the response times and the allocated VMs, respectively. In both figures, the dotted black line represents the first day, the dashed red line the second day, and the solid green line the last day. Whereas the distributions in CSPC and EC2 are similar, they differ from the distributions in MMEE. This can be explained by the scaling behavior depicted in Figure 15.6: during the first day, the autoscaler allocates too few instances; during the second day, it almost satisfies the demand; and during the third day, it overprovisions the system. Table 15.2 shows the average metrics and their standard deviation.

Table 15.2: Average metric (and standard deviation) for a day in each scenario

Metric	CSPC	EC2	MMEE
θ_U (accuracy$_U$) [%]	2.39 (1.54)	14.05 (1.82)	19.42 (5.04)
θ_O (accuracy$_O$) [%]	43.22 (4.38)	10.09 (1.75)	54.98 (11.87)
τ_U (time share$_U$) [%]	9.76 (4.77)	57.20 (2.60)	42.16 (1.76)
τ_O (time share$_O$) [%]	82.95 (5.46)	27.53 (4.42)	53.06 (3.08)
υ (instability) [%]	14.00 (0.66)	18.12 (0.66)	13.01 (1.43)
ψ (SLO violations) [%]	2.70 (3.68)	49.30 (1.71)	53.02 (7.11)
Avg. response time [s]	0.60 (0.17)	2.68 (0.08)	2.32 (0.68)
# Adaptations	25.67 (1.88)	80.66 (3.40)	39.67 (7.54)
Avg. #VMs [VMs]	10.53 (0.44)	8.84 (0.07)	11.01 (0.12)

We now apply the one-factor ANOVA technique (cf. Chapter 5, Section 5.1) to evaluate the impact of the environment on the elasticity of the autoscaler. Table 15.3 shows for each elasticity metric the proportion of observed variation explained by the impact of varying the environment as well as the respective *p-value*. The *p-value* is the minimum significance level (with $1 - p$ corresponding to the maximum confidence level) for which the observed variation due to actual differences in the environment is statistically significant. Given that each *p-value* is less than 1%, and a high proportion of the observed variation is due to the environment, we conclude that the scaling behavior of a standard, reactive, CPU utilization-rule-based autoscaler is significantly impacted by the environment in which the autoscaler is deployed.

Table 15.3: ANOVA results per metric

Statistic	θ_U	θ_O	τ_U	τ_O
p-value	0.006	0.001	0.003	0.003
Prop. of variation due to env. [%]	82	84	98	97

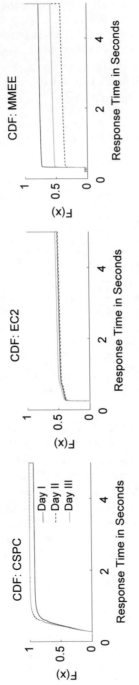

Fig. 15.7: Distribution of response times per day

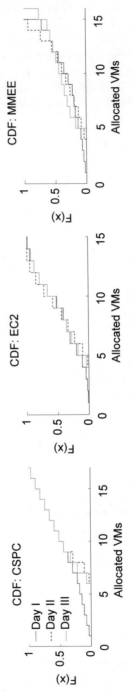

Fig. 15.8: Distribution of allocated VMs per day

15.6 Concluding Remarks

This chapter started with defining elasticity as an important attribute of cloud computing platforms and presented a comprehensive set of elasticity metrics. We introduced a set of intuitive metrics enabling detailed assessment of the elastic behavior of autoscalers based on the Bungee benchmarking methodology. We illustrated the use of the metrics in a compact case study investigating the question of whether standard reactive autoscalers behave differently in different infrastructure cloud environments.

References

Almeida, R. F., Sousa, F. R., Lifschitz, S., and Machado, J. C. (2013). "On Defining Metrics for Elasticity of Cloud Databases". In: *Proc. of the 28th Brazilian Symposium on Databases (SBBD 2013)*. (Recife, Pernambuco, Brazil) (cited on p. 319).

Bauer, A., Herbst, N. R., Spinner, S., Ali-Eldin, A., and Kounev, S. (2019). "Chameleon: A Hybrid, Proactive Auto-Scaling Mechanism on a Level-Playing Field". *IEEE Transactions on Parallel and Distributed Systems*, 30(4). IEEE: Piscataway, New Jersey, USA, pp. 800–813 (cited on p. 322).

Chandler, D., Coskun, N., Baset, S., Nahum, E., Khandker, S. R. M., Daly, T., Paul, N. W. I., Barton, L., Wagner, M., Hariharan, R., and Chao, Y.-s. (2012). *Report on Cloud Computing to the OSG Steering Committee*. Tech. rep. Gainesville, VA, USA (cited on p. 319).

David, H. A. (1987). "Ranking from Unbalanced Paired-Comparison Data". *Biometrika*, 74(2). Oxford University Press: Oxford, UK, pp. 432–436 (cited on p. 329).

Duboc, L., Rosenblum, D., and Wicks, T. (2007). "A Framework for Characterization and Analysis of Software System Scalability". In: *Proceedings of the 6th Joint Meeting of the European Software Engineering Conference and the ACM SIGSOFT Symposium on the Foundations of Software Engineering (ESEC-FSE 2007)*. (Dubrovnik, Croatia). ACM: New York, NY, USA, pp. 375–384 (cited on p. 320).

Galante, G. and Bona, L. C. E. de (2012). "A Survey on Cloud Computing Elasticity". In: *Proceedings of the 2012 IEEE/ACM Fifth International Conference on Utility and Cloud Computing (UCC 2012)*. (Chicago, IL, USA). IEEE Computer Society: Washington, DC, USA, pp. 263–270 (cited on p. 319).

Herbst, N. R., Bauer, A., Kounev, S., Oikonomou, G., Eyk, E. van, Kousiouris, G., Evangelinou, A., Krebs, R., Brecht, T., Abad, C. L., and Iosup, A. (2018). "Quantifying Cloud Performance and Dependability: Taxonomy, Metric Design, and Emerging Challenges". *ACM Transactions on Modeling and Performance*

Evaluation of Computing Systems, 3(4). ACM: New York, NY, USA, 19:1–19:36 (cited on p. 322).

Herbst, N. R., Kounev, S., and Reussner, R. (2013). "Elasticity in Cloud Computing: What it is, and What it is Not". In: *Proceedings of the 10th International Conference on Autonomic Computing (ICAC 2013)*. (San Jose, CA, USA). USENIX, pp. 23–27 (cited on p. 320).

Herbst, N. R., Kounev, S., Weber, A., and Groenda, H. (2015). "BUNGEE: An Elasticity Benchmark for Self-adaptive IaaS Cloud Environments". In: *Proceedings of the 10th International Symposium on Software Engineering for Adaptive and Self-Managing Systems (SEAMS 2015)*. (Florence, Italy). IEEE: Piscataway, NJ, USA, pp. 46–56 (cited on p. 330).

Herbst, N. R., Krebs, R., Oikonomou, G., Kousiouris, G., Evangelinou, A., Iosup, A., and Kounev, S. (2016). *Ready for Rain? A View from SPEC Research on the Future of Cloud Metrics*. Tech. rep. SPEC-RG-2016-01. Gainesville, VA, USA: SPEC RG—Cloud Working Group, Standard Performance Evaluation Corporation (SPEC) (cited on p. 322).

Islam, S., Lee, K., Fekete, A., and Liu, A. (2012). "How a Consumer Can Measure Elasticity for Cloud Platforms". In: *Proceedings of the 3rd ACM/SPEC International Conference on Performance Engineering (ICPE 2012)*. (Boston, MA, USA). ACM: New York, NY, USA, pp. 85–96 (cited on p. 319).

Janert, P. (2013). *Feedback Control for Computer Systems*. O'Reilly and Associates: Sebastopol, California (cited on p. 325).

Jennings, B. and Stadler, R. (2015). "Resource Management in Clouds: Survey and Research Challenges". *Journal of Network and Systems Management*, 23(3). Springer US: New York, NY, USA, pp. 567–619 (cited on p. 319).

Jogalekar, P. and Woodside, M. (2000). "Evaluating the Scalability of Distributed Systems". *IEEE Transactions on Parallel and Distributed Systems*, 11(6), pp. 589–603 (cited on p. 320).

Lorido-Botran, T., Miguel-Alonso, J., and Lozano, J. A. (2014). "A Review of Auto-scaling Techniques for Elastic Applications in Cloud Environments". *Journal of Grid Computing*, 12(4). Springer Netherlands: Amsterdam, The Netherlands, pp. 559–592 (cited on p. 319).

Papadopoulos, A. V., Versluis, L., Bauer, A., Herbst, N. R., Kistowski, J. von, Ali-Eldin, A., Abad, C., Amaral, J. N., Tuma, P., and Iosup, A. (2019a). "Methodological Principles for Reproducible Performance Evaluation in Cloud Computing". *IEEE Transactions on Software Engineering*. IEEE Computer Society: Washington, DC, USA (cited on p. 333).

– (2019b). *Methodological Principles for Reproducible Performance Evaluation in Cloud Computing - A SPEC Research Technical Report*. Tech. rep. SPEC-RG-2019-04. Gainesville, VA, USA: SPEC RG—Cloud Working Group, Standard Performance Evaluation Corporation (SPEC) (cited on p. 333).

Chapter 16
Performance Isolation

Rouven Krebs and Samuel Kounev

Cloud computing enables resource sharing at different levels of a data center infrastructure. Hardware and software resources in a data center can be shared based on server virtualization, application containerization, or multi-tenant software architectures.

Multi-tenancy is an approach to share one application instance among multiple customers by providing each of them with a dedicated view. Tenants expect to be isolated in terms of the application performance they observe; therefore, a provider's inability to offer performance guarantees can be a major obstacle for potential cloud customers. A *tenant* is a group of users sharing the same view onto an application. This view includes the data they access, the application configuration, the user management, application-specific functionality, and related non-functional properties. Usually, the tenants are members of different legal entities. This comes with restrictions (e.g., concerning data security and privacy). In this chapter, multi-tenancy is understood as an approach to share an application instance between multiple tenants by providing every tenant with a dedicated share of the instance isolated from other shares with regard to performance, appearance, configuration, user management, and data privacy (Krebs et al., 2012). Some publications use a broader definition of the term multi-tenancy; however, in this chapter, we focus on the case of shared application instances as described above.

Hypervisors and virtual machines provide another way of sharing resources between customers. In contrast to multi-tenant applications, a hypervisor runs multiple virtual machines (VMs) on the same hardware. By leveraging virtualization technology, the VMs can run in parallel and share the underlying physical resources. This technology is used to provide multiple customers access to Software-as-a-Service (SaaS) offerings whereby several instances of an application are used to serve user requests. Furthermore, virtualization is an enabling technology for Infrastructure-as-a-Service (IaaS) where customers rent VMs from cloud providers.

Despite the use of shared resources, users expect to have the feeling of control over their own and separate environment, with their own Service-Level Agreements (SLAs) and regulations as known from private data centers, both in virtualized and multi-tenant application scenarios. In addition, they expect to be *isolated* from other customers with regard to functional and non-functional aspects. However, due to the sharing of resources, performance-related issues may appear when a customer

S. Kounev et al., *Systems Benchmarking*, https://doi.org/10.1007/978-3-030-41705-5_16

sends a high number of requests generating load on the system. This is because the load generated by one customer competes for resources also used by others. Especially in the cloud context, where resources are shared intensively among customers, it is not easy to maintain reliable performance. This is a serious obstacle for cloud customers, especially for users of multi-tenant applications.

This chapter presents metrics to quantify the degree of performance isolation a system provides. The metrics are based on Krebs et al. (2014), Krebs (2015), and Herbst, Bauer, et al. (2018), and they have been endorsed by the SPEC Research Group (Herbst, Krebs, et al., 2016). In an ideal case, one should be able to measure performance isolation externally, that is, by running benchmarks from the outside and treating the system as a black box. This enables their use for a broad set of applications given that no internal knowledge of the system is required. The metrics and the thought process to create them serve as a practical example illustrating the metric attributes and principles introduced in Chapter 3.

The metrics presented in this chapter are applicable for use in performance benchmarks that measure the performance without requiring internal knowledge. They are preferable in situations where different request sources use the functions of a shared system with a similar call probability and demand per request but with a different load intensity. These characteristics are typical for multi-tenant applications but can also occur in other shared resource systems. This chapter introduces the metrics and provides a case study showing how they can be used in a real-life environment.

16.1 Definition of Performance Isolation

To avoid distrust in a multi-tenant application provider, it is necessary to ensure fair behavior of the system with respect to its different tenants. It is assumed that each tenant is assigned a *quota* that specifies the maximum load the tenant is allowed to place on the system, for example, the maximum number of service requests that can be sent per second. In this chapter, the following definition of *fairness* is used:

Definition 16.1 (Fairness) A system is considered to be *fair* if all of the following conditions are met:

1. Tenants working within their assigned quotas must not suffer performance degradation due to other tenants exceeding their quotas.
2. Tenants exceeding their quotas may suffer performance degradation; tenants exceeding their quotas more should suffer higher performance degradation than tenants exceeding their quotas less.
3. Tenants exceeding their quotas may suffer performance degradation only if other tenants that comply with their quotas would otherwise be affected.

The term *quota* refers to the amount of workload a tenant is allowed to execute (e.g., number of user requests or transactions per second).

Tenants working within their quotas will be referred to as *abiding tenants*, whereas tenants that exceed their quotas will be referred to as *disruptive tenants*. The term *guarantee* refers to the negotiated performance level as part of SLAs with the provider. The main focus of this chapter is on the first fairness criterion, which is achieved by performance isolation.

Definition 16.2 (Performance Isolation) Performance isolation is the ability of a system to ensure that tenants working within their assigned quotas (i.e., abiding tenants) will not suffer performance degradation due to other tenants exceeding their quotas (i.e., disruptive tenants).

A system is usually expected to be somewhere in between being completely performance isolated and non-isolated. A system where the influence of a tenant on other tenants is lower is considered to provide a better performance isolation compared to a system where the influence is higher.

SLAs are of major importance for shared services. Therefore, it may be useful to reflect this in the previous definitions. This would imply that the performance of tenants working within their quotas is allowed to be reduced as long as the guaranteed level of performance is maintained. The latter is essential in order to allow overcommitment of resources. Note that, in a non-isolated system, the guaranteed performance for abiding tenants eventually will be violated if the disruptive tenants continue to increase their workload. In contrast, an isolated system will maintain the guaranteed performance independent of the disruptive tenants' workload.

16.2 Performance Isolation Metrics

The performance isolation metrics we present in this chapter are not necessarily coupled to performance and they do not express the system's capability to accomplish useful work. They rather express the influence a tenant has on the ability of another tenant to accomplish useful work.

Existing benchmarks and metrics in the field of shared resources and cloud computing focus on specific aspects like database performance (Cooper et al., 2010). Some works discuss metrics for cloud features like elasticity (Herbst, Kounev, et al., 2013; Islam et al., 2012; Kupperberg et al., 2011), as discussed in Chapter 15, or performance variability (Iosup, Ostermann, et al., 2011; Schad et al., 2010). Performance variability characterizes the changes in performance over time while the workload is assumed to be constant. However, these changes are not set in relation to the workload induced by others and thus a new approach is required.

In the following, the goals and requirements for the new isolation metrics are discussed. After that, the definitions of the metrics are presented. A case study measuring performance isolation in virtualized environments serves as an example showing the metrics in action. Based on the practical experiences from the case study, we then perform a final assessment of the usability of the metrics before concluding this chapter.

16.2.1 Metrics Goals and Requirements

To improve an existing performance isolation mechanism, application developers need isolation metrics in order to compare different variants of an isolation approach. For stakeholders involved in operations, the impact an increasing workload has on other tenants can be of interest in order to define SLAs or to manage the system's capacity.

As per our definition, a system is performance isolated if each tenant working within his quota is not negatively affected in terms of performance when other tenants increase their workloads beyond their quotas. A decreased performance for the tenants exceeding their quotas is fair with regard to the second fairness property (see Section 16.1). Moreover, as mentioned earlier, it is possible to link the definition of performance isolation to the assumed performance guarantees using SLAs. As a result, a decreased performance for tenants working within their quotas would be acceptable as long as it is within their SLA-defined guarantees. These aspects have to be reflected by performance isolation metrics.

The metrics should be designed to support answering the following questions:

Q1 How much can a tenant's workload influence the performance of other tenants?
Q2 How much potential exists for improving a system's performance isolation?
Q3 Which performance isolation technique is better?

Besides these metric-specific requirements, several general quality attributes and criteria for good metrics were introduced in Chapter 3 (Section 3.4.2): *ease of measurement, repeatability, reliability, linearity, consistency*, and *independence*.

For the measurement of performance isolation, one has to distinguish between groups of *disruptive* and *abiding* tenants as defined in Section 16.1. The presented metrics are based on the influence of the disruptive tenants on the abiding tenants. Thus, the influence on one group as a function of the workload of the other group must be evaluated. This is a major difference to traditional performance benchmarking. For the definition of the metrics, a set of symbols is defined in Table 16.1.

The metrics presented in the rest of this chapter can be applied to quantify isolation with respect to any measurable QoS-related property of a system that is shared between different entities. As such, the metrics are not limited to performance isolation in multi-tenant applications, although the latter are used as an example in this chapter.

Assume a non-isolated system and the situation illustrated in Figure 16.1 where disruptive tenants increase their workload over time. Assuming that the system is not isolated, the response time for the abiding tenants and their users would increase in the same way as if these users would belong to the disruptive tenants.

Table 16.1: Overview of variables and symbols for performance isolation metrics

Symbol	Meaning
D	Set of disruptive tenants exceeding their quotas (i.e., tenants inducing more than the allowed maximum requests per second); in the context of measuring performance isolation, we assume that $|D| > 0$
A	Set of abiding tenants not exceeding their quotas (i.e., tenants inducing less than the allowed maximum requests per second); in the context of measuring performance isolation, we assume that $|A| > 0$
t	A tenant in the system; we assume that $t \in D$ or $t \in A$
w_t	The workload caused by tenant t represented as a numeric value in $\mathbb{R}_0^+$; the value is considered to increase with higher loads on the system (e.g., request rate or job size); $w_t \in W$
W	The total system workload as a set of the workloads induced by all individual tenants
$z_t(W)$	A numeric value describing the Quality-of-Service (QoS) (e.g., request response time) provided to tenant t; the individual QoS a tenant observes depends on the aggregate workload W of all tenants; QoS metrics with lower values of $z_t(W)$ correspond to better QoS (e.g., faster response time); $z_t : W \to \mathbb{R}_0^+$
I	The degree of isolation provided by the system; an index is added to distinguish different types of isolation metrics (the various indices are introduced later; a numeric suffix to the index is used in some places to express the load level under which the isolation is measured)

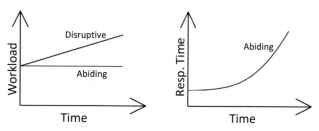

Fig. 16.1: Influence of disruptive tenants on the response time of abiding tenants in a non-isolated system

16.2.2 QoS-Impact-Based Isolation Metrics

QoS-impact-based isolation metrics depend on at least two measurements: First, the observed QoS for every abiding tenant $t \in A$ at an application-wide reference workload W_{ref}; second, the QoS for every abiding tenant $t \in A$ at a modified workload W_{disr} where a subset of the tenants have increased their load to challenge the system's isolation mechanisms. W_{ref} and W_{disr} are composed of the aggregate workload of the same set of tenants, that is, the union of A and D. In W_{disr}, the workload of the disruptive tenants is increased.

The relative difference in the QoS for abiding tenants at the reference workload compared to the disruptive tenant workload can be computed as

$$\Delta z_A = \frac{\sum\limits_{t \in A} \left[z_t(W_{disr}) - z_t(W_{ref}) \right]}{\sum\limits_{t \in A} z_t(W_{ref})}. \tag{16.1}$$

The relative difference of the load induced by the two workloads is given by

$$\Delta w = \frac{\sum\limits_{w_t \in W_{disr}} w_t - \sum\limits_{w_t \in W_{ref}} w_t}{\sum\limits_{w_t \in W_{ref}} w_t}. \tag{16.2}$$

Based on these two quantities, the influence of the increased workload on the QoS of the abiding tenants is expressed as follows:

$$I_{QoS} := \frac{\Delta z_A}{\Delta w}. \tag{16.3}$$

A low value of this metric represents a good isolation, as the impact on the QoS of abiding tenants in relation to the increased workload is low. If the value is 0, the isolation is perfect. Accordingly, a high value of the metric indicates a bad isolation of the system. In principle, the upper bound of the metric is unlimited. A negative value may occur if a mechanism reduces the performance of the disruptive tenants more than expected, thus providing the abiding tenants an even better performance.

The metric provides a result for two specified workloads (W_{ref} and W_{disr}), and thus the selection of the workloads plays an important role. However, only one measurement for a given workload tuple (W_{ref}, W_{disr}) is not sufficient if the exact workloads of interest are unknown or variable. To address this, one can consider the arithmetic mean of I_{QoS} for m different disruptive tenant workloads as follows:

$$I_{avg} := \frac{\sum\limits_{i=1}^{m} I_{QoS_m}}{m}. \tag{16.4}$$

This metric provides an average isolation value for the entire considered space of workloads and provides one representative numeric value. The disruptive tenant workload is increased in equidistant steps within a lower and upper bound. However, the curve's shape is not reflected in the average value and it may thus lead to misleading results for some ranges of disruptive tenant workload.

It is conceivable that a provider might be interested in the relative difference of disruptive tenant workload Δw at which abiding tenants receive a predefined proportion Δz_A of the promised QoS. This is conceptually similar to the already described metrics and could be used to extend them with further metrics.

16.2.3 Workload-Ratio-Based Isolation Metrics

The metrics we introduce in the following are not directly associated with the QoS impact resulting from an increased workload of disruptive tenants. Instead, the idea is to compensate for the increased workload of disruptive tenants by decreasing the workload of the abiding ones such that the QoS for abiding tenants can remain unaffected. Figure 16.2 illustrates this. For simplicity, we assume that in a non-isolated system, resources are equally shared among the tenants; therefore, the response time would maintain a constant value if abiding tenants decrease their workload by the same amount as the amount by which disruptive tenants increase theirs. The better the performance isolation, the less abiding tenants would have to reduce their workload. Naturally, this is only possible with the support of the abiding tenants and such a behavior would not be expected in productive systems. Thus, these metrics are planned to be applied in benchmarks with artificial workloads where a load driver simulates the tenants and can be programmed to follow the described behavior.

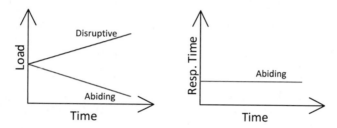

Fig. 16.2: Influence of disruptive tenants when abiding tenants adapt their workload accordingly

In the following, the idea is described in more detail. We start by measuring the isolation behavior of a non-isolated system by continuously increasing the disruptive tenant workload W_d. In such a situation, $z_t(W)$ remains unaffected if the workload of the abiding tenants W_a is adjusted accordingly to compensate for the increase in the disruptive tenant workload.

The x-axis in Figure 16.3 shows the amount of workload W_d caused by the disruptive tenants, whereas the y-axis shows the amount of the workload W_a caused by the abiding tenants. The *Non-Isolated* line depicts how W_a has to decrease in order to maintain the same QoS as in the beginning. In a non-isolated system this function decreases linearly; that is, for every additional unit of work added to the disruptive tenant workload, one has to remove the same amount from the abiding tenant workload. In a perfectly isolated system, the increased disruptive tenant workload W_d would have no influence on $z_t(W)$ for all $t \in A$. Thus, W_a would be constant in this case as reflected by the *Isolated* line in the figure. The *Isolated* and *Non-Isolated* lines provide exact upper and lower bounds, which correspond to a perfectly isolated and a non-isolated system, respectively. Figure 16.3 shows some important data points, which are described in Table 16.2.

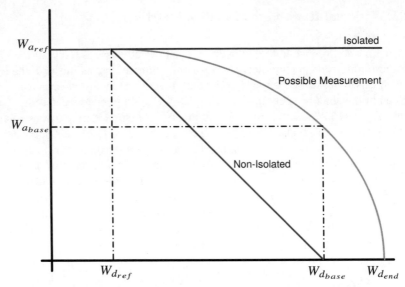

Fig. 16.3: Fictitious isolation curve including upper and lower bounds

Table 16.2: Description of relevant data points in Figure 16.3

Symbol	Meaning
W_d	The total workload induced by the disruptive tenants; $W_d = \sum\limits_{t \in D} w_t$
$W_{d_{base}}$	The level of the disruptive tenant workload at which the abiding tenant workload in a non-isolated system must be reduced to 0 in order to avoid SLA violations
$W_{d_{end}}$	The level of the disruptive tenant workload at which the abiding tenant workload in the system under test (SUT) must be reduced to 0 in order to avoid SLA violations
$W_{d_{ref}}$	The value of the disruptive tenant workload at the reference point in the SUT with respect to which the degree of isolation is quantified; it is defined as the disruptive tenant workload at which, in a non-isolated system, the abiding tenant workload would have to start being reduced to avoid SLA violations
W_a	The total workload induced by the abiding tenants; $W_a = \sum\limits_{t \in A} w_t$
$W_{a_{ref}}$	The value of the abiding tenant workload at the reference point $W_{d_{ref}}$ in the SUT; $W_{a_{ref}} = W_{d_{base}} - W_{d_{ref}}$
$W_{a_{base}}$	The value of the abiding tenant workload corresponding to $W_{d_{base}}$ in the SUT

Based on this approach, several metrics are defined in the following. As discussed before, the workload scenarios play an important role and it may therefore be necessary to consider multiple different scenarios.

16.2.3.1 Metrics Based on Edge Points

The edge points $W_{d_{end}}$, $W_{d_{base}}$, $W_{a_{ref}}$, and $W_{a_{base}}$ in Figure 16.3 provide several ways to define an isolation metric by themselves. I_{end} is a metric derived from the point at which the workloads of abiding tenants have to be reduced to 0 to compensate for the disruptive tenant workload. The metric describes a relationship between $W_{d_{end}}$ and $W_{a_{ref}}$. Due to the discussed relationship of the workloads in a non-isolated system and the definition of the various points, the condition $W_{a_{ref}} = W_{d_{base}} - W_{d_{ref}}$ holds. This relation helps to simplify the formulas. With Figure 16.3 in mind, the metric I_{end} is defined as follows:

$$I_{end} := \frac{W_{d_{end}} - W_{d_{base}}}{W_{a_{ref}}}. \tag{16.5}$$

A value of 0 for I_{end} reflects a non-isolated system. Higher values reflect better isolated systems. A value of 1 is interpreted as being twice as good as a non-isolated system. In case of a perfectly isolated system, the metric value tends to infinity. This makes it hard to interpret the value of the metric for a given system. A negative value may occur if, for some reason, the performance of the abiding tenants is reduced more than the disruptive tenant workload is increased. This may happen in case the system runs into an overloaded and trashing state.

Another approach to define an isolation metric uses $W_{a_{base}}$ as a reference. Setting this value and $W_{a_{ref}}$ in relation results in the following isolation metric having a value in the interval [0, 1]:

$$I_{base} := \frac{W_{a_{base}}}{W_{a_{ref}}}. \tag{16.6}$$

A value of 0 for I_{base} reflects a non-isolated system, while a value of 1 corresponds to perfect isolation. Both metrics have some drawbacks resulting from the fact that they do not take the curve's form into account. Consider a system that behaves like a perfectly isolated system until a short distance from $W_{d_{base}}$ and then suddenly drops to $W_a = 0$. In such a system, both metrics would have the same value as for a completely non-isolated system, which obviously is unfair in this case. Moreover, a well-isolated system requires a very high disruptive tenant workload before W_a drops to 0, which makes it hard to measure the metric in an experimental environment. I_{base} has some further disadvantages given that it is only representative for the behavior of the system within the range between $W_{d_{ref}}$ and $W_{d_{base}}$. Given that the metric does not reflect what happens after $W_{d_{base}}$, it may lead to misleading results in the case of well-isolated systems for which the respective $W_{d_{end}}$ points differ significantly.

For systems that exhibit a linear degradation of the abiding tenant workload, it is also possible to use isolation metrics based on the angle between the observed abiding tenant workload's line segment and the line segment representing a non-isolated system. However, typically, a linear behavior cannot be assumed.

16.2.3.2 Metrics Based on Integrals

Next, we define two metrics addressing the discussed disadvantages of the above metrics. They are based on the area under the curve derived for the measured system $A_{measured}$ set in relation to the area under the curve corresponding to a non-isolated system $A_{non-isolated}$. The area under the curve corresponding to a non-isolated system is calculated as $W_{a_{ref}}^2/2$.

Integral Limited to $W_{d_{base}}$ The first metric $I_{intBase}$ represents the isolation as the ratio of $A_{measured}$ and $A_{non-isolated}$ within the interval $[W_{d_{ref}}, W_{d_{base}}]$. $f_m : W_d \rightarrow W_a$ is defined as a function that returns the residual workload for the abiding tenants based on the workload of the disruptive tenants. Based on this function, we define the metric $I_{intBase}$ as follows:

$$I_{intBase} := \frac{\left(\int_{W_{d_{ref}}}^{W_{d_{base}}} f_m(W_d)dW_d \right) - W_{a_{ref}}^2/2}{W_{a_{ref}}^2/2}. \tag{16.7}$$

$I_{intBase}$ has a value of 0 in case the system is not isolated and a value of 1 if the system is perfectly isolated within the interval $[W_{d_{ref}}, W_{d_{base}}]$. The metric's major advantage is that it helps to set the system directly in relation to an isolated and non-isolated system. This metric, again, has the drawback that it only captures the system behavior within $[W_{d_{ref}}, W_{d_{base}}]$. Again, a negative value may occur if, for some reason, the performance of the abiding tenants is reduced to a greater degree than the disruptive tenant workload is increased.

Integral Without Predefined Intervals In a well-isolated system, it would be of interest to measure the system behavior beyond the point $W_{d_{base}}$. The following metric $I_{intFree}$ allows the use of any predefined artificial upper bound $p_{end} > W_{d_{base}}$ representing the highest value of W_d that was measured in the SUT. The metric is defined as follows:

$$I_{intFree} := \frac{\left(\int_{W_{d_{ref}}}^{p_{end}} f_m(W_d)dW_d \right) - W_{a_{ref}}^2/2}{W_{a_{ref}} \cdot (p_{end} - W_{d_{ref}}) - W_{a_{ref}}^2/2}. \tag{16.8}$$

This metric quantifies the degree of isolation provided by the system for a specified maximum level of injected disruptive tenant workload p_{end}. A value of 1 represents a perfect isolation; a value of 0 represents a non-isolated system. Negative values for $I_{intFree}$ have the same interpretation as negative values for $I_{intBase}$.

16.2.4 Further Isolation Quality Aspects

Although the metrics described in Sections 16.2.2 and 16.2.3 allow one to quantify isolation, they do not adequately describe the behavior of a system over time. Several methods for performance isolation employ an adaptive approach that dynamically adapts the system configuration to ensure isolation often based on a closed control loop—see, for example, Krebs, Spinner, et al. (2014). Consequently, one can assume the existence of situations where the system requires a certain amount of time to adapt to changes in the workload. Therefore, two additional metrics allowing one to quantify the dynamic aspects of performance isolation mechanisms are discussed.

Some commonly discussed issues in the context of system control theory in the literature are *stability/oscillation*, *settling time/performance*, and *accuracy/steady-state error* (Janert, 2013, pp. 19–21). In our context, the accuracy (steady-state error) is already covered by the metrics in Sections 16.2.2 and 16.2.3. The other two issues are discussed in the following two sections.

16.2.4.1 Settling Time

The settling time describes the time a system needs to achieve an output value within a defined error range after a sudden change in input levels. A system with a faster settling time is generally considered to be better.

Ideally, a Dirac impulse would be used for the input. In our context, the input value is the workload of the tenants, whereas the output value is the observed value of the QoS metric under investigation (e.g., response time). Naturally, it is not possible to generate a Dirac impulse for such a system; therefore, a step function must be used. However, a significant increase of the workload to a constant value in a very short time may not be feasible. Therefore, the start event for measuring the settling time is defined as the point in time at which the workload again achieves stability. An observation of the QoS metric reaching a stable value can then be used as the trigger to stop the measurement of the settling time. In these measurements, a certain error is acceptable. It is possible to relate the start and stop events to the QoS guarantee provided to a tenant. In this case, the start event is triggered if the observed QoS is worse than the guarantee, whereas the end event is triggered when it meets the guarantee again.

However, a different approach would be required should the considered QoS metric not be related to any QoS guarantees. The proposed metric considers the average response time of the sample of next m to n observations in the future and compares it with the current one. The values of m and n should be selected in a way to fulfill the following conditions: (1) there should be enough sample data in the floating window to compute a stable average value; (2) m should be far enough in the future to ensure that the average value is already stable before the impulse is triggered; and (3) in cases of an online calculation, m should not be too far in the future in order to be able to obtain a timely result for the metric.[1] If the load increases, one can expect a higher response time, which will decrease as the method tries to compensate this problem. At some point in time, this value will be close to the computed average or even cross this line, which marks the end event.

Figure 16.4a,b shows an example throughput over time for an abiding tenant. The two vertical lines mark the beginning and the end of the time span where the workload changed. Note that the workload-related lines are based on the amount of simulated users in the benchmark, and it takes a few seconds to start them. The throughput itself needs even longer before adapting to the new workload.

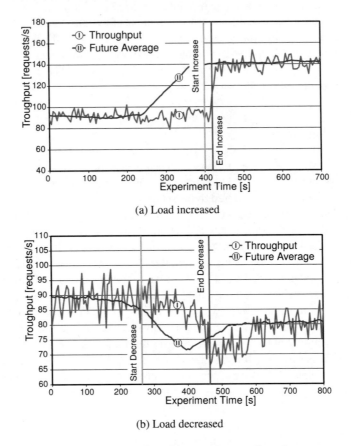

(a) Load increased

(b) Load decreased

Fig. 16.4: Examples of measuring settling times

---

[1] Note that in the case of offline analysis with just one single impulse (e.g., benchmarking), the selection of m and n is less important and the threshold may even be computed by a separate measurement run.

Metrics similar to settling time were already used in the past for adaptive IT systems in the context of QoS metrics. One example is the CloudScale consortium (Brataas, 2014), which uses a metric referred to as MTTQR to describe the time an elastic system needs to become SLA-compliant after the occurrence of an SLA violation. Although MTTQR focuses on different scenarios, it is comparable to the interpretation of settling time presented here.

16.2.4.2 Oscillation

Oscillation can happen if feedback from the system is used to adapt it to changing scenarios. Figure 16.5 shows an example of oscillating throughput for abiding tenants.

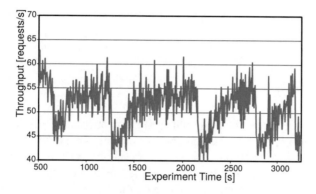

Fig. 16.5: Example of oscillation

Oscillation is the repetitive variation of the system between two or more different states. It is a common phenomenon in control theory (Janert, 2013, pp. 19–21). For this reason, controllers are usually designed to damp the oscillation and ensure that the amplitude converges to zero. If this is the case, the *settling time* is a useful metric. Otherwise, the controller maintains an unstable state.

Discrete systems with random inputs, like an interactive web application, can be in a steady state concerning the average values of QoS metrics, while the input is still subject to random processes. Furthermore, in closed systems, the output may influence the input. This increases the risk that the isolation method never converges to a steady state. The amplitude and the frequency of resulting oscillations are indicators to compare different methods. For the purpose of performance isolation mechanisms, the amplitude would be based on the average relative change of the QoS metric of interest. An average value for all tenants can be considered. Although this seems intuitively correct, such a metric would lack in objectivity. This is because in real systems, oscillation is mixed with noise in the measurements and a clear oscillation might not be visible at all. Furthermore, if the system reacts very fast to minor and possibly random changes, no repeatable pattern may occur. Thus, it is likely that a precise identification of the highest and lowest point of the oscillation is not possible. Consequently, it may be difficult to clearly identify patterns caused by the active control mechanisms as opposed to normal random processes. Thus, a human would have to define which signals are relevant and which are not, raising the question of objectivity and reliability of the metric. Furthermore, the distribution of the measured data would be unknown and potentially different for different isolation mechanisms.

Therefore, we consider the length of the interval between the 25% and 75% percentiles set in relation to the observed arithmetic mean or median value of the QoS metric of interest. In case of high oscillation or high variability of the metric, the length of the interval would be higher in comparison to scenarios with low oscillation. This approach does not rely on the assessment of a human. The drawback is that very strong noise may be classified wrongly as oscillation. This metric is closely related to an existing approach for quantifying performance variability (Iosup, Yigitbasi, et al., 2011).

16.3 Case Study

We now present a case study—the initial version of which was published in Krebs et al. (2014)—showing the metrics in action by applying them to virtualization-based systems. The case study demonstrates the applicability of the metrics in real-life environments and provides some insights on the isolation capabilities of the widely used hypervisor Xen. Furthermore, it is an example of how the metrics can be employed by system operators to make decisions in a deployment scenario.

Beside multi-tenancy, the sharing of hardware resources by running several operating systems on the same physical host is a widely adopted technology providing the foundation for IaaS clouds. Xen[2] is a widely used hypervisor for Linux environments enabling resource sharing at the hardware level. The goal of the case study we present in this section is to stress Xen in order to evaluate its performance isolation capabilities. More precisely, we quantify the degree of isolation for various Xen configurations and deployments based on a black-box measurement approach employing the isolation metrics introduced in the previous section. We deploy several instances of the TPC-W benchmark on different virtual machines (VMs) hosted by one Xen hypervisor and measure how they influence each other. The case study demonstrates the wide range of scenarios supported by the metrics and how the latter can be used to reason about the isolation capabilities of IaaS clouds running on Xen.

In the following, we describe some details on the Xen hypervisor, the chosen benchmark, and the system landscape we consider in our case study. We then present and discuss the evaluation results.

---

[2] Xen hypervisor: https://xenproject.org

16.3.1 Xen Hypervisor

A hypervisor is a software enabling the execution of several virtual machines (VM) as guests on one physical host. Xen is one of the most popular hypervisors for Linux environments. The operating systems installed within VMs are decoupled from each other and have no permission for administrative tasks on the hardware or the hypervisor's configuration. In order to configure the hypervisor and to execute administrative tasks, the first VM started in Xen (referred to as *domain-0* or *dom0*) has special privileges. Furthermore, dom0 provides a driver abstraction for the different guest systems. The drivers in Xen are divided into two parts. The drivers actually accessing the hardware are installed in dom0; the guest systems (referred to as *domU* domains) communicate with dom0 to access the hardware. Consequently, dom0 might become a bottleneck for various activities. Especially I/O-intensive tasks are known to produce high overhead in dom0; thus, the independent guest VMs are likely to influence each other when executing such tasks. Such a behavior was observed by Huber et al. (2011) and Gupta et al. (2006). By default, VMs have access to all existing resources on the host. To increase performance and isolation, it is possible to pin a core exclusively to a domain. It is worth mentioning that dom0 usually does not host any services for end users due to its special administrative role.

16.3.2 TPC-W Benchmark

The TPC-W benchmark was introduced in Chapter 9, Section 9.3.3. In the specific setup of this chapter, TPC-W's bookshop consists of a Java Servlet-based application and an SQL database. Instead of using the usual performance metric, which is the number of web interactions processed per second, we consider the average response time of the requests for TPC-W's three profiles. The load can be varied by the amount of emulated browsers (EB) accessing the system. One EB simulates one user calling various web transactions in a closed workload. Based on the benchmark's heavy I/O demands, we expect to observe the influence of the different VMs on each other.

16.3.3 Experimental Environment

The experimental environment in our case study comprises two servers with two physical quad core CPUs (2,133 MHz with two threads per core) and 16 GB of main memory. On both servers, Xen 4.1 is installed and Suse Linux Enterprise Server (SLES) 11 SP2 is used as a guest operating system. The servers are connected with a 1 Gbit Ethernet link. One server hosts the load driver for the TPC-W benchmark. The various domains of the second server are described below as part of the scenario-specific configuration. The database schema is refreshed before every measurement and filled with 100,000 items and 300,000 customers.

In total, we study three different configuration scenarios in our case study. In the *pinned* scenario, the server hosts four guest systems (dom1, dom2, dom3, dom4) and dom0. Every domU domain has a fixed memory allocation of 3,096 MB and hosts a MySQL 5.0 database and an SAP-specific customized Tomcat web server. The various domains were pinned exclusively to the existing cores. Thus, no competition for the same CPU resources was possible. Based on this run-time environment, four separate instances of the TPC-W bookshop application were deployed.

In the *unpinned* scenario, all domU domains and dom0 were not pinned to a specific CPU and were thus free to use all available hardware resources. Xen's credit scheduler was chosen to allocate resources to the various domains.

In addition to this, we investigated an *unpinned two-tier* scenario, which also does not have a fixed CPU pinning and likewise uses the Xen credit scheduler. However, the database and the application server in this case were deployed in separate domains. Every domU domain with an application server has a fixed memory allocation of 2,024 MB and the database domain uses 1,024 MB. This memory setup was chosen because of the small database size.

Table 16.3 shows the values we used to define the reference and disruptive tenant workloads for the three scenarios. The number of emulated browsers (EBs) at the maximum aggregated throughput of all domains is presented in the second column; the corresponding throughput per domain and the average response time are listed next. The last column shows the disruptive domain's amount of EBs at which we observed a high proportion of failed requests. In the unpinned two-tier scenario, we observed different values for the QoS-impact-based and workload-ratio-based metrics. The relevant QoS for our analysis is the average response time of the tenants. The additional information is shown only for the sake of better system understanding.

Table 16.3: Scenario setup and configuration

Scenario	EBs per domU	Total throughput	Throughput per domU	Avg. resp. time	Max. load disruptive
Pinned	3,000	1,195 r/s	299	1,104 ms	15,000
Unpinned	1,600	721 r/s	180	843 ms	13,500
Unpinned two-tier	1,300	617 r/s	154	833 ms	8,000 (QoS-based), 11,050 (ratio-based)

In the pinned scenario, the highest difference in throughput for one domain compared to the mean was around 4.5%, and the highest difference in response time was around 6.5%. In the unpinned scenario, we observed 2.2% (one-tier) and 2.7% (two-tier) difference in throughput. The difference in response time was at 8.2% (one-tier) and 9.4% (two-tier).

As a consequence of these observations p_{end} is set to 15,000 for the pinned scenario and to 13,500 for the unpinned. In the unpinned two-tier scenario, we had to set p_{end} to 11,050 and stop our test for the I_{QoS} metrics at 8,000 users. It is worth mentioning that in both unpinned scenarios, p_{end} is very close to nine times the load of the maximum throughput for one domain.

In all presented examples, one tenant has been used to generate the disruptive load. All other tenants have been classified as abiding tenants.

16.3.4 Performance Isolation Metrics in Action

We now provide an overview of the measurement results and the observed isolation metrics. Figure 16.6 combines the results for both unpinned scenarios based on normalized values for the abiding and disruptive tenant workloads. Table 16.4 presents the QoS-impact-based metrics based on the same values for Δw. Thus, the results provide a comparable view for the two deployments.

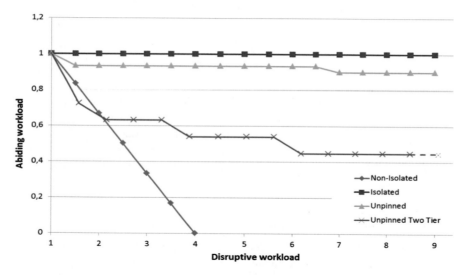

Fig. 16.6: Normalized reduction of abiding tenant workload in the unpinned and the unpinned two-tier scenario

Table 16.4 contains the values of I_{QoS} for all three scenarios. The first column of Table 16.4 shows the scenario, the second column shows the number of users in the disruptive domain, and the third column shows the average response time of all abiding domains followed by the results for Δw, Δz, I_{QoS}, and I_{avg}. For the pinned scenario, we collected only one measurement due to the very good isolation. The I_{avg} values were calculated based on interpolation of the depicted measurements in the table as supporting points including the reference workload ($\Delta w = 0$ with $\Delta z = 0$).

For the pinned scenario, we assume a behavior of the isolation between $\Delta w = 0$ and $\Delta w = 1$.

Table 16.4: Results of I_{QoS} in the different scenarios

Scenario	Disruptive load	Response time	Δw	Δz	I_{QoS}	I_{avg}
Pinned	15,000	1,317 ms	1.00	0.19	0.19	0.10
Unpinned	3,200	927 ms	0.25	0.10	0.40	
	4,800	942 ms	0.50	0.12	0.24	0.21
	7,500	914 ms	0.92	0.09	0.09	
	10,000	1,173 ms	1.31	0.39	0.30	
Unpinned two-tier	3,000	1,011 ms	0.33	0.21	0.64	
	4,400	3,784 ms	0.60	3.54	5.90	3.06
	6,750	4,354 ms	1.05	4.22	4.02	

16.3.4.1 Pinned Scenario

Overall, this scenario presented a nearly perfect isolation throughout the whole range. The I_{QoS} metric presented in Table 16.4 at a disruptive tenant workload of 15,000 users was below 0.2 and the I_{avg} resulted in 0.1. The workload-ratio-based metric decreased for the abiding tenant workload only once at 12,000 disruptive tenant users. The related metrics $I_{intFree15000}$ and $I_{intBase}$ resulted in a value slightly below 1.

16.3.4.2 Unpinned Scenario

For the metrics based on the QoS impact, we determined the isolation at various disruptive tenant workloads shown in Table 16.4. We observed two significant characteristics. The first one is the increasing response time when the disruptive tenant workload is set to 3,200 users. The second one is the increasing response time at 10,000 users. Accordingly, the isolation becomes better between 3,200 users and 10,000 users. This is due to the widely stable response times at increasing load, which changes the ratio of $\Delta z/\Delta w$. On average, the isolation I_{avg} is 0.21.

Figure 16.6 presents the total abiding tenant workload W_a based on the disruptive tenant users. Similar to the I_{QoS}-based results, two significant points can be observed at the same position. In both cases, W_a decreased because of an increasing response time of the abiding tenants. At a disruptive tenant workload of 13,500 users (corresponding to 9 in the figure), the disruptive domain failed to successfully handle incoming requests. Therefore, the results are not valid for higher disruptive tenant workloads. The overall isolation values are $I_{intFree13500} = 0.89$ and $I_{intBase} = 0.86$.

16.3.4.3 Unpinned Two-Tier Scenario

Table 16.4 shows the various disruptive tenant workloads used to evaluate I_{QoS}. We configured the disruptive tenant workloads in a way to result in the same Δw as in the unpinned single-tier scenarios. Due to the increasing number of timeouts and exceptions in the disruptive domain, we had to stop at 6,750 users. For this workload range, we observed continuously increasing response times. Nevertheless, from 4,400 to 6,750 users, the isolation improved, as Δw increased more than Δz. Over the entire range of measurements, the average isolation I_{avg} was 3.06.

Figure 16.6 presents the total abiding tenant workload W_a based on the disruptive tenant users for the workload-ratio-based metrics. Analogous to the response times in Table 16.4, we can see a continuously decreasing amount of abiding tenant workload in Figure 16.6. At a disruptive tenant workload of 2, we can see the observed isolation curve crossing the respective curve for a non-isolated system. This is due to the selected step width for reducing the number of users in the disruptive domain. At a disruptive tenant workload of 11,050 users (corresponding to 8.5 in Figure 16.6), the disruptive domain failed to successfully handle incoming requests. The results are no longer valid for higher disruptive tenant workloads and are therefore illustrated using a dashed line. The overall isolation values were $I_{intFree1105} = 0.42$ and $I_{intBase} = 0.36$.

16.3.5 Effectiveness of the Deployment Options

Overall, the *pinned* scenario exhibited the best results, whereas the *unpinned two-tier* scenario exhibited the worst ones. The selected size of the database was small enough for data to be mostly cached. The memory was not overcommitted in our setup and the network I/O did not reach the critical point at which the CPUs for dom0 became a bottleneck in the one-tier scenarios. Therefore, the isolation was nearly perfect with pinned CPUs. In the *unpinned* scenario, the resources of the domU domain were shared with those for dom0; therefore, the slightly increased I/O overhead for dom0 was competing for resources and had some minor effect. The credit scheduler was not able to compensate completely for this. By splitting the domU domain into application server and database server, we noticeably increased the network I/O. In this setup, we observed a significant impact of the disruptive domain on the others, whereby the handling of the network I/O in dom0 led to a bottleneck and/or it requested additional processing resources from the guest domains.

When an administrator has to decide for one of the mentioned deployments, various considerations might be of importance. In a pinned setup, the overall performance and isolation is the best. However, unused resources of one domain cannot be used by other domains and thus this setup might lack in terms of efficiency. The *unpinned* scenario overcomes this drawback at the expense of performance and isolation. From a separation-of-concerns point of view, it might be beneficial to separate the database and application server. On the other hand, as can be seen from Table 16.3, a distributed deployment provides less performance and the worst isolation. These example measurements show how the isolation metrics provide the opportunity to quantify one more dimension in the framework of multiple trade-off decisions a system provider has to make. An additional result is that an administrator can increase isolation by hard resource allocations, which also lead to reduced I/O.

16.4 Assessment of the Metrics

For the assessment of the metrics, we concentrate on the following aspects: First, the practical usability of the metrics for the target group of system owners/providers or developers/researchers; and second, the expressiveness of the metrics in terms of the type of evidence they provide; third, the number of measurements required to obtain a valid value; fourth, situations in which the metrics are not meaningful. In the following, we evaluate the metrics of each category with respect to these aspects.

16.4.1 QoS-Impact-Based Metrics

These metrics show the influence of disruptive tenant workloads on the QoS of abiding tenants. This helps system owners to manage their systems, because it indicates the influence of disruptive tenant workloads on the QoS, which is important for capacity planning. QoS-impact-based metrics can show that a system is perfectly isolated; however, they fail in ranking a system's isolation capabilities in the range between perfectly isolated and non-isolated. Thus, it is hard to estimate the potential of an isolation method. A single I_{QoS} metric can be derived with only two measurements to obtain evidence for one point of increased workload. However, to obtain some more detailed information on the system's performance isolation capabilities, more measurements are required. Therefore, I_{avg} describes the average isolation value for multiple different scenarios of interest. Nevertheless, the metric is not suitable to describe a system's impact of different disruptive tenant workloads on the abiding tenants, because these workloads cannot be set into relation for a concrete scenario.

16.4.2 Edge-Point-Based Metrics

The metric I_{end} might not be practically usable for quantifying isolation in well-isolated systems. Furthermore, it is not possible to directly deduce from it relevant system behaviors such as response time behavior. If this metric is provided, it could help to compare two systems regarding the maximum disruptive tenant workload they can handle. However, to quantify I_{end}, more measurements are required than would be the case for the QoS-impact-based metrics.

I_{base} orders a system within the range of perfectly isolated and non-isolated systems for one specific point in the diagram. Nevertheless, it does not provide information about the behavior of the system before that point. It is limited to comparing the isolation behavior of the systems at one selected load level and it is also inadequate to derive direct QoS-related metrics. The usefulness of this metric is limited compared to the integral-based metrics.

16.4.3 Integral-Based Metrics

$I_{intBase}$ and $I_{intFree}$ are widely comparable metrics $I_{intBase}$ has the advantage to be measured at a predefined point. For $I_{intFree}$, the endpoint of the interval must be additionally specified in order to have a fully defined metric. Both metrics provide good evidence of the isolation within the considered interval ordered between the magnitudes of perfectly isolated and non-isolated systems. However, they lack in providing information concerning the degree of SLA violations. For example, the SLA violations could be very low and acceptable or critically high in each iteration as we reduce W_a. However, in both cases, the results of the metrics would be similar. This limits the value of $I_{intBase}$ and $I_{intFree}$ for system owners/providers. Nevertheless, for comparison of systems and analyzing their behavior, the metrics are very useful and can be exploited by developers or researchers. Finally, on the negative side, a disadvantage of these metrics is that their measurement may be a time-consuming task. In our Xen-based case study, we had experiment series of around 15 h.

16.4.4 Discussion

The various metrics show their advantages in different fields of applications and express various semantics. The I_{QoS} and I_{avg} metrics capture the reduced QoS due to disruptive tenant workload. They cannot provide a ranking within the range of fully isolated and non-isolated systems. However, for a system operator this might be helpful to estimate the impact of disruptive tenant workloads on the system. The I_{end} metric shows how many times a system is better than a non-isolated one. This information may be helpful to compare different systems if one has to decide for one. The integral-based metrics rank a system within the range of fully isolated and non-isolated. This knowledge is beneficial for the developer of a system to estimate the potential for improvements.

The presented isolation metrics are not limited to multi-tenant environments. They are also applicable in other scenarios where a system is shared, for example, a web service triggered by other components, virtual machines hosted on the same hypervisor instance (as shown in our case study), or network devices serving packets from various sources. However, practical limitations might appear, for example, due to non-uniform workload behavior with work arriving from different sources.

16.5 Concluding Remarks

This chapter presented metrics to quantify the degree of performance isolation a system provides. The metrics are applicable for use in performance benchmarks that measure the performance without requiring internal knowledge. They are preferable in situations where different request sources use the functions of a shared system with similar demands per request but with a different load intensity. These characteristics are typical for multi-tenant applications but can also occur in other shared resource systems. The presented metrics are based on observing the influence of disruptive tenants (i.e., tenants exceeding their assigned quotas) on the abiding tenants (i.e., tenants working within their quotas). Thus, the influence on one group as a function of the workload of the other group must be evaluated. This is a major difference to traditional performance benchmarking. We presented a case study showing the metrics in action by applying them to evaluate the performance isolation of virtual machines running on a shared physical host. The case study demonstrated the applicability of the metrics in real-life environments and provided some insights on the isolation capabilities of the widely used virtualization platform Xen. Furthermore, it showed an example of how the metrics can be employed by system operators to make decisions in a deployment scenario. The performance isolation metrics presented in this chapter can be applied to quantify isolation with respect to any measurable QoS-related property of a system shared between different entities.

References

Brataas, G. (2014). *CloudScale: Design Support Deliverable D1.2.* EU FP7, Collaboration Project CloudScale. FP7-ICT-2011-8-317704 (cited on p. 353).

Cooper, B., Silberstein, A., Tam, E., Ramakrishnan, R., and Sears, R. (2010). "Benchmarking Cloud Serving Systems with YCSB". In: *Proceedings of the 1st ACM Symposium on Cloud Computing (SoCC 2010).* (Indianapolis, Indiana, USA). ACM: New York, NY, USA, pp. 143–154 (cited on p. 343).

Gupta, D., Cherkasova, L., Gardner, R., and Vahdat, A. (2006). "Enforcing Performance Isolation Across Virtual Machines in Xen". In: *Proceedings of the ACM/IFIP/USENIX 2006 International Conference on Middleware.* (Melbourne, Australia). Springer US: New York, NY, USA, pp. 342–362 (cited on p. 355).

Herbst, N. R., Bauer, A., Kounev, S., Oikonomou, G., Eyk, E. van, Kousiouris, G., Evangelinou, A., Krebs, R., Brecht, T., Abad, C. L., and Iosup, A. (2018).

"Quantifying Cloud Performance and Dependability: Taxonomy, Metric Design, and Emerging Challenges". *ACM Transactions on Modeling and Performance Evaluation of Computing Systems*, 3(4). ACM: New York, NY, USA, 19:1–19:36 (cited on p. 342).

Herbst, N. R., Kounev, S., and Reussner, R. (2013). "Elasticity in Cloud Computing: What it is, and What it is Not". In: *Proceedings of the 10th International Conference on Autonomic Computing (ICAC 2013)*. (San Jose, CA). USENIX (cited on p. 343).

Herbst, N. R., Krebs, R., Oikonomou, G., Kousiouris, G., Evangelinou, A., Iosup, A., and Kounev, S. (2016). *Ready for Rain? A View from SPEC Research on the Future of Cloud Metrics*. Tech. rep. SPEC-RG-2016-01. Gainesville, VA, USA: SPEC RG—Cloud Working Group, Standard Performance Evaluation Corporation (SPEC) (cited on p. 342).

Huber, N., von Quast, M., Hauck, M., and Kounev, S. (2011). "Evaluating and Modeling Virtualization Performance Overhead for Cloud Environments". In: *Proceedings of the 1st International Conference on Cloud Computing and Services Science (CLOSER 2011)*. (Noordwijkerhout, The Netherlands). SciTePress, pp. 563–573 (cited on p. 355).

Iosup, A., Ostermann, S., Yigitbasi, M. N., Prodan, R., Fahringer, T., and Epema, D. (2011). "Performance Analysis of Cloud Computing Services for Many-Tasks Scientific Computing". *IEEE Transactions on Parallel and Distributed Systems*, 22(6). IEEE: Piscataway, New Jersey, USA, pp. 931–945 (cited on p. 343).

Iosup, A., Yigitbasi, N., and Epema, D. (2011). "On the Performance Variability of Production Cloud Services". In: *2011 11th IEEE/ACM International Symposium on Cluster, Cloud and Grid Computing (CCGrid 2011)*. (Newport Beach, CA, USA). IEEE: Piscataway, New Jersey, USA, pp. 104–113 (cited on p. 354).

Islam, S., Lee, K., Fekete, A., and Liu, A. (2012). "How a Consumer Can Measure Elasticity for Cloud Platforms". In: *Proceedings of the 3rd ACM/SPEC International Conference on Performance Engineering (ICPE 2012)*. (Boston, MA, USA). ACM: New York, NY, USA, pp. 85–96 (cited on p. 343).

Janert, P. (2013). *Feedback Control for Computer Systems*. O'Reilly and Associates: Sebastopol, California (cited on pp. 351, 353).

Krebs, R. (2015). "Performance Isolation in Multi-Tenant Applications". PhD thesis. Karlsruhe, Germany: Karlsruhe Institute of Technology (KIT) (cited on p. 342).

Krebs, R., Momm, C., and Kounev, S. (2012). "Architectural Concerns in Multi-Tenant SaaS Applications". In: *Proceedings of the 2nd International Conference on Cloud Computing and Services Science (CLOSER 2012)*. (Setubal, Portugal). SciTePress (cited on p. 341).

– (2014). "Metrics and Techniques for Quantifying Performance Isolation in Cloud Environments". *Science of Computer Programming*, Vol. 90, Part B. Elsevier Science: Amsterdam, The Netherlands, pp. 116–134 (cited on pp. 342, 354).

Krebs, R., Spinner, S., Ahmed, N., and Kounev, S. (2014). "Resource Usage Control In Multi-Tenant Applications". In: *Proceedings of the 14th IEEE/ACM International Symposium on Cluster, Cloud and Grid Computing (CCGrid 2014)*. (Chicago, IL, USA). IEEE: Piscataway, New Jersey, USA, pp. 122–131 (cited on p. 351).

Kupperberg, M., Herbst, N. R., Kistowski, J. von, and Reussner, R. (2011). *Defining and Quantifying Elasticity of Resources in Cloud Computing and Scalable Platforms*. Tech. rep. 2011-16. Karlsruhe, Germany: Karlsruhe Institute of Technology (KIT) (cited on p. 343).

Schad, J., Dittrich, J., and Quiané-Ruiz, J.-A. (2010). "Runtime Measurements in the Cloud: Observing, Analyzing, and Reducing Variance". *Proceedings of the VLDB Endowment*, 3(1-2). VLDB Endowment, pp. 460–471 (cited on p. 343).

Chapter 17
Resource Demand Estimation

Simon Spinner and Samuel Kounev

As discussed in Chapter 7, resource demands, also referred to as service demands, play a key role in operational analysis and queueing theory. Most generally, the *resource demand* or *service demand* of a unit of work (e.g., request, job, or transaction) at a given resource in a system refers to the average time the respective unit of work spends obtaining service from the resource over all visits to the latter, excluding any waiting times (cf. Chapter 7, Section 7.1.2). Resource demands are normally quantified based on measurements taken on the system under consideration; however, the accurate quantification of resource demands poses many challenges. The resource demand for processing a request in a computing system is influenced by different factors, for example: (1) the application logic, which specifies the sequence of instructions to process a request; (2) the hardware platform, which determines how fast individual instructions are executed; and (3) platform layers (hypervisor, operating system, containers, or middleware systems), which may introduce additional processing overhead. While the direct measurement of resource demands is feasible in some systems, it requires an extensive instrumentation of the application, and it typically introduces significant overheads that may distort measurements. For instance, performance profiling tools (cf. Section 6.3 in Chapter 6) can be used to obtain execution times of individual application functions when processing a request. However, the resulting execution times are not broken down into processing times at individual resources, and profiling tools typically introduce high overheads, influencing the system performance.

In this chapter, we survey, systematize, and evaluate different approaches to the statistical estimation of resource demands based on easy to measure system-level and application-level metrics. We consider resource demands in the context of computing systems; however, the methods we present are also applicable to other types of systems. We focus on generic methods to approximate resource demands without relying on dedicated instrumentation of the application. The goal is to estimate the resource demands based on *indirect measurements* (cf. Section 6.1 in Chapter 6) derived from commonly available metrics (e.g., end-to-end response time or resource utilization).

© Springer Nature Switzerland AG 2020

S. Kounev et al., *Systems Benchmarking*, https://doi.org/10.1007/978-3-030-41705-5_17

The methods we consider face the following challenges:

- The value of a resource demand is platform-specific (i.e., only valid for a specific combination of application, operating system, hardware platform, etc.). The hardware platform determines how fast a piece of code executes in general. Furthermore, each platform layer on top (e.g., hypervisor, operating system, and middleware systems) may add additional overheads, influencing the resource demands of an application.
- Applications often serve a mix of different types of requests (e.g., read or write transactions), which also differ in their resource demands. For resource management purposes, it is beneficial to be able to distinguish between different types of requests. Quantifying resource demands separately for each type of request (i.e., workload class) often poses technical challenges due to the lack of fine-granular monitoring data.
- Modern operating systems can provide only aggregate resource usage statistics on a per-process level. Many applications, especially the ones running in data centers, serve different requests with one or more operating system processes (e.g., HTTP web servers). The operating system is unaware of the requests served by an application and therefore cannot attribute the resource usage to individual requests.
- Many applications allow only the collection of time-aggregated request statistics (e.g., throughput or response time) while they are serving production workloads. A tracing of individual requests is often considered too expensive for a production system, as it may influence the application performance negatively.
- Resource demands may change over time due to platform reconfigurations (e.g., operating system updates) or dynamic changes in the application state (e.g., increasing database size). Therefore, resource demands need to be updated continuously at system run time based on up-to-date measurement data.

In the rest of this chapter, we survey the state of the art in resource demand estimation and provide a systematization of existing estimation methods discussing their pros and cons with respect to how well they deal with the above challenges. The goal of the systematization is to help performance engineers select an estimation method that best fits their specific requirements. We first survey existing estimation methods and describe their modeling assumptions and their underlying statistical techniques. Then, we introduce three dimensions for systematization: (1) input parameters, (2) output metrics, and (3) robustness to anomalies in the input data. For each dimension, we first describe its features and then categorize the estimation methods accordingly. In addition to the systematization, we compare and evaluate the different estimation methods in terms of their accuracy and execution time. The presented systematization and comparison of estimation methods are based on Spinner et al. (2015) and Spinner (2017). Finally, we briefly discuss a recent approach to resource demand estimation that relies on multiple statistical techniques for improved robustness and uses a cross-validation scheme to dynamically select the technique that performs best for the concrete scenario (Spinner, 2017).

In the following, we use a consistent notation for the description of the different approaches to resource demand estimation. We denote resources with the index $i = 1 \ldots I$ and workload classes with the index $c = 1 \ldots C$. The variables used in the description are listed in Table 17.1, which are consistent with the notation we used in Chapter 7 (Section 7.2.2) in the context of queueing networks. As usual, we assume that the considered system is in operational equilibrium (i.e., over a sufficiently long period of time, the number of request completions is approximately equal to the number of request arrivals). As a result, the arrival rate λ_c is assumed to be equal to the throughput X_c. Furthermore, as mentioned earlier, we use the term resource demand as a synonym for service demand, and for simplicity of exposition, we assume $V_{i,c} = 1$; that is, no distinction is made between service demand and service time.

Table 17.1: Notation used in resource demand estimation

Symbol	Meaning
$D_{i,c}$	Average resource demand of requests of workload class c at resource i
$U_{i,c}$	Average utilization of resource i due to requests of workload class c
U_i	Average total utilization of resource i
$\lambda_{i,c}$	Average arrival rate of workload class c at resource i
$X_{i,c}$	Average throughput of workload class c at resource i
$R_{i,c}$	Average response time of workload class c at resource i
R_c	Average end-to-end response time of workload class c
$A_{i,c}$	Average queue length of requests of workload class c seen upon arrival at resource i (excluding the arriving job)
$V_{i,c}$	Average number of visits of a request of workload class c at resource i
I	Total number of resources
C	Total number of workload classes

17.1 Estimation Methods

In this section, we describe the most common methods for resource demand estimation that exist in the literature. Table 17.2 gives an overview of the different methods.

Table 17.2: Overview of estimation methods categorized according to the underlying statistical techniques

Technique	Variant	References
Approximation with response times		Urgaonkar et al. (2007) Nou et al. (2009) Brosig et al. (2009)
Service demand law		Lazowska et al. (1984) Brosig et al. (2009)
Linear regression	Least squares	Bard and Shatzoff (1978) Rolia and Vetland (1995) Pacifici et al. (2008) Kraft et al. (2009); Pérez, Pacheco-Sanchez, et al. (2013)
	Least absolute differences	Stewart et al. (2007); Q. Zhang et al. (2007)
	Least trimmed squares	Casale et al. (2008); Casale et al. (2007)
Kalman filter		Zheng et al. (2008) Kumar, Tantawi, et al. (2009) Wang, Huang, Qin, et al. (2012); Wang, Huang, Song, et al. (2011)
Optimization	Non-linear constrained optimization	L. Zhang et al. (2002) Menascé (2008)
	Quadratic programming	Liu et al. (2006); Wynter et al. (2004) Kumar, L. Zhang, et al. (2009)
Machine learning	Clusterwise linear regression	Cremonesi, Dhyani, et al. (2010)
	Independent component analysis	Sharma et al. (2008)
	Support vector machine	Kalbasi, Krishnamurthy, Rolia, and Richter (2011)
	Pattern matching	Cremonesi and Sansottera (2012, 2014)
Maximum likelihood estimation		Kraft et al. (2009) Pérez, Pacheco-Sanchez, et al. (2013)
Gibbs sampling		Sutton and Jordan (2011) Wang and Casale (2013)
Demand estimation with confidence (DEC)		Kalbasi, Krishnamurthy, Rolia, and Dawson (2012); Rolia, Kalbasi, et al. (2010)

17.1.1 Approximation with Response Times

Assuming a single queue and insignificant queueing delays compared to the resource demands, we can approximate the resource demands with the observed response times. However, this trivial approximation only works with systems under light load where a single resource dominates the observed response time. This approximation is used by Nou et al. (2009), Urgaonkar et al. (2007), and Brosig et al. (2009).

17.1.2 Service Demand Law

The service demand law (cf. Chapter 7, Sections 7.1.2 and 7.2.3) is an operational law that can be used to directly calculate the demand $D_{i,c}$ given the utilization $U_{i,c}$ and the throughput $X_{i,c}$. However, modern operating systems can report the utilization only on a per-process level. Therefore, we usually cannot observe the per-class utilization $U_{i,c}$ directly, given that single processes may serve requests of different workload classes. Given a system serving requests of multiple workload classes, Lazowska et al. (1984) and Menascé et al. (2004) recommend to use additional per-class metrics if available (e.g., in the operating system) to apportion the aggregate utilization U_i of a resource between workload classes. Brosig et al. (2009) use an approximate apportioning scheme based on the assumption that the observed response times are proportional to the resource demands.

17.1.3 Linear Regression

Given a linear model $\mathbf{Y} = \mathbf{X}\boldsymbol{\beta} + \boldsymbol{\epsilon}$, where $\boldsymbol{\beta}$ (cf. Chapter 2, Section 2.7.1) is a vector of resource demands $D_{i,r}$ and $\mathbf{Y}$, $\mathbf{X}$ contain observations of performance metrics of a system, we can use linear regression to estimate the resource demands. Two alternative formulations of such a linear model have been proposed in the literature:

- The utilization law (cf. Chapter 7, Sections 7.1.1 and 7.2.3) requires observations of the aggregate utilization U_i and the throughputs $\lambda_{i,c}$. This is a classical model used by different authors (Bard and Shatzoff, 1978; Casale et al., 2007; Kraft et al., 2009; Pacifici et al., 2008; Rolia and Vetland, 1995; Stewart et al., 2007; Q. Zhang et al., 2007). Some of the authors include a constant term $U_{i,0}$ in the model in order to estimate the utilization caused by background work.
- Kraft et al. (2009) and Pérez, Pacheco-Sanchez, et al. (2013) propose a linear model based on a multi-class version of the response time equation $R_i = D_i(1+A_i)$ requiring observations of the queue length A_i seen by a newly arriving job and its response time R_i. In their initial work, Kraft et al. (2009) assume a FCFS scheduling strategy; Pérez, Pacheco-Sanchez, et al. (2013) generalize the model to PS queueing stations.

Bard and Shatzoff (1978), Rolia and Vetland (1995), Pacifici et al. (2008), and Kraft et al. (2009) use nonnegative least squares regression for solving the linear model. Other regression techniques, such as least absolute differences regression (Stewart et al., 2007; Q. Zhang et al., 2007) or least trimmed squares (Casale et al., 2008; Casale et al., 2007), were proposed to increase the robustness of regression-based estimation techniques to multi-collinearities, outliers, or abrupt changes in the demand values.

17.1.4 Kalman Filter

The resource demands of a system may vary over time, for example, due to changing system states or changing user behavior. These variations may be abrupt or continuous. In order to track time-varying resource demands, Zheng et al. (2008), Kumar, Tantawi, et al. (2009), and Wang, Huang, Qin, et al. (2012) use a Kalman filter (cf. Chapter 2, Section 2.7.2). The authors assume a dynamic system where the state vector $\mathbf{x}$ consists of the hidden resource demands $D_{i,c}$ that need to be estimated. Given that no prior knowledge about the dynamic behavior of the system state exists, they assume a constant state model; that is, Equation (2.49) on page 40 is reduced to $\mathbf{x}_k = \mathbf{x}_{k-1} + \mathbf{w}_k$.

The observation model $\mathbf{z} = h(\mathbf{x})$ requires a functional description of the relationship between the observations $\mathbf{z}$ and the system state $\mathbf{x}$. Wang, Huang, Qin, et al. (2012) use the observed utilization U_i as vector $\mathbf{z}$ and define $h(\mathbf{x})$ based on the utilization law (cf. Equation 7.38 on page 167). Given the linear model, a conventional Kalman filter is sufficient. Zheng et al. (2008) and Kumar, Tantawi, et al. (2009) use an observation vector consisting of the observed response time $R_{i,c}$ of each workload class and the utilization U_i of each resource. The function $h(\mathbf{x})$ is defined based on the solution of a M/M/1 queue (cf. Equation 7.43 on page 168) and the utilization law. Due to the non-linear nature, it requires an extended Kalman filter design—see Equation (2.51) on page 40.

17.1.5 Optimization

Given a general queueing network, we can formulate an optimization problem to search for values of the resource demands so that the differences between performance metrics observed on the real system and the ones calculated using the queueing network are minimized. The main challenge is the solution of the queueing network. Depending on the structure of the queueing network, its solution may be computationally expensive and the optimization algorithm may need to evaluate the queueing network with many different resource demand values in order to find an optimal solution. Existing approaches (Kumar, L. Zhang, et al., 2009; Liu et al., 2006; Menascé, 2008; Wynter et al., 2004) assume a product-form queueing network with an open workload. Then, the equations in Chapter 7, Section 7.2.4, can be used to calculate the end-to-end response times.

Given N observations of the end-to-end response time $\tilde{R}_c$ and the utilization $\tilde{U}_i$, Liu et al. (2006) propose the following objective function:

$$\min_{\mathbf{D}} \sum_{n=1}^{N} \left(\sum_{c=1}^{C} p_c \left(R_c(\mathbf{D}) - \tilde{R}_c^{(n)} \right)^2 + \sum_{i=1}^{I} \left(U_i(\mathbf{D}) - \tilde{U}_i^{(n)} \right)^2 \right). \qquad (17.1)$$

The function $R_c(\mathbf{D})$ is based on the solution of a M/M/1 queue—see Equation (7.43) on page 168—and $U_i(\mathbf{D})$ on the utilization law.

The factor p_c introduces a weighting according to the arrival rates of workload classes $p_c = \lambda_c / \sum_{d=1}^{C} \lambda_d$. The resulting optimization problem can be solved using quadratic programming techniques.

Kumar, L. Zhang, et al. (2009) extend this optimization approach to estimate load-dependent resource demands. Their approach requires prior knowledge of the type of function (e.g., polynomial, exponential, or logarithmic) that best describes the relation between arriving workloads and resource demands.

Menascé (2008) formulates an alternative optimization problem that depends only on response time and arrival rate measurements:

$$\min_{\mathbf{D}} \sum_{c=1}^{C} \left(R_c(\mathbf{D}) - \tilde{R}_c \right)^2 \text{ with } R_c(\mathbf{D}) = \sum_{i=1}^{I} \frac{D_{i,c}}{1 - \sum_{d=1}^{C} \lambda_{i,d} D_{i,d}} \qquad (17.2)$$

$$\text{subject to } D_{i,c} \geq 0 \quad \forall i, c \text{ and } \sum_{c=1}^{C} \lambda_{i,c} D_{i,c} < 1 \quad \forall i.$$

In contrast to Liu et al. (2006), this formulation is based on a single sample of the observed response times. Menascé (2008) proposes to repeat the optimization for each new sample using the previous resource demand estimate as the initial point. To solve this optimization problem we depend on a non-linear constrained optimization algorithm.

17.1.6 Machine Learning

Cremonesi, Dhyani, et al. (2010) use clusterwise regression techniques to improve the robustness to discontinuities in the resource demands due to system configuration changes. The observations are clustered into groups where the resource demands can be assumed constant, and the demands are then estimated for each cluster separately. In Cremonesi and Sansottera (2012) and Cremonesi and Sansottera (2014) an algorithm is proposed based on a combination of change-point regression methods and pattern matching to address the same challenge.

Independent Component Analysis (ICA) is a method to solve the *blind source separation* problem (i.e., to estimate the individual signals from a set of aggregate measurements). Sharma et al. (2008) describe a way to use ICA for resource demand estimation using a linear model based on the utilization law. ICA can provide estimates solely based on utilization measurements when the following constraints hold (Sharma et al., 2008): (1) the number of workload classes is limited by the number of observed resources, (2) the arrival rate measurements are statistically independent, and (3) the inter-arrival times have a non-Gaussian distribution while the measurement noise is assumed to be zero-mean Gaussian. ICA not only provides estimates of resource demands, but also automatically categorizes requests into workload classes.

Kalbasi, Krishnamurthy, Rolia, and Richter (2011) consider the use of Support Vector Machines (SVM) (Smola and Schölkopf, 2004) for estimating resource demands. They compare it with results from LSQ and LAD regression and show that it can provide better resource demand estimates depending on the characteristics of the workload.

17.1.7 Maximum Likelihood Estimation (MLE)

Kraft et al. (2009) and Pérez, Pacheco-Sanchez, et al. (2013) use Maximum Likelihood Estimation (MLE) (cf. Chapter 2, Section 2.7.3) to estimate resource demands based on observed response times and queue lengths seen upon arrival of requests. Given N response time measurements $R_i^1, \ldots, R_i^N$ of *individual* requests, the estimated resource demands $D_{i,1}, \ldots, D_{i,C}$ are the values that maximize the likelihood function $\mathbb{L}(D_{i,1}, \ldots, D_{i,C})$ defined as follows:

$$\max \mathbb{L}(D_{i,1}, \ldots, D_{i,C}) = \sum_{k=1}^{N} \log f(R_i^k \mid D_{i,1}, \ldots, D_{i,C}). \qquad (17.3)$$

The density function f is obtained by constructing a phase-type distribution. The phase-type distribution describes the time to absorption in a Markov chain representing the current state of the system. Observations of the queue lengths are necessary in order to be able to construct the corresponding phase-type distribution. Kraft et al. (2009) describe the likelihood function for queueing stations with FCFS scheduling. Pérez, Pacheco-Sanchez, et al. (2013) generalize this approach to PS scheduling.

17.1.8 Gibbs Sampling

Sutton and Jordan (2011) and Wang and Casale (2013) both propose approaches to resource demand estimation based on Bayesian inference techniques (cf. Section 2.7.4). Sutton and Jordan (2011) assume an open, single-class queueing network. They develop a deterministic mathematical model allowing for the calculation of service times and waiting times of individual requests given the arrival times, departure times, and the path of queues of all requests in a queueing network. They assume that this information can be only observed for a subset of requests. Therefore, they propose a Gibbs sampler to sample the missing departure times of requests that were not observed. Given the posterior distribution of the departure times of all requests, they then derive the expected resource demands at the individual queues.

Wang and Casale (2013) assume a multi-class, closed queueing network that fulfills the BCMP theorem (cf. Chapter 7, Section 7.2.2). Under this assumption, the probability distribution of the queue lengths for given resource demands is well-known (see Equation 7.36 on page 166). They assume the availability of queue-length samples from a real system and construct a Gibbs sampler for the posterior distribution $f(\mathbf{D}|\mathbf{A})$, where $\mathbf{D}$ is a vector of resource demands $D_{i,c}$ and $\mathbf{A}$ is a vector of observed queue lengths $A_{i,c}$. They propose an approximation for the conditionals of the posterior distribution as required by the Gibbs sampling algorithm. A main challenge is the calculation of the normalization constant G for the steady-state probabilities (cf. Equation 7.36 on page 166), which is nontrivial for a closed queueing network. Wang and Casale (2013) propose a Taylor expansion of G and apply an algorithm based on mean-value analysis (MVA) to determine its value.

17.1.9 Other Approaches

Rolia, Kalbasi, et al. (2010) and Kalbasi, Krishnamurthy, Rolia, and Dawson (2012) propose a technique called Demand Estimation with Confidence (DEC) for estimating the aggregate resource demand of a given workload mix. This technique assumes that a set of benchmarks is available for the system under study. Each benchmark utilizes a subset of the different functions of an application. DEC expects the measured demands of the individual benchmarks as input and then derives the aggregate resource demand of a given workload mix as a linear combination of the demands of the individual benchmarks. DEC is able to provide confidence intervals of the aggregate resource demand (Kalbasi, Krishnamurthy, Rolia, and Dawson, 2012; Rolia, Kalbasi, et al., 2010).

17.2 Input Parameters

Methods for resource demand estimation often differ in terms of the set of input data they require. We do not consider parameters of the underlying statistical techniques (e.g., parameters controlling an optimization algorithm) because they normally are specific to the concrete implementation of an estimation method.

Figure 17.1 depicts the main types of input parameters for demand estimation algorithms. The parameters are categorized into *model parameters* and *measurements*. In general, parameters of both types are required. Model parameters capture information about the performance model for which we estimate resource demands.

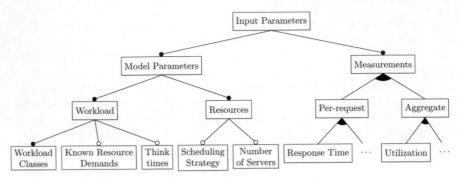

Fig. 17.1: Types of input parameters

Measurements consist of samples of relevant performance metrics obtained from a running system, either a live production system or a test system.

Before estimating resource demands, it is necessary to decide on certain modeling assumptions. As a first step, resources and workload classes need to be identified. This is typically done as part of the workload characterization activity when modeling a system. It is important to note that the observability of performance metrics may influence the selection of resources and workload classes for the system under study. In order to be able to distinguish between individual resources or workload classes, observations of certain per-resource or per-class performance metrics are necessary. At a minimum, information about the number of workload classes and the resources for which the demands should be determined is required as input to the estimation. Depending on the estimation method, more detailed information on resources and workload classes may be expected as input (e.g., *scheduling strategies*, *number of servers*, or *think times*).

Measurements can be further grouped on a *per-request* or *aggregate* basis. Common per-request measurements used in the literature include response times, arrival rates, visit counts, and queue lengths seen upon arrival. Aggregate measurements can be further distinguished in *class-aggregate* and *time-aggregate* measurements. Class-aggregate measurements are collected as totals over all workload classes processed at a resource. For instance, utilization is usually reported as an aggregate value because the operating system is agnostic of the application internal logic and is not aware of different request types in the application. Time-aggregate measurements (e.g., average response times or average throughput) are aggregated over a sampling period. The sampling period can be evenly or unevenly spaced.

Categorization of Existing Methods

We consider the methods for resource demand estimation listed in Table 17.2 and examine their input parameters. Table 17.3 shows an overview of the input param-

Table 17.3: Input parameters of estimation methods

Estimation method	Measurements					Parameters		
	U_i	R_c	X_c/λ_c	$A_{i,c}$	$V_{i,c}$	$D_{i,c}$	Z	P
Approximation with response times								
Urgaonkar et al. (2007)		✗[1]			✗			
Nou et al. (2009)	✗	✗						
Brosig et al. (2009)		✗						
Service demand law								
Lazowska et al. (1984)				✗		✗[2]		
Brosig et al. (2009)	✗	✗			✗			
Linear regression								
Bard and Shatzoff (1978)								
Rolia and Vetland (1995)								
Pacifici et al. (2008)	✗		✗					
Q. Zhang et al. (2007)								
Stewart et al. (2007)	✗		✗					
Kraft et al. (2009); Pérez, Casale, et al. (2015)		✗		✗				✗
Casale et al. (2008); Casale et al. (2007)	✗		✗					
Kalman filter								
Zheng et al. (2008)	✗	✗	✗					
Kumar, Tantawi, et al. (2009)	✗	✗	✗					
Wang, Huang, Qin, et al. (2012)	✗		✗					
Optimization								
L. Zhang et al. (2002)	✗	✗	✗			$(✗)^5$		✗
Liu et al. (2006); Wynter et al. (2004)	✗	✗	✗		✗			✗
Menascé (2008)		✗	✗			✗[3]		
Kumar, L. Zhang, et al. (2009)	✗	✗	✗					✗
Machine learning								
Cremonesi, Dhyani, et al. (2010)	✗		✗					
Sharma et al. (2008)	✗							
Kalbasi, Krishnamurthy, Rolia, and Richter (2011)	✗		✗					
Cremonesi and Sansottera (2012, 2014)	✗		✗					
Maximum likelihood estimation								
Kraft et al. (2009)		✗[4]		✗[4]			✗	✗
Pérez, Casale, et al. (2015)		✗[4]		✗[4]			✗	✗
Gibbs sampling								
Sutton and Jordan (2011)		✗[4]	✗[4]					✗
Wang and Casale (2013)				✗[4]			✗	
Kalbasi, Krishnamurthy, Rolia, and Dawson (2012); Rolia, Kalbasi, et al. (2010)				✗	✗			

[1] Response time per resource
[2] Measured with accounting monitor—system overhead not included
[3] A selected set of resource demands is known a priori
[4] Non-aggregated measurements of individual requests
[5] Requires coefficient of variation of resource demands in case of FCFS scheduling

eters of each estimation method (utilization U_i, response time R_c, throughput X_c, arrival rate λ_c, queue length $A_{i,c}$, visit counts $V_{i,c}$, resource demands $D_{i,c}$, think time Z, and scheduling policy P). Parameters common to all estimation methods, such as the number of workload classes and the number of resources, are not included in this table. The required input parameters vary widely between different estimation methods. Depending on the system under study and on the available performance metrics, one can choose a suitable estimation method from Table 17.3. Furthermore, approaches based on optimization can be adapted by incorporating additional constraints into the mathematical model capturing the knowledge about the system under study. For example, the optimization approach by Menascé (2008) allows one to specify additional known resource demand values as input parameters. These a priori resource demands may be obtained from the results of other estimation methods or from direct measurements.

Another approach that requires resource demand data is described by Lazowska et al. (1984, Chapter 12) who assume that the resource demands are approximated based on measurements provided by an accounting monitor; however, such an accounting monitor does not include the system overhead caused by each workload class. The system overhead is defined as the work done by the operating system for processing a request. Lazowska et al. (1984) describe a way to distribute unattributed computing time among the different workload classes, providing more realistic estimates of the actual resource demands.

Approaches based on response time measurements, such as those proposed by L. Zhang et al. (2002), Liu et al. (2006), Wynter et al. (2004), and Kumar, L. Zhang, et al. (2009), require information about the scheduling strategies of the involved resources abstracted as queueing stations. This information is used to construct the correct problem definition for the optimization technique. The estimation methods proposed by Kraft et al. (2009), Pérez, Pacheco-Sanchez, et al. (2013), and Wang and Casale (2013) assume a closed queueing network. Therefore, they also require the average think time and the number of users as input.

In addition to requiring a set of specific input parameters, some approaches also provide a rule of thumb regarding the number of required measurement samples. Approaches based on linear regression (Kraft et al., 2009; Pacifici et al., 2008; Rolia and Vetland, 1995) need at least $K + 1$ linear independent equations to estimate K resource demands. When using robust regression methods, significantly more measurements might be necessary (Casale et al., 2008; Casale et al., 2007). Kumar, L. Zhang, et al. (2009) provide a formula to calculate the number of measurements required by their optimization-based approach. The formula provides only a minimum bound on the number of measurements and more measurements are normally required to obtain good estimates (Stewart et al., 2007).

17.3 Output Metrics

Approaches to resource demand estimation are typically used to determine the mean resource demand of requests of a given workload class at a given resource. However, in many situations, the estimated mean value may not be sufficient. Often, more information about the confidence of estimates and the distribution of the resource demands is required. The set of output metrics an estimation method provides can influence the decision to adopt a specific method.

Generally, resource demands cannot be assumed to be deterministic (Rolia, Kalbasi, et al., 2010); for example, they may depend on the data processed by an application or on the current state of the system (Rolia and Vetland, 1995). Therefore, resource demands are described as random variables. Estimates of the mean resource demand should be provided by every estimation method. If the distribution of the resource demands is not known beforehand, estimates of higher moments of the resource demands may be useful to determine the shape of their distribution.

We distinguish between point and interval estimators of the real resource demands. Generally, confidence intervals would be preferable; however, it is often a challenge to ensure that the statistical assumptions underlying a confidence interval calculation hold for a system under study (e.g., distribution of the regression errors).

In certain scenarios, for example, if DVFS or hyperthreading techniques are used (Kumar, L. Zhang, et al., 2009), the resource demands are load-dependent. In such cases, the resource demands are not constant; they are rather a function that may depend, for example, on the arrival rates of the workload classes (Kumar, L. Zhang, et al., 2009).

Categorization of Existing Methods

Table 17.4 provides an overview of the output metrics of the considered estimation methods. Point estimates of the mean resource demand are provided by all approaches. Confidence intervals can be determined for linear regression using standard statistical techniques as mentioned by Rolia and Vetland (1995) and Kraft et al. (2009). These techniques are based on the Central Limit Theorem (cf. Section 2.5 in Chapter 2), assuming an error term with a Normal distribution. Resource demands are typically not deterministic, violating the assumptions underlying linear regression. The influence of the distribution of the resource demands on the accuracy of the confidence intervals is not evaluated for any of the approaches based on linear regression. DEC (Kalbasi, Krishnamurthy, Rolia, and Dawson, 2012; Rolia, Kalbasi, et al., 2010) is the only approach for which the confidence intervals have been evaluated in the literature. The MLE approach (Kraft et al., 2009) and the optimization approach described by L. Zhang et al. (2002) are capable of providing estimates of higher moments. This additional information comes at the cost of a higher amount of required measurements.

Table 17.4: Output metrics of estimation methods

Estimation method	Resource demands			
	Point estimates	Confidence interval	Higher moments	Load-dependent
Response time approximation				
Urgaonkar et al. (2007)	✗			
Nou et al. (2009)	✗			
Brosig et al. (2009)	✗			
Service demand law				
Lazowska et al. (1984)	✗			
Brosig et al. (2009)	✗			
Linear regression				
Bard and Shatzoff (1978)				
Rolia and Vetland (1995),				
Pacifici et al. (2008)	✗	$✗^2$		
Q. Zhang et al. (2007)	✗	$✗^2$		
Kraft et al. (2009); Pérez, Casale, et al. (2015);	✗	$✗^2$		
Pérez, Pacheco-Sanchez, et al. (2013)				
Casale et al. (2008); Casale et al. (2007)	✗	$✗^2$		
Kalman filter				
Zheng et al. (2008)	✗			
Kumar, Tantawi, et al. (2009)	✗			
Wang, Huang, Qin, et al. (2012)	✗			
Optimization				
L. Zhang et al. (2002)	✗		$✗^1$	
Liu et al. (2006); Wynter et al. (2004)	✗			
Menascé (2008)	✗			
Kumar, L. Zhang, et al. (2009)	✗			✗
Machine learning				
Cremonesi, Dhyani, et al. (2010)	✗			
Sharma et al. (2008)	✗			
Kalbasi, Krishnamurthy, Rolia, and Richter (2011)	✗			
Cremonesi and Sansottera (2012, 2014)	✗			
Maximum likelihood estimation				
Kraft et al. (2009)	✗		✗	
Pérez, Casale, et al. (2015)	✗		✗	
Gibbs sampling				
Sutton and Jordan (2011)	✗			
Wang and Casale (2013)	✗			
Kalbasi, Krishnamurthy, Rolia, and Dawson (2012); Rolia, Kalbasi, et al. (2010) (DEC)	✗	✗		

[1] Only feasible if a priori knowledge of the resource demand variance is available.
[2] The accuracy of the confidence intervals is not evaluated.

All of the estimation methods in Table 17.2 can estimate load-independent mean resource demands. Additionally, the enhanced inferencing approach (Kumar, L. Zhang, et al., 2009) also supports the estimation of load-dependent resource demands, assuming a given type of function.

17.4 Robustness

Usually, it is not possible to control every aspect of a system while collecting measurements. This can lead to anomalous behavior in the measurements. Casale et al. (2007), Casale et al. (2008), and Pacifici et al. (2008) identified the following issues with real measurement data:

- presence of outliers,
- background noise,
- non-stationary resource demands,
- collinear workload, and
- insignificant flows.

Background activities can have two effects on measurements: the presence of outliers and background noise. Background noise is created by secondary activities that utilize a resource only lightly over a long period of time. Outliers result from secondary activities that stress a resource at high utilization levels for a short period of time. Outliers can have a significant impact on the parameter estimation resulting in biased estimates (Casale et al., 2007). Different strategies are possible to cope with outliers. It is possible to use special filtering techniques in an upstream processing step or to use parameter estimation techniques that are inherently robust to outliers. However, tails in measurement data from real systems might belong to bursts (e.g., resulting from rare but computationally complex requests). The trade-off decision as to when an observation is to be considered an outlier has to be made on a case-by-case basis, taking into account the characteristics of the specific scenario and application.

The resource demands of a system may be non-stationary over time (i.e., not only the arrival process may change over time, but also the resource demands, which, for example, can be described by a $M_t/M_t/1$ queue). Different types of changes are observed in production systems. Discontinuous changes in the resource demands can be caused by software and hardware reconfigurations, for example, the installation of an operating system update (Casale et al., 2007). Continuous changes in the resource demands may happen over different time scales. Short-term variations can often be observed in cloud computing environments where different workloads experience mutual influences due to the underlying shared infrastructure. Changes in the application state (e.g., database size) or the user behavior (e.g., increased number of items in a shopping cart in an online shop during Christmas season) may result in long-term trends and seasonal patterns (over days, weeks, and months). When using the estimated resource demands to forecast the required resources of an application over a longer time period, these non-stationary effects need to be considered in order to obtain accurate predictions. In order to detect such trends and seasonal patterns, it is possible to apply forecasting techniques on a time series resulting from the repeated execution of one considered estimation method over a certain time period. An overview of such forecasting approaches based on time series analysis can be found in Box et al. (2015).

Another challenge for estimation methods is the existence of collinearities in the arrival rates of different workload classes. There are two possible reasons for collinearities in the workload: low variation in the throughput of a workload class or dependencies between workload classes (Pacifici et al., 2008). For example, if we model *login* and *logout* requests each with a separate workload class, the resulting classes would normally be correlated. The number of logins usually approximately matches the number of logouts. Collinearities in the workload may have negative effects on resource demand estimates. A way to avoid these problems is to detect and combine workload classes that are correlated.

Insignificant flows are caused by workload classes with very small arrival rates in relation to the arrival rates of the other classes. Pacifici et al. (2008) experience numerical stability problems with their linear regression approach when insignificant flows exist. However, it is noteworthy that there might be a dependency between insignificant flows and the length of the sampling time intervals. If the sampling time interval is too short, the variance in arrival rates might be high.

Categorization of Existing Methods

Ordinary least-squares regression is often sensitive to outliers. Stewart et al. (2007) come to the conclusion that least-absolute-differences regression is more robust to outliers. Robust regression techniques, as described in Casale et al. (2007) and Casale et al. (2008), try to detect outliers and ignore measurement samples that cannot be explained by the regression model. Liu et al. (2006) also include an outlier detection mechanism in their estimation method based on optimization.

In general, sliding window or data aging techniques can be applied to the input data to improve the robustness to non-stationary resource demands (Pacifici et al., 2008). In order to detect software and hardware configuration discontinuities, robust and clusterwise regression approaches are proposed by Casale et al. (2007), Casale et al. (2008), and Cremonesi, Dhyani, et al. (2010). If such discontinuities are detected, the resource demands are estimated separately before and after the configuration change. Approaches based on Kalman filters (Kumar, Tantawi, et al., 2009; Zheng et al., 2008) are designed to estimate time-varying parameters. Therefore, they automatically adapt to changes in the resource demands after a software or hardware discontinuity. None of the considered estimation methods is able to learn long-term trends or seasonal patterns (over days, weeks, or months).

Collinearities are one of the major issues when using linear regression (Chatterjee and Price, 1995). A common method to cope with this issue is to check the workload classes for collinear dependencies before applying linear regression. If collinearities are detected, the involved workload classes are merged into one class. This is proposed by Pacifici et al. (2008) and Casale et al. (2007). The DEC approach (Rolia, Kalbasi, et al., 2010) mitigates collinear dependencies, since it estimates the resource demands only for mixes of workload classes.

Pacifici et al. (2008) also consider insignificant flows. They call a workload class insignificant if the ratio between the throughput of the workload class and the throughput of all workload classes is below a given threshold. They completely exclude insignificant workload classes from the regression in order to avoid numerical instabilities.

17.5 Estimation Accuracy and Execution Time

Depending on the concrete application scenario, the presented methods for resource demand estimation can differ significantly in terms of their accuracy and execution time. Spinner et al. (2015) present a comprehensive experimental comparison, evaluating the different estimation methods in terms of their accuracy and overhead. The aim of the evaluation is to answer the following questions:

- How do the different methods compare in terms of estimation accuracy and execution time?
- Which factors influence the estimation accuracy of the different methods?
- How to automatically decide which set of estimation methods to apply in a given scenario?

To address these questions, the influence of the following factors on the estimation accuracy is evaluated: length of sampling interval, number of samples, number of workload classes, load level, collinearity of workload classes, missing workload classes for background activities, and presence of delays during processing at a resource. Table 17.5 lists the estimation methods considered in the experimental evaluation.

Table 17.5: Estimation methods considered in the experimental evaluation

Abbreviation	Estimation method
SDL	Service demand law (Brosig et al., 2009)
UR	Utilization regression (Rolia and Vetland, 1995)
KF	Kalman filter (Kumar, Tantawi, et al., 2009)
MO	Menascé optimization (Menascé, 2008)
LO	Liu optimization (Liu et al., 2006)
RR	Response time regression (Kraft et al., 2009)
GS	Gibbs sampling (Wang, Huang, Qin, et al., 2012)

In the following, we summarize the results of the experimental comparison by Spinner et al. (2015):

- When using estimation methods based on time-aggregated observations (e.g., UR, KF, MO, or LO), the length of the sampling interval is an important parameter that needs to be adjusted to the system under study. A good sampling interval length depends on the response times of requests and the number of requests observed in one interval. The sampling interval should be significantly larger than the response times of requests to avoid end effects, and it should be long enough to be able to calculate the aggregate value based on the observations of a significant number of requests (more than 60 requests per sampling interval has proven to provide good results).
- Most estimation methods (except MO and LO) are negatively influenced when reducing the experiment length to 10 min (i.e., 10 samples). However, they still yield results with acceptable accuracy (relative demand error below 8%).
- All estimation methods are sensitive to the number of workload classes. The linear regression method UR, which uses only utilization and throughput observations, generally yields a degraded accuracy in scenarios with several workload classes. Observations of the response times of requests can help to improve the estimation accuracy significantly even in situations with a very high number of workload classes. However, it is crucial to ensure that the modeling assumptions of the estimation methods using response times are fulfilled as they are highly sensitive to violated assumptions (e.g., incorrect scheduling strategies). Furthermore, insignificant flows can impair resource demand estimation. Workload classes with a small contribution to the total resource demand of a system should therefore be excluded from resource demand estimation.
- When a system operates at a high utilization level (80% or higher), the estimation methods KF, MO, LO, and GS may yield inaccurate results.
- Collinearities in throughput observations of different workload classes impair the estimation accuracy of UR. While it correctly estimates the total resource demand, the apportioning between workload classes is wrong. The other estimation methods are much less sensitive to collinearities in throughput observations.
- Methods that rely on response time observations (e.g., MO, RR, and GS) are more robust to missing workload classes than methods based on utilization.
- Delays due to non-captured software or hardware resources have a strong influence on the estimation accuracy of estimation methods based on observed response times. While some estimation methods (e.g., L. Zhang et al. (2002), Liu et al. (2006), and Menascé (2008)) consider scenarios where multiple resources contribute to the observed end-to-end response time, only Pérez, Pacheco-Sanchez, et al. (2013) consider contention due to *software* resources.
- There are significant differences in the computational complexity of the different estimation methods. In the considered datasets, the estimation takes between under 1 ms and up to 20 s depending on the estimation method. When using resource demand estimation techniques on a production system (e.g., for online performance and resource management), the computational effort needs to be taken into account (especially in data centers with a large number of systems).

In summary, the evaluation shows that using response times can improve the accuracy of the estimated resource demands significantly compared to the traditional approach based on the utilization law using linear regression, especially in cases with multiple workload classes. However, estimation methods employing response time measurements are very sensitive if assumptions of the underlying mathematical model are violated (e.g., incorrect scheduling strategy).

17.6 Library for Resource Demand Estimation (LibReDE)

While the presented systematization and experimental comparison provide a solid basis for selecting the right resource demand estimation method for a given scenario, the selection is still not trivial and requires expertise on the underlying statistical techniques and their assumptions. Also, in many cases, it may be infeasible to determine the right method in advance, as the respective input data may only be available at system run time and the decision would have to be made on-the-fly. Furthermore, the system and its workload may change over time requiring a dynamic switchover to a different estimation method.

Spinner (2017) presents an approach to resource demand estimation that relies on multiple statistical techniques for improved robustness and uses a cross-validation scheme to dynamically select the technique that performs best for the concrete scenario. This simplifies the usage of resource demand estimation methods for performance engineers. Furthermore, it is a crucial building block for Application Performance Management (APM) techniques that automatically estimate resource demands at system run time and use them for online resource management. The approach has been implemented as an open-source tool called LibReDE.[1] The tool includes a library for resource demand estimation, providing ready-to-use implementations of eight common estimation methods.

The main idea of LibReDE is to leverage *multiple statistical techniques* combined with a *feedback loop* to improve the accuracy of the resource demand estimation by iteratively: (1) adapting the estimation problem, (2) selecting suitable statistical methods to be applied, and (3) optimizing the configuration parameters of each method. LibReDE uses *cross-validation* techniques with an error metric based on the deviation between the observed response times and utilization, on the one hand, and the respective predicted metrics using the resource demand estimates, on the other hand.

LibReDE applies multiple statistical techniques in an online setting, automatically combining, weighting, and iteratively refining their results (in a feedback loop) to produce as accurate estimates as possible. Further details on LibReDE and the respective estimation approach it implements can be found in Spinner (2017).

---

[1] http://descartes.tools/librede

17.7 Concluding Remarks

In this chapter, we surveyed, systematized, and evaluated different approaches to the statistical estimation of resource demands based on easy to measure system-level and application-level metrics. The goal of the presented systematization is to help performance engineers select an estimation method that best fits their specific requirements. We first surveyed existing estimation methods and described their modeling assumptions and their underlying statistical techniques. Then, we introduced three dimensions for systematization: (1) input parameters, (2) output metrics, and (3) robustness to anomalies in the input data. For each dimension, we first described its features and then categorized the estimation methods accordingly. We considered resource demands in the context of computing systems; however, the methods we presented are also applicable to other types of systems. We focused on generic methods to determine resource demands without relying on dedicated instrumentation of the application. The goal was to estimate the resource demands based on *indirect measurements* derived from commonly available metrics (e.g., end-to-end response time or resource utilization). We summarized the results of a comprehensive experimental comparison evaluating the different estimation methods in terms of their accuracy and overhead. The evaluation revealed that using response times can improve the accuracy of the estimated resource demands significantly compared to the traditional approach based on the utilization law using linear regression, especially in cases with multiple workload classes. However, estimation methods employing response time measurements are very sensitive if assumptions of the underlying mathematical model are violated.

References

Bard, Y. and Shatzoff, M. (1978). "Statistical Methods in Computer Performance Analysis". In: *Current Trends in Programming Methodology Vol. III: Software Modeling*. Ed. by K. M. Chandy and R. T.-Y. Yeh. Prentice-Hall: NJ, Englewood Cliffs, pp. 1–51 (cited on pp. 368–370, 375, 378).

Box, G. E. P., Jenkins, G. M., Reinsel, G. C., and Ljung, G. M. (2015). *Time Series Analysis: Forecasting and Control*. Fifth edition. Wiley Series in Probability and Statistics. John Wiley & Sons: Hoboken, New Jersey, USA (cited on p. 380).

Brosig, F., Kounev, S., and Krogmann, K. (2009). "Automated Extraction of Palladio Component Models from Running Enterprise Java Applications". In: *Proceedings of the Fourth International Conference on Performance Evaluation Methodologies and Tools (VALUETOOLS 2009)—ROSSA 2009 Workshop*. (Pisa, Italy). ICST/ACM (cited on pp. 368, 369, 375, 378, 381).

Casale, G., Cremonesi, P., and Turrin, R. (2008). "Robust Workload Estimation in Queueing Network Performance Models". In: *Proceedings of the 16th Euromicro*

Conference on Parallel, Distributed and Network-Based Processing (PDP 2008). (Toulouse, France). IEEE: Piscataway, New Jersey, USA, pp. 183–187 (cited on pp. 368, 370, 375, 376, 378–380).

Casale, G., Cremonesi, P., and Turrin, R. (2007). "How to Select Significant Workloads in Performance Models". In: *Proceedings of the 33rd International Computer Measurement Group Conference (CMG 2007).* (San Diego, CA, USA) (cited on pp. 368–370, 375, 376, 378–381).

Chatterjee, S. and Price, B. (1995). *Praxis der Regressionsanalyse.* Second Edition. Oldenbourg Wissenschaftsverlag: Munich, Germany (cited on p. 380).

Cremonesi, P., Dhyani, K., and Sansottera, A. (2010). "Service Time Estimation with a Refinement Enhanced Hybrid Clustering Algorithm". In: *Analytical and Stochastic Modeling Techniques and Applications—17th International Conference, ASMTA 2010—Proceedings.* (Cardiff, UK). Ed. by K. Al-Begain, D. Fiems, and W. J. Knottenbelt. Vol. 6148. Lecture Notes in Computer Science. Springer-Verlag: Berlin, Heidelberg, pp. 291–305 (cited on pp. 368, 371, 375, 378, 380).

Cremonesi, P. and Sansottera, A. (2012). "Indirect Estimation of Service Demands in the Presence of Structural Changes". In: *Proceedings of the 2012 Ninth International Conference on Quantitative Evaluation of Systems (QEST 2012).* IEEE Computer Society: Washington, DC, USA, pp. 249–259 (cited on pp. 368, 371, 375, 378).

– (2014). "Indirect Estimation of Service Demands in the Presence of Structural Changes". *Performance Evaluation*, 73. Elsevier Science: Amsterdam, The Netherlands, pp. 18–40 (cited on pp. 368, 371, 375, 378).

Kalbasi, A., Krishnamurthy, D., Rolia, J., and Dawson, S. (2012). "DEC: Service Demand Estimation with Confidence". *IEEE Transactions on Software Engineering*, 38(3). IEEE Computer Society: Washington, DC, USA, pp. 561–578 (cited on pp. 368, 373, 375, 377, 378).

Kalbasi, A., Krishnamurthy, D., Rolia, J., and Richter, M. (2011). "MODE: Mix Driven On-line Resource Demand Estimation". In: *Proceedings of the 7th International Conference on Network and Service Management (CNSM 2011).* (Paris, France). IEEE: Piscataway, New Jersey, USA (cited on pp. 368, 372, 375, 378).

Kraft, S., Pacheco-Sanchez, S., Casale, G., and Dawson, S. (2009). "Estimating Service Resource Consumption from Response Time Measurements". In: *Proceedings of the 4th International Conference on Performance Evaluation Methodologies and Tools (VALUETOOLS 2009).* (Pisa, Italy). ICST/ACM, p. 48 (cited on pp. 368–370, 372, 375–378, 381).

Kumar, D., Tantawi, A. N., and Zhang, L. (2009). "Real-Time Performance Modeling for Adaptive Software Systems with Multi-Class Workload". In: *Proceedings of the 17th Annual Meeting of the IEEE/ACM International Symposium on Modelling, Analysis and Simulation of Computer and Telecommunication Systems*

(MASCOTS 2009). (London, UK). IEEE Computer Society: Washington, DC, USA, pp. 1–4 (cited on pp. 368, 370, 375, 378, 380, 381).

Kumar, D., Zhang, L., and Tantawi, A. N. (2009). "Enhanced Inferencing: Estimation of a Workload Dependent Performance Model". In: *Proceedings of the 4th International Conference on Performance Evaluation Methodologies and Tools (VALUETOOLS 2009)*. (Pisa, Italy). ICST/ACM (cited on pp. 368, 370, 371, 375–379).

Lazowska, E. D., Zahorjan, J., Graham, G. S., and Sevcik, K. C. (1984). *Quantitative System Performance: Computer System Analysis Using Queueing Network Models*. Prentice-Hall: Upper Saddle River, NJ, USA (cited on pp. 368, 369, 375, 376, 378).

Liu, Z., Wynter, L., Xia, C. H., and Zhang, F. (2006). "Parameter Inference of Queueing Models for IT Systems using End-to-End Measurements". *Performance Evaluation*, 63(1). Elsevier Science: Amsterdam, The Netherlands, pp. 36–60 (cited on pp. 368, 370, 371, 375, 376, 378, 380–382).

Menascé, D. A. (2008). "Computing Missing Service Demand Parameters for Performance Models". In: *Proceedings of the 34th International Computer Measurement Group Conference (CMG 2008)*. (Las Vegas, Nevada, USA), pp. 241–248 (cited on pp. 368, 370, 371, 375, 376, 378, 381, 382).

Menascé, D. A., Almeida, V. A., and Dowdy, L. W. (2004). *Performance by Design: Computer Capacity Planning By Example*. Prentice Hall: Upper Saddle River, NJ, USA (cited on p. 369).

Nou, R., Kounev, S., Julià, F., and Torres, J. (2009). "Autonomic QoS Control in Enterprise Grid Environments using Online Simulation". *Journal of Systems and Software*, 82(3). Elsevier Science: Amsterdam, The Netherlands, pp. 486–502 (cited on pp. 368, 369, 375, 378).

Pacifici, G., Segmuller, W., Spreitzer, M., and Tantawi, A. N. (2008). "CPU Demand for Web Serving: Measurement Analysis and Dynamic Estimation". *Performance Evaluation*, 65(6-7). Elsevier Science: Amsterdam, The Netherlands, pp. 531–553 (cited on pp. 368–370, 375, 376, 378–381).

Pérez, J. F., Casale, G., and Pacheco-Sanchez, S. (2015). "Estimating Computational Requirements in Multi-Threaded Applications". *IEEE Transactions on Software Engineering*, 41(3). IEEE Computer Society: Washington, DC, USA, pp. 264–278 (cited on pp. 375, 378).

Pérez, J. F., Pacheco-Sanchez, S., and Casale, G. (2013). "An Offline Demand Estimation Method for Multi-threaded Applications". In: *Proceedings of the 2013 IEEE 21st International Symposium on Modelling, Analysis and Simulation of Computer and Telecommunication Systems (MASCOTS 2013)*. (San Francisco, CA, USA). IEEE Computer Society: Washington, DC, USA, pp. 21–30 (cited on pp. 368, 369, 372, 376, 378, 382).

Rolia, J., Kalbasi, A., Krishnamurthy, D., and Dawson, S. (2010). "Resource Demand Modeling for Multi-Tier Services". In: *Proceedings of the First Joint WOSP/SIPEW International Conference on Performance Engineering (ICPE 2010)*. (San Jose, CA, USA). ACM: New York, NY, USA, pp. 207–216 (cited on pp. 368, 373, 375, 377, 378, 381).

Rolia, J. and Vetland, V. (1995). "Parameter Estimation for Performance Models of Distributed Application Systems". In: *Proceedings of the 1995 Conference of the Centre for Advanced Studies on Collaborative Research (CASCON 1995)*. (Toronto, Ontario, Canada). IBM Press, p. 54 (cited on pp. 368–370, 375–378, 381).

Sharma, A. B., Bhagwan, R., Choudhury, M., Golubchik, L., Govindan, R., and Voelker, G. M. (2008). "Automatic Request Categorization in Internet Services". *SIGMETRICS Performance Evaluation Review*, 36(2). ACM: New York, NY, USA, pp. 16–25 (cited on pp. 368, 372, 375, 378).

Smola, A. J. and Schölkopf, B. (2004). "A Tutorial on Support Vector Regression". *Statistics and Computing*, 14(3). Kluwer Academic Publishers: Hingham, MA, USA, pp. 199–222 (cited on p. 372).

Spinner, S. (2017). "Self-Aware Resource Management in Virtualized Data Centers". PhD thesis. Würzburg, Germany: University of Würzburg (cited on pp. 366, 383).

Spinner, S., Casale, G., Brosig, F., and Kounev, S. (2015). "Evaluating Approaches to Resource Demand Estimation". *Performance Evaluation*, 92. Elsevier Science: Amsterdam, The Netherlands, pp. 51–71 (cited on pp. 366, 381, 382).

Stewart, C., Kelly, T., and Zhang, A. (2007). "Exploiting Nonstationarity for Performance Prediction". In: *ACM SIGOPS Operating Systems Review - Proceedings of the 2nd ACM SIGOPS EuroSys European Conference on Computer Systems*. (Lisbon, Portugal). Vol. 41. 3. ACM: New York, NY, USA, pp. 31–44 (cited on pp. 368–370, 375, 376, 380).

Sutton, C. and Jordan, M. I. (2011). "Bayesian Inference for Queueing Networks and Modeling of Internet Services". *The Annals of Applied Statistics*, 5(1). The Institute of Mathematical Statistics, pp. 254–282 (cited on pp. 368, 372, 375, 378).

Urgaonkar, B., Pacifici, G., Shenoy, P. J., Spreitzer, M., and Tantawi, A. N. (2007). "Analytic Modeling of Multitier Internet Applications". *ACM Transactions on the Web*, 1(1). ACM: New York, NY, USA (cited on pp. 368, 369, 375, 378).

Wang, W., Huang, X., Qin, X., Zhang, W., Wei, J., and Zhong, H. (2012). "Application-Level CPU Consumption Estimation: Towards Performance Isolation of Multi-tenancy Web Applications". In: *Proceedings of the 2012 IEEE Fifth International Conference on Cloud Computing (CLOUD 2012)*. (Honolulu, HI, USA). IEEE Computer Society: Washington, DC, USA, pp. 439–446 (cited on pp. 368, 370, 375, 378, 381).

Wang, W., Huang, X., Song, Y., Zhang, W., Wei, J., Zhong, H., and Huang, T. (2011). "A Statistical Approach for Estimating CPU Consumption in Shared Java Middleware Server". In: *Proceedings of the 2011 IEEE 35th Annual Computer Software and Applications Conference (COMPSAC 2011)*. (Munich, Germany). IEEE Computer Society: Washington, DC, USA, pp. 541–546 (cited on p. 368).

Wang, W. and Casale, G. (2013). "Bayesian Service Demand Estimation Using Gibbs Sampling". In: *Proceedings of the 2013 IEEE 21st International Symposium on Modelling, Analysis and Simulation of Computer and Telecommunication Systems (MASCOTS 2013)*. IEEE Computer Society: Washington, DC, USA, pp. 567–576 (cited on pp. 368, 372, 373, 375, 376, 378).

Wynter, L., Xia, C. H., and Zhang, F. (2004). "Parameter Inference of Queueing Models for IT Systems using End-to-End Measurements". In: *Proceedings of the ACM SIGMETRICS International Conference on Measurements and Modeling of Computer Systems (SIGMETRICS 2004)*. ACM: New York, NY, USA, pp. 408–409 (cited on pp. 368, 370, 375, 376, 378).

Zhang, L., Xia, C. H., Squillante, M. S., and Mills, W. N. (2002). "Workload Service Requirements Analysis: A Queueing Network Optimization Approach". In: *Proceedings of the 10th IEEE International Symposium on Modeling, Analysis and Simulation of Computer and Telecommunications Systems (MASCOTS 2002)*. (Fort Worth, TX, USA). IEEE Computer Society: Washington, DC, USA, pp. 23–32 (cited on pp. 368, 375–378, 382).

Zhang, Q., Smirni, E., and Cherkasova, L. (2007). "A Regression-Based Analytic Model for Dynamic Resource Provisioning of Multi-Tier Applications". In: *Proceedings of the Fourth International Conference on Autonomic Computing (ICAC 2007)*. IEEE Computer Society: Washington, DC, USA, p. 27 (cited on pp. 368–370, 375, 378).

Zheng, T., Woodside, C. M., and Litoiu, M. (2008). "Performance Model Estimation and Tracking Using Optimal Filters". *IEEE Transactions on Software Engineering*, 34(3). IEEE Computer Society: Washington, DC, USA, pp. 391–406 (cited on pp. 368, 370, 375, 378, 380).

Chapter 18
Software and System Security

Aleksandar Milenkoski and Samuel Kounev

Evaluation of computer security mechanisms is an active research area with many un-resolved issues. The research community has produced many results that contribute towards addressing these issues. In this chapter, we systematize the accumulated knowledge and current practices in the area of evaluating computer security mech-anisms. We define a design space structured into three parts: workload, metrics, and measurement methodology. We provide an overview of the current practices by surveying and comparing evaluation approaches and methods related to each part of the design space.

Computer security mechanisms—referred to as security mechanisms—are crucial for enforcing the properties of confidentiality, integrity, and availability of system data and services. A common security mechanism is an intrusion detection sys-tem (IDS). IDSes monitor on-going activities in the protected networks or hosts, detecting potentially malicious activities. The detection of malicious activities en-ables the timely reaction in order to stop an on-going attack or to mitigate the impact of a security breach. Other common security mechanisms include firewalls and access control (AC) systems.

To minimize the risk of security breaches, methods and techniques for evaluating security mechanisms in a realistic and reliable manner are needed. The benefits of evaluating security mechanisms are manifold. For instance, in the case of IDSes, one may compare different IDSes in terms of their attack detection accuracy in order to deploy an IDS that operates optimally in a given environment, thus reducing the risks of a security breach. Further, one may tune an already deployed security mechanism by varying its configuration parameters and investigating their influence through evaluation tests. This enables a comparison of the evaluation results with respect to the configuration space of the mechanism and can help to identify an optimal configuration.

The evaluation of security mechanisms is of interest to many different types of users and professionals in the field of information security. This includes researchers, who typically evaluate novel security solutions; industrial software architects, who typically evaluate security mechanisms by carrying out internationally standardized large-scale tests; and IT security officers, who evaluate security mechanisms in order to select a mechanism that is optimal for protecting a given environment, or to optimize the configuration of an already deployed mechanism.

© Springer Nature Switzerland AG 2020

S. Kounev et al., *Systems Benchmarking*, https://doi.org/10.1007/978-3-030-41705-5_18

In this chapter, we survey existing knowledge on the evaluation of security mechanisms by defining an evaluation design space that puts existing work into a common context. Given the significant amount of existing practical and theoretical work, the presented systematization is beneficial for improving the general understanding of the topic by providing an overview of the current state of the field. The evaluation design space that we present is structured into three parts, that is, workload, metrics, and measurement methodology—the standard components of any system evaluation scenario. The discussions in this chapter are relevant for the evaluation of a wide spectrum of security mechanisms, such as firewalls and AC systems.

This chapter is structured as follows: in Section 18.1, we provide the background knowledge essential for understanding the topic of evaluating security mechanisms; in Section 18.1.1, we discuss different types of attacks and put the different security mechanisms into a common context; in Section 18.1.2, we demonstrate the wide applicability of evaluation of security mechanisms; and in Sections 18.2.1–18.2.3, we compare multiple approaches and methods that evaluation practitioners can employ.

The chapter is a compact summary of Milenkoski, Vieira, et al. (2015), Milenkoski, Payne, et al. (2015), and Milenkoski (2016). These publications provide more details on the topics discussed in this chapter.

18.1 Essential Background

We start with some background relevant for understanding the context of the content presented in the rest of the chapter. We first introduce attacks and common security mechanisms used to protect against them. Following this, we describe real-life practical scenarios where techniques for evaluating security mechanisms are needed, demonstrating the wide applicability of such techniques and their broad relevance.

18.1.1 Attacks and Common Security Mechanisms

A given system (i.e., a host) is considered secure if it has the properties of confidentiality, integrity, and availability of its data and services (Stallings, 2002). *Confidentiality* means the protection of data against its release to unauthorized parties. *Integrity* means the protection of data or services against modifications by unauthorized parties. Finally, *availability* means the protection of services such that they are ready to be used when needed. Attacks are deliberate attempts to violate the previously mentioned security properties (Shirey, 1999).

There are many security mechanisms used to enforce the properties of confidentiality, integrity, and availability of system data and services. Kruegel et al. (2005) classify security mechanisms by taking an attack-centric approach distinguishing between attack prevention, attack avoidance, and attack detection mechanisms. Based on this classification, we put the different security mechanisms into a common context, as depicted in Figure 18.1.

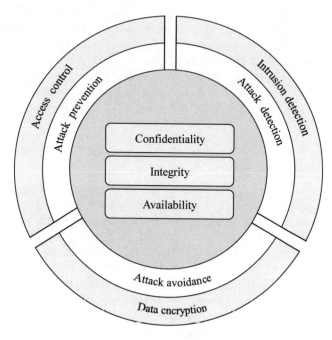

Fig. 18.1: Common security mechanisms

The attack prevention class includes security mechanisms that prevent attackers from reaching, or gaining access to, the targeted system. A representative mechanism that belongs to this class is access control, which uses the concept of identity to distinguish between authorized and unauthorized parties. For instance, firewalls distinguish between different parties trying to reach a given system over a network connection based, for example, on their IP addresses. According to access control policies, firewalls may allow or deny access to the system.

The attack avoidance class includes security mechanisms that modify the data stored in the targeted system such that it would be of no use to an attacker in case of an intrusion. A representative mechanism that belongs to this class is data encryption, which is typically implemented using encryption algorithms, such as RSA (Rivest–Shamir–Adleman) and DES (Data Encryption Standard).

The attack detection class includes security mechanisms that detect on-going attacks under the assumption that an attacker can reach, or gain access to, the targeted system and interact with it. A representative security mechanism that belongs to this class is intrusion detection. There are several different types of IDSes. For example, according to the target platform that IDSes monitor, they can be categorized into *host-based* (IDSes that monitor the activities of the users of the host where they are deployed), *network-based* (IDSes that monitor the network traffic that is destined for, and/or originates from, a single host or a set of hosts that constitute a network environment), or *hybrid* IDSes. According to the employed attack detection method, IDSes can be categorized into *misuse-based* (IDSes that evaluate system and/or network activities against a set of signatures of known attacks), *anomaly-based* (trained IDSes that use a profile of regular network and/or system activities as a reference to distinguish between regular activities and anomalous activities, the latter being treated as attacks), or *hybrid* IDSes.

This chapter surveys existing knowledge on the evaluation of security mechanisms that belong to the attack prevention and attack detection class. It treats the topic of IDS evaluation as a single sub-domain of evaluation of security mechanisms.

18.1.2 Application Scenarios

We now present various application scenarios of evaluation of security mechanisms in order to demonstrate its wide applicability and broad relevance. This evaluation helps to determine how well a security mechanism performs and how well it performs when compared to other mechanisms. The answer to this question is of interest to many different types of professionals in the field of information security. These include designers of security mechanisms, both researchers and industrial software architects, as well as users of security mechanisms, such as IT security officers.

Researchers design novel security mechanisms. They typically focus on designing mechanisms that are superior in terms of given properties that are subject of research, for example, attack detection accuracy or workload processing capacity. To demonstrate the value of the research outcome, researchers typically perform small-scale evaluation studies comparing the proposed security mechanisms with other mechanisms in terms of the considered properties. For instance, Meng and Li (2012) measure workload processing throughput, Mohammed et al. (2011) measure power consumption, and Sinha et al. (2006) measure memory consumption. Further, in order to demonstrate that the proposed security mechanisms are practically useful, researchers also evaluate properties that are not necessarily in the focus of their research but are relevant from a practical perspective. For example, Lombardi and Di Pietro (2011) measure the performance overhead incurred by the IDS they propose.

Industrial software architects design security mechanisms with an extensive set of features according to their demand on the market. Security mechanisms, in this context, are typically evaluated by carrying out tests of a large scale. The latter are part of regular quality assurance procedures. They normally use internationally standardized tests for evaluating security mechanisms in a standard and comprehensive manner. For instance, Microsoft's Internet Security and Acceleration (ISA) Server 2004 has been evaluated according to the *Common Criteria* international standard for evaluating IT security products.[1] Standardized tests are performed in

---

[1] https://www.iso.org/standard/50341.html

strictly controlled environments and normally by independent testing laboratories, such as NSS Labs,[2] to ensure credibility of the results.

In contrast to evaluation studies performed by researchers, evaluation studies in industry normally include the evaluation of mechanism properties that are relevant from a marketing perspective. An example of such a property is the financial cost of deploying and maintaining an IDS or a firewall, which is evaluated as part of the tests performed by NSS Labs (NSS Labs, 2010).

IT security officers use security mechanisms to protect environments of which they are in charge from malicious activities. They may evaluate mechanisms, for example, when designing security architectures in order to select a mechanism that is considered optimal for protecting a given environment. Further, if a security architecture is already in place, an IT security officer may evaluate the performance of the selected mechanism for different configurations in order to identify its optimal configuration. The performance is typically very sensitive to the way the mechanism is configured.

In addition to security and performance-related aspects, as part of evaluation studies, further usability-related aspects may also be considered. This is to be expected since IT security officers deal with security mechanisms on a daily basis. For instance, security officers in charge of protecting large-scale environments may be cognitively overloaded by the output produced by the deployed security mechanisms (Komlodi et al., 2004). Thus, the ability to produce structured output that can be analyzed efficiently is an important property often considered when evaluating security mechanisms.

18.2 Current State

In this section, we put the existing practical and research work related to the evaluation of security mechanisms into a common context. Since such an evaluation is a highly complex task, any evaluation experiment requires careful planning in terms of the selection of workloads, tools, metrics, and measurement methodology. We provide a comprehensive systematization of knowledge in the respective areas providing a basis for the efficient and accurate planning of evaluation studies. We define an evaluation design space structured into three parts: workloads, metrics, and measurement methodology, considered to be standard components of any evaluation experiment.

The proposed design space structures the evaluation components and features they may possess with respect to different properties expressed as variability points in the design space. Note that we do not claim complete coverage of all variability points in the design space. We instead focus on the typical variability points of evaluation approaches putting existing work related to the evaluation of security mechanisms

---

[2] https://www.nsslabs.com

into a common context. We illustrate the defined design space categories by referring to evaluation experiments that fit each of the considered categories.

18.2.1 Workloads

In Figure 18.2, we depict the workload part of the design space. In order to evaluate a security mechanism, one needs both malicious and benign workloads. One can use them separately, for example, as *pure malicious* and *pure benign workloads* for measuring the capacity of the mechanism (Bharadwaja et al., 2011; Jin, Xiang, Zou, et al., 2013) or its attack coverage. Alternatively, one can use *mixed* workloads to subject the mechanism to realistic attack scenarios. A more detailed overview of typical use cases of different workload forms is provided in Section 18.2.3 in the context of measurement methodologies.

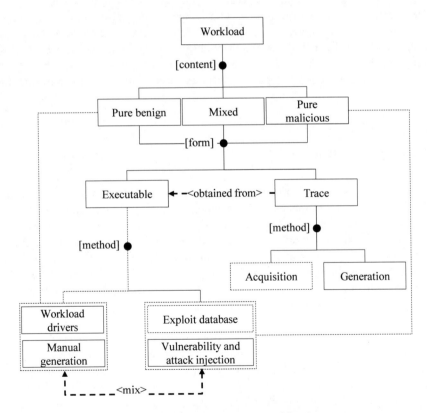

Fig. 18.2: Design space—workloads

Workloads for evaluating security mechanisms normally take an *executable* form for live testing, or a recorded form (i.e., a *trace*) generated by recording a live execution of workloads for later replay. A major advantage of using workloads in executable form is that they closely resemble a real workload as monitored by a security mechanism during operation. However, a malicious workload in executable form requires a specific victim environment, which can be expensive and time-consuming to setup.[3] In contrast, such an environment is not always required for replaying workload traces. Further, replicating evaluation experiments when using executable malicious workloads is usually a challenge since the execution of attack scripts might crash the victim environment or render it in an unstable state. The process of restoring the environment to an identical state as before the execution of the attack scripts may be time-consuming. At the same time, multiple evaluation runs would be typically required to ensure statistical significance of the observed system behavior. We refer the reader to Mell et al. (2003) for further comparison of workloads in executable and trace form. In the following, we discuss different methods for generating benign and malicious workloads in executable form: use of *workload drivers* and *manual generation* approaches for generation of pure benign workloads and use of an *exploit database* and *vulnerability and attack injection* techniques for generating pure malicious workloads (Figure 18.2).

18.2.1.1 Workload Drivers

For the purpose of live testing, a common practice is to use benign workload drivers in order to generate pure benign workloads with different characteristics. We surveyed evaluation experiments (e.g., Jin, Xiang, Zhao, et al. (2009), Lombardi and Di Pietro (2011), Jin, Xiang, Zou, et al. (2013), Griffin et al. (2003), Patil et al. (2004), Riley et al. (2008), Reeves et al. (2012), and Zhang et al. (2008)) concluding that some of the commonly used workload drivers are the following (and alike): SPEC CPU2000[4] for generation of CPU-intensive workloads; IOzone[5] and Postmark (Katcher, 1997) for generation of file I/O-intensive workloads; httpbench,[6] dkftpbench,[7] and ApacheBench for generation of network-intensive workloads; and UnixBench[8] for generation of system-wide workloads that exercise not only the hardware but also the operating system. A major advantage of using benign workload drivers is the ability to customize the workload in terms of its temporal and intensity characteristics. For instance, one may configure a workload driver to gradually

---

[3] While setting up their workbench for evaluation of IDSes, Debar et al. (1998) concluded that "*Transforming exploit scripts found in our database into attack scripts requires some work but setting up a reliable and vulnerable server has also proved to be a difficult task!*"

[4] https://www.spec.org/cpu2000

[5] http://www.iozone.org

[6] http://freecode.com/projects/httpbench

[7] http://www.kegel.com/dkftpbench

[8] http://code.google.com/p/byte-unixbench

increase the workload intensity over time, as typically done when evaluating the capacity of a security mechanism.

18.2.1.2 Manual Generation

An alternative approach to using workload drivers is to manually execute tasks that are known to exercise specific system resources. For example, a common approach is to use file encoding or tracing tasks to emulate CPU-intensive tasks (e.g., Dunlap et al. (2002) perform ray tracing, while Lombardi and Di Pietro (2011) perform encoding of a .mp3 file); file conversion and copying of large files to emulate file I/O-intensive tasks (e.g., Lombardi and Di Pietro (2011) and Allalouf et al. (2010) use the UNIX command *dd* to perform file copy operations), and kernel compilation to emulate mixed (i.e., both CPU-intensive and file I/O-intensive) tasks (e.g., performed by Wright et al. (2002), Lombardi and Di Pietro (2011), Riley et al. (2008), Reeves et al. (2012), and Dunlap et al. (2002)). This approach of benign workload generation enables the generation of workloads with behavior as observed by the security mechanism under test during regular system operation; however, it does not support workload customization and might require substantial human effort.

18.2.1.3 Exploit Database

As pure malicious workloads in executable form, security researchers typically use an exploit database. They have a choice of assembling an exploit database by themselves or using a readily available one.

A major disadvantage of the *manual assembly* is the high cost of the attack script collection process. For instance, when collecting publicly available attack scripts, the latter typically have to be adapted to exploit vulnerabilities of a specific victim environment. This includes modification of shell codes, adaptation of employed buffer overflow techniques, and similar. Depending on the number of collected attack scripts, this process may be extremely time-consuming. Mell et al. (2003) report that in 2001 the average number of attack scripts in common exploit databases was in the range of 9–66, whereas some later works, such as the one of Lombardi and Di Pietro (2011), use as low as four attack scripts as a malicious workload.

To alleviate the above-mentioned issues, many researchers employ penetration testing tools to use a *readily available* exploit database. The Metasploit framework (Maynor et al., 2007) is a popular penetration testing tool that has been used in evaluation experiments (Görnitz et al., 2009). The interest of security researchers in Metasploit (and in penetration testing tools in general) is not surprising since Metasploit enables customizable and automated platform exploitation by using an exploit database that is maintained up-to-date and is freely available. Metasploit is very well accepted by the security community not only due to the large exploit database it provides but also because it enables rapid development of new exploits. However, although penetration testing frameworks might seem like an ideal solution for generating malicious workloads, they have some critical limitations. Gad El Rab (2008) analyzes the Metasploit's exploit database to discover that most of the exploits are executed from remote sources and exploit only implementation and design vulnerabilities, neglecting operation and management vulnerabilities (Shirey, 1999). Such characteristics are common for many penetration testing tools, which indicates their limited usefulness in evaluating security mechanisms.

An effort to provide an extensive collection of exploits to security researchers has been driven by Symantec. Dumitras and Shou (2011) present Symantec's WINE datasets, which contain a collection of malware samples that exploit various novel vulnerabilities. The large scale of this project is indicated by the fact that Symantec's sensors continuously collect malware samples from 240,000 sensors deployed in 200 countries worldwide. Due to the continuous nature of the malware collection process, this malware database is useful not only as a basis for generating extensive malicious workloads but also for providing an up-to-date overview of the security threat landscape. However, since the malware samples are collected from real platforms and contain user data, Symantec's malware samples can be accessed only on-site at the Symantec Research Lab to avoid legal issues.

18.2.1.4 Vulnerability and Attack Injection

An alternative approach to the use of an exploit database is the use of vulnerability and attack injection techniques.

Vulnerability injection enables live testing by artificially injecting exploitable vulnerable code in a target platform. Thus, this technique is useful in cases where the collection of attack scripts that exploit vulnerabilities is unfeasible. However, this method for generation of malicious workloads is still in an early phase of research and development. Vulnerability injection relies on the basic principles of the more general research area of fault injection. Since it enables estimation of fault-tolerant system measures (e.g., fault coverage, error latency) (Arlat et al., 1993), fault injection is an attractive approach to validate specific fault handling mechanisms and to assess the impact of faults in actual systems. In the past decades, research on fault injection has been focused on the emulation of hardware faults. Carreira et al. (1998) and Rodríguez et al. (1999) have shown that it is possible to emulate these faults in a realistic manner. The interest in software fault injection has been increasing and has been a foundation for many research works on the emulation of software faults (e.g., Durães and Madeira (2003)). In practice, software fault injection deliberately introduces faults into a software system in a way that emulates real software faults. A reference technique, proposed by Durães and Madeira (2006), is G-SWFI (Generic Software Fault Injection Technique), which enables injection of realistic software faults using educated code mutation. The injected faults are specified in a library derived from an extensive field study aimed at identifying the types of bugs that are usually found in many software systems.

A specific application of software fault injection is a security assessment in which of central importance are software faults that represent security vulnerabilities. Fonseca and Vieira (2008) analyzed 655 security patches of 6 web applications to discover that only 12 generic software faults are responsible for all security problems of the applications. This finding has motivated further research in software fault injection as a method for security evaluation. Fonseca, Vieira, and Madeira (2009) proposed a procedure that enables automatic vulnerability injection and attack of web applications. To accurately emulate real-world web vulnerabilities, this work relies on results obtained from a field study on real security vulnerabilities (Fonseca and Vieira, 2008). Fonseca, Vieira, and Madeira (2009) built a Vulnerability and Attack Injector, a mechanism that automatically exploits injected vulnerabilities. In order to inject vulnerabilities in the source code of web applications, first the application source code is analyzed searching for locations where vulnerabilities can be injected. Once a possible location is found, a vulnerability is injected by performing a code mutation. The code mutation is performed by vulnerability operators that leverage a realistic field data of vulnerable code segments. For more details on the vulnerability injection procedure, we refer the reader to Fonseca, Vieira, and Madeira (2009). Aware of the injected vulnerability, the Attack Injector interacts with the web application in order to deliver attack payloads.

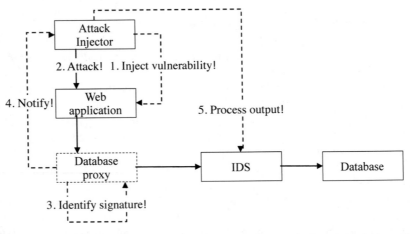

Fig. 18.3: Use of vulnerability injection to evaluate a security mechanism (an IDS)

Fonseca, Vieira, and Madeira (2009) also demonstrated a preliminary approach for automated (i.e., without human intervention) evaluation of a security mechanism that detects SQL (Structured Query Language) injection attacks. We depict a procedure that follows this approach in Figure 18.3. First, the Vulnerability Injector injects a vulnerability in the web application, followed by the Attack Injector that delivers an attack payload with a given signature, that is, an attack identifier. Fonseca, Vieira, and Madeira (2009) developed a database proxy that monitors the communication between the application and the database in order to identify the presence of an attack signature. In case it identifies such signature, it notifies the Attack Injector that the injected vulnerability is successfully exploited. In this way, the Attack Injector builds a ground truth knowledge. Given that Fonseca, Vieira, and Madeira (2009) customized the Attack Injector to process the output of the security mechanism that monitors the traffic to the database, the Attack Injector can automatically calculate values of attack detection accuracy metrics (see Section 18.2.2).

Attack injection, as an approach separate from vulnerability injection, enables the generation of workloads for evaluating security mechanisms that contain benign and malicious activities such that attacks, crafted with respect to representative attack models, are injected during regular operation of a given system. Same as vulnerability injection, this technique is useful in cases where the collection of attack scripts that exploit vulnerabilities is unfeasible.

In Milenkoski, Payne, et al. (2015), we proposed an approach for the accurate, rigorous, and representative evaluation of hypercall security mechanisms designed to mitigate or detect hypercall attacks. Hypercalls are software traps from the kernel of a virtual machine (VM) to the hypervisor. For instance, the execution of an attack triggering a vulnerability of a hypervisor's hypercall handler may lead to a crash of the hypervisor or to altering the hypervisor's memory. The latter may enable the execution of malicious code with hypervisor privilege. In Milenkoski, Payne, et al. (2015), we presented *HInjector*, a customizable framework for injecting hypercall attacks during regular operation of a guest VM in a Xen-based environment.[9] The goal of HInjector is to exercise the sensors of a security mechanism that monitors the execution of hypercalls. The attacks injected by *HInjector* conform to attack models based on existing Xen vulnerabilities. We distinguish the following attack models:

- Invoking hypercalls from irregular call sites. Some hypercall security mechanisms (e.g., Bharadwaja et al. (2011)) may consider hypercalls invoked from call sites unknown to them, for example, an attacker's loadable kernel module (LKM), as malicious.
- Invoking hypercalls with anomalous parameter values (a) outside the valid value domains or (b) crafted for exploiting specific vulnerabilities not necessarily outside the valid value domains. This attack model is based on the Xen vulnerabilities described in CVE-2008-3687, CVE-2012-3516, CVE-2012-5513, and CVE-2012-6035.
- Invoking a series of hypercalls in irregular order, including repetitive execution of a single or multiple hypercalls. This attack model is based on the Xen vulnerability described in CVE-2013-1920. The repetitive execution of hypercalls, for example, requesting system resources, is an easily feasible attack that may lead to resource exhaustion of collocated VMs.

In Figure 18.4, we depict the architecture of HInjector, which consists of the components *Injector*, *LKM*, *Identificator*, *Configuration*, and *Logs*. We refer to the VM injecting hypercall attacks as malicious VM (MVM). The security mechanism under test (an IDS) is deployed in a secured VM (SVM) collocated with MVM.

The *Injector*, deployed in the hypercall interface of MVM's kernel, intercepts hypercalls invoked by the kernel during regular operation and modifies hypercall pa-

---

[9] https://xenproject.org

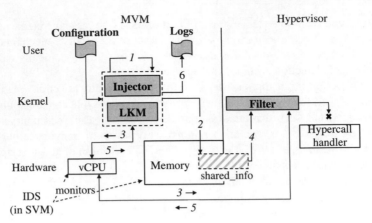

Fig. 18.4: Architecture of HInjector

rameter values on-the-fly, making them anomalous. The Injector is used for injecting hypercalls invoked from a regular call site.

The loadable kernel module (*LKM*), a module of MVM's kernel, invokes regular hypercalls, hypercalls with anomalous parameter values, or hypercalls in irregular order. The LKM is used for injecting hypercalls invoked from an irregular call site.

The *Identificator*, deployed in Xen's hypercall interrupt handler (i.e., 0x82 interrupt), identifies hypercalls injected by the Injector or the LKM, blocks their execution, and returns a valid error code. The latter is important for preventing MVM crashes by allowing the control flow of MVM's kernel to handle failed hypercalls that have been invoked by it. The Identificator blocks the execution of Xen's hypercall handlers to prevent Xen crashes. The Identificator identifies injected hypercalls based on information stored by the Injector/LKM in the *shared_info* structure, a memory region shared between a guest VM and Xen. To this end, we extended *shared_info* with a string field named *hid* (hypercall identification).

The *configuration* is a set of user files containing configuration parameters for managing the operation of the Injector and the LKM. Currently, it allows for specifying the duration of an injection campaign, valid parameter value domains and/or specifically crafted parameter values for a given hypercall (relevant to the Injector and the LKM), and valid order of a series of hypercalls (relevant to the LKM).

The *logs* are user files containing records about injected hypercalls—that is, hypercall IDs (hypercall identification numbers assigned by Xen) and parameter values as well as timestamps. The logged data serves as reference data (i.e., as "ground truth") used for calculating attack detection accuracy metrics.

In Figure 18.4, we depict the steps involved in injecting a single hypercall by the Injector/LKM. An illustrative example of the Injector injecting a hypercall with a parameter value outside of its valid domain is as follows: (1) The Injector intercepts a hypercall invoked by MVM's kernel and replaces the value, for example, of the first parameter, with a generated value outside the parameter's valid value domain specified in the configuration; (2) The Injector stores the ID of the hypercall, the number of the parameter with anomalous value (i.e., one), and the parameter value itself in *hid*; (3) The Injector passes the hypercall to MVM's virtual CPU, which then issues a 0x82 interrupt and passes control to Xen; (4) The Identificator, using the data stored in *hid*, identifies the injected hypercall when it arrives at Xen's 0x82 interrupt handler; (5) The Identificator returns a valid error code without invoking the hypercall's handler; and (6) After the return code arrives at MVM's kernel, the Injector stores in the log files, the ID and parameter values of the injected hypercall, and a timestamp.

We now discuss methods for obtaining pure benign, pure malicious, or mixed workloads in trace form. We distinguish between trace *acquisition* and trace *generation*.

18.2.1.5 Trace Acquisition

Under trace acquisition, we understand the process of obtaining trace files from an industrial organization, that is, real-world traces, or obtaining publicly available traces.

Real-world traces subject a security mechanism under test to a workload as observed during operation in a real deployment environment. However, they are usually very difficult to obtain mainly due to the unwillingness of industrial organizations to share operational traces with security researchers because of privacy and similar legal concerns. Thus, real-world traces are usually anonymized by using various techniques, which are known to introduce inconsistencies in the anonymized trace files. Another challenge is that the attacks in real-world traces are usually not labeled and may contain unknown attacks, making the construction of the "ground truth" challenging. Lack of ground truth information severely limits the usability of trace files; for example, one could not quantify the false negative detection rate. To quote from Sommer and Paxson (2010): "*If one cannot find a sound way to obtain ground-truth for the evaluation, then it becomes questionable to pursue the work at all, even if it otherwise appears on a solid foundation.*" Among many other things, the labeling accuracy and feasibility depend on the capturing method used to record the traces, that is, on the richness of the information regarding the recorded activity itself (e.g., network packet timestamps, system call arguments). For instance, Sperotto et al. (2009) argue that when it comes to evaluating a network-based IDS that differentiates between network flows, traces captured in honeypots enable much more efficient labeling than traces captured in real-world environments, since honeypots are able to record relevant activity information that is not usually provided with real-world production traces. An interesting derived observation is that one may tend to prioritize trace generation in an isolated and a specialized environment (e.g., a honeypot). This is due to the increased feasibility of trace labeling, overusing real-world traces that are representative of the real world, even in the hardly achievable case when real-world production traces are available.[10] We discuss more on honeypots and on trace generation approaches in general in Section 18.2.1.6.

In contrast to proprietary real-world traces, one can obtain publicly available traces without any legal constraints. However, the use of such traces has certain risks. For instance, publicly available traces often contain errors, and they quickly become outdated after their public release; that is, attacks have limited shelf-life, and further, the characteristics of the benign background activities and the mix of malicious and benign activities change significantly over time. Since such activities are recorded permanently in trace files for later reuse, traces lose on representativeness over time. Some of the most frequently used publicly available traces include the DARPA (MIT Lincoln Laboratory, 1999) and the KDD Cup'99 (University of California, 1998) datasets, which are currently considered outdated (Sommer and Paxson, 2010).[11] However, these traces have been used in many evaluation experiments over the last two decades (e.g., Alserhani et al. (2010), Yu and Dasgupta (2011), and Raja et al. (2012)). We also conclude that the trend of overusing these datasets continues up to the current date despite the past criticism of their poor representativeness. For instance, Sommer and Paxson (2010) referred to the DARPA dataset as *"no longer adequate for any current study"* and *"wholly uninteresting if a network-based IDS detects the attacks it [the DARPA dataset] contains,"* stressing the overuse of these datasets due to lack of alternative publicly available datasets for security research. The DARPA and the KDD Cup'99 datasets have also been extensively criticized. For instance, McHugh (2000) criticizes the DARPA dataset for unrealistic distribution of probe/surveillance attacks in the benign background activity. The KDD Cup'99 dataset is known for lack of precise temporal information on the attacks recorded in the trace files, which is crucial for attack detection to many IDSes. Despite all criticism, some researchers are still looking for usage scenarios of these datasets. For instance, Engen et al. (2011) identify the KDD Cup'99 dataset as useful in the evaluation of the learning process of anomaly-based IDSes (e.g., learning from a very large dataset, incremental learning, and similar).

18.2.1.6 Trace Generation

Under trace generation, we understand the process of generating traces by the evaluator himself. In order to avoid the previously mentioned issues related to acquiring

---

[10] A worthy point to mention is that real-world traces of a "small" size may still be labeled in a reasonable time; however, such traces would contain a small amount of attacks. To quote from Sperotto et al. (2009): *"... labeling is a time-consuming process: it could easily be achieved on short traces, but these traces could present only a limited amount of security events."* The amount of (human) resources that one has available for labeling plays a central role in determining the acceptable size of real-world traces that can be labeled in a time-efficient manner.

[11] We focus on the DARPA and the KDD Cup'99 datasets because of their popularity. However, we stress that the risk of a dataset to become outdated soon after its public release is *not* a characteristic of the DARPA and the KDD Cup'99 datasets in particular, but to the contrary, of all datasets in general.

traces, researchers generate traces in a testbed environment or deploy a honeypot in order to capture malicious activities.

The generation of traces in a testbed environment is challenged by several concerns. For instance, the cost of the resources needed to build a testbed that scales to realistic production environment may be high. Further, the approach for the generation of traces may produce faulty or simplistic workloads. For instance, Sommer and Paxson (2010) warn that activities captured in small testbed environments may differ fundamentally from activities in a real-world platform. Finally, the methods used to generate traces are not flexible enough to timely follow the current attack and benign activity trends. This issue, in particular, has motivated one of the major current research directions that deals with the generation of traces in a testbed environment in a customizable and scientifically rigorous manner. Such research is mainly motivated by the fact that the characteristics of attacks and of benign workloads are rapidly changing over time, making the one-time datasets inappropriate for evaluation on a long-term basis. To this end, Shiravi et al. (2012) proposed the use of workload profiles that enable customization of both malicious and benign network traffic. This includes customization of the distribution of network traffic from specific applications and protocols as well as customization of intrusive activities.

Honeypots enable recording of malicious activities performed by an attacker without revealing their purpose. By mimicking real operating systems and vulnerable services, honeypots record the interaction between the attack target and the attack itself. Security researchers often use honeyd,[12] a low-interaction honeypot that can emulate a network of an arbitrary number of hosts, where each host may run multiple services. Honeyd is attractive to security researchers since it is open-source and is well equipped with many logging and log processing utilities. Maybe the most extensive deployment of honeyd up-to-date is in the frame of the Leurre.com project,[13] which at the time of writing consists of 50 active honeyd instances in 30 countries worldwide. Since honeypots are usually isolated from production platforms, almost all of the interactions that they observe are malicious, making honeypots ideal for generation of pure malicious traces. However, since low-interaction honeypots use complex scripts to interact with attacks, they are often unable to interact with and record zero-day attacks. Under a zero-day attack, we understand an attack that exploits a vulnerability that has not been publicly disclosed before the execution of the attack. The notion "zero-day" indicates that such an attack occurs on "day zero" of public awareness of the exploited vulnerability. A promising solution of this issue is the work of Leita et al. (2006) where they incorporate unsupervised learning mechanism in the interaction state machine of ScriptGen, a framework for automatic generation of honeyd scripts with the benefit to capture zero-day attacks. ScriptGen was later enhanced and implemented in the honeyd instances of the Leurre.com project.

---

[12] http://www.honeyd.org

[13] http://www.leurrecom.org

18.2.2 Metrics

In Figure 18.5, we depict the metrics part of the design space. We distinguish between two metric categories: (1) performance-related and (2) security-related.

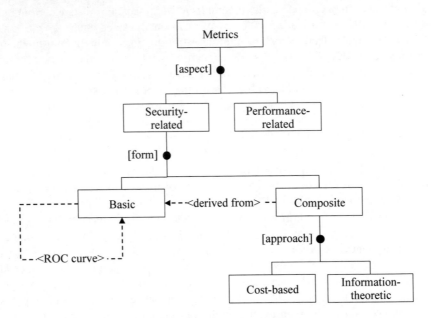

Fig. 18.5: Design space—metrics

Under performance-related metrics, we consider metrics that quantify the non-functional properties of a security mechanism under test, such as capacity, performance overhead, resource consumption, and similar. The metrics that apply to these properties, such as processing throughput and CPU utilization, are typical for traditional performance benchmarks. The practice in the area of evaluating security mechanisms has shown that they are also applicable to security evaluation. For instance, Meng and Li (2012) measure workload processing throughput, Lombardi and Di Pietro (2011) measure performance overhead, Mohammed et al. (2011) measure energy consumption, and Sinha et al. (2006) measure memory consumption. In the context of this chapter, we focus on the systematization and analysis of security-related metrics.

Under security-related metrics, we assume metrics that are used exclusively in security evaluation. In this chapter, we focus on metrics that quantify attack detection accuracy. These are relevant for evaluating security mechanisms that feature attack detection and issue attack alerts, such as IDSes. We distinguish between *basic* and *composite* security-related metrics. We provide an overview of these metrics in Table 18.1, where we annotate an attack (or an intrusion) with I and an attack alert with A.

Table 18.1: Security-related metrics

	Metric	Annotation/Formula
Basic	True positive rate	$1 - \beta = P(A|I)$
	False positive rate	$\alpha = P(A|\neg I)$
	True negative rate	$1 - \alpha = P(\neg A|\neg I) = 1 - P(A|\neg I)$
	False negative rate	$\beta = P(\neg A|I) = 1 - P(A|I)$
	Positive predictive value (PPV)	$P(I|A) = \frac{P(I)P(A|I)}{P(I)P(A|I)+P(\neg I)P(A|\neg I)}$
	Negative predictive value (NPV)	$P(\neg I|\neg A) = \frac{P(\neg I)P(\neg A|\neg I)}{P(\neg I)P(\neg A|\neg I)+P(I)P(\neg A|I)}$
Composite	Cost-based Expected cost	$C_{exp} = Min(C\beta B, (1 - \alpha)(1 - B)) + Min(C(1 - \beta)B, \alpha(1 - B))$
	Information-theoretic Intrusion detection capability	$C_{ID} = \frac{I(X;Y)}{H(X)}$

Basic Security-Related Metrics The basic metrics are most common, and they quantify various individual attack detection properties. For instance, the true positive rate $P(A|I)$ quantifies the probability that an alert is really an intrusion. The false positive rate $P(A|\neg I)$ quantifies the probability that an alert is not an intrusion but a regular benign activity. Alternatively, one can use the respective complementary metrics, that is, the true negative rate $P(\neg A|\neg I)$ and the false negative rate $P(\neg A|I)$. In evaluation experiments, the output of the security mechanism under test is compared with a ground truth information in order to calculate the above-mentioned probabilities. Other basic metrics are the positive predictive value (PPV), $P(I|A)$, and the negative predictive value (NPV), $P(\neg I|\neg A)$. The former quantifies the probability that there is an intrusion when an alert is generated, whereas the latter quantifies the probability that there is no intrusion when an alert is not generated. These metrics are normally calculated once one has already calculated $P(A|I)$, $P(A|\neg I)$, $P(\neg A|\neg I)$, and $P(\neg A|I)$ by using the Bayesian theorem for calculating the conditional probability (Table 18.1). Thus, PPV and NPV are also known as Bayesian positive detection rate and Bayesian negative detection rate, respectively. PPV and NPV are useful from a usability perspective, for example, in situations when an alert automatically triggers an attack response. In such situations, low values of PPV and NPV indicate that the considered security mechanism is not optimal for deployment. For example, a low value of PPV (therefore a high value of its complement $1 - P(I|A) = P(\neg I|A)$) indicates that the considered IDS may often cause the triggering of attack response actions when no real attacks have actually occurred.

Composite Security-Related Metrics Security researchers often combine the above presented basic metrics in order to analyze relationships between them. Such analysis is used to discover an optimal operating point (e.g., a configuration of the mechanism under test that yields optimal values of both the true and the false positive detection rate) or to compare multiple security mechanisms. It is a common practice to use a Receiver Operating Characteristic (ROC) curve in order to investigate the relationship between the true positive and the false positive detection rate. However, some argue that a ROC curve analysis is often misleading (e.g., Gu et al. (2006), Gaffney and Ulvila (2001), and Stolfo et al. (2000)) and propose alternative approaches based on (1) metrics that use cost-based measurement methods or (2) metrics that use information-theory measurement methods. In the following, we briefly analyze two of the most prominent metrics that belong to these categories— that is, the expected cost metric (Gaffney and Ulvila, 2001) and the intrusion detection capability metric (Gu et al., 2006)—presented in Table 18.1. We focus on comparing the applicability of ROC curves and these metrics for the purpose of comparison of multiple IDSes. We assume as a goal the comparison of two IDSes: IDS_1 and IDS_2. For that purpose, we analyze the relationship between the true positive and the false positive detection rate denoted by $1 - \beta$ and α, respectively (Table 18.1). We assume that for IDS_1, $1 - \beta$ is related to α with a power function; that is, $1 - \beta = \alpha^k$ such that $k = 0.002182$. Further, we assume that for IDS_2, $1 - \beta$ is related to α with an exponential function; that is, $1 - \beta = 1 - 0.00765e^{-208.32\alpha}$. We take the values of k, α, and the coefficients of the exponential function from Gaffney and Ulvila (2001).

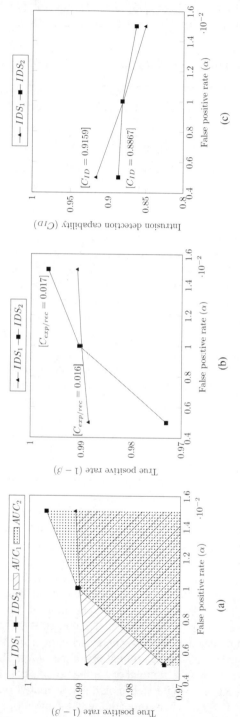

Fig. 18.6: IDS comparison with: (a) ROC curves, (b) expected cost metric, and (c) intrusion detection capability metric

We calculate the values of $1 - \beta$ for IDS_1 and IDS_2 for $\alpha = \{0.005, 0.010, 0.015\}$. We depict the values of $1 - \beta$ for IDS_1 and IDS_2 in Table 18.2.

Table 18.2: Values of $1 - \beta$, C_{exp}, and C_{ID} for IDS_1 and IDS_2

	IDS_1			IDS_2		
α	$1 - \beta$	C_{exp}	C_{ID}	$1 - \beta$	C_{exp}	C_{ID}
0.005	0.9885	**0.016**	**0.9159**	0.973	0.032	**0.8867**
0.010	0.99	0.019	0.8807	0.99047	0.019	0.8817
0.015	0.9909	0.022	0.8509	0.99664	**0.017**	0.8635

In Figure 18.6a, we depict the ROC curves that express the relationship between $1 - \beta$ and α for IDS_1 and IDS_2. One may notice that the ROC curves intersect approximately at $1 - \beta = 0.99$ and $\alpha = 0.01$. Thus, one could not identify the better IDS in a straightforward manner. Note that an IDS is considered better than another if it features higher positive detection rate $(1 - \beta)$ than the other IDS at all operating points along the ROC curve. An intuitive solution to this problem, as suggested by Durst et al. (1999), is to compare the area under the ROC curves, that is, $AUC_1 : \int_{\alpha=0.005}^{\alpha=0.015} \alpha^{0.002182} d\alpha$ and $AUC_2 : \int_{\alpha=0.005}^{\alpha=0.015} (1 - 0.00765e^{-208.32\alpha}) d\alpha$. However, Gu et al. (2006) consider such a comparison as unfair, since it is based on all operating points of the compared IDSes, while in reality, a given IDS is configured according to a single operating point. Moreover, ROC curves do not express the impact of the rate of occurrence of intrusion events $(B = P(I))$, known as the base rate, on α and $1 - \beta$. As suggested by Axelsson (2000), the attack detection performance of an IDS should be interpreted with respect to a base rate measure due to the base-rate fallacy phenomenon.

In order to overcome the above-mentioned issues related to ROC curve analysis, Gaffney and Ulvila (2001) propose the measure of cost as an additional comparison parameter. They combine ROC curve analysis with cost estimation by associating an estimated cost with an operating point (i.e., with a measure of false negative and false positive rates); that is, they introduce a cost ratio $C = C_\beta/C_\alpha$, where C_α is the cost of an alert when an attack has not occurred, and C_β is the cost of not detecting an attack when it has occurred. Gaffney and Ulvila (2001) use the cost ratio to calculate the expected cost C_{exp} of a security mechanism operating at a given operating point (see Table 18.1). For further explanation of the analytical formula of C_{exp}, we refer the reader to Gaffney and Ulvila (2001). By using C_{exp}, one can determine which mechanism performs better by comparing the estimated costs when each mechanism operates at its optimal operating point. The mechanism that has lower C_{exp} associated with its optimal operating point is considered to be better. A given operating point of a single mechanism is considered optimal if it has the lowest C_{exp} associated with it when compared with the other operating points.

To determine the optimal operating points of IDS_1 and IDS_2, we calculate the values of C_{exp} for each operating point of the two IDSes. Note that C_{exp} depends on the base rate B as well as the cost ratio C (Table 18.1). Thus, to calculate the values of C_{exp}, we assume that $C = 10$, that is, the cost of not responding to an attack is 10 times higher than the cost of responding to a false alert, and $B = 0.10$. We present the values of C_{exp} in Table 18.2. One may conclude that the optimal operating point of IDS_1 is $(0.005, 0.9885)$ and of IDS_2 is $(0.015, 0.99664)$; that is, the associated expected cost with these points is minimal. Since the minimal C_{exp} of IDS_1 (0.016) is smaller than the minimal C_{exp} of IDS_2 (0.017), one may conclude that IDS_1 performs better. We depict the ROC curves annotated with the minimal C_{exp} of IDS_1 and of IDS_2 in Figure 18.6b.

Although the discussed cost-based metric enables straightforward comparison of multiple security mechanisms, it strongly depends on the cost ratio C. To calculate the cost ratio, one would need a cost-analysis model that can estimate C_α and C_β. We argue that in reality, it might be extremely difficult to construct such a model. Cost-analysis models normally take multiple parameters into consideration that often might not be easy to measure or might not be measurable at all (e.g., man-hours, system downtime, and similar). Further, if the cost model is not precise, the calculation of C_{exp} would be inaccurate. Finally, C_{exp} provides a comparison of security mechanisms based on a strongly subjective measure (i.e., cost), making the metric unsuitable for objective comparisons. This issue is also acknowledged by Gu et al. (2006). We argue that the above-mentioned issues apply not only to the considered cost-based metric but also to all metrics of similar nature.

Another approach for quantification of attack detection performance is the information-theoretic approach. In this direction, Gu et al. (2006) propose a metric called intrusion detection capability (denoted by C_{ID}, Table 18.1). Gu et al. (2006) model the input to an IDS as a stream of a random variable X ($X = 1$ denotes an intrusion, $X = 0$ denotes benign activity) and the IDS output as a stream of a random variable Y ($Y = 1$ denotes IDS alert, $Y = 0$ denotes no alert). It is assumed that both the input and the output stream have a certain degree of uncertainty reflected by the entropies $H(X)$ and $H(Y)$, respectively. Thus, Gu et al. (2006) model the number of correct guesses by an IDS (i.e., $I(X;Y)$) as a piece of mutually shared information between the random variables X and Y; that is, $I(X;Y) = H(X) - H(X|Y)$. An alternative interpretation is that the accuracy of an IDS is modeled as a reduction of the uncertainty of the IDS input, $H(X)$, after the IDS output Y is known. Finally, by normalizing the shared information $I(X;Y)$ with the entropy of the input variable $H(X)$, the intrusion detection capability metric C_{ID} is obtained (Table 18.1). Note that C_{ID} incorporates the uncertainty of the input stream $H(X)$ (i.e., the distribution of intrusions in the IDS input) and the accuracy of an IDS under test $I(X;Y)$. Thus, one may conclude that C_{ID} incorporates the base rate B and many basic metrics, such as the true positive rate $(1 - \beta)$, the false positive rate (α), and similar. For the definition of the relationship between C_{ID} and B, $1 - \beta$, and α, we refer the reader to Gu et al. (2006). Given this relationship, a value of C_{ID} may be assigned to any operating point of an IDS in a ROC curve. With this assignment, one obtains a new curve, that is, a C_{ID} curve. Assuming a base rate of $B = 0.10$, we calculated C_{ID}

for various operating points of IDS_1 and IDS_2 (Table 18.2). In Figure 18.6c, we depict the C_{ID} curves of IDS_1 and IDS_2. A C_{ID} curve provides a straightforward identification of the optimal operating point of an IDS, that is, the point that marks the highest C_{ID}. Further, one can compare IDSes by comparing the maximum C_{ID} of each IDS. An IDS is considered to perform better if its optimal operating point has a higher C_{ID} associated with it. From Table 18.2, one would consider the IDS_1 as a better performing IDS since it has greater maximum C_{ID} (0.9159) than the maximum C_{ID} of IDS_2 (0.8867).

Note that, in contrast to the expected cost metric, the intrusion detection capability metric is not based on subjective measures such as cost, which makes it suitable for objective comparisons. However, this also implies that this metric lacks expressiveness with respect to subjective measures such as the cost of not detecting an attack, which may also be of interest. For instance, the IDS evaluation methodology of NSS labs (NSS Labs, 2010) advocates the comparison of IDSes by taking into account the costs associated with IDS operation at a given operating point.

18.2.3 Measurement Methodology

Under measurement methodology, we understand the specification of the security mechanism properties that are of interest (e.g., attack detection accuracy, capacity) as well as the specification of the employed workloads and metrics for evaluating a given property. In Sections 18.2.1 and 18.2.2, we presented a workload and metric systematization with respect to their characteristics (e.g., workload content, metric aspect, metric form). In this section, we systematize different, commonly evaluated security mechanism properties. We also indicate the applicability of different workload and metric types with respect to their inherent characteristics. Thus, we round up and finalize the evaluation design space.

We identify the following security mechanism properties as most commonly evaluated in studies: attack detection, resource consumption, capacity, and performance overhead. In Table 18.3, we provide a more fine-granular systematization of these properties. Next, we briefly discuss current methodologies for evaluating the properties listed in Table 18.3.

18.2.3.1 Attack Detection

This property is relevant for evaluating IDSes since these security mechanisms feature attack detection. We classify the attack detection property of IDSes into four relevant categories: (1) attack detection accuracy (attack detection accuracy under normal working conditions, that is, in presence of mixed workloads); (2) attack coverage (attack detection accuracy under ideal conditions, that is, in the presence of attacks without any benign background activity); (3) resistance to evasion techniques; and (4) attack detection speed. In Table 18.3, we provide an overview of the workload

Table 18.3: Design space—measurement methodology

Measurement methodology	Workloads	Metrics	
Variability point	Variability point	Variability point	
[Property]	[Content]	[Aspect]	[Form]
Attack detection			
Attack detection accuracy	Mixed	Security-related	Basic, composite
Attack coverage	Pure malicious	Security-related	Basic
Resistance to evasion techniques	Pure malicious, mixed	Security-related	Basic, composite
Attack detection speed	Mixed	Performance related	/
Resource consumption			
CPU consumption			
Memory consumption	Pure benign	Performance-related	/
Network consumption			
Hard disk consumption			
Performance overhead	Pure benign	Performance-related	/
Capacity			
Workload processing capacity	Pure benign	Performance-related	/

and metric requirements for evaluating these properties. For instance, in contrast to the case of evaluating the attack detection accuracy, if one is interested in evaluating the attack coverage of an IDS, only pure malicious workloads and (basic) metrics that do not contain measures of false alerts would be required.

When it comes to evaluating the attack detection ability of an IDS, the detection of novel, unseen attacks is of central interest. Thus, the security research community has invested efforts in designing various anomaly-based detection techniques, a process that is still underway (e.g., Avritzer et al. (2010) in 2010 designed system for intrusion detection that uses performance signatures, Raja et al. (2012) in 2012 leveraged statistical patterns for detection of network traffic abnormalities). Since it is practically unfeasible to execute a workload that contains unseen attacks in order to train anomaly-based IDSes, in such cases, researchers use benign workloads that are considered normal whereby any deviation from such workloads is assumed as malicious. This assumption, denoted as "closed world" assumption, is considered unrealistic by Witten et al. (2011). They argue that real-life situations rarely involve "closed worlds." Thus, measurement methodologies that follow this assumption might yield unrealistic results. Furthermore, the prioritization of the attack detection properties of IDSes, with respect to their importance in case of limited available resources, is gaining increasing attention. Due to limited resources (e.g., lack of various malicious workloads), security researchers currently tend to evaluate only one or two of the attack detection properties (Table 18.3). Thus, to obtain the highest benefits from evaluation efforts, a proper prioritization of these properties is in order.

Sommer and Paxson (2010) provide an interesting insight on this matter, stating that resistance to evasion techniques is a stimulating research topic, but of limited importance from a practical perspective since most of the real-life attacks perform mass exploitation instead of targeting particular IDS flaws in handpicked target platforms. We tend to agree with this statement, which is also supported by many reports. As an example, an IBM X-Force report, that is, the 2012 Mid-Year Trend and Risk Report (IBM, 2012), states that the greatest portion of system exploitations are due to automated SQL injection attacks. Thus, similarly to Sommer and Paxson (2010), we argue that a representative workload on a global scale would contain a very small amount of evasive attacks, which decreases the priority of evaluating resistance to evasion techniques in case of limited resources.

18.2.3.2 Resource Consumption

Resource consumption is evaluated by using workloads that are considered normal for the environment in which the evaluated security mechanism is deployed; that is, such workloads should not exhibit extreme behavior in terms of intensity or in terms of the exercised hardware components (i.e., CPU-intensive, memory-intensive). Dreger et al. (2008) show that the resource consumption of many IDSes is often sensitive to the workload behavior. Thus, in order to avoid unrealistic and irrelevant resource consumption observations, one must be assured that the workloads used in evaluation experiments are representative of the target deployment environment.

There are mainly two approaches for evaluating resource consumption: black-box testing and white-box testing. The black-box testing is fairly simplistic since one measures the resource consumption of the evaluated security mechanism as resource consumption of a single entity that operates in a given environment (e.g., the resource consumption of the process of a host-based IDS in an operating system). Although practical, this approach does not provide insight into the resource consumption of the individual components of the security mechanism under test. Such insight is important for optimizing the configuration of the mechanism. To the contrary, the white-box testing usually assumes the use of a model that decomposes the mechanism under test; that is, it abstracts individual mechanism components and estimates the respective resource consumption. Dreger et al. (2008) construct an IDS model that can estimate CPU and memory consumption of an IDS with a relative error of 3.5%. Maybe the greatest benefit of the model-based white-box testing approach is that it can be used to predict resource consumption for varying workloads. The model of Dreger et al. (2008) assumes orthogonal IDS decomposition; that is, it does not model the relations between individual IDS components. Although it would be of great scientific interest to devise a model of a security mechanism that supports inter-component relations, it would require extensive modeling due to the great architectural complexity of modern mechanisms. Alternatively, one may opt for instrumentation of the code of the evaluated security mechanism, making it possible to capture the resource demands of the individual mechanism components. However, this approach might be unfeasible in case the mechanism under test is not open-source or if it has a complex codebase.

18.2.3.3 Performance Overhead

Performance overhead is evaluated by using workloads that do not exhibit extreme behavior in terms of intensity but are extreme in terms of the exercised set of hardware resources; that is, depending on the evaluated security mechanism, an overhead evaluation experiment may consist of five independent experiments, where in each experiment, one executes a task whose workload is CPU-intensive, memory-intensive, disk I/O-intensive, network-intensive, or mixed. We provided an overview of such tasks in Section 18.2.1. The execution of these tasks is performed twice, once with the mechanism under test being inactive and once with it being active. The differences between the measured task execution times reveal the performance overhead caused by the operation of the mechanism.

18.2.3.4 Capacity

Workload processing capacity is evaluated by using workloads that exhibit extreme behavior in terms of intensity; that is, their intensity increases over time. The goal is to identify a specific workload intensity after which the workload processing performance of the evaluated security mechanism degrades. Similar to resource consumption, capacity may be evaluated using a black-box or a white-box testing approach. With white-box testing, typically multiple live tests that target specific components of the evaluated security mechanism are used. Hall and Wiley (2002) propose a methodology consisting of individual tests for measuring the packet flow, the packet capture, the state tracking, and the alert reporting components of network IDSes. Although such tests enable identification of workload processing bottlenecks in a security mechanism, they require time-consuming experimentation.

In addition to investigating the individual properties of security mechanisms listed in Table 18.3, security researchers are often interested in evaluating trade-offs between these properties. For instance, Hassanzadeh and Stoleru (2011) propose an IDS for resource-constrained wireless networks with a focus on achieving an optimal trade-off between network performance, power consumption, and attack detection effectiveness. Also, Doddapaneni et al. (2012) analyze the trade-off between the attack detection efficiency and the energy consumption of security mechanisms for wireless networks. Due to the increasing complexity and the enhanced detection abilities of modern security mechanisms, the set of requirements considered to be crucial for an effective mechanism operation (e.g., low resource consumption, low performance overhead) is also growing. Thus, simple measurement methodologies, such as the evaluation of a single mechanism property in isolation, are normally insufficient. We observe that currently many research efforts, such as the ones that we previously mentioned, are focusing on evaluating relationships between a small set of properties. This trend is justified given the various evaluation requirements and the great number of (often insurmountable) challenges to satisfy them.

18.3 Concluding Remarks

There are three inter-related points in the planning of every evaluation study: (1) *goals* of the study; (2) existing *approaches* to realize the set goals (i.e., approaches for generating workloads and for measuring performance metrics, see Section 18.2); and (3) *requirements* that need to be met. Under the goals of an evaluation study, we understand the properties of a security mechanism that one aims to evaluate. Besides the desired extensiveness of an evaluation study, the selection of mechanism properties for evaluation is normally done by considering the *design objectives* and the *target deployment environments* of the mechanisms under test.

We now discuss the requirements that have to be met for the different approaches for evaluating security mechanisms discussed in Section 18.2. We emphasize that the ability of an evaluator to satisfy the requirements that we present significantly affects both the planning and the execution of an evaluation experiment. We systematize requirements for evaluating security mechanisms as follows:

- *Availability of required resources*, mainly related to the generation or adaptation of workloads. There are three major types of resources:

  - *Financial resources*: For instance, the financial costs of building a testbed that scales to realistic production environments are typically significant (Section 18.2.1.6);
  - *Time resources*: For instance, when an exploit database is manually assembled, the attack script collection process and the adaptation of collected attack scripts to exploit vulnerabilities of the target victim environment may be very time-consuming (Section 18.2.1.3); and
  - *Human resources*: For instance, the amount of human resources that one has available for labeling attacks in traces is a key deciding factor whether the traces can be labeled in a time-efficient manner (Section 18.2.1.5).

- *Access to confidential data:* This requirement applies when real-world production traces are used. Organizations are often unwilling to share operational traces with security researchers, or with the public in general, because of privacy concerns and legal issues (Section 18.2.1.5).
- *Availability of knowledge* about:

  - *The architecture and inner working mechanisms of the security mechanism under test*: For instance, when the IDS property resistance to evasion techniques is evaluated, the decision about which evasion techniques should be applied is based on knowledge of the workload processing mechanism of the tested IDS and of the decision-making process of the IDS for labeling an activity as benign or malicious (Section 18.2.3.1);

- *The characteristics of the employed workloads*: For instance, information about the attacks used as malicious workloads (e.g., time of execution of the attacks) must be known in order to calculate any security-related metric (Section 18.2.2); and
- *The implications of different behavior exhibited by the security mechanism under test*: For instance, the cost of the IDS missing an attack must be known in order to calculate the expected cost metric (Section 18.2.2).

The requirements mentioned above often cannot be fully satisfied. This is understandable given the big investment of resources that typically needs to be made. We observed that in case of limited resources, sacrifices are often made in:

- *The representativeness or scale of the employed workloads*: An example is the typically low number of attack scripts used in evaluation studies (Section 18.2.1.3) and
- *The number of evaluated properties of security mechanisms* (Section 18.2.3).

Trade-offs made between the quality of evaluations and the invested resources should be clearly stated when reporting results from evaluation studies so that the results can be interpreted in a fair and accurate manner. We emphasize that robust techniques for evaluating security mechanisms are essential not only to evaluate specific mechanisms but also as a driver of innovation in the field of computer security by enabling the identification of issues and the improvement of existing security mechanisms.

References

Allalouf, M., Ben-Yehuda, M., Satran, J., and Segall, I. (2010). "Block Storage Listener for Detecting File-Level Intrusions". In: *Proceedings of the 2010 IEEE 26th Symposium on Mass Storage Systems and Technologies (MSST 2010)*. (Incline Village, NV, USA). IEEE Computer Society: Washington, DC, USA, pp. 1–12 (cited on p. 396).

Alserhani, F., Akhlaq, M., Awan, I. U., Cullen, A. J., and Mirchandani, P. (2010). "MARS: Multi-stage Attack Recognition System". In: *Proceedings of the 24th IEEE International Conference on Advanced Information Networking and Applications (AINA 2010)*. (Perth, WA, Australia). IEEE Computer Society: Washington, DC, USA, pp. 753–759 (cited on p. 402).

Arlat, J., Costes, A., Crouzet, Y., Laprie, J.-C., and Powell, D. (1993). "Fault Injection and Dependability Evaluation of Fault-Tolerant Systems". *IEEE Transactions on Computers*, 42(8). IEEE: Piscataway, New Jersey, USA, pp. 913–923 (cited on p. 397).

Avritzer, A., Tanikella, R., James, K., Cole, R. G., and Weyuker, E. J. (2010). "Monitoring for Security Intrusion using Performance Signatures". In: *Proceedings of the First Joint WOSP/SIPEW International Conference on Performance Engineering (ICPE 2010)*. (San Jose, CA, USA). ACM: New York, NY, USA, pp. 93–104 (cited on p. 411).

Axelsson, S. (2000). "The Base-Rate Fallacy and the Difficulty of Intrusion Detection". *ACM Transactions on Information and System Security*, 3(3). ACM: New York, NY, USA, pp. 186–205 (cited on p. 408).

Bharadwaja, S., Sun, W., Niamat, M., and Shen, F. (2011). "Collabra: A Xen Hypervisor Based Collaborative Intrusion Detection System". In: *Proceedings of the 2011 Eighth International Conference on Information Technology: New Generations (ITNG 2011)*. (Las Vegas, NV, USA). IEEE Computer Society: Washington, DC, USA, pp. 695–700 (cited on pp. 394, 399).

Carreira, J., Madeira, H., and Silva, J. G. (1998). "Xception: A Technique for the Experimental Evaluation of Dependability in Modern Computers". *IEEE Transactions on Software Engineering*, 24(2). IEEE Computer Society: Washington, DC, USA, pp. 125–136 (cited on p. 397).

Debar, H., Dacier, M., Wespi, A., and Lampart, S. I. (1998). *An Experimentation Workbench for Intrusion Detection Systems*. Tech. rep. RZ 2998. IBM T.J. Watson Research Center (cited on p. 395).

Doddapaneni, K., Ever, E., Gemikonakli, O., Mostarda, L., and Navarra, A. (2012). "Effects of IDSs on the WSNs Lifetime: Evidence of the Need of New Approaches". In: *Proceedings of the 2012 IEEE 11th International Conference on Trust, Security and Privacy in Computing and Communications (TrustCom 2012)*. (Liverpool, UK). IEEE: Piscataway, New Jersey, USA, pp. 907–912 (cited on p. 413).

Dreger, H., Feldmann, A., Paxson, V., and Sommer, R. (2008). "Predicting the Resource Consumption of Network Intrusion Detection Systems". In: *Proceedings of the 2008 ACM International Conference on Measurement and Modeling of Computer Systems (SIGMETRICS 2008)*. (Annapolis, MD, USA). Vol. 36. ACM SIGMETRICS Performance Evaluation Review. ACM: New York, NY, USA, pp. 437–438 (cited on p. 412).

Dumitras, T. and Shou, D. (2011). "Toward a Standard Benchmark for Computer Security Research: The Worldwide Intelligence Network Environment (WINE)". In: *Proceedings of the First Workshop on Building Analysis Datasets and Gathering Experience Returns for Security (BADGERS 2011)*. (Salzburg, Austria). ACM: New York, NY, USA, pp. 89–96 (cited on p. 397).

Dunlap, G. W., King, S. T., Cinar, S., Basrai, M. A., and Chen, P. M. (2002). "ReVirt: Enabling Intrusion Analysis Through Virtual-Machine Logging and Replay". In: *Proceedings of the 5th Symposium on Operating Systems Design and Implementation (OSDI)*. (Boston, Massachusetts). Vol. 36. ACM SIGOPS

Operating Systems Review. ACM: New York, NY, USA, pp. 211–224 (cited on p. 396).

Durães, J. A. and Madeira, H. (2003). "Definition of Software Fault Emulation Operators: A Field Data Study". In: *Proceedings of the 2003 International Conference on Dependable Systems and Networks (DSN 2003)*. (San Francisco, CA, USA). IEEE Computer Society: Washington, DC, USA, pp. 105–114 (cited on p. 397).

– (2006). "Emulation of Software Faults: A Field Data Study and a Practical Approach". *IEEE Transactions on Software Engineering*, 32(11). IEEE Computer Society: Washington, DC, USA, pp. 849–867 (cited on p. 397).

Durst, R., Champion, T., Witten, B., Miller, E., and Spagnuolo, L. (1999). "Testing and Evaluating Computer Intrusion Detection Systems". *Communications of the ACM*, 42(7). ACM: New York, NY, USA, pp. 53–61 (cited on p. 408).

Engen, V., Vincent, J., and Phalp, K. (2011). "Exploring Discrepancies in Findings Obtained with the KDD Cup'99 Data Set". *Intelligent Data Analysis*, 15(2). IOS Press: Amsterdam, The Netherlands, pp. 251–276 (cited on p. 402).

Fonseca, J. and Vieira, M. (2008). "Mapping Software Faults with Web Security Vulnerabilities". In: *Proceedings of the 2008 IEEE International Conference on Dependable Systems and Networks (DSN 2008)*. (Anchorage, AK, USA). IEEE Computer Society: Washington, DC, USA, pp. 257–266 (cited on p. 398).

Fonseca, J., Vieira, M., and Madeira, H. (2009). "Vulnerability and Attack Injection for Web Applications". In: *Proceedings of the 2009 IEEE/IFIP International Conference on Dependable Systems and Networks (DSN 2009)*. (Lisbon, Portugal). IEEE Computer Society: Washington, DC, USA, pp. 93–102 (cited on pp. 398, 399).

Gad El Rab, M. (2008). "Evaluation des systèmes de détection d'intrusion". PhD thesis. Toulouse, France: Université Paul Sabatier - Toulouse III (cited on p. 397).

Gaffney, J. and Ulvila, J. (2001). "Evaluation of Intrusion Detectors: A Decision Theory Approach". In: *Proceedings of the 2001 IEEE Symposium on Security and Privacy*. (Oakland, CA, USA). IEEE: Piscataway, New Jersey, USA, pp. 50–61 (cited on pp. 406, 408).

Görnitz, N., Kloft, M., Rieck, K., and Brefeld, U. (2009). "Active Learning for Network Intrusion Detection". In: *Proceedings of the 2nd ACM Workshop on Security and Artificial Intelligence (AISec 2009)*. (Chicago, Illinois, USA). ACM: New York, NY, USA, pp. 47–54 (cited on p. 396).

Griffin, J. L., Pennington, A., Bucy, J. S., Choundappan, D., Muralidharan, N., and Ganger, G. R. (2003). *On the Feasibility of Intrusion Detection inside Workstation Disks*. Tech. rep. CMU-PDL-03-106. Pittsburgh, PA, USA: Parallel Data Laboratory, Carnegie Mellon University (cited on p. 395).

Gu, G., Fogla, P., Dagon, D., Lee, W., and Skorić, B. (2006). "Measuring Intrusion Detection Capability: An Information-Theoretic Approach". In: *Proceedings of the 2006 ACM Symposium on Information, Computer and Communications Security (ASIACCS 2006)*. (Taipei, Taiwan). ACM: New York, NY, USA, pp. 90–101 (cited on pp. 406, 408, 409).

Hall, M. and Wiley, K. (2002). "Capacity Verification for High Speed Network Intrusion Detection Systems". In: *Recent Advances in Intrusion Detection—5th International Symposium, RAID 2002—Proceedings*. (Zurich, Switzerland). Ed. by A. Wespi, G. Vigna, and L. Deri. Vol. 2516. Lecture Notes in Computer Science. Springer-Verlag: Berlin, Heidelberg, pp. 239–251 (cited on p. 413).

Hassanzadeh, A. and Stoleru, R. (2011). "Towards Optimal Monitoring in Cooperative IDS for Resource Constrained Wireless Networks". In: *Proceedings of 20th International Conference on Computer Communications and Networks (ICCCN 2011)*. (Maui, HI, USA). IEEE: Piscataway, New Jersey, USA, pp. 1–8 (cited on p. 413).

IBM (2012). *IBM X-Force 2012 Mid-Year Trend and Risk Report* (cited on p. 412).

Jin, H., Xiang, G., Zhao, F., Zou, D., Li, M., and Shi, L. (2009). "VMFence: A Customized Intrusion Prevention System in Distributed Virtual Computing Environment". In: *Proceedings of the 3rd International Conference on Ubiquitous Information Management and Communication (ICUIMC 2009)*. (Suwon, Korea). ACM: New York, NY, USA, pp. 391–399 (cited on p. 395).

Jin, H., Xiang, G., Zou, D., Wu, S., Zhao, F., Li, M., and Zheng, W. (2013). "A VMM-based Intrusion Prevention System in Cloud Computing Environment". *The Journal of Supercomputing*, 66(3). Springer US: New York, NY, USA, pp. 1133–1151 (cited on pp. 394, 395).

Katcher, J. (1997). *PostMark: A New File System Benchmark*. Tech. rep. TR3022. Sunnyvale, USA: Network Appliance (cited on p. 395).

Komlodi, A., Goodall, J. R., and Lutters, W. G. (2004). "An Information Visualization Framework for Intrusion Detection". In: *CHI'04 Extended Abstracts on Human Factors in Computing Systems*. (Vienna, Austria). ACM: New York, NY, USA, p. 1743 (cited on p. 393).

Kruegel, C., Valeur, F., and Vigna, G. (2005). *Intrusion Detection and Correlation—Challenges and Solutions*. Vol. 14. Advances in Information Security. Springer US: New York, NY, USA (cited on p. 390).

Leita, C., Dacier, M., and Massicotte, F. (2006). "Automatic Handling of Protocol Dependencies and Reaction to 0-day Attacks with ScriptGen Based Honeypots". In: *Recent Advances in Intrusion Detection—9th International Symposium, RAID 2006, Proceedings*. Ed. by D. Zamboni and C. Kruegel. Vol. 4219. Lecture Notes in Computer Science. Springer-Verlag: Berlin, Heidelberg, pp. 185–205 (cited on p. 403).

Lombardi, F. and Di Pietro, R. (2011). "Secure Virtualization for Cloud Computing". *Journal of Network and Computer Applications*, 34(4). Academic Press Ltd.: London, UK, pp. 1113–1122 (cited on pp. 392, 395, 396, 404).

Maynor, D., Mookhey, K. K., Cervini, J., Roslan, F., and Beaver, K. (2007). *Metasploit Toolkit for Penetration Testing, Exploit Development, and Vulnerability Research*. Syngress Publishing: Rockland, MA, USA (cited on p. 396).

McHugh, J. (2000). "Testing Intrusion Detection Systems: A Critique of the 1998 and 1999 DARPA Intrusion Detection System Evaluations as Performed by Lincoln Laboratory". *ACM Transactions on Information and System Security*, 3(4). ACM: New York, NY, USA, pp. 262–294 (cited on p. 402).

Mell, P., Hu, V., Lippmann, R., Haines, J., and Zissman, M. (2003). *An Overview of Issues in Testing Intrusion Detection Systems*. NIST Interagency/Internal Report (NISTIR) 7007. Gaithersburg, MD, USA: National Institute of Standards and Technology (NIST) (cited on pp. 395, 396).

Meng, Y. and Li, W. (2012). "Adaptive Character Frequency-Based Exclusive Signature Matching Scheme in Distributed Intrusion Detection Environment". In: *Proceedings of the IEEE 11th International Conference on Trust, Security and Privacy in Computing and Communications (TrustCom 2012)*. (Liverpool, UK). IEEE: Piscataway, New Jersey, USA, pp. 223–230 (cited on pp. 392, 404).

Milenkoski, A. (2016). "Evaluation of Intrusion Detection Systems in Virtualized Environments". PhD thesis. Würzburg, Germany: University of Würzburg (cited on p. 390).

Milenkoski, A., Payne, B. D., Antunes, N., Vieira, M., Kounev, S., Avritzer, A., and Luft, M. (2015). "Evaluation of Intrusion Detection Systems in Virtualized Environments Using Attack Injection". In: *Research in Attacks, Intrusions, and Defenses—18th International Symposium, RAID 2015—Proceedings*. (Kyoto, Japan). Ed. by H. Bos, F. Monrose, and G. Blanc. Vol. 9404. Lecture Notes in Computer Science. Springer-Verlag: Berlin, Heidelberg (cited on pp. 390, 399).

Milenkoski, A., Vieira, M., Kounev, S., Avritzer, A., and Payne, B. D. (2015). "Evaluating Computer Intrusion Detection Systems: A Survey of Common Practices". *ACM Computing Surveys*, 48(1). ACM: New York, NY, USA, 12:1–12:41 (cited on p. 390).

MIT Lincoln Laboratory (1999). *1999 DARPA Intrusion Detection Evaluation Dataset*. URL: https://www.ll.mit.edu/r-d/datasets/1999-darpa-intrusion-detection-evaluation-dataset (cited on p. 402).

Mohammed, N., Otrok, H., Wang, L., Debbabi, M., and Bhattacharya, P. (2011). "Mechanism Design-Based Secure Leader Election Model for Intrusion Detection in MANET". *IEEE Transactions on Dependable and Secure Computing*, 8(1). IEEE Computer Society: Washington, DC, USA, pp. 89–103 (cited on pp. 392, 404).

NSS Labs (2010). *Network Intrusion Prevention System Test Methodology v.6.1.* http://www.nsslabs.com/assets/Methodologies/nss2010 (cited on pp. 393, 410).

Patil, S., Kashyap, A., Sivathanu, G., and Zadok, E. (2004). "FS: An In-Kernel Integrity Checker and Intrusion Detection File System". In: *Proceedings of the 18th USENIX Conference on System Administration (LISA 2004)*. (Atlanta, GA). USENIX Association: Berkeley, CA, USA, pp. 67–78 (cited on p. 395).

Raja, N., Arulanandam, K., and Rajeswari, B. (2012). "Two-Level Packet Inspection Using Sequential Differentiate Method". In: *Proceedings of the Intl. Conference on Advances in Computing and Communications (ICACC 2012)*. (Cochin, Kerala, India). IEEE: Piscataway, New Jersey, USA, pp. 42–45 (cited on pp. 402, 411).

Reeves, J., Ramaswamy, A., Locasto, M., Bratus, S., and Smith, S. (2012). "Intrusion Detection for Resource-Constrained Embedded Control Systems in the Power Grid". *International Journal of Critical Infrastructure Protection*, 5(2). Elsevier Science: Amsterdam, The Netherlands, pp. 74–83 (cited on pp. 395, 396).

Riley, R., Jiang, X., and Xu, D. (2008). "Guest-Transparent Prevention of Kernel Rootkits with VMM-Based Memory Shadowing". In: *Recent Advances in Intrusion Detection—11th International Symposium, RAID 2008—Proceedings*. (Cambridge, MA, USA). Ed. by R. Lippmann, E. Kirda, and A. Trachtenberg. Vol. 5230. Lecture Notes in Computer Science. Springer-Verlag: Berlin, Heidelberg, pp. 1–20 (cited on pp. 395, 396).

Rodríguez, M., Salles, F., Fabre, J.-C., and Arlat, J. (1999). "MAFALDA: Microkernel Assessment by Fault Injection and Design Aid". In: *Dependable Computing——EDCC-3—Third European Dependable Computing Conference—Proceedings*. Ed. by J. Hlavička, E. Maehle, and A. Pataricza. Vol. 1667. Lecture Notes in Computer Science. Springer-Verlag: Berlin, Heidelberg, pp. 143–160 (cited on p. 397).

Shiravi, A., Shiravi, H., Tavallaee, M., and Ghorbani, A. A. (2012). "Toward developing a systematic approach to generate benchmark datasets for intrusion detection". *Computers and Security*, 31(3). Elsevier Science: Amsterdam, The Netherlands, pp. 357–374 (cited on p. 403).

Shirey, R. (1999). *Internet Security Glossary*. Internet Engineering Task Force, RFC 2828, http://tools.ietf.org/html/draft-shirey-security-glossary-01 (cited on pp. 390, 397).

Sinha, S., Jahanian, F., and Patel, J. M. (2006). "WIND: Workload-aware INtrusion Detection". In: *Recent Advances in Intrusion Detection—9th International Symposium, RAID 2006—Proceedings*. (Hamburg, Germany). Ed. by D. Zamboni and C. Kruegel. Vol. 4219. Lecture Notes in Computer Science. Springer-Verlag: Berlin, Heidelberg, pp. 290–310 (cited on pp. 392, 404).

Sommer, R. and Paxson, V. (2010). "Outside the Closed World: On Using Machine Learning For Network Intrusion Detection". In: *Proceedings of the 2010 IEEE Symposium on Security and Privacy*. (Oakland, California). IEEE Computer Society: Washington, DC, USA, pp. 305–316 (cited on pp. 401–403, 412).

Sperotto, A., Sadre, R., Vliet, F., and Pras, A. (2009). "A Labeled Data Set for Flow-Based Intrusion Detection". In: *IP Operations and Management—9th IEEE International Workshop, IPOM 2009—Proceedings*. (Venice, Italy). Ed. by G. Nunzi, C. Scoglio, and X. Li. Vol. 5843. Lecture Notes in Computer Science. Springer-Verlag: Berlin, Heidelberg, pp. 39–50 (cited on pp. 401, 402).

Stallings, W. (2002). *Cryptography and Network Security: Principles and Practice*. 3rd edition. Pearson Education: London, UK (cited on p. 390).

Stolfo, S., Fan, W., Lee, W., Prodromidis, A., and Chan, P. (2000). "Cost-Based Modeling for Fraud and Intrusion Detection: Results from the JAM Project". In: *Proceedings of the DARPA Information Survivability Conference and Exposition (DISCEX)*. (Hilton Head, SC, USA). Vol. 2. IEEE: Piscataway, New Jersey, USA, pp. 130–144 (cited on p. 406).

University of California (1998). *KDD Cup 1999 Data: Data Set Used for The Third International Knowledge Discovery and Data Mining Tools Competition*. URL: http://kdd.ics.uci.edu/databases/kddcup99/kddcup99.html (cited on p. 402).

Witten, I. H., Frank, E., and Hall, M. A. (2011). *Data Mining: Practical Machine Learning Tools and Techniques*. 3rd edition. Morgan Kaufmann Series in Data Management Systems. Morgan Kaufmann: Burlington, MA, USA (cited on p. 411).

Wright, C., Cowan, C., Smalley, S., Morris, J., and Kroah-Hartman, G. (2002). "Linux Security Modules: General Security Support for the Linux Kernel". In: *Proceedings of the 11th USENIX Security Symposium*. (San Francisco, California). USENIX Association: Berkeley, CA, USA, pp. 17–31 (cited on p. 396).

Yu, S. and Dasgupta, D. (2011). "An effective network-based Intrusion Detection using Conserved Self Pattern Recognition Algorithm augmented with near-deterministic detector generation". In: *Proceedings of the 2011 IEEE Symposium on Computational Intelligence in Cyber Security (CICS 2011)*. (Paris, France). IEEE: Piscataway, New Jersey, USA, pp. 17–24 (cited on p. 402).

Zhang, Y., Wang, H., Gu, Y., and Wang, D. (2008). "IDRS: Combining File-level Intrusion Detection with Block-level Data Recovery based on iSCSI". In: *Proceedings of the Third International Conference on Availability, Reliability and Security (ARES 2008)*. (Barcelona, Spain). IEEE Computer Society: Washington, DC, USA, pp. 630–635 (cited on p. 395).

Index